# Superwomen

# Superwomen

*Gender, Power, and Representation*

Carolyn Cocca

Bloomsbury Academic
An imprint of Bloomsbury Publishing Inc

# B L O O M S B U R Y

NEW YORK · LONDON · OXFORD · NEW DELHI · SYDNEY

**Bloomsbury Academic**
An imprint of Bloomsbury Publishing Inc

| 1385 Broadway | 50 Bedford Square |
|---|---|
| New York | London |
| NY 10018 | WC1B 3DP |
| USA | UK |

**www.bloomsbury.com**

**BLOOMSBURY and the Diana logo are trademarks of Bloomsbury Publishing Plc**

First published 2016

**Library of Congress Cataloging-in-Publication Data**
Names: Cocca, Carolyn, 1971- author.
Title: Superwomen: gender, power, and representation / Carolyn Cocca.
Description: New York: Bloomsbury Academic, an imprint of Bloomsbury
Publishing Inc., 2016. | Includes bibliographical references and index.
Identifiers: LCCN 2016007660 (print) | LCCN 2016012839 (ebook) | ISBN
9781501316562 (hardback) | ISBN 9781501316593 (ePDF) | ISBN 9781501316586
(ePUB) | ISBN 9781501316586 (ePub)
Subjects: LCSH: Comic books, strips, etc.–United States–History and
criticism. | Women heroes–Comic books, strips, etc. | Women heroes in
literature. | Women heroes in motion pictures. | BISAC: PERFORMING ARTS /
Film & Video / General. | SOCIAL SCIENCE / Media Studies. | LITERARY
CRITICISM / Comics & Graphic Novels. | SOCIAL SCIENCE / Gender Studies.
Classification: LCC PN6725 .C585 2016 (print) | LCC PN6725 (ebook) | DDC
741.5/973–dc23
LC record available at http://lccn.loc.gov/2016007660

ISBN: HB: 978-1-5013-1656-2
PB: 978-1-5013-1657-9
ePDF: 978-1-5013-1659-3
ePUB: 978-1-5013-1658-6

Cover design: Alice Marwick

Typeset by Deanta Global Publishing Services, Chennai, India
Printed and bound in the United States of America

# Contents

# Acknowledgments

In some ways, I've been writing this book my whole life. I was writing it in elementary school when I played *Star Wars* with Vaughn, Brian, and Eric. I was writing it in junior high when Heath and I talked about *Star Trek,* and in high school when Matthew and Don and I read *The Dark Knight Returns* and Stratton and I saw the *Batman* movie. I continued it in college when I dressed as Princess Leia and Ellen dressed as Luke Skywalker for Halloween, and in graduate school when Margaret and I watched *Buffy* every week. Today, I'm surrounded by these characters and others on TV, on film, and on physical and virtual bookshelves. I grew older, but my love for superhero stories never changed. A lot of adults and kids apparently feel the same way, with their passions fueling a multibillion dollar industry.

In terms of actual typing, I started writing about this topic a few years ago because of my partner Steve's friend, Bill Shea. If it weren't for Bill I wouldn't have met Kent Worcester and started talking to another academic about superheroes and comics, one who encouraged me to write about them. Kent and Matthew Costello edited a symposium for *PS: Political Science and Politics* to which I contributed, and they were both helpful and gracious in giving me feedback not only on that article but also on the proposal for this book. Research for that article led me to a conference at which I met three people who have been similarly helpful to my work and gracious with their time: Chris Gavaler, Jeffrey Brown, and Trina Robbins. My paper from that conference went into *Heroines of Film and Television*, and Norma Jones' editing improved my chapter as well as the book proposal. Claudia Bucciferro, editor of *X-Men Films: A Cultural Analysis*, likewise gave me feedback on my chapter in that book that figures into the analysis of X-Men in this one. Junot Díaz was also very encouraging about the overall themes of the book, stressing the importance of authentic storytelling. I also benefited greatly from the many comics creators and fans with whom I have spoken over the last few years.

I am thankful to have been welcomed into a knowledgeable and kind geek community by Melissa Megan, Maria Norris, Huw Perry, Bob Reyer, Steve Seigh, Bobby Shortle, and Mara Wood from *Talking Comics*. On their podcasts and on the *Talking Comics* website I had to dial back the jargon-laden way in which I was trained to speak and write, and hopefully this book is more readable because of that. Special thanks are due to "the doctors": Maria, for inviting me to write for the London School of Economics and Political Science *Human Rights Blog*; and Mara, for contributing her *Star Wars* expertise to Chapter 3.

This book simply could not have happened without *Talking Comics'* Bob Reyer. He lent me at least a thousand comics from his own archives, giving me crucial access not only to their stories but also to their letter columns, ads, and sales figures. He read the manuscript more than once and was nothing but supportive for the entire journey.

My editors at Bloomsbury, Katie Gallof, Mary Al-Sayed, and Michelle Chen, all eased the book-production process with their professionalism and kindness. Chris Gavaler read the final manuscript with painstaking care, and his many insightful suggestions as well as his overall support have strengthened it.

I am grateful to my longtime friends Khalen Gloeckner and Stratton Danes for their feedback as well as their encouragement, and to Don LaVoie and Matthew Wilkening for contributing their Bat-family expertise to the Barbara Gordon chapter.

My immediate family also gave me comments and suggestions on the manuscript and were supportive throughout: Amelia, Theo, and Steve Goodman. Amelia also used her gender studies expertise to compile the index. My mother, Anne Swinton, has read everything I've written, many times each, and is unfailingly there for me. For countless reasons beyond this, my mother is and always has been my favorite superhero.

My daughter Anna's contribution lay less in reviewing the manuscript and more in reading comics and watching TV shows and films with me (although I kept her away from many 1990s–2010s comics, for reasons described within). She has stated repeatedly that her favorite characters are the ones who look like her, and the ones with whom she has certain traits in common. This is because, she says, she likes to see herself in the story, in place of those characters. She likes to be the hero, as do we all.

This book is for Anna. I hope that there are many creators out there who will produce fantastic works for her and others to read and watch, with diverse and nuanced characters who show all of us that anybody can be a hero. We need to support those creators as well as to push others to consider the breadth of their potential readership and how much representation matters. We need to support equity in hiring and promotion practices that diversify the ranks of the companies producing superhero-related media and merchandise, and also to support creators who work outside of a corporate structure.

If you don't see yourself in someone else's stories, write your own and put them out in the world. That would benefit not just you, but all of us.

# List of Illustrations

Figure 1.1. In a brief animated appearance, a 1940s-esque Wonder Woman engaged in some of her most iconic activities. Here, as she often did in the comics, she carries Steve Trevor and subverts "traditional" gender roles (*Batman: The Brave and the Bold*, "Curse of the Star Sapphire," S03E04, 2011).

Figure 1.2. Lynda Carter, as Wonder Woman, in the more revealing costume of the TV show's second season, pushing with her superstrength against rapidly closing walls ("The Man Who Made Volcanoes," S02E09, 1977).

Figure 1.3. Wonder Woman in the *Justice League* animated series, which highlighted her superstrength ("The Savage Time, Part Two," S01E25, 2002).

Figure 1.4. Wonder Woman, the "battle-scarred" and "intimidating warrior," played by Gal Gadot in *Batman v Superman: Dawn of Justice* (2016).

Figure 2.1. Yvonne Craig as the petite, balletic, purple-clad Batgirl on *Batman*'s third season ("Enter Batgirl, Exit Penguin," S03E01, 1967).

Figure 2.2. The short-lived *Birds of Prey* TV show, starring (left to right) Ashley Scott as Helena/Huntress, Rachel Skarsten as Dinah (here, the daughter of the Black Canary), and Dina Meyer as Barbara/Oracle ("Pilot," S01E01, 2002).

Figure 2.3. The younger and slighter Barbara as Batgirl in *The New Batman Adventures* ("Old Wounds," S01E18, 1998).

Figure 2.4. Oracle's sole appearance in animated form: 2007's *The Batman* ("Artifacts," S04E07).

Figure 3.1. Princess Leia (Carrie Fisher) is a rebel leader positioned between the two main male characters, Han (Harrison Ford) and Luke (Mark Hamill). (*Star Wars: A New Hope*, 1977).

Figure 3.2. The sole woman in a sea of white men, Leia (Carrie Fisher) explains the plan they are to follow (*The Empire Strikes Back*, 1980).

Figure 3.3. Queen Padmé Amidala (Natalie Portman), mother of Princess Leia, in her elaborate royal garb and white makeup (*The Phantom Menace*, 1999).

Figure 3.4. Senator Padmé Amidala in the *Clone Wars* series, in which she engaged in action, diplomacy, and romance ("Destroy Malevolence," S01E04, 2008).

Figure 3.5. Jabba the Hutt forces Leia (Carrie Fisher) to wear a metal bikini and puts a chain around her neck. She later strangles him with that same chain (*Return of the Jedi*, 1983).

she is here jealous of her boyfriend Captain Marvel's attention to another woman ("Another Order of Evil Part 2," S02E02, 2010).

Figure 6.3. Ms. Marvel in *Earth's Mightiest Heroes*, wearing her second comics outfit—a bare-legged version of Captain Marvel's costume (see Figure 6.2). The first Captain Marvel wears his native uniform ("Welcome to the Kree Empire," S02E04, 2012).

Figure 6.4. Carol as Captain Marvel, wearing her redesigned uniform in 2015's *Frost Fight*.

# Introduction: Representation Matters

As a little kid, I spent most of my time with three boys who lived on my street. When we played *Star Wars*, the boys were Luke, Han, and Chewbacca, and I was Leia. When we played *Super Friends*, they were Superman, Batman, and Aquaman, and I was Wonder Woman. When we played *Battle of the Planets*, they were Mark, Jason, and Tiny, and I was Princess. At the time, I didn't question that these fictional superwomen were only one-quarter of their ensembles, or that they showed more skin than the supermen, or that they were all by name or by birth "princesses." I didn't question that I was always "the girl." It fit our group numerically, and it fit me as a young white girl with dark hair identifying with and trying to emulate superheroic white women with dark hair.

But now—as a political scientist who writes and teaches about the politics of gender, as a mother of a daughter who is the same age now as I was then—now, I'm questioning why the proportion of female superheroes as compared to male ones hasn't really changed, why they tend to be super-sexualized along with being superstrong, and why most of them are white and heterosexual and upper middle class and able-bodied.

Now is the time to ask these questions, because between comics, films, live-action and animated television shows, conventions, and licensed merchandise, superheroes are billion-dollar, transmedia, global commodities. In 2016, there were over twenty-five television shows on air or in development, and over fifty films set to star comics-based superhero characters. About 7 percent of these are solo vehicles for female superheroes. Of the rest, about half have white male leads, and the other half have almost entirely white and male ensemble casts.[1] The percentage of mainstream superhero comics starring female characters is at a high of about 12 percent.[2]

Increasingly, some fans, authors, editors, and publishers have been pushing for characters, settings, and plots that would broaden the diversity of the superhero universe. Others have been actively pushing back against such appeals, some with benign words and some with violent threats.[3]

For all of these people, representation matters. And representations of superheroes—particularly ones who look like them and with whom they may more strongly identify—matter. They can perpetuate "traditional" ideas about gender and sexuality and race and disability by portraying stereotypes, such as, women are always weaker than men, or heterosexuality is the only acceptable form of a loving relationship, or people of color are never as capable as white people, or people with disabilities are bitter and dependent. They can also subvert those stereotypes in ways that empower those who have been marginalized because of them. And they are currently doing both at the same time, as savvy parent companies can capitalize on the current profitability of superheroes to reach ever-larger audiences.

The superhero genre in comics, television, and film is among the many areas in our culture that underrepresents women in positions of power, both as real-life creators and as fictional characters. It is a site at which passionate struggles take place over characters and stories in which fans feel enormously invested.

This book explores the corporate productions, creator representations, and audience receptions of female superheroes in mainstream superhero comics, television shows, and films.[4] It examines how and why they're created and sold the way they are, how and why they sound and look the way they do, and how and why different audiences make meaning from them the ways they do.

Each chapter covers a different hero, and her circle of allies and villains: Wonder Woman, the Batgirls and the Birds of Prey, Princess Leia, the "X-Women," Buffy the Vampire Slayer, and Captain Marvel and Ms. Marvel. Through these heroic figures, editorial boards, writers and artists, parent companies, and different audience groups have all struggled over the meaning of gender and how gender intersects with other identity categories, such as race, ethnicity, sexuality, and disability.[5] There is push and pull, changing over time through different political contexts and cultural moments, between all of these players and their ideas about what kinds of roles they want female superheroes to perform and why. Each has their own biases and their own agendas; each can learn from the others and be moved as well. Producers and consumers are not necessarily equal in this space, but each enables and constrains the other in different ways.[6]

Examining the interplay between how comics are produced, what kinds of characters are portrayed and how, where comics are sold, who is buying them, and how this has changed over the time provides a fuller picture of the world of mainstream superheroes. This includes looking at representations of superwomen in comics as well as in related television and films; at interviews with writers, artists, and editors; at writers' websites, tumblrs, instagrams, blogs, and tweets; and at fan letters, websites, tumblrs, instagrams, blogs, tweets, and podcasts.[7] It also means taking into account the political economy of superheroes—that is, how it is that superhero characters make money, and how companies assume they make money. Representations of female superheroes are affected by the ways in which they are produced for maximum relevance, and therefore maximum profit, by parent companies, editors, artists, and writers, as well as how their manufacture and distribution has changed over time.

Through exploring all of these aspects of portrayals of superwomen in comics, this book analyzes how and why such characters have become more numerous but are still not close to real-world numbers; how and why their representations have become a flashpoint in the comics world and increasingly, in the mainstream as well; what has changed, if anything, in terms of how female superheroes are produced and received; and how and why such an examination of the superhero genre is of real-world consequence.

In short, the market for superheroes is shifting. Blockbuster superhero films, downloadable television shows based on different production models, trade paperback collections of comics sold in bookstores and accessible at libraries, wide availability of supporting merchandise, and the digitization of comics have brought in new fans and empowered old ones. And these fans, due to changing population demographics and gains of civil rights movements, are not only more diverse but also more vocal with their desires and their dollars. They're going to comic conventions in increasing numbers, some of them in costume as their favorite characters, and some of them spending quite a bit of money on superhero-related products. Technology has amplified their voices: web-based comics journalism and their message boards, as well as various social media all allow fans to communicate with each other as well as with creators, and allow creators to cultivate their fandom. Superhero comic creators and producers are slightly more diverse themselves than in the past. They themselves may want change, and they also cannot afford to ignore how much the fan base has changed just over the last several years. So they have begun to diversify superhero titles, but not without backlash from the more "traditional" fan base, overrepresented in media representations as well as in positions of social, political, and economic power. Negotiations between all of these players, particularly about representations of female superheroes, are at the heart of this study and show the ways in which we continue to struggle over the "place" of women in society.

Throughout, the book emphasizes the need for more diverse representations in these media, the tensions inherent in increased diversity in what are both artistic and corporate products, and the caution with which we should approach more diverse representations when they may be progressive or stereotypical or both at the same time. There are more female superhero characters, and some of them are strong, nuanced, and less domesticated and objectified than they used to be. But female superhero characters are still small in number, are still often posed as sex objects in ways in which male characters are not, and are still most likely to be white, heterosexual, nondisabled, and cisgender (that is, when one's gender identity conforms to the gender one was assigned at birth). The superhero genre has come far in a number of ways, but has far to go. A critical examination of why female superhero representations are the way they are, why they matter so much to their fans and their potential fans, and why we should keep working to make them the best they can be is the heart of the book.

## Representation matters

*Superwomen* is grounded in the premise that representation matters. While you do not have to have a perfect demographic match with a fictional character to identify with her or him, seeing someone who looks like you can have a positive impact on self-esteem and seeing no one who looks like you can have a negative impact on self-esteem.[8] You are more likely to imagine yourself as a hero if you see yourself represented as a hero. Marginalized groups have been forced to "cross-identify" with those different from them while dominant groups have not. That is, because white males have been so overrepresented, women and people of color have had to identify with white male protagonists.[9] But white males have not had to identify with the small number of women and people of color protagonists. This is not only unfair, but can curtail imagination. If you see heroes who look nothing like you, it may be easier to imagine someone in that group being a hero too. If you don't, it may be more difficult. Diverse representation benefits everyone, because it shows all of us that anyone can be a hero.

But if, over and over in a variety of media, we see women represented only a fraction as often as men; if we never see a woman portrayed as a leader, a mentor, a professional; if we see women written and drawn and acted only as supportive, interested in their own looks and in romance, in need of rescue, and emotional; and if we never see women as heroes, what happens to our imagination for ourselves and our world? And if we do see female heroes, but those heroes are almost never people of color, people with disabilities, people who identify as gender-fluid or transgender or queer, what happens to our imagination for ourselves and our world?

We need to ask these questions because while women are, of course, half of the population of the world, they are greatly underrepresented in positions of power as well as underrepresented and stereotyped across fiction, particularly in books, television and film. Across thousands of children's books over the last century, females were only about one-third of the characters (McCabe et al. 2011: 197). People of color, male or female, were only about 1–3 percent of main characters across thousands of children's and adults' books in the 2010s (Cooperative Children's Book Center 2014). Children's animated series displayed the same disparities in the 2000s, with females only about one-fifth of characters in the "traditional adventure" genre, and about one-third of characters in "educational" shows or "animal character" shows (Leaper et al. 2002: 1659). In animated superhero series, females were about one-third of the characters, acted as team leaders or mentors only 10 percent of the time, and were twice as likely as male characters to have a mentor (Baker and Raney 2007: 37). Women were about one-third of broadcast leads and people of color were less than 10 percent of broadcast leads (Hunt, Ramon, and Price 2014), barely higher than the 1970s and 1980s, and about the same as in the 1990s (Signorielli 2012: 344). Only one-tenth of the seven hundred top-grossing films of 2007–14 had gender-balanced casts or featured girls/women in roughly half of the speaking roles. Women had less than one-third of speaking roles in those seven hundred films—and that includes characters who spoke only one word. The women were almost always younger than the men, almost always white, and almost always heterosexual. Less than one-quarter of the films had a woman or girl as a main character driving the plot. Only about one-quarter showed women working, and those portraying professional work showed women holding about one-seventh of such jobs (Smith et al. 2014a; Smith, Choueiti, and Pieper 2014b, 2015). Only about one-third of all of the superhero films from 2000 to 2015 pass the three-part "Bechdel-Wallace test:" that there must be (1) at least two female characters (2) who talk to each other (3) about something other than a man.[10] In a sample of mainstream superhero comics with ensemble casts from 1993 to 2013, females were less than one-quarter of the characters and drawn in about one-quarter of the panels (Cocca 2014a: 6). Black, Latina, and Asian female superheroes, even more underrepresented, have often been portrayed in ways that reinforce both racial and gendered stereotypes (Brown 2013). Across media, these same studies found, females are portrayed stereotypically as well: more fearful, more supportive, more interested in romance, and more sexualized. That is, they were more prone than male characters to be in revealing attire, to be nude, and to have their looks referenced by other characters. Repeated objectification could not only make some readers and viewers feel unwelcome and others feel less empathy for the objectified group, but also correlates with closer body monitoring and body shame among the objectified group.[11]

The repetition of stereotypes exerts power. Writer Chimamanda Ngozi Adichie (2014) describes how she has interacted with Europeans and Americans who hold stereotypes of Africa and Africans and therefore of her. They had only ever seen one type of story about Africans, she realized: one that whites told of backwardness, barbarism, victimhood, poverty, and rescue by benevolent whites.

> So that is how to create a single story, show a people as one thing—as only one thing—over and over again, and that is what they become. . . . Power is the ability not just to tell the story of another person, but to make it the definitive story of that person. . . . The single story creates stereotypes, and the problem with stereotypes is not that they are untrue, but that they are incomplete. They make one story become the only story. . . . The consequence of the single story is this: It robs people of dignity. It makes our recognition of our humanity difficult. It emphasizes how we are different rather than how we are similar.

This power has generally been exercised by the same groups over and over, marginalizing other groups. Dominant groups have been telling not only their own stories but the stories of those whom they have marginalized as well: whites telling the stories of people of color, men telling stories of women, heterosexuals telling stories of queers, nondisabled people telling stories of disabled people. Sometimes they are terrific stories. But often their lack of authenticity means they're not only inaccurate, but harmful.

When an underrepresented group of people is repeatedly reduced to objects, when the narrative's point of view is consistently *at* that group instead of *from* that group, the objectified group's story is not being told, empathy for that group is less likely, and the group's power is subverted. If the constantly repeated story is that women and girls are not leaders, are not working in professional settings, are not agents of their own lives but merely adjuncts to others, and are sometimes not even present at all, it can reinforce or foster societal undervaluing of women and girls.[12] It can naturalize inequalities. In other words, it can make it seem as if a world where women and girls are weak and incapable and emotional, and where fewer women and girls are in charge of their own lives and in positions of power, is "natural" and normal. But it is not. The underrepresentation of women, the reliance on stereotypes of gender, and the repetition of inequalities in fiction as in other areas of life are unacceptable and can and must be changed.[13]

This is not to say that any audience swallows whole what it sees portrayed in media. Much of this book, and many others, show that different people receive media in very different ways. You may wholly believe what you see and hear, agree with some parts and not others, or dismiss it completely because your own experience is opposed to what you are seeing. But fiction is part of our world. And as with other institutions in our world, people within them can be pressured to varying degrees by people both within and outside of them. Creators and consumers can use a variety of means to either push for stereotypical portrayals of gender, of race, of sexuality, or to push for portrayals that subvert those stereotypes.

We should not focus only on the number and visibility of diverse characters, though, because as Peggy Phelan notes, "If representational visibility equals power, then almost-naked young white women should be running Western culture. The ubiquity of their image, however, has hardly brought them political or economic power" (1993: 10). We need to increase not only the number of new female characters but also their diversity, depth, and quality. Part of the problem is the low percentages of female creators and executives, and low percentages of creators of color, involved in the creation of fictional media.[14] But the multiyear film study referenced above found that films with a female screenwriter or female lead had more female characters on screen, and that films with a director of color had more people of color on screen as well (Smith, Choueiti, and Pieper 2015). We need more diverse creators across media that not only foreground previously underrepresented groups, but also tell authentic stories. This does not mean that men are not capable of telling good stories about women. Clearly, many have, can, and do, and some of those men are highlighted in this book. But the end result across media is, for the most part, underrepresentation and stereotyping. For so many years, women, and especially women of color, have not been able to tell their own stories and to challenge the ways in which others have been telling their stories.

There is power in telling stories. "Our social world, with its rules, practices, and assignments of prestige and power, is not fixed; rather, we construct it with words, stories, and silence. But we need not acquiesce in arrangements that are unfair. By writing and speaking against them, we may hope to contribute to a better, fairer world" (Delgado 2000: xvii). Our fictional superwomen can and must be more representative than the "fair maidens" rescued by princes in antiquated fairy tales and the often-sexualized "women warriors" of today's media. Not only must they be more numerous, but also they must represent the universe of all those who would identify as female so as to contribute to broadening our imaginations about who can be a hero.

## A brief history of (female) superheroes

While this book does discuss male superheroes, the specific texts it focuses on are those starring well-known, transmedia, female superheroes. There are a number of reasons for this. If you ask someone to name a superhero, that person will probably name Superman, Spider-Man, Batman, Captain America, or Wolverine. The word "superhero" pretty much assumes that the hero in question is male, and white, and heterosexual, and able-bodied. That's why many people—myself included—don't generally feel the need to say "male superheroes" but tend to clarify when they're talking about "female superheroes" or "black superheroes" or "queer superheroes" or "disabled superheroes." Microsoft Word and my iPhone say that "superheroine" isn't even a word by underlining it in red, but both accept "superhero" as a word. Google accepts "superheroine" but not "superwomen." It asks if I meant "superwoman" (due to a much-watched YouTube user with the name, and due to DC Comics having copyrighted the name). I use the words superhero, female superhero, superheroine, and superwoman to refer to the characters described within. But just as "stewardess" became "flight attendant" and "policeman" became "police officer," there's no reason that the word "superhero" couldn't suffice for all of these characters. This book, like many of the characters it studies, seeks to disrupt assumptions about the gendered connotation of the word "superhero."

Portrayals of female superheroes are embedded in particular moments in the history and the struggles over women's roles and women's power at particular times. Comics don't just simply reflect "real life," though, nor do they simply affect "real life." Rather, they are part of real life, in that they are an institution in our world (like schools or like mainstream news media) through which ideas about gender, sexuality, race, religion, disability, and power circulate. Portrayals of female superhero characters, as produced by artists, writers, editors, publishers, and parent companies, are a part of our culture just as their creators are and as we are. These various actors are pushing and pulling at the boundaries of how they and those around them see, read, and experience gender at a particular time. Dominant cultural narratives of gender, sexuality, race, class, and disability can be and have been read, recognized, reworked, reformed, and/or resisted by readers in variable and unpredictable ways.[15]

Over time, as this book demonstrates, different audiences have pushed for more traditional readings of gender as well as more fluid ones, sometimes in concert with authors and editors, sometimes in conflict with them and with each other. Some like what they see exactly as it appears, some perform what comics writer Gail Simone (2014a) calls "mental surgery" to enjoy what they like and reject what they don't, some change their points of view due to the reactions of those around them, some are engaged in other tasks at the same time and are barely paying attention to a given character, some approach the medium with what bell hooks (1992) named an "oppositional gaze" because they are so accustomed to offensive and stereotypical representations that they are on guard to ignore or dismiss more of the same.

There are some overarching trends in representations of female superheroes (see Madrid 2009, Robbins 1996, and Robbins 2013), which are illustrated in much more depth in the book's substantive chapters. In short, while there are a number of popular, strong, complex female superheroes, in general what we see is underrepresentation, domestication, sexualization, and heteronormativity. That is, there are far fewer women than men, the women are portrayed as interested in romance or as less-powerful adjuncts to male characters, the women are shown in skimpy clothing and in poses that accentuate their curves while the male characters are portrayed as athletic and action-oriented, and both women and men are almost always portrayed as very different from one another and interested only in opposite-sex romance and sex.

## The 1940s–60s: The "Golden Age" and the "Silver Age" of comics

Female superheroes in the 1940s were generally clever, strong, and independent-minded, no doubt encouraged by women's contributions to the war effort and the wartime flux in gender roles.[16] Wonder Woman was and remains the most prominent (see Chapter 1). But there were others, such as Miss Fury, Black Cat, Mysta of the Moon, and Gale Allen and the Girl Squadron, all of which were drawn by women. Mary Marvel, Phantom Lady, Black Widow, Liberty Belle, and Miss America launched at this time as well. All were fair-skinned and long-haired, able-bodied and beautiful, and mostly in skirts. Comics were sold on newsstands and in grocery and drugstores, easily accessible to a wide variety of people. They were sent overseas to soldiers as well. "Reading comic books was a cultural practice that was practically universal among American preadolescents and adolescents of both sexes at this time" (Gabilliet 2010: 198).

The postwar era was marked by a reassertion of "traditional" values as male war veterans were integrated back into American life and female workers were pushed back into the home. This included a heavily idealized emphasis on the heterosexual middle-class nuclear family, and the more strictly binary, unequal, and supposedly "natural" gender roles of the prewar years. The comics market was oversaturated with superhero books while reader tastes turned to horror and crime and romance comics, the rise of television competed for fan attention, and a moral panic over comics wrought the industry-created Comics Code. In combination, this meant that by the mid-1950s, once-popular horror comics had been scaled back, the number of female creators and female superheroes had fallen off, and the most prominent one that remained, Wonder Woman, was a shadow of her former self.[17] Softer and more feminized in appearance, she and female side characters such as "Superman's girlfriend" Lois Lane portrayed women as far more oriented toward marriage, like the popular romance books of the time, than toward fighting injustice.

At this time, fans communicated with creators through their buying habits as well as through letters to the publisher, some of which were chosen by editors to be printed in the letter columns in the back of single issues of comics. As Matthew Pustz notes, editors' choices had multiple aims, "Letters can reveal editors' ideas about a comic's intended audience and about how it will be read [as well as] to mobilize fans" (1999: 167). When editors began publishing fans' addresses under their reprinted letters, fans could and did communicate with one another as well. This was not simultaneous and could be slow. Later, when comic conventions began, fans and creators could be face to face with one another once a year or so. All of this meant that the relationship between comics producers and consumers was different from, and tighter than, those in other media (Brown 2000; Gordon 2012; Pustz 1999).

The late 1950s and early 1960s superhero revival (sometimes referred to as the "Silver Age" of comics by fans, in contrast to the "Golden Age" of the late 1930s and 1940s), pushed for in those letter columns and elsewhere by fans, began in part to fill the void left by the scaling back of crime and horror comics due to the Code (Duncan and Smith 2009: 45). This brought teams to the forefront: the Justice League, the Fantastic Four, the X-Men, and the Avengers. The overrepresentation of whiteness and the underrepresentation of women was in high relief among writers and artists as well as in the books. Ramona Fradon drew at DC, and Marie Severin colored at Marvel. They were it, for many years. DC Comics' Justice League had one female character (Wonder Woman) and nine males. Marvel Comics' Fantastic Four had one female

(Invisible Girl) and three males, their X-Men had one female (Marvel Girl) and four males, and their Avengers had one female (Wasp) and four males. These proportions have changed little, fifty years later.

Female superheroes of the early 1960s suffered both quantitatively and qualitatively. They were not at all diverse, and they were markedly less threatening in their names and powers. Four of them, Marvel's Invisible Girl and Marvel Girl, and DC's Supergirl and Bat-Girl, had "girl" right in their names. This was in contrast to, say, the teenage Spider-Man and Iceman, who were not labeled "boys." Invisible Girl's power was to turn invisible, and she often fainted when taxed, as did Marvel Girl. Supergirl and Bat-Girl were less-powerful female knockoffs of previously existing male characters. Supergirl was the young cousin of Superman and was just as strong as he was, but she was limited by his lack of confidence in her abilities and his control of her. Bat-Girl was introduced as a love interest for Robin, as her aunt Batwoman was for Batman. Not much different from the 1950s Wonder Woman, these superheroes were written and drawn as weaker, more emotional, in need of rescue, more geared toward romance with men, more interested in domestic chores like cooking and sewing (Donaldson 2013; Madrid 2009; Robbins 1996; Wright 2001). This is not to say that readers didn't see heroism and strength in these characters. Indeed, the very presence of female superheroes during these times showed readers at least some sense of an alternative to the romanticization of the married, white, middle-class homemaker and mother.

The late 1960s, though, were quite different from the early 1960s in terms of negotiations of gender, due to what is usually labeled the "Second Wave" of feminism that sought equal opportunities for women through changing discriminatory laws and societal norms about "proper" gender roles.[18] This is generally dated from the publication of Betty Friedan's *The Feminine Mystique*, the report from the Presidential Commission on the Status of Women, the passage of the Equal Pay Act and the Civil Rights Act of 1964, the founding of the National Organization for Women, and the introduction into Congress of the Equal Rights Amendment. In comics, Scarlet Witch, Black Widow, Carol Danvers (later, Ms. Marvel) and Zatanna made their first appearances, and the producers of the *Batman* television show introduced a new Batgirl, Barbara Gordon (see Chapter 2). The following year Wonder Woman was relaunched without her powers, but with martial arts training like that of Batgirl. Supergirl was de-powered as well. In all three cases, as put onto the page by liberal-leaning male artists and writers, these white, able-bodied, heterosexual characters were indeed more able and independent than their 1950s counterparts. But they also exhibited numerous stereotypically "feminine" weaknesses.

## The 1970s–80s: The "Bronze Age" of comics

Due to lobbying by various feminist and civil rights groups, as well as a new wave of creators at Marvel and DC (who were almost universally male), the number of superheroines did begin to increase in the comics. Representation of women and people of color across media did as well. And the "old" superheroines were strengthened in this so-called "Bronze Age" of comics. They remained small in number. In 1972,

Batgirl/Barbara Gordon ran for Congress and won, and in 1973 Supergirl and Wonder Woman got their powers back. Particularly after the Comics Code was relaxed in 1971, they were drawn curvier than before, sometimes less than fully dressed and posed more provocatively. Letters printed in DC's *Wonder Woman* and *Supergirl* comics at this time display a number of male letter writers praising these sexier versions of the heroes (Hollon 2012: 123, 129). Marvel's *X-Men* relaunched in 1975 with a new team that included six males and one female: Storm, who would become the first prominent African American X-Man, female superhero, and team leader, and whose costume was akin to a bikini and thigh-high boots (see Chapter 4). Captain Marvel/Monica Rambeau would be the first African American female Avenger (see Chapter 6), and African American Vixen would join the Justice League. African American Misty Knight and Asian American Colleen Wing would open their detective agency. Their very representation was important, but at the same time, each in their own ways, these new characters suffered from the "contrived exoticism" and "weak emulation of blaxploitation" not uncommon to characters of color (Svitavsky 2013: 154; see also Brown 2013: 134, 137). In general, their body types were the same as those of their white counterparts.

Ms. Marvel and Mystique (discussed in Chapters 4 and 6), as well as Spider-Woman and Power Girl debuted in the late 1970s–early 1980s as well, all white and with similar curvaceous bodies. Two who did not conform to being scantily clad or in skintight clothing—yet—were the new young X-Men, Jewish teen Kitty Pryde and white American southerner Rogue. The trend of representations of increased capability coupled with increasingly exaggerated female bodies, the discomfort with and backlash to Second Wave feminism, and a changing fan base, would only intensify over the coming decades.

As newsstand comic sales began to decline in the 1970s and early 1980s, publishers increased the reach of their properties across different media (Lopes 2009: 74). Parent companies developed more animated and live-action television series, as well as films. The animated *Super Friends* and the live-action *Wonder Woman* both featured that classic character, often the only female on screen. The first *Star Wars* comic was released just before the film in 1977, with Princess Leia the only woman on screen for almost the entire film (see Chapter 3). Overall, there was virtually no diversity in terms of race, ethnicity, gender, sexuality, body type, or ability across these shows and films.[19]

## The 1980s–2000s: The "Dark Age" (or "Modern Age") and the direct market

The last decades of the twentieth century were marked by the explosive growth and decline of local comic shops, which fostered a narrower fan base and coincided with more sexualized and more violent depictions of female superheroes. Rather than sell comics to newsstands and drugstores and grocery stores, who could return unsold merchandise, publishers increasingly turned to distribute comics to specialty stores that could order a specific number of heavily discounted comics of their choosing but could not return unsold merchandise. This "direct market" for comics benefited the new specialty stores (many started by fans) who could target their ordering, it benefited the publishers who no longer worried about unsold merchandise, and it benefited the dedicated fans who would buy from the specialty stores. In 1972, there were twenty-three such stores; by 1983, there were at least 2000; by 1993, about 10,000 (Beerbohm 2015; Smith and Duncan 2012; Stroup 2015). The shops fostered interactions between some fans, as had letter columns and conventions, but many also fostered exclusionary cultures that deterred new and/or demographically different readers.

Comic fandom had been widespread and diverse in the 1940s. But the intertwining of an increasing number of specialized comic shops, higher sticker prices due to higher paper costs, suburbanization, a royalty system and a focus on high sales of superhero comics and merchandise tended to concentrate the comic fan base—it seemed to be mostly male, white, and older (Brooker 2000; Gabilliet 2010; Krensky 2008; Lopes 2009). The question was how creators and producers within the crosscutting pressures of the time period would push comics: toward the increasingly homogenous fan market and the conservatism that could be inferred by its demographics, or toward a more inclusive readership and authorship. The latter was represented by the underground comix movement, identity politics activism and the "Third Wave" of feminism, and the growing diversity of writers and artists who had launched initiatives such as the African American artist and writers' Milestone Comics and the women in comics' organization Friends of Lulu.

In short, the growth of the direct market intersected with the broader conservative backlash against the gains of the Second Wave of feminism, civil rights movements, and gay rights movements. Most mainstream superhero comics began to display very particular and very binary representations of gender: hypermuscular men and hypersexualized women. Storylines were dark, a trend ushered in by the successful "graphic novels" of *Watchmen* and *Batman: The Dark Knight Returns*. Many writers have referred to the predominantly heterosexual male authorship and readership of comic art at this time, and the possible desires and insecurities of some in that readership, to explain these trends.[20] A medium and genre that had been read by most male and female eight- to twelve-year-olds in the 1940s was now read much more by a subset of males in their twenties (Gabilliet 2010: 208).

This was the era of "Bad Girl" comic art, sometimes referred to as "Image house style" (after the founding of Image Comics in 1992) due to its artists' frequent use of it. The term "Bad Girl" derives from the so-called "Good Girl" comic art of the 1940s and 1950s, in which attractive women were sometimes objectified. But while the older drawings featured voluptuous women, they did not reveal anywhere near as much skin and curves as that which supermodels and the mainstreaming of pornography brought to mass attention in the 1990s (Madrid 2009). Nor did Good Girl art feature anatomically impossible proportions or anatomically impossible poses, while Bad Girl art did. Even the X-Women, touted in the 1970s and 1980s as more "real" in body types and personalities, were drawn to conform to the trend as superstar artists began to eclipse writers in terms of attention and sales.

To be sure, mainstream superhero comics portrayed both male and female superheroes as strong, active subjects. However, as comics writer Greg Rucka has put it, these comics are also "a medium that in the main depicts men as asexualized Adonises and presents women with incredibly prominent sexual characteristics" (Talking Comics 2013b). The males were generally drawn facing front with a focus on their musculature, while the scantily clad females were often drawn from the back or from the side, large-breasted and small-waisted, long-haired and long-legged, sometimes without their faces shown at all.[21] Comics writer Kelly Sue DeConnick has noted that there should be a "sexy lamp test" for comics: "Never mind the Bechdel test, try this: if you can replace your female character with a sexy lamp and the story still basically works, maybe you need another draft" (Hudson 2012). Indeed, the much smaller number of female characters were often posed in ways that males simply were not: unnaturally twisted and arched to display all of their curves in front and back simultaneously. One's back would have to be broken to contort in such a way, which is why it would come to be labeled the "broke back" pose.

Seeing Wonder Woman flying and punching a villain while she is falling out of the top of her costume and arching her thonged backside up in the air can lead to a variety of responses, depending on the reader. She or he might identify with the strength of the female superhero, note that such strength coexists with posing in a sexually appealing way, skip over the female body with indifference, gaze at the female body with prurient interest, feel turned off and taken out of the story by the near nudity and posing, or do all of these things in the course of one issue. These comics, then, often showed readers dialogue and plot that depicted a strong, active, often violent female character, while also showing that character "broke back" and with her curves hanging out of her clothes—exaggerating traits associated with masculinity and femininity simultaneously. Female superhero bodies in action show strength and sexiness at some times, but in such poses their power is undercut as the reader is prodded to see them primarily as sex objects (see Brown 2004 and 2011; Madrid 2009; Pennell and Behm-Morawitz 2015; Stanley 2005). Given that there are many fewer female than male characters, the repetition of their being posed in these ways makes it seem as if female superheroes are objects to be looked at rather than subjects to view the story through. Such portrayals have persisted through the present.

At the same time, these female characters were subject to sexualized violence and/ or "killed, maimed, or depowered" at much higher rates than their more numerous male counterparts, generally as a plot point to further a male character's development. Comics fan and future comics writer Gail Simone began a list of such characters, called "Women in Refrigerators" after hero Green Lantern's girlfriend who had been killed and stuffed into a refrigerator for him to find, get upset about, and avenge. She linked the "fridging" with the sexualization and the direct market, seeing them as discouraging women from buying and reading mainstream superhero comics, "Combine this trend with the 'Bad Girl' comics and you have a very weird, slightly hostile environment for women down at the friendly comics shoppe" (1999).

The comics market crashed by the mid-to-late 1990s amid overexpansion, higher prices, and speculation boom-and-bust. As noted, there were about 10,000 comic shops in 1993; by 1996 when Marvel declared bankruptcy, about 4000; by 2002, about 2300; by 2015, about 2000 (Duncan and Smith 2009: 77; Gabilliet 2010: 152; O'Leary 2015). This left parent companies again looking to other media to make money (see Gordon, Jancovich, and McAllister 2007). The Spider-Man, X-Men, and Batman film franchises in particular showed that there was a market for superhero fare outside of the assumed core audience for comics, but the idea that female-led titles wouldn't sell due to that core audience remained as conventional wisdom in the industry. This was supposedly "proven" by the failed films *Elektra* and *Catwoman* (and their sole predecessor, *Supergirl*). However, in the 2000s, there were almost thirty movies based on Marvel or DC Comics that starred male characters while only these two starred female characters. More than two of those starring male characters were bad movies, but the main characters' gender was not blamed for their failure.

There were new superheroine titles in the 2000s, following the conventional wisdom-busting success of young female leads in such TV series as *Xena: Warrior Princess, Buffy the Vampire Slayer, Dark Angel,* and *Alias.* The all-female team book and short-lived TV show *Birds of Prey* included Barbara Gordon not as Batgirl but as the wheelchair-using information broker Oracle, alongside Black Canary, Huntress, and others. Sometimes they worked with Detective Renee Montoya, a lesbian Latina character who starred as herself in *Gotham Central* and as a masked crimefighter in *The Question.* Two different *Batgirl* books, *Ms. Marvel, Power Girl, Spider-Girl,* and *Buffy the Vampire Slayer* launched. *Supergirl* and *Wonder Woman* relaunched with #1 issues. New team books included females, but not at or near parity with males. *Justice League* was reconceptualized with Wonder Woman, Black Canary, Vixen, and Hawkgirl as members. *New Avengers* was created with Spider-Woman, and later, Ms. Marvel and Mockingbird. *New X-Men* featured Jean Grey and Emma Frost and *Astonishing X-Men* included Kitty Pryde, and then Storm. For the most part, though, comics in the 2000s continued to underrepresent, sexualize, and fridge female characters. The sheer repetition of these three elements to the exclusion of others, apparently resonant to many readers, made them appear natural and timeless.[22]

## The new Golden Age or the Dark Age continued? The 2010s

Some superhero comic readers began to push back strongly on such portrayals, while others became accustomed to and liked them. In the 2010s, many more conversations over such representations were enabled by a number of broader demographic and political changes wrought by the gains of various civil rights movements. Within that context, the fan base has broadened due to the increase in superhero blockbuster films, downloadable television shows, and trade paperbacks available in bookstores (Johnson 2007: 75; Duncan and Smith 2012: 149). These new media for superhero characters and their further availability at libraries, along with their supporting merchandise, continued to grow and diversify the audiences for the characters. Best-selling "indie" trade paperbacks and young adult novels have pushed the big comics companies to expand into these formats as well. The digitization of comics furthered this trend, as anyone with access to a computer or mobile device can buy (or torrent) and read a comic. If one is deterred by the perceived or actual culture of a local comic shop, or if one lives nowhere near such a shop, one can still access the content in ways that one could not before the advent of this technology. Web-based comics journalism and fan websites have grown tremendously, both informing fans about their favorite characters as well as providing electronic forums for comments and other types of interaction. The virtually synchronous communication enabled by social media broadens access to creators for formerly marginalized fans as well as changing the ways in which fans negotiate with one another and with producers (Jenkins 2007; Johnson 2007a; Lackaff and Sales 2013; Milestone and Meyer 2012). This media savvy and this use of technology as a base for organization can be perceived either as an extension of "Third Wave" feminism, or as heralding a "Fourth Wave." Producers use social media as well to cultivate their fan bases and create hype for their products (Gordon, Jancovich, and McAllister 2007; Jenkins 2007; Johnson 2007b; Salkowitz 2012). And while superhero comics producers are still overwhelmingly white and male, diversity among writers, artists, and editors has increased. Convention attendance has both multiplied and diversified as well (Asselin 2014; Emerald City Comic Con tumblr 2014; ReedPop 2014; Siuntres 2015).

As a result, there have been a number of changes for some superhero characters and in some superhero comics. To ease acceptance of some of the transitions to diversity and to capitalize on preexisting fan bases, Marvel Comics for instance has substituted a female or nonwhite character for a formerly white male character such as the Pakistani-American Ms. Marvel, the African American Captain America, the white female Thor, and the African American Latino Spider-Man Miles Morales.[23] New or relaunched female-headed titles such as *Angela, Black Widow, Captain Marvel, Ms. Marvel, Moon Girl and Devil Dinosaur, Patsy Walker AKA Hellcat, She-Hulk, Silk, Spider-Gwen, Spider-Woman, The Unbeatable Squirrel Girl, Storm, Mighty Thor, All-New Wolverine, Red Sonja, Batgirl, Black Canary, Catwoman, Sensation Comics: Wonder Woman,* and *Supergirl* all present more complex and less sexualized characters, although most of them are similar in terms of age, race, ethnicity, sexuality, and body type. Slightly more diversity in these terms is evident across the ensembles in 2010s team books such as *Young Avengers, A-Force, Mighty Avengers,* and *Ultimates.*

The decrease in the underrepresentation, sexualization, and objectification of female characters, I would argue, is due to all of the changes in the comics world noted above, fostering new types of interactions between creators and consumers that have pushed parent companies to diversify their titles. However, as this book discusses throughout, this has mostly occurred at the margins thus far. Most superhero titles have white male-dominated teams and white male leads, and tend to portray female characters as weaker and in a sexualized manner (Hanley n.d.; Hickey 2014; Brown 2013; Cocca 2014a).

Changes in the industry in terms of different creators or new titles or different portrayals have been small, but they have been described as part of a zeitgeist by some comics producers, fans, and journalists as well as in the mainstream media.[24] DC copublishers Dan DiDio and Jim Lee blogged to fans who protested that their fifty-two relaunched titles had only one female creator, "We hear you . . . we're committed to telling diverse stories with a diverse point of view" (DCE Editorial 2011). But they did little at the time. Marvel Comics editor-in-chief Axel Alonso, echoing others, stated in 2014 that "fans' appetite for diversity and change is re-shaping the market, and we're doing our best to nudge that change along" (Alonso 2014). By 2015, DC's DiDio was stating, "We recognize there's a massively changing audience going on here" and Lee said that they would shortly have "as diverse a group of creators, characters, stories and approaches to storytelling that I've seen in the history of DC" (Ching 2015). Some fans have welcomed such promises and continue to lobby for more. But others have been angered and offended by the diversifying moves. This "fantagonism" has in some cases replicated social hierarchies while also giving voice to those from more historically marginalized groups (Johnson 2007a: 286; see also Milestone and Meyer 2012: 183, Gosling 2007).

Those who pushed back saw no problem with the titles and characters as they were. They felt as if their tastes were being put down, and they felt threatened that what they liked would be taken away by "social justice warriors" who didn't belong in their comics world. Like the similar conversation occurring in the gaming world, some of these defenses were neutrally phrased. But some of these commenters escalated from disdain to rudeness to harassment, including threats of (usually gender-based) violence against those whom they ironically portrayed as being oversensitive hysterical aggressors. Many of them felt attacked, as if such representations were occurring in a vacuum in which every group is represented in proportion to their actual demographics, in which male superheroes were also sexualized and subjected to sexualized violence, and in which a new "vocal minority" was suddenly being "pandered" to.

These assertions are simply false. Objections to the underrepresentation of women and people of color, and the representation of women as objects are happening in a world in which such groups are still discriminated against professionally, socially, and culturally, in which sexual violence against women is something that occurs, statistically, every minute of every day, and women are still more often than not blamed for inviting it. They are happening in a world in which those whose voices have been silenced for years and years and years—the voices of those who have been never portrayed at all, or only portrayed in very small numbers, or only portrayed in objectified, stereotypical ways—are speaking up and being heard. People in the most privileged groups have been able to ignore much of this before now. It is they who have been pandered to, with the luxury of seeing themselves overrepresented not only in fiction, but also in social, political, and economic positions of power.[25]

There have been changes to superhero portrayals. The number and frequency of panels depicting female characters in sexually objectifying ways has decreased since the 1990s. However, such representations are still pervasive, especially on covers and in superhero-team titles, with no corresponding depictions of male characters (Cocca 2014a).[26] The amount of coverage and commentary on comic news sites about such portrayals has increased greatly, along with critical fan parodic art. Three tumblrs in particular have garnered millions of views: "The Hawkeye Initiative," which posts readers' own drawings of the male superhero Hawkeye in the same pose as (and side-by-side with) published art of female superheroes; and "The Brokeback Pose" and

"Escher Girls," which post the editors' and readers' submitted examples of exaggerated curves and other impossible distortions of female anatomy.[27] Such parodies serve to disrupt, with humor rather than polemics, readers' assumptions about and comfort with what have become very common portrayals of gender in superhero comics.

Because women are only a fraction of superhero characters, the impact of their repetition as objects is even greater. Such portrayals can circulate, reinforce and/or construct stereotypes of men as active and heroic subjects and women (or just parts of women) as objects valued for their sex appeal. As there are fewer female characters to begin with, each is overburdened with representing women as a group. That such art is embedded in a culture in which some claim that movements for equality are no longer necessary should give us pause.[28] Reception is complicated, as is much-discussed in this book, when traditional gender norms are simultaneously unsettled (by a woman being portrayed as a strong subject) and reinforced (by a woman being portrayed as sexualized object) at the same time (see Brown 2011).

Comics audiences are not merely passive consumers. They can decide how they will receive and analyze objectified images, and they can decide how they will accede to or reinvent or protest those images. They can actively communicate with writers, artists, and publishers through letters, blog posts, tweets, podcasts, and face-to-face interactions at comic conventions. They can also communicate with their dollars by spending them on certain comics and withholding them from others. The interactions between these various groups ultimately shapes representations of superwomen, whether and how female characters in mainstream superhero comics are depicted as subjects, objects, or both, and whether and how they are written and drawn to display the diversity of peoples in real life.

# Plan of the book

The substantive chapters of this book engage with the complex interplay of all of these issues as laid out above: the broader political and cultural context of a given time period and the ways in which interactions between producers and consumers within that context can change representations, the impact of the direct market and of subsequent developments in digitization and social media, the changes in the fan base and in the ways in which fans communicate with each other and with creators. Sometimes these interactions have wrought more diversity and complex storytelling, and at other times more stereotyping, underrepresentation and sexualization of female characters. The chapters are each organized around a single character and a small number of related characters, providing details on each of those characters while also analyzing them as a site through which to explore fan-creator interactions. Embedded in their times and subject to the push and pull between various actors with various interests, each illuminates historically specific struggles over gender, race, class, sexuality, and disability, while also providing a window into the nature and importance of representation. These chapters as a whole are meant to foster a critical understanding of how and why certain representations occur, informing and empowering fans to advocate for and even create authentic, non-stereotypical stories with heroes that embody privileged groups as well as formerly marginalized groups.

The specific superheroes in this book were chosen because: (1) they are transmedia properties in terms of their decades-long presence in comics, novels, animated or live-action television series, animated or live-action films, and/or merchandise; (2) their comics have been published by different companies, but most are published by DC and Marvel ("the Big Two") who command the superhero genre; (3) they represent, while skewing heavily toward privilege, a variety of heroisms; and (4) their supporting casts, often near in prominence to the superwomen themselves, make for a more well-rounded investigation of various categories of identities and the ways in which they intersect with gender.

Chapter 1 is about Wonder Woman: the quintessential and most recognized female superhero. This chapter explores the politics of gender in Wonder Woman by examining the ways in which different groups have worked through ideas about gender, race, class, and sexuality through Wonder Woman comics, and finds that moments of more fluid representations of gender in most of Wonder Woman's history were followed by periods of backlash and containment. Created as a feminist character, she is a lightning rod for arguments over the meanings of feminism and the boundaries of gender. She conforms to "traditional" cultural narratives of gender as an attractive, white, heterosexual, middle-to-upper class woman, but she also unsettles those narratives by representing a determined, astute, formidable warrior at the same time. This becomes something of a standard for how female superheroes are written, as do the ways in which the print versions of the character differ from those on television. The chapter covers a sweep of Wonder Woman's history since her first appearance in 1941, and unlike most writings on the character, focuses more heavily on her transmedia representations, receptions, and sales and distribution of the character since 1987, the year in which DC Comics relaunched all of their superhero comics. It concludes by addressing the so-called "trickiness" of writing the character, who for some is an aspirational figure and for others, a threatening one.

Chapter 2 is centered on Barbara Gordon, the Batgirl, who debuted on TV and in comics in 1967. Similar to Wonder Woman, she chooses to become a hero not because of tragedy but because she wants to help others. Different from Wonder Woman, she is a librarian with a PhD and without superstrength, relying on her brains, martial arts training, and gadgetry to fight crime. Since the 1990s, she has been portrayed as a continuously younger and slighter Batgirl in various animated series. But in comics, following an infamously violent assault (or, "fridging") that caused her to use a wheelchair, she was relaunched as the computer-savvy strategist, Oracle, in 1989. In 2011, Barbara rose from her wheelchair to again don Batgirl's boots. This chapter examines writers and artists' portrayals of Barbara as a woman and girl with (and temporarily without) disabilities over the last four decades, as well as the debates among creators and fans over her gender and disability, over her more recent "cure," over the de-sexualization of her costume, and overrepresentations of her fridging in the mid-2010s. It also discusses differences in portrayals of super "girls" and super "women," and differences in her comics, TV, and film incarnations.

*Star Wars* debuted simultaneously in the comics and on film in 1977, to record sales in both media. Princess Leia Organa, her mother Padmé Amidala, and her daughter Jaina Solo are central characters in the incredibly well-known and lucrative expanded universe of *Star Wars*, including the theatrical films, comics, animated series, and novels. Chapter 3 illustrates the ways in which these three characters disrupt gender stereotypes as young leaders and rebel warriors. Indeed, Princess Leia might be considered the prototype of the cinematic female action hero. Quite privileged, these three characters face no discrimination even as numerical imbalances between male and female characters imply that they must be exceptional. And they are: two, like other superheroes, are born with special abilities (i.e., the Force); two are royalty; all are strong and heroic. All three are also white, petite, and able-bodied, and have character arcs culminating in marriage to white men. Diversity manifests itself more through aliens than through humans, and the novelized and comic versions of the female characters are more numerous and diverse than those in the animated series and in the films. Fan debates over these characters and over George Lucas' dominant creative vision (until late 2012 when he sold the property to Disney), as well as post-2012 creator-and-fan negotiations, illuminate struggles over late twentieth-century feminisms and their increasing intersectionality.

The X-Men character base is widely touted as having more diversity than other superhero teams. It is certainly more diverse than the characters discussed thus far. Chapter 4 explores the female characters of Mystique, Jean Grey, Storm, Rogue, and Kitty Pryde in the *X-Men* comics, animated series, and films. Its "mutant metaphor" allows the characters to represent various real-life "others" misunderstood, feared, and stereotyped by the "mainstream." *X-Men* writers and artists have pushed and pulled at binary gendered stereotypes, particularly with the female characters' powers, strengths, leadership, and friendships, as well as through their bodies and sexualities. But, quantitatively speaking, most of the X-Men teams over time have been dominated by white males. The X-Women also conform to stereotypes of race, gender, and sexuality, as race goes unacknowledged and heteronormativity—the idea that heterosexuality is normal, natural, and expected—is explicitly portrayed. The direct market for comics sales in the 1990s, and catering to its assumed customers, played a strong role in the increasing sexualization of these characters in the 1990s and 2000s. This chapter analyzes the portrayals of these women and girls in the comics, and the writer-artist-reader interactions around those portrayals, particularly in the period after 1975 when the team was relaunched and diversified. It focuses on characters and storylines that transitioned from 1970s and 1980s comics to the 1990s animated series to the 2000s films, and the ways in which the films carry forward the underrepresentation and stereotyping of female superhero characters.

The inheritor of all of the themes explored in the previous chapters is Buffy the Vampire Slayer. Like Wonder Woman, Buffy was created to unsettle gender boundaries and to persuade males to embrace the character. Buffy's creator Joss Whedon pushed it further in having his hero be a slight, blond, white, California cheerleader, the kind that usually gets killed in horror movies. He has said that the character is based on Kitty Pryde of the X-Men, his description of her as "Barbie with kung-fu grip" casts her in the mold of Batgirl, and her youth and petite physicality are reminiscent of the *Star Wars* women. While the slogan "girl power" was used by some feminists early in the 1990s, it rather quickly became depoliticized and commodified but probably also enabled shows such as Buffy to get on the air in 1997. Chapter Five explores letter columns in the comics, fan websites, and interviews with creators that illustrate a variety of points of view about representations of gender, sexuality, and race in the TV and comics series from 1997 to 2015. Like the female characters of *Star Wars*, Buffy's portrayals were dominated by one man's creative vision, and like *Star Wars*, the series has displayed less sexualization and more diversity in its later years and in print.

This self-awareness about creating female characters to challenge stereotypes continues in the 2010s Captain Marvel and Ms. Marvel. Chapter Six illustrates the ways in which these two represent not only the changing face of superhero comics, but the changing face of superhero comics authorship and fandom. Captain Marvel (Carol Danvers) doesn't seem all that different from other superheroes: white, blond, heterosexual, tall, attractive, strong, smart, and determined. But her striving to be "the best of the best" has resonated with female and male fans looking for a hero in the 2010s. Many of these fans, who call themselves the "Carol Corps," and push for more diversity in superhero media, enabled the 2014 launch of the extremely successful *Ms. Marvel* title starring Pakistani-American Muslim teen Kamala Khan. Both have fans who purchase the book digitally, such that both books upend conventional wisdom that comic buyers are most likely to be older white males who buy male superhero titles in brick-and-mortar stores. This chapter analyzes Captain Marvel (called Ms. Marvel from 1977 to 2009) from her origin to the present, examining the numerous changes in her portrayals in various comics and animated series. It compares negotiations over both the current Captain Marvel (white Carol Danvers) and the first female Captain Marvel (African American Monica Rambeau) alongside the new Ms. Marvel (Kamala Khan). This allows for an examination of race, ethnicity, religion, gender, and heroism, as well as the political economy of digital comics.

This chapter order tracks roughly with the origin dates of the characters: Wonder Woman in the 1940s, Batgirl in the 1960s, then Princess Leia in the 1970s. These three conform the most to norms of race, class, sexuality and at their outset tended to be less-nuanced "strong female characters," while those who launched after them break various parts of that mold. The X-Men chapter focuses on the period after its relaunch in 1975 and particularly on the comics' heyday in the 1980s and 1990s, hence its placement after 1977's *Star Wars*. *Buffy the Vampire Slayer* follows from there because its lead character was inspired by one of the X-Women from the 1980s, and because it launched in the late 1990s. The Carol Danvers/Ms. Marvel/Captain Marvel chapter is last because although Carol first appeared as Ms. Marvel in 1977, her incarnation as Captain Marvel from 2012 and the subsequent launch of Kamala Khan as the new Ms. Marvel in 2014 illustrate many of the ways in which production, representation, and reception of female superhero characters has changed over time, and changed quite rapidly in the 2010s.

Finally, the conclusion focuses on the ways in which there have been changes in the superhero universe in some ways, but not in others. There are more female superhero characters, and some of them are less sexualized in their own titles. However, female characters are still small in number, many of them are sexualized in ways that male characters are not, and most of them are white, cisgender, heterosexual, and nondisabled. The victories for diversity celebrated by fans stem from the interactions of producer predilections and fan demands and buying habits, many of which are grounded in new technologies for purchasing comics and films as well as new technologies enabling virtually instant conversations between fans and creators and between fans themselves. Such interactions, in an era of increasing tolerance for diversity (but also of vociferous backlash in some quarters), contribute to shaping the varied productions and receptions of female superhero characters. Those interactions are then marketized by profit-oriented parent companies. As such, there are limits to this type of change when the change is based on consumerism and access to technology. Inequalities can be reproduced in both areas, as those with more resources may pull more weight than those with fewer.

## Notes

1   Of almost thirty shows, four star women (*Supergirl, Jessica Jones,* the superhero-related *Marvel's Agent Carter,* and the animated short *Vixen*), and one will star a male of color (*Static,* a live-action digital short). Of the films, *Black Panther* and *Cyborg* star African American males. *Captain Marvel* and *Wonder Woman* star white females. *Ant-Man and Wasp* stars a white man and white woman. The ensemble cast of *The Avengers* stars five white men and one white woman; *Justice League* stars four white men, one Polynesian-American man, one black man, and one white woman.

2   Superhero books on the shelves at the close of 2015 starring female superheroes were *A-Force, Angela, Captain Marvel, Ms. Marvel, Moon Girl and Devil Dinosaur, Patsy Walker AKA Hellcat, Silk, Unbeatable Squirrel Girl, All-New Wolverine, Scarlet Witch, Spider-Gwen, Spider-Woman,* and *Mighty Thor* from Marvel. The first eight of these have either a female writer or artist. DC Comics had *Batgirl, Black Canary, DC Bombshells, Harley Quinn, Starfire,* and *Wonder Woman,* all with at least one female creative, as well as *Catwoman. Buffy the Vampire Slayer* from Dark Horse had a female artist. Most of these teams and books are quite new. Almost no other superhero comics (i.e., starring males or ensembles) have female creatives. Of the top 200 comics distributed through comic shops in 2015, about 170 could be classified as superhero comics. Of those 170, the above 21 starred women (12 percent). In 2010, the figure was 9 out of about 160 (6 percent); in 2005, 10 out of about 150 (7 percent); in 2000, 8 out of about 160 (5 percent). Figures computed from John Jackson Miller's Comichron: http://www.comichron.com/monthlycomicssales.html.

3   See, for instance, threats of sexual violence against former DC editor Janelle Asselin for her critique of a comic cover depicting a teen girl in a sexualized manner: http://www.xojane.com/it-happened-to-me/janelle-asselin-comic-book-rape-threats, http://www.npr.org/2014/10/10/353497842/wheres-thor-when-you-

need-her-women-in-comics-fight-an-uphill-battle, and examples of some of the threats and a broader critique of some men's treatment of women in the comics world: http://comicsalliance.com/sexual-harassment-online-rape-threats-comics-superheroes-lessons-men-geek-culture/. See coverage over polarized reactions to the new Thor character being female rather than male: http://www.scpr.org/news/2014/07/15/45364/fans-creators-react-to-marvel-making-thor-a-woman/. See coverage over the similarly polarizing variant cover for the *Batgirl* comic depicting the Joker holding a gun to a crying Batgirl (discussed in Chapter 2): http://www.washingtonpost.com/news/comic-riffs/wp/2015/03/17/batgirl-artist-sides-with-fans-in-canceling-variant-cover-of-joker-still-angry-surely-you-jest/.

4    This work puts into practice a suggestion of critical theorist Douglas Kellner, "Conjoining production/audience/text perspectives can help provide a more complex sense of how culture and media actually operate in everyday life" (Kellner and Durham 2012: 4).

5    I approach comics as "interactive public spheres" where negotiation over cultural narratives takes place among a variety of players. The phrase "public spheres" draws from Habermas 1962. "Interactive public spheres" draws from Duggan (2000)'s analysis of mass circulation newspapers. The reference to the production/reception binary as being more of a collaboration and negotiation draws from Brown (2000)'s analysis in *Black Superheroes*, and the idea of "competing constituent audiences" draws from Reed (2009)'s analysis of gender in *The L Word*.

6    See, e.g., Brooker 2000, Brown 2000, Duggan 2000, Fiske 2002 [1989], Hall 2003 [1997], Hall ed. 2003 [1997], Jenkins 2007, Johnson 2007a, Kellner and Durham 2012, Smith 1994 on reception, resistance, and constraints. Edited works with a variety of points of view on this subject include Brooker and Jermyn 2002; Gray, Sandvoss, and Harrington 2007; Durham and Kellner 2012. Those focusing more on gender include Jones 2010 and Milestone and Meyer 2012.

7    This could also include looking at video games and at fanfiction; both are beyond the scope of this book.

8    See, e.g., Ghee 2013 and Hains 2012 citing dozens of studies; see Martins and Harrison 2012 for one on superheroes.

9    See, e.g., Showalter 1971 on literature, Case 1988 on theater, Aubrey and Harrison 2004 summarizing decades of research on kids' television consumption.

10   The test is taken from Alison Bechdel's *Dykes To Watch Out For*, specifically, the 1985 strip "The Rule" which was inspired by the author's conversation with her friend Liz Wallace. Certainly, there are problems with the test. Terrible movies can pass, and movies can pass when two female characters say only one sentence to each other. But it is useful for identifying the broader trend of underrepresentation. See Baker-Whitelaw 2014b.

11   A number of studies have found correlations (with no claims made about causation) between exposure to sexually objectifying media and higher self-objectification, body shame and surveillance, and eating disorder symptoms, particularly among young women (see, e.g., Moradi and Huang 2008). See Heflick and Goldenberg 2009, consistent with Nussbaum (1999) finding that "objectifying women led others to perceive them as less competent and less fully human." See Heldman and Cahill 2007, finding that "self-objectification also has a negative effect on internal and external political efficacy." See Pennell and Behm-Morawitz 2015, finding that women watching a montage of superheroines in action then reported lower body self-esteem.

12   Other costs from the underrepresentation and stereotyping of female characters
     include that "children [may] accept the invisibility of women and girls and believe
     they are less important than men and boys" (McCabe et al. 2011: 199, 200; see also
     Aubrey and Harrison 2004, Leaper et al. 2002, Signorielli 2012). Showalter wrote that
     literature for women readers "confirms what everything else in society tells them:
     that the masculine viewpoint is considered normative and the feminine viewpoint
     divergent" (1971: 856; see also Case 1988). Further, "children's amount of television
     viewing [correlates with their own] gender stereotyping" (Leaper et al. 2002: 1653–54;
     see also Signorielli 2012: 352).

13   Because of the book's orientation toward the importance of representation and the
     ways in which such portrayals are embedded in real-life inequalities, I employ the
     insights of feminist theory, queer theory, critical race theory, and disability theory.
     Each of these theories is "intersectional" in striving to take into account the ways
     in which different types of discrimination interact differently for different people—
     women of different races and abilities and sexualities may have some life experiences
     in common, but have probably also faced different kinds of discrimination and
     stereotyping as well. Each highlights the real-world consequences for those whose
     economic and political marginalization is in part undergirded by stories that use
     stereotypes and shorthand labels, or dominant "cultural narratives."
         This work seeks to disrupt those dominant cultural narratives, and "socially
     constructed" binaries. That is, I assume that certain labels for people were created in
     certain places at certain times, that they are not natural or timeless or universal, and
     that they tend to support inequalities. Many if not most of these labels are based on
     binaries of two, positioned in opposition to another such that one is made superior to
     the other not just in naming but in real-life discrimination, such as: male and female,
     white and black, heterosexual and homosexual, able-bodied and disabled. While I
     approach these identity categories as historically contingent and unstable, I do use
     labels (like "woman" or "white") for demographic categories in this book partly for
     ease of description and partly to stress that such labels do carry significance for how
     people have been and continue to be treated in the world. Lastly, each of the theories
     noted above stresses the importance of "counternarratives," stories and evidence that
     challenge and subvert dominant stereotypes.
         Most useful here are not just foundational works in these theories, but those that
     are most intersectional. On feminist theories: hooks 1981, Lorde 1984, Moraga and
     Anzaldúa 1981, Butler 1990, Heywood and Drake 1997, Walker 1992 and Walker
     1995, Halberstam 1998, Nestle et al. 2002. On critical race theories: Crenshaw et al.
     1996, Delgado and Stefancic 2013. On queer theories: Duggan 2003, Hall and Jagose
     2012. On disability theories: Garland-Thomson 1997, McRuer 2006, Clare 2009,
     Davis 2010.

14   See, e.g., Children's Cooperative Book Center 2014, Hanley n.d., Hickey 2014, Hunt
     et al. 2014 and 2015, and Smith et al. 2014a, Smith, Choueiti, and Pieper, 2014b, 2015.

15   See note 6 on reception.

16   This is not to say that these were the first-ever female adventure heroes or
     superheroes. There were several of the first type in the 1910s and a few of the second
     in the 1930s, and superheroes' roots reach back centuries. See Gavaler 2015.

17   See Chapter 1 for how Wonder Woman figured into the panic over comics. For
     overviews of comics and the comics industry grounded in this time period, see
     Costello 2009, DiPaolo 2011, Gabilliet 2010, Hajdu 2008, Krensky 2008, Wright

2001. Lopes 2009 and Madrid 2009 address gender more directly and at more length than these.

18  I employ the "wave" terminology because of its common usage, but as Springer 2002 and Snyder 2008 among others have pointed out, the metaphor is problematic. The word "wave" may imply that the ideas of the different time periods are distinct and separate from one another without commonalities that carry through. Also, the usual dates placed on the first two "waves" of feminism (1848–1920, 1965–80s) are centered on white women's activism and thereby marginalize the activities of women of color.

19  Lynda Carter (born Linda Jean Córdova Carter) as Wonder Woman was the first Latina in a superhero role, as her mother was of Spanish and Mexican heritage.

20  See, e.g., Brooker 2000: 260, Brown 2004: 61, 2011: 68, Gabilliet 2010: 208, Kaveney 2008: 20, Lopes 2009: 122, Madrid 2009: 290, Robbins 1996: 166, 2002: 1, Salkowitz 2012: 78, Taylor 2007: 345, Wright 2001: 262.

21  There are a few male superheroes that are usually drawn as less hypermuscular and are sometimes posed differently from the other males: the more acrobatic, more lithe, less hugely muscular Robin, Nightwing, Daredevil, and Spider-Man. Swinging from rooftops or vaulting over villains, they have been drawn from behind or with their legs spread. However, they are not drawn with scanty costumes, nor posed in physically impossible or sexually submissive ways. See Cocca 2014a.

22  Anna Marie Smith notes, "If one sex/gender/sexuality articulation appears as a 'natural' position, it has only won that appearance through the violent suppression of alternatives as 'unnatural'" (1994: 104). See also Butler 1990.

23  This is not confined to this era, but had been practiced earlier with male characters: John Stewart as the Green Lantern, James Rhodes as Iron Man, Ryan Choi as the Atom, Jaime Reyes as the Blue Beetle. See Svitavsky 2013: 157–58.

24  See, e.g., Scott 2015, Associated Press 2014, Hickey 2014, Simone 2014, Weiland 2014, Yu 2014. See also Jenkins 2007: 357, Brooker and Jermyn 2002: 168.

25  See note 3 on harassment of fans pushing for more diversity in a variety of media.

26  See Cocca 2014a for a quantitative study of female-headed titles and ensemble titles from 1993 to 2013. In short, almost every issue in the sample had sexually objectifying portrayals of female characters: about two-thirds of the time they were depicted on ensemble-title covers and about half of the time on female-headed-title covers; about one-third of the time they were depicted in ensemble-title panels and about one-quarter of the time in female-headed title panels—an average of once every three panels and once every four panels that portrayed women, respectively.

27  See Cocca 2014a. See the Hawkeye Initiative, http://thehawkeyeinitiative. com/; "What If The Male Avengers Posed Like The Female One?", http://twitpic. com/9i8dcn; "What if Male Superheroes Were Posed Like Wonder Woman?" http:// coelasquid.tumblr.com/post/8420220692/dreamsofawesome-wonder-womans-new-costume-looks); "If Male Superheroes Were Drawn Like Female Superheroes," http://www.thegeektwins.com/2011/09/if-male-superheroes-were-drawn-like.html; "10 Most Ridiculous Broken Back Superheroine Poses," http://www.thegeektwins. com/2012/03/10-most-ridiculous-broken-back.html. See also The Brokeback Pose, http://thebrokebackpose.tumblr.com/ and Escher Girls, http://eschergirls.tumblr. com/. There has been more mainstream coverage as well, such as when Buzzfeed photoshopped real women into comic book bodies; it became one of their top posts: http://www.buzzfeed.com/kristinchirico/superheroes#.ilz4AVVpjO.

28  See notes 11 and 12 on the costs of underrepresentative and stereotypical media.

# 1

# "The Sexier the Outfit, the Fewer Questions Asked": Wonder Woman[1]

Wonder Woman tends to be the first female superhero people think of, whether or not they have ever read a comic or seen her portrayed on television. Her very name has become synonymous with a woman who does it all, and does it all well. She is often referred to as an icon, representing female power, and by implication, female equality with males.

She's a brave, strong, decisive, smart superpowered hero fighting for truth and justice and protecting the innocent. But that isn't what makes her special, because Batman and Superman were both doing that before her and they still do. What's special is that she does those things through a female body. She's not a distaff version of a male character, and she's not just "one of the guys." This makes her anti-normative, or, against long-standing cultural norms, about who is or who should be more powerful than whom. She is, therefore, a potentially threatening figure, even as she is written as approaching all situations with an open heart, an open mind, and an open hand. In a world in which women have been treated unequally by law and by custom for far too long, she has demonstrated since the 1940s that intelligence and strength and leadership are not "male" traits. Rather, they are human traits that can be performed by anyone. Anyone can be a hero.

One might argue, though, that Wonder Woman has demonstrated only that superheroism can be performed by a woman who is white, of royal birth, nearly nude, attractive, heterosexual, and able-bodied. In this way she embodies a variety of privileges that many women do not have. Written and drawn mostly by men, she has often been the only female character in a given story, surrounded by male characters. Often sexualized, her portrayal has not necessarily foregrounded the idea that women in general are equal to men, but just that this particular, exceptional, beautiful, bathing-suit clad white woman is as physically powerful as men.

These seeming contradictions have led to a number of writers exploring whether Wonder Woman is a feminist character.[2] In short, sometimes she is and sometimes she isn't. This complexity is summed up by Metropolis' star reporter Lois Lane as written by Phil Jimenez and Joe Kelly, "Wonder Woman is a mirror . . . a mirror of human truth. She reflects the contradictions of the world—the person staring at her—takes them onto herself, and gives you truth, love, and respect in return" (2001, *Wonder Woman* Volume 2 #170). More so than any other female superhero, she is an inspirational figure to a variety of readers and viewers, representing the power of "truth, love, and respect," and she is particularly resonant to those who have been historically underrepresented and stereotyped. For others, though, her challenge to the traditional boundaries of gender causes discomfort.

This chapter explores the politics of gender in *Wonder Woman*—comics, live-action series, and animated series—by examining her production, distribution, representations and audience receptions over time. It begins with her progressive origins in the 1940s, her domestication in the 1950s and 1960s, and her expansion into TV in the 1970s. It emphasizes the period after 1987 when DC Comics relaunched their superhero characters, including an expansion of the title's feminism in the late 1980s, increasing sexualization in the 1990s, and renewed emphasis on challenging gender norms in the 2000s. It concludes with debates over her varied transmedia portrayals in the 2010s. Within the contexts of changing political and cultural moments and changing methods of comics distribution, the chapter analyzes the ways in which writers, artists, editors, corporate owners, and fans have worked through differing ideas not only about Wonder Woman's stories themselves but also about the "proper" place of women in society. The stories of male superheroes, by contrast, have not historically engendered similar debates about the "proper" place of men in society. Over time, somewhat cyclically, Wonder Woman has both reinforced traditional ideas about women as well as creating space for more fluid gender possibilities. Sometimes, both have occurred at the same time.

## Feminism and its containment in Wonder Woman, 1941–68

Created by lawyer and psychologist William Moulton Marston, Wonder Woman was introduced in 1941 "as lovely as Aphrodite, as wise as Athena, with the speed of Mercury and the strength of Hercules" (Marston and Harry G. Peter 1941–42, *All Star Comics* #8). Marston saw females and "feminine" love as superior to males and "masculine" violence. He thought that women needed to be taught to see their potential, and that men needed to be taught to accept "female love power" (Richard 1942). Indeed, not long after the character's debut, Marston would change Wonder Woman's page-one description to, "beautiful *as* Aphrodite, wise *as* Athena, stronger *than* Hercules, and swifter *than* Mercury," leaving no doubt as to her equality with the female gods and supremacy over the male gods (italics mine).[3] Marston lived with two women, both of whom were suffragists and feminists, and had children with both of them. After his death the two women continued to live together for decades. Marston's chosen artist for drawing Wonder Woman, Harry Peter, had a background not only in drawing hourglass-figured, pouty-mouthed Gibson Girls, but also in drawing suffragist cartoons with women breaking out of the chains of their oppression (Lepore 2015: 57, 85–86). From the start, the character was grounded in feminist advocacy for seeing women and men as equal in worth, and critiquing the subordination of women.

Wonder Woman's original mission is to aid the American effort in the Second World War, and to teach the Amazon values of peace, love, and equality to those in "Man's World." Looking fit, but not particularly curvaceous or muscular, "Diana the Wonder Woman" debuted wearing a flat red bustier with a gold eagle, a blue split skirt with white stars, heeled red boots, a gold tiara with a red star, and bracelets. An Amazon from the all-female and technologically advanced Paradise Island, she is light-skinned and blue-eyed, with shoulder-length black hair. Centuries before, men had enslaved the Amazons, but with the help of Aphrodite and the condition that they separate themselves from the world of men and wear bracelets as a reminder of their enslavement, they freed themselves. Diana's mother, the Amazon queen Hippolyte (later spelled Hippolyta), formed her from clay and the goddess of love Aphrodite brought her to life. The adult Diana finds injured American army intelligence pilot Steve Trevor on Paradise Island and falls in love with him. Waking, he calls her an "angel." She wins a contest among all of the Amazons to bring him back to Man's World. Her mother makes her iconic costume, based on Steve's uniform, and sends her off with an invisible plane not only to bring Steve back, but also because "America, the last citadel of democracy, and of equal rights for women, needs your help!" (Marston and Peter 1942, *WW* [hereafter, *WW*] #1). To stay near him, she uses the identity of "Diana Prince" and becomes a secretary. As Wonder Woman, she runs like the wind and swims like a fish, jumps tremendous distances, deflects bullets with her bracelets, communicates telepathically, pilots her plane, uses a magic lasso, and occasionally punches or kicks a villain in the face. As an "outsider," she questions and comments on norms about gender that Americans take for granted. With her lasso that compels people to obey, she says, "I can change human character! I can make bad men good and weak women strong!" (Marston and Peter 1942, *Sensation Comics* #6; see also *WW* #13, 1945).

She is always surrounded by women in these stories: sometimes Amazons, sometimes villains, and often, a group of sorority women led by the short, stout, blonde, candy-loving Etta Candy. While Etta is Diana's "sister," she is also her foil, as her body type contrasts completely with Diana's and thereby constructs the latter's as the more "normal." Etta's women's college world, in which she and her friends are seen talking only about having fun and subduing male criminals, can be read as not "properly" female or ladylike or heterosexual. She doesn't care about her weight or marriage, "When you've got a man, there's nothing you can do with him—but candy you can eat!" (Marston and Peter 1942, *WW* #1). By contrast, Diana falls in love with the first man she sees. While deploring the inequality of men and women, she confesses envy for being a "wife and mother" (Marston and Peter 1942, *Sensation Comics* #9), softening her challenges to American gender roles.

Characters representing the Axis powers become Wonder Woman's second type of foil (or "other") in that they are constructed as un-American and nonwhite. Women are being underpaid at a department store due to the machinations of an apparently Italian man, Guigi del Slimo (Marston and Peter 1942, *Sensation Comics* #8). A German doctor is described by Etta, "That big heinie was going to shoot me full of germs or something!" (Marston and Peter 1942, *Sensation Comics* #9). The Japanese characters are portrayed with darker skin, very large teeth, and sometimes round glasses. Several times, they forge alliances with Mexicans and South Americans such that the latter appear naïve or unintelligent (see, e.g., Marston and Peter 1942, *WW* #1; *Sensation Comics* #16 (1943), #18 (1943), #45 (1945)). In contrast, small side panels in select comics during these years assume readers are "all-American," exhorting them to buy war bonds and stamps.

The small number of African American characters who appear are caricatures. The porter who carries Etta's bag is black-ink-skinned with large pink lips, "Dis suitcase show am heaby!" (Marston and Peter 1943, *Sensation Comics* #18). A large, handkerchiefed "mammy" archetype cares for her charges more than their society-climbing white mother, telling her, "Mis Mod'n yo' chillum done run 'way in de canoe!" (Marston and Peter 1944, *Sensation Comics* #31). With these portrayals of non-Americans and African Americans, and to some extent, the portrayal of Etta in contrast to that of Diana, the comic circulates dominant "American" ideas about gender, race, and class.

At the same time, though, confrontations of stereotypes of gender were embedded in these early comics. Space for such subversion was created in a unique cultural moment, through the wartime flux of gender roles, as Rosie the Riveters and other women worked for the war effort. Diana is superstrong and confident. Alongside her, Etta is fearless, capable, and an instrumental part of our hero's successes. Both, along with Etta's friends, battle Nazis, Japanese spies, a group of female criminals calling themselves Villainy Incorporated, and various mythical and alien characters. They generally subdue these characters not by overt violence but rather, by tying them up, and work to redeem the female criminals and help women and children in general.[4] When Wonder Woman is captured, she usually rescues herself, or sometimes, Etta and her friends rescue her. As noted, they are not oriented toward romance, but toward fun as well as fighting injustice, and this can be read as broadening possibilities for women. Their sisterhood replicates that of the Amazons, and is in stark contrast to many more recent portrayals of women as competitive and catty. It is not just Wonder Woman who is strong and capable, but all women. Submitting to men is constructed as women's undoing, literally: if a man chains Diana's bracelets together, "she becomes weak as other women in a man-ruled world" (Marston and Peter 1942, *WW* #2). Diana often tells women that they can be as strong and independent as she is if they believe in themselves and have proper physical training. She shows her own strength through throwing cars, lassoing planes, smothering bombs in her hands, and standing up for a cause; for instance, when she insists at the aforementioned department store, "For humanity's sake, why don't you give these girls a living wage?" (Marston and Peter 1942, *Sensation Comics* #8). Steve Trevor, too, subverts gender roles to an extent. He is a heroic military man in love with a beautiful woman. But he is shown as interested in romance and marriage, and with someone who is clearly stronger than him and in no way submissive to him. She rescues him frequently. He is a "mansel" in distress. While she loves him, Diana refuses him for three reasons. First, he isn't interested in her alter ego Diana Prince. Second, her mission to fight injustice must come first. Third, she says, "If I married, you, Steve, I'd have to pretend that I'm weaker than you are to make you happy—and that, no woman should do" (Marston and Peter 1945, *WW* #13).

Comics' distribution on newsstands, and for some, also in newspaper comic strips, required that their appeal be quite broad. A lot of people were reading these comics: during the war, about 90 percent of comics had superheroes in them, and sales may have been between 25 and 40 million per month (Wright 2001: 31; Hajdu 2008: 5).

**Figure 1.1** In a brief animated appearance, a 1940s-esque Wonder Woman engaged in some of her most iconic activities. Here, as she often did in the comics, she carries Steve Trevor and subverts "traditional" gender roles (*Batman: The Brave and the Bold*, "Curse of the Star Sapphire," S03E04, 2011).

In the war years, an average of two to three comics per week were read by over 90 percent of six- to eleven-year-olds, 84 percent of twelve- to seventeen-year-olds, and 35 percent of those eighteen and older. In each age group, the numbers of males and females reading comics were roughly equal (Gabilliet 2010: 198). It is difficult to get exact circulation numbers. But Wonder Woman was so successful in her first title, *Sensation Comics*, the publisher also launched *Wonder Woman*, and she appeared in *All Star Comics* and *Comic Cavalcade* as well. As the general sales manager for the King Features Syndicate pitched it to newspapers, "It is a strip that will appeal to women for the strength and character of Wonder Woman; to men for her magnificent beauty and her sinuous agility, her daring exploits and her charm; to all boys for the sheer thrill and excitement of Wonder Woman; and to girls who will take her for their idol and prototype" (Mullaney 2014: 9). It is probable that Wonder Woman as a character was selling in the six figures, and maybe even seven figures,[5] and her reach was further extended through the syndicated newspaper strip.

After the war, all of this changed as the more fluid gender possibilities embodied by the wartime Diana and Steve were shut down by Robert Kanigher, who would become the character's editor and writer for over twenty years. Marston was physically weak by 1945, with his assistant Joye Murchison probably authoring a number of comics credited to him at the time, and he died in 1947. With him died an insistence on the character's feminism at the same time that "traditional" gender roles were being reconstructed and reenforced in a variety of institutions, pushing women out of work and into the kitchen to act as the supportive homemakers and mothers they were supposedly born to be. Comic tastes turned away from superheroes and toward romance (portraying women as desiring heterosexual relationships to complete them) and horror (portraying women as attractive victims). A years-long moral panic over comics culminated in the industry-adopted Comics Code. Although the sources of the comics panic were many, its touchstone was manufactured social science by psychologist Fredric Wertham that linked comics and juvenile delinquency (Tilley 2012). Wonder Woman was part of the problem: "She is physically very powerful, tortures men, has her own female following, is the cruel, 'phallic' woman. While she is a frightening figure for boys, she is an undesirable ideal for girls, being the exact opposite of what they are supposed to want to be" (Wertham 2008 [1954]: 54). He also expressed some concern about Diana's all-female college girl entourage and their sexuality—he said they were lesbians and that Batman and Robin were gay, casting them all outside of American Cold War–era propriety. To be fair, Wertham also criticized the sexualization of women and the subordinate portrayals of people of color, but those critiques did not make the same impact at the time as those targeted at violent content and at the "nontraditional" nature of prominent genres and characters.

"Traditional" femininity, masculinity, and marriage were central to the Kanigher's *Wonder Woman* in the 1950s and 1960s. He thought that the Amazons were lesbians (Robbins 2014: 145), and wanted to write "a real love story with real people" (Daniels 2000: 93). Steve Trevor's marriage proposals to Diana became constant, and she left the military to work for a romance column and as a stunt woman in Hollywood. *Sensation Comics* was canceled, and artist Harry Peter was fired. On covers drawn by Irwin Hasen and panels by Ross Andru, Diana's boots were replaced with delicate laced sandals, her formerly flat bustier was drawn with more defined curves, her hair was longer and her eyes and mouth larger, and more dynamic posing allowed for more focus on her curves.[6] The feature in the back of the comic that profiled famous women, called "Wonder Women of History," was replaced in 1950 by "Marriage a la Mode," which documented marriage customs around the world. Similar romance supplements continued for twenty years.[7]

In her post–Second World War incarnation, Wonder Woman is no longer anti-normative or antiestablishment. The origin story of her being "made from clay by her mother and brought to life by goddesses" was wiped away as her mother tells her tearfully that she had a father who was lost at sea (Robert Kanigher and Ross Andru 1959, *WW* #105). Her mission to teach peace and equality was replaced by a mission to "battle crime and injustice" (Kanigher and Andru 1958, *WW* #98). Her powers became more "super" and were bestowed by the gods, rather than being earned through Amazon training. She battled fantastic monsters like a giant centipede, a giant squid, a giant bird, and a giant egg with a mustache named Egg Fu. Etta and the girls were jettisoned such that she had no peers, and numerous stories focused on Wonder Woman as a "Wonder Tot" and also a "Wonder Girl," juggling suitors such as Mer-Boy and Amoeba-Boy, going to birthday parties and flying kites. She was put in the role of a child through the Wonder Girl and Wonder Tot characters, which are her at younger ages, but she was also put into the role of a mother as she was shown alongside them, caring for her "Wonder Family." The feminizing costume shift and body changes, the romance and the addition of a father, and the Wonder Family all serve to put her squarely inside a "heteronormative" frame—the idea that strict male and female gender roles as well as heterosexuality are normal and natural. This meant that for the most part, the character did not present the same kinds of resistance to gendered inequalities as she had in the 1940s. Comics were among the many institutions circulating Cold War ideologies that worked to reestablish "traditional" order after the multiple challenges of the war years.

Printed fan letters grew increasingly critical (Valcour 2013: 73–75) and Kanigher recast the book back to a more Golden Age veneer. As Pustz notes, "It is important to remember that the letters pages offer readers a site for mediated (if not manipulated) interaction. Editors decide which letters to publish and which to ignore" (1999: 177). A fan letter after the change expressed uncertainty about this direction and concern that the Wonder Family would no longer be in the book, along with asserting that the character was held in "extremely low opinion" by its fandom (Joseph Arul, *WW* #162). Kanigher replied, "I want to see whether it is possible to recreate a golden era for a golden super heroine. . . . If my head rolls for it, I'll try to stick it back on and move in the direction you've mentioned" (*WW* #162). The recast book did not, however, have its "golden era" feminism without Marston.

Sales were mediocre throughout the 1960s (Hanley 2014: 157). Through the changes, her intro line remained, "Beautiful as Aphrodite, wise as Athena, swifter than Mercury, and stronger than Hercules." Her next incarnation would portray her mostly as the first one and less as the other three, all in the name of a more modern feminism.

## Wonder Woman in the Second Wave of feminism: 1968–86[8]

"I'll lose him forever if I don't do something to keep him interested in me!" laments Diana in 1968, as she gives up her powers and "mystical skills" to be with Steve (Dennis O'Neil and Mike Sekowsky 1968, *WW* #178 and 179). On the cover, her hair is longer and teased up, and she wears a purple tunic with black leggings and boots, "Wow, I'm gorgeous! I should have done this ages ago!" Diana uses martial arts, gadgets, and detective skills to defeat criminals, like the TV characters Emma Peel in *The Avengers* and Batgirl in *Batman* ['66]. Superman watches her take down some muggers, thinking "Guess I was wrong worrying about Diana! The lass doesn't need superpowers!" (O'Neil and Dick Dillin 1971, *World's Finest* #204). During the day, she owns and operates a clothing boutique. She is her own boss, and financially independent.

As noted in the Introduction, the Second Wave of feminism beginning in the mid-1960s was united in its insistence on equal opportunities for men and women and in its deconstruction of the "feminine mystique" that glorified different and unequal roles for men and women. Through lobbying, court cases, rallies, publications, alternative institutions and safe spaces, and consciousness-raising, these feminists did make headway in changing laws that overtly discriminated against women. Changing norms about gender was, and remains, not so easy. In particular, for questioning inequality and discrimination, feminists were and still are often demonized as not being "proper" women. This one-note stereotype of "man-hating" and "angry feminist" would surface repeatedly in Wonder Woman's portrayals, but not quite yet.

The first writer and later, editor of this period, Dennis O'Neil, defined the new direction for the title as feminist, "I saw it as taking a woman and making her independent, and not dependent on superpowers. I saw it as making her thoroughly human and then an achiever on top of that [which was] very much in keeping with the feminist agenda" (Daniels 2000: 126). Editors' responses to letters reflect this mind-set as well (Hollon 2012: 102). Indeed, this was one year after the new Batgirl had appeared on the *Batman* ['66] TV show: a working woman who was attractive and not superpowered, fighting crime—and owned by the same company, DC (see Chapter 2). O'Neil spoke about his goals for the title in the same way in 2013, but added that while he had been on the left politically and felt at the time that he was serving the cause of feminism, in retrospect he saw that his ideas about gender politics were not quite as advanced as he thought they were (Denver Comic Con Panel 2013).

In some ways, the new *Wonder Woman* team had made a feminist move. But in other ways they were writing a very stereotypical woman: she gives up power to keep a man, she often looks frightened or is crying, she is geared toward fashion, and she is secondary to an older male mentor. For most of this lengthy "depowered" period (October 1968 to December 1972), she wears a white dress or jumpsuit and is trained in martial arts by a short, blind, elderly, wise Asian man named I-Ching. He serves as another foil for Diana's all-American, nondisabled white woman, but rather than being demonized as per early *Wonder Woman* comics, he is exoticized. Both types of portrayals had roots in Western fiction and were having a resurgence at this time. He is written as more powerful than her: more sage, more physically capable, more rational. The cover of issue #180 has as its title *The Incredible I-Ching and . . . The New Wonder Woman* and remains so for the next few issues, setting her up as secondary in her own book. I-Ching explains as he trains her, "I am last surviving member of ancient sect! Our monastery was hidden high in mountain! It was our task to maintain ageless knowledge lost for centuries past!" (O'Neil and Sekowski, *WW* #179). The character is stereotyped even as he is set up to be interesting and sympathetic. So is Diana: she cries over the dead Steve Trevor even as she has a succession of dates (with whom she tends to fall in love and over whom she tends to cry). The above-mentioned story in which Superman observes her taking down muggers ends with him protecting her from their bullets, and both of them lamenting how he'd like to kiss her but shouldn't. She resigns from the Justice League because she has no superpowers. Apparently, the superpower-less Batman felt no such compulsion. Diana does have moments of happiness, since "happiness for any healthy red-blooded young gal is bedecking herself in the latest fashion finery" (Sekowski 1969, *WW* #182). If the character had started out this way, gaining confidence and skill via I-Ching and growing stronger and more decisive, sort of like a proto-Buffy the Vampire Slayer (see Chapter 5), the comic may have been received more positively by more people. But an all-male creative team reducing a long-standing, iconic, superpowered female character's strength and confidence, and having Diana secondary to a multiply stereotyped male character, subverted the "independent" and "feminist" character the writers and artists were striving for.

This "New Wonder Woman" wasn't fighting for democracy or peace or for equal rights for women, though. Indeed, she was rarely around women at all. Then in the 1972 "Special Women's Lib Issue," Diana is asked to join a "lib" group (drawn as diverse in skin color, age, and body type), but declines to join their protest for better pay at a department store, "I'm for equal wages too! But I'm not a joiner. I wouldn't fit in with your group. In most cases, I don't even like women" (Samuel Delany and Dick Giordano 1972, *WW* #203). Diana does change across the story: she joins the group and protests the injustice. But the contrast with her 1940s incarnation—the Amazon from all-female Paradise Island, who called all women "Sister," who fought Nazis and Japanese spies with a group of women, who tried to redeem female criminals, who stood up for better pay for women, and who exhorted women to believe in themselves and their own strength—is quite stark. Although this was supposed to be the first of a multipart series on women's issues, it was rather the last issue of this era. Its usual letter column page announced that the next issue would be helmed again by Robert Kanigher, who as noted produced much more traditional and binary depictions of gender and sexuality in the title from the late 1940s to the late 1960s. With this move, DC turned away from both Marston's brand of First Wave feminism and O'Neil's brand of Second Wave feminism.

Demonstrating the ways in which audience reception is neither predictable nor simplistic, letters show that some fans embraced the depowered portrayal while others wanted Diana's superpowers back. *Wonder Woman* editor (for two issues) Dorothy Woolfolk wanted to return the powers in 1971. At the same time, Gloria Steinem was launching *Ms.* magazine, with the classic costumed Wonder Woman on the cover (Edgar 1972). Generating publicity for both of them, *Ms.* and DC Comics copublished a collection of *Wonder Woman* stories, with a heartfelt introduction by Steinem on what the character's strength, compassion, and sense of justice meant to her and other young women. Not long after, Diana's powers were restored and the old costume was back, as was the overwhelmingly white (without I-Ching) character base. Nubia— Wonder Woman's twin sister, molded from "black clay" as Diana was molded from "white," and shoeless and clad in leopard print to further exoticize her dark skin—was introduced but quickly discarded (Robert Kanigher and Don Heck, *WW* #204–06). Restoring Wonder Woman's powers didn't mean restoring her feminism or the title's 1940s sensibility about the fluidity of gender. Indeed, Wonder Woman was drawn to look somewhat younger and prettier, with a slightly smaller costume. Within a few years, she was decidedly curvier and often posed more suggestively.

These changes were enabled by the liberalization of the Comics Code in 1971 as it amended the Code of 1954, by different artists, by whom DC felt their audience was at the time, and by who they wanted their audience to be. Ads and fan letters in the *Wonder Woman* comics had shifted. Gender-neutral public service announcements and romance supplements were being replaced by ads for BB guns and bodybuilding, and letter authors were more often male and adult (Hollon 2012: 93, 96; Hanley 2014: 153, 155). Some letters praised the new portrayals and requested more full-page pictures for pin-ups. Only six letters from 1974 to 1983 referred to Wonder Woman as feminist, while twenty-six letters from 1968 to 1983 requested Steve Trevor (who was dead for about half of these years) be empowered (Hollon 2012: 106, 113, 119,

120, 123). For instance, "I agree with the reader who would like to see Steve develop super powers. I'm really tired of seeing a woman in a superior position to a man. What this must be doing to Steve's ego!" (Lester Tracy, *WW* #178). Due to these reader sentiments and apparently his own feelings, new editor Julius Schwartz felt no need to empower the character to align her more with her origins or with Second Wave feminism, admitting, "I never particularly cared for Wonder Woman."

Years later, some letter writers still found her antimale, with one saying she had "man-hating tendencies" (Mark Rogers, *WW* #240). The response, unsigned but presumably by post-Schwartz editor Larry Hama, was, "Wonder Woman does NOT hate men! . . . the Amazons and Wonder Woman hate the violence perpetrated by men and their wars. It is the love of mankind (of humankind, if you will) that prompted the Amazons to send Princess Diana to the outside world it the first place." This did not make much of an impact on some readers, such as a later letter writer who saw the comic differently, "I am sick and tired of her moaning and whining about men and her self-righteous belief that women are superior" (Dan Beck, *WW* #284). This letter and the one noted just above both referred to issues by writer Gerry Conway, who in 1977 would launch *Ms. Marvel* at Marvel Comics (see Chapter 6). But these and similar letters didn't cite specific text or art in which Wonder Woman was "man-hating," which implies that either it was so obvious to them they felt they didn't need to, or if it was her overall demeanor and strength alongside and against males that gave them that impression.

During this same time period, the *Super Friends* cartoon aired on Saturday mornings (1973–86), and Lynda Carter portrayed Diana in the evenings (1975–79), both with high ratings. Both may have been more palatable to viewers than the comic and its increasingly older and male readers, albeit for different reasons. On the animated show, she was the only female "Super Friend": at the beginning, as one of the original five Super Friends, and at the end, one of eleven. Most of the time, there were no female characters who could have been considered her peers and the show usually failed the "Bechdel test," such that there were not at least two female characters who talk about something other than a man. Like the comics of the 1950s and 1960s that had no peer female characters around Wonder Woman, the cartoon put tremendous pressure on the character to represent "all" women and girls on Saturday mornings to millions of kids, an important but impossible task in a time of both successes by and backlashes to feminist initiatives. She was capable and intelligent, and one episode showcased her origin story in its Marston version. Made by her mother from clay, with Athena and Aphrodite's guidance, she was "strong as Hercules and swifter than Mercury" (Jeffrey Scott 1978, "Secret Origins," *Challenge of the Super Friends*). But it seems in their initial effort to make sure she was perceived as strong, she was often written and directed as one-note, no-nonsense, and humorless, and her eyebrows were drawn quite arched in a perpetual frown. Wonder Woman voice actor Shannon Farnon noted,

> The director made the choices as how to play her. . . . We did change Wonder Woman along the way from very butch to somewhat softer. It often depended on the people at the network in any given year. . . . I liked her to keep the feminine side and show young women it's ok to be strong. (Whipple n.d.)

The cartoon's success wrought the *Super Friends* comics (1976–81), where Wonder Woman was usually written by E. Nelson Bridwell and drawn by Ramona Fradon, who tends to be unacknowledged as the first woman to draw the character because she did not work on the eponymous title.[9] In the print version, Diana wasn't as ultra-serious in text or in art. Her look was more feminized, with Fradon displaying her body in active but not sexualized poses as she flies her invisible plane, lassoes large objects and villains, and uses her bracelets to deflect bullets and lasers. Her strength was unquestioned by the others, shown as on par with Superman's, and she was an integral part of the team. As on the cartoon, she was usually the only female Super Friend. This is the "Smurfette principle," an unfortunately not uncommon representation of one token and privileged female amid a sea of males, such that her main character trait is simply "being" the female: "Boys are the norm, girls the variation; boys are central, girls peripheral; boys are individuals, girls types. Boys define the group, its story and its code of values. Girls exist only in relation to boys" (Pollitt 1991).

While both the *Super Friends* cartoon and comic were successes, where Wonder Woman exploded in terms of popularity was in the live-action show starring Lynda Carter as the titular character. The show has been referred to as "jiggle tv" and later *Wonder Woman* writer John Byrne recalled "fond memories of Lynda Carter running in slo-mo" (Daniels 2000: 193). But unlike her animated counterpart, Carter's Diana was multifaceted: strong, confident, smart, humble, sexy, fierce, diplomatic, sweet, funny, and regal all at once, pushing the boundaries of traditional narratives of gender on prime-time TV. The first season of the show on ABC (which also aired the *Super Friends*) was set during the Second World War, and portrayed not only Diana but also her mother, sister, and other Amazons as well as Etta Candy. Diana sometimes lectured villains about equality, peace, and tolerance, but the show had plenty of action along with Carter's iconic "spin" that magically changed her clothes. The first season of the show has some similarities to the 1940s Marston comics. Two season-opening episodes portray Wonder Woman winning a contest of strength and skill to leave the all-female Paradise Island and return Steve Trevor to the United States, although they do not reference her birth from clay (Stanley Ralph Ross 1975, "The New Original Wonder Woman" and Stephen Kandel 1977, "The Return of Wonder Woman"). Diana reaches out to women by appealing to sisterhood, most famously with Fausta, "The Nazi Wonder Woman." Steve is knocked out or requires rescue in many episodes, but he is updated to be more appreciative of Wonder Woman's alter ego Diana Prince.

The writer of the *Wonder Woman* comic at the time, Martin Pasko, has said he was directed to capitalize on the show's success by recasting the comic back to the 1940s to mirror it (Siuntres 2012). Indeed, much of the editor's column of issue #228 is taken up with addressing this and with a section called "Meet Lynda Carter"; and in the next issue there is a similar section for readers to "Meet Lyle Waggoner," who played Steve Trevor. The show's success seems to have increased comic sales somewhat, as well as enabling the *Super Friends* cartoon, canceled in 1974, to get picked back up. But it was expensive to produce as a period piece. In its second and third season, the show's setting was fast-forwarded to the 1970s by CBS after ABC had passed, in order

**Figure 1.2** Lynda Carter, as Wonder Woman, in the more revealing costume of the TV show's second season, pushing with her superstrength against rapidly closing walls ("The Man Who Made Volcanoes," S02E09, 1977).

to save money. At that point, while Carter still wore her classic comics outfit at some points—with a slightly lower cut top and higher cut bottoms—the show became more like a 1970s cop show, with her and Steve more like detectives. It began to feature much more diverse casting than the comic, particularly in its third season, and as it went along, greatly scaled back the earnestness. Like her animated counterpart, Wonder Woman became the only continuing female character. The comic editors apparently received dozens of letters from fans about the TV series' changed time period. Some wanted the comic series to stay in the 1940s and some wanted it updated to the 1970s to match what they saw on TV. DC chose the latter, announcing on the letters page that they would align the comic with the show, the *Justice League* comic, and the *Super Friends* cartoon and comic (*WW* #240, 241, 242). But the TV show could not float the comic forever. Sales declined.

By 1980, just about every printed letter in *Wonder Woman* was from a male writer. One rare letter from a woman read, "You said Wonder Woman wasn't selling very well. . . . In one year it has gone from my favorite comic to worst and there are many reasons. . . . She has no friends and no life . . . there are no supporting characters. Even the villains are forgettable" (Suzanne Missert, *WW* #273). Indeed, by 1981, the sales were only about half of what they were in 1976–77 while the TV show was on.[10] The 1970s and early 1980s portrayals were somewhat campy and action-oriented, and often portrayed curvy women fighting one another or fighting men in a kind of "battle of the sexes" that negatively stereotyped feminism.[11] In *Wonder Woman*'s last issue before a company-wide relaunch of its superhero comics, she and Steve get married, framing the event as her ultimate achievement or dream come true.

As a letter writer in 1986 summed up the previous two decades of *Wonder Woman* comics,

> She should be one of the most successful, interesting, thought provoking characters in comics. Instead, we have seen her presented as everything from a female Superman . . . to a man-hating belligerent female chauvinist. We have seen her stripped of power and we have seen her prove that Diana Prince can be a hundred times more boring than Clark Kent. We have seen her comic format changed to WWII to fit a tv show. "When," scream her remaining faithful, "will we see a real wonder of a woman?" (Donald Shelton, *WW* #329)

The portrayals he cites were not uncommon in mass media portrayals of women and feminism at the time, indicative of misunderstandings of and backlash against the civil rights movements of the previous decades, particularly by all-male creative teams.

## Third Wave feminism in *Wonder Woman* in the 1980s and 1990s

Struggles over the representations and resonance of Wonder Woman would continue in the 1980s and 1990s, related not just to creators' different goals, but also to the contentious politics of the times and a change in the distribution methods for comics. Amid declining sales across its books, DC Comics wiped out the histories of its superhero titles with a 1985 event called *Crisis on Infinite Earths*, and rebooted its superhero universe. The new *Wonder Woman* was helmed by writer/artist and self-described feminist George Pérez and the title's first female editor Karen Berger. Of the sixty-two issues he wrote, Pérez drew about twenty, as did Jill Thompson, making her the first female artist on the ongoing title. Mindy Newell, the first female writer on the title due to three issues she'd written before *Crisis*, cowrote about a dozen issues with Pérez. The *Wonder Woman 1989 Annual* would credit Pérez along with about twenty women as writers, pencilers, inkers, and letterers. Berger summed up the new team's approach in the second issue: "Wonder Woman [is] a great role model to young women, but also contains many elements that appeal to males as well. Wonder Woman crosses the gender line." Harkening back to Marston's first stories from the 1940s, Pérez's Diana works with friends and allies to spread the "power of peace" around the world with her "brains, brawn, and beauty" (Pérez 1987, *WW* Vol. 2 #7). Specifically, she would teach "lessons of peace and equality" while also being prepared to fight humans, monsters, and gods—particularly, God of War Ares—if compassion and diplomacy failed (Pérez and Len Wein 1988, *WW* Vol. 2 #17). This combination of actions traditionally thought of as "feminine" and "masculine" highlights how the connotations of those words are constructed, and creates space for questioning what is feminine, what is masculine, and whether there isn't more of a spectrum of gender rather than two neat boxes with accompanying traits (Brown 2004 and 2011; Inness 2004; Robinson 2004; Stuller 2010; see also Butler 1990; Halberstam 1998).

Pérez says he had great freedom because no one else wanted to take on the *Wonder Woman* title, so he drew Diana as more "ethnic" to show that "she is not American," drew the Amazons and other supporting characters as more racially diverse, and introduced the dark-skinned Phillipus as Diana's mother's trusted female companion (Supanova 2010). None of these characters was sexualized, but rather, beautiful, strong, capable, and regal in bearing. He also implied that some Amazons were in romantic and/or sexual relationships with each other (see, e.g., Pérez, Newell, and Chris Marrinan 1990, *WW* Vol. 2 #38). Further, his Amazons were created by the Greek goddesses from the souls of women who'd been abused and murdered by their male partners, and he renamed Man's World "Patriarch's World" to underscore its gendered inequalities. Diana's mother, Queen Hippolyta, is still the sole ruler of the Amazons, but she makes clear that her decisions are based on majority rule. All of these elements exhibited some of the sensibilities of the Third Wave of feminism, which beginning in the 1980s encompassed those who opposed discrimination and supported equality like its Second Wave, but also emphasized diversity and was more open to celebrating femininity. The comic appears to have been read as such.

Most of the first fan letters printed after the reboot specifically praised the new Diana as a strong feminine and feminist woman. For instance, "Feminism has been Wonder Woman's credo since 1942 . . . she should go on promoting equality for women" (Jeff Turner, *WW* Vol. 2 #4). "I fully agree with your perception of Wonder Woman as a positive and strong model for girls/women. It also, hopefully, will take some of the chauvinism out of the male readers brought up on macho men and weak women" (Malcolm Bourne, *WW* Vol. 2 #5). "The core positive feminist perspective has been a great joy for me . . . . The women you portray are affirming yet independent women—not the castrating lesbian that seems to be the macho-male's greatest fear, nor the stereotypical simpering patriarchal feminine" (Daniel Brian Eddy, *WW* Vol. 2 #26). Most of the early letters were from men, prompting one female fan to write, "I would like to see more comments from women. I know I'm not alone out here, am I?" (Mary Griffin, *WW* Vol. 2 #15). Editor Karen Berger responded in #28,

> George is an ardent feminist, supporting women's rights more than a lot of women I know, and he is a true believer in equality between the sexes. As for the majority of letters written by men, that's because 99% of those who write in are male, and I print as many letters from women as I can. I wish more women would write in.

Sales were high, about the same as those in 1976–77 during the Lynda Carter TV show and about double those of the early 1980s.[12] Fan letters were specifically enthusiastic about the book's politics, its return to a more Marston-esque character, its emphasis on peace and love and compassion, and its characters and their characterizations, all of which pushed back on the antifeminist backlash of the late 1970s and early 1980s.

DC printed a few negative letters that described Diana as "man-hating," but they were outnumbered by the negative letters that wanted *more* diversity across and tolerance by the characters.[13] Elements that would have drawn praise from early Second Wave feminists were now perceived as not going far enough. For instance, the still-stout Etta Candy and Steve Trevor would marry one another, which not only removed Steve from being linked with Diana, but also foreclosed the possibilities of the queerness that Marston had implied for Etta. Diana would acquire a new circle of friends and "sisters," the strong supporting characters of the older single mother and academic Julia Kapatelis and her daughter Vanessa, and the high-powered fashionable businesswomen Myndi Mayer, in particular. They and other new characters were female and of differing ages, but were also mostly white, educated, and middle class. It is these kinds of moves that are both welcomed and critiqued by feminism's Third Wave.

As conservative politics in the late 1980s and early 1990s clashed with liberal identity politics, the sensibilities of Third Wave feminism and of queer theory gained resonance for some on the left. But as comics writer Grant Morrison observed, superhero comics at the time would lean to the right: "The gender confusions and reorganizations of masculine-feminine boundaries that marked the eighties had outgrown their welcome, so men became lads and women were babes" (2011: 235). The shift in direction, within the political and social context outlined above, was pushed along further by changes in comics distribution. As newsstand sales declined and direct market sales to local comic shops increased, the active fan base frequenting such shops became more homogenous: mostly male, white, heterosexual, and adult.[14] Comic art began to display a hypergendered backlash to the gains of the feminist movements: hypermuscular men and hypersexualized women. Wonder Woman had been out of step with the trend and still selling well, but her story and the ways in which it would be represented would soon become the embodiment of it.

The new "Bad Girl" portrayal of Wonder Woman was drastically different from that by George Pérez and Jill Thompson. By the mid-1990s, superhero comic sales had begun to crash, and reliance on the loyal customers of the direct market and local comic shops was high. Sales initially went up as DC "tried to make the character more accessible to the largely male, conservative comic-book-buying audience by emphasizing her sexuality and downplaying her feminism" (DiPaolo 2011: 83; see also Madrid 2009: 210). These stories were less about Greek myths, about questions of morality and power and peace, and more about simply fighting criminals in a hyperviolent and hypersexualized manner, often with a facial expression that has been described as "porn face."

Many fans thought that writer William Messner-Loebs gave the character "a harder edge . . . without compromising her basic code of honor" (Paul Girard, *WW* Vol. 2 #0) and praised his writing. From 1992 to 1995, after George Pérez and editor Karen Berger left, Loebs and a variety of artists worked on the title. Loebs had Diana lead a female slave rebellion on another planet, work in the fast food restaurant Taco Whiz, and compel a mobster to pay child support. But it was the last artist on Loebs' run, Mike Deodato, Jr., who garnered the most attention for the way he objectified Diana and the Amazons in sexualized poses, and incorporated more and bloodier violence. Wearing little, they were often drawn in the "broke back" fashion described in the Introduction: a twisted, physically impossible posture allowing the reader to see all of a woman's curves in the front and back at the same time (Loebs and Deodato 1996a, b).[15]

Deodato's portrayal was in line with many other superhero comics, mainstream movies, and video games at the time. He later remarked,

> They gave me freedom to do whatever I want. . . . I kept making her more . . . um . . . hot? Wearing thongs. I talked to Bill Loebs at a convention, and he said his friends call his run on *Wonder Woman* with me "porn Wonder Woman" [laughter]. . . . Every time the bikini was smaller, the sales got higher. (*Newsarama* 2006)

Clearly, many readers liked Diana in a thong and posed with her back very arched and her buttocks upturned. But many others may have dropped the title over such representations. Comics writer, artist, and herstorian Trina Robbins summarized this portrayal as a "barely-clothed hypersexual pinup" (1996: 166).

Two letters in particular represent the different ways in which readers received "porn Wonder Woman." One embraced Diana's embodiment of traits that had historically been constructed as conflicting, "Deodato drew at once a beautiful princess and a fierce warrior" (Eric Gerbershagen, *WW* Vol. 2 #104). A second wrote at length about the female characters' sexualization: "Costumes. Kindly get them out of their butts. Glancing through the comic, every woman's cheeks are out flapping in the breeze. Give them some rear coverage and some dignity . . . [12-inch] Waists. Please give them more realistic waistlines" (Kate Payne, *WW* Vol. 2 #95). Both readers represent Third Wave feminist ideas, but they conflict with one another. The first letter writer is in line with the Third Wave's celebration of a person's individual choices and of sexy images of women. The second represents the Third Wave's push for cultural critique of the objectification of women. The art style was not seen as a problem by the comic's editor, Paul Kupperberg. He responded to Kate Payne's letter: "Uh-huh, and all men have 42-inch chests, 30-inch waists, and bulging pecs . . . not! Comic book heroes tend to be idealized versions of men and women both." True, males in 1990s comics were drawn in an exaggeratedly muscular way. They were not, however, drawn scantily clad or with excessive attention to their sex organs, nor were they posed in "broke back" fashion or in sexually submissive poses as their female counterparts often were.

A further complication was that these letter writers (along with many others) praised the storyline that was illustrated by these images. The plot concerned Artemis, an Amazon like Diana, but who was raised in poverty and had to fight constantly against invaders. She is light-skinned like Diana, but taller and more muscular, with impossibly long red hair and a darker personality. They are "two sides of the same coin" and both purposely named for the same goddess, acknowledged editor Kupperberg (#102). Artemis is given the title of Wonder Woman, replacing the titular hero not unlike the situations in *The Death of Superman* and *Batman: Knightfall*, both of which had been recently released to high sales. Although Artemis tries to carry the mantle of Wonder Woman, she faces two major challenges. One is her generally more brusque and violent approach that is constructed to be a result of her harsh upbringing. The second is that those around her constantly compare her to Diana, which causes her both to resent them and seek to earn their respect through her fighting skills. She is defeated, attacked and dying bloodily on about one-third of her last issue's pages, with her costume progressively more shredded. Artemis' death, like her life, was enmeshed in its "Bad Girl" times as capitalized on by Deodato. On the final page, only some parts of her breasts are covered and only a small strip of fabric runs down the middle of her crotch. Yet while bloodied and dead, she is still posed arching her back so as to accentuate her curves (Loebs and Deodato 1995, *WW* Vol. 2 #100). Her dying words to Diana are that she (Artemis) had not deserved the title of Wonder Woman.

But fans didn't read Artemis as undeserving. Even if the characterization of Artemis was supposed to shore up Diana's "proper" portrayal of the female hero, fans loved both characters and embraced the idea that there's more than one way to be a hero. "Thanks for giving Artemis an honorable death. . . . She could have been the true Wonder Woman" (Kati Lovegrove, *WW* Vol. 2 #104.) And, "I really like her! She's headstrong, arrogant, and has a chip on her shoulder, but she's also honest, brave, and has ideals just as strong (if not stronger) than Diana's own. Don't kill her off—Keep her around as a supporting character" (Jim Headrick, *WW* Vol. 2 #101). In reference to talk of resurrecting Artemis, many fans wrote in to agree.

Writers and editors listened. Artemis "got better," as the saying goes when dead comic characters are brought back to life. Loebs wrote and Ed Benes drew a miniseries starring her, John Byrne wrote and drew her in the main title, and Eric Luke wrote and Yanick Paquette drew her in the main title as well. Artemis is part of Diana's circle, even training the new Wonder Girl, Cassie Sandsmark. In all three of these 1990s portrayals, Artemis is still portrayed as the "darker" Amazon and is still quite sexualized. Diana is as well, less so in Byrne's book.

The "girls" remained "bad" through the end of the 1990s. The 2000s, having reaped some successes of Third Wave feminism, would be a time of backlash to the backlash. In other words, the 2000s comics writers pushed back against the 1990s Bad Girl portrayals and sought to again recapture the feminism of Pérez's and Marston's Wonder Woman. Representations of Wonder Woman, and struggles over her story and her significance to broader cultural debates about the role of women, would change yet again.

## Race, sexuality, and gender politics in *Wonder Woman* in the 2000s

The main writers of Wonder Woman in the 2000s, Phil Jimenez, Greg Rucka, and Gail Simone, were strongly influenced by George Pérez's time on the book, and were all established voices in the comics industry who wanted to write the character. They also generally subscribed to the ideas and aesthetics of the Third Wave of feminism. Mobilized by the backlash to the Second Wave of feminism in the 1980s and the continuing devaluation of women and girls into the 1990s, the Third Wave is not only open to spectrums of race, gender, and sexuality but also the reclaiming of womanhood and femininity as empowering. Cultural critique and cultural production, often laced with parody or irony, are important aspects of the Third Wave as well (see, e.g., hooks

1981, Lorde 1984, Moraga and Anzaldúa 1981, Baumgartner and Richards 2000, Heywood and Drake 1997, Walker 1992 and 1995; see also Kinser 2004, Purvis 2004, Snyder 2008).[16] Jimenez, Rucka, and Simone all displayed these types of concerns and sensibilities through the comics they produced.

When writer and artist Phil Jimenez took over the title in 2000, he reiterated that the character was "stronger than Hercules, swifter than Hermes, wise as Athena, and beautiful as Aphrodite" and drew her as beautiful and sexy but not sexualized. He made Diana's politics explicitly feminist and queer through her founding the Wonder Woman Foundation to help women be "economically self-sufficient and in control of their bodies and reproductive lives" and to promote

> the liberation of men, women, and children from the terrible problems that stem from antiquated religious philosophies and patriarchal fear—by educating them about alternatives. All human beings deserve to live on this planet without threat of violation, physical or spiritual, simply because of the body they were born in, the gender they were born to, or the region in which they live. (Jimenez and Joe Kelly 2001, *WW* Vol. 2 #170)

Subversions of narratives of gender are not just about women, of course. A number of gay male Wonder Woman fans, Phil Jimenez among them, have said that they found in her a strong role model without her strength being linked to being macho, that she was nonjudgmental, and that she didn't bow to cultural expectations or stereotypes of gender but broke them.[17] This issue received almost entirely positive and encouraging fan responses. A few were negative, such as "Little did I expect to find Diana on a neo-fascist diatribe about [Christianity] or sub-Marxist gibberish about 'valuing each other simply because we exist'" (Chris Jackson, *WW* Vol. 2 #173).

Jimenez also sought to increase the diversity in the title. He had the Amazons choose Artemis and Phillipus, the impoverished, rough warrior and the black military leader, to replace Queen Hippolyta and Diana as leaders. He wrote a scene of two Amazons talking that made it clear they were in a relationship. A letter writer reacted negatively, "Should you continue to advance the homosexual agenda . . . you will be able to include me along with Chris Jackson as an ex-longtime reader" (Seth Richard, *WW* Vol. 2 #177). The editor, either Eddie Berganza or Tom Palmer, Jr., scolded the letter writer for being intolerant, and wrote, "For the record, Phil is working on giving Diana a *boy*friend." Indeed, Diana had a new love interest, not white Steve Trevor but black Trevor Barnes, her colleague at the UN. There was largely positive fan feedback to the idea, says Jimenez, but also very "negative and often racist reactions" as well, that "undermined my goals" (Singh 2002). The very negative feedback was not printed. Instead, a typical letter read, "The most attractive part of Jimenez's latest storyline is the African American love interest. . . . Speaking as an African American reader, I hope that this becomes a very strong storyline for Diana" (Terry Hagan, *WW* Vol. 2 #180). On the other side were letters such as, "One thing has me troubled, this whole losing the virginity thing. . . . I just don't like this Trevor guy" (Tim Holl, *WW* Vol. 2 #181). What finally appeared was a panel in which Trevor's parents find the two on the couch, mostly clothed—an image that can be read in different ways and takes into account that negotiation between producers and consumers.

Jimenez' writing and art pushed for the fluidity of gender and sexuality, portrayed diversity, drew Diana as a strong woman not gratuitously sexualized, and used the genre to comment on cultural norms. Many, but not all, readers were on board with those ideals and the ideals remained despite criticism. Many, but not all, readers were willing to see a (hetero)sexually active Diana, but were not given the opportunity due to other readers' criticism. "Diana is an inherently political character—she's about feminist politics, humanist politics, sex politics, the politics of war, etc.—and that fact is probably her downfall. What makes her fascinating and endearing to me is also what makes her so controversial and unlikeable to some; it's also one of the things that make her such a difficult property commercially" (DiPaolo 2011: 86), says Jimenez, summing up the contested nature of her reception by different audiences.

Seeking to explicitly portray the politics of Wonder Woman, a character that he (like Jimenez) describes as "a political figure . . . designed to be a feminist character," Greg Rucka began writing *Wonder Woman* in 2002 (Talking Comics 2013b). He had Diana work as a diplomat at the UN with a strong diverse supporting cast, battling gods, teaching nonviolent conflict resolution to kids, and recording PSAs for Amnesty International. The non-sexualized but still brusque Artemis and partner of Diana's mother, Phillipus, remain the leaders of the Amazons. Rucka's highly praised run was grounded in the real world as it portrayed those for and against Diana's ideals as explicated in the book she writes within the world of the comic. Diana nixes the first book cover suggested by the publisher, which showed her lying on her stomach, parts of her breasts and buttocks exposed as a small pink drape covers very little of her—a meta image that plays on the readers' savvy in recognizing the objectification of women and being amused by its use as a marketing ploy. She counters this with a plain white cover depicting her lasso (Rucka and Drew Johnson 2003, *WW* Vol. 2 #195). Some characters frame her and her book as "nontraditional": Greek, pagan, disrespectful of authority, probably lesbian, vegetarian. Within the comic, people protest in the streets for and against her, while Rucka's text comments on the character both within and outside of the comic: "For everyone who loves her, there's someone who hates her, who's scared of her, of what she says and what she represents" (Rucka and Johnson, *WW* Vol. 2 #198). One of the latter says on a talk show, "I have no problem with her heroics, but the moment that woman gets in front of children to promote a life style and a belief system that right-thinking Americans find, frankly, disgusting, well, enough is enough. . . . She flies in the face of core family values . . . . She needs to remember her place." He is then asked, "Her place as a woman?" (Rucka and Johnson 2003, *WW* Vol. 2 #198). In other words, if she just punches things and saves people, that is acceptable because it fits long-standing cultural ideas of what (male) superheroes do, but if she speaks about beliefs different from long-standing cultural ideas, she is a threat. Later, blinded from a dramatic fight with Medusa, she breaks up a slave traffic ring and is asked by the media not about the women she has helped or the men she has brought to justice, but about how she does her hair without being able to see (Rucka and Rags Morales 2015, *WW* Vol. 2 #215). Her place as a woman is made clear here as well, echoing the ways in which female public figures are asked about fashion and diet while their male counterparts are not. While creators and fans had debated overrepresentations of Wonder Woman for decades by this point, Rucka made those struggles over the character and over women part of the story itself.

Rucka's run is most famous for its plotline that was part of a high-selling crossover event, which had similarities to a number of post-9/11 comics that had explored a lack of trust in governmental authority and in superheroes (Costello 2009; Lewis 2012). Wonder Woman kills a human being, Maxwell Lord, who had sought to show why people should not trust superheroes by controlling Superman and forcing him into increasingly destructive actions. Compelled to tell the truth by Diana's lasso, Lord told her that the only way to stop him was to kill him. But Batman and Superman (and much of the world) turn against her for this action, saying she should have found another way (Rucka et al. 2005, *WW* Vol. 2 #219; *Adventures of Superman* #643; *The Omac Project*). Given the stakes, and given that Wonder Woman always, more than any of the others, would open her hand to enemies and try to resolve conflict with diplomacy while using force only when necessary and as a last resort, some fans felt the level of their disapproval was a bit forced. Others agreed with their condemnation. This story was editorially mandated, mostly for the effects it would have on Batman and Superman and how they felt about what she had done. Rucka had planned about eighteen more months of stories about Wonder Woman dealing with the fallout from the killing but did not get to write them (Talking Comics 2013a). The result, then, was a short-term focus on Batman and Superman's anger, a softer version of the phenomenon called "Women in Refrigerators," when a female character's actions, or what happens to her, just furthers the development of a male character.

The phrase "Women in Refrigerators" was coined by hairdresser and comics fan Gail Simone in 1999, just before Jimenez began his run. She compiled a list of female superheroes subject to repeated and often sexualized violence (like Artemis) and to long-term depowerment (like Wonder Woman), in ways that their male counterparts had not been (http://www.lby3.com/wir/index.html). The list got its name from the storyline of when Green Lantern's girlfriend was killed and put in his refrigerator for him to find. Simone sent it to dozens of comic creators, whose reactions ranged from defensive to neutral to agreement. This list exploded online such that Simone began to write a weekly column for the *Comic Book Resources* website. Several years later, she was writing *Wonder Woman*. Sixty years after the character was created, Simone was her first ongoing female writer. The only previous credited female writers had been Mindy Newell for three issues before Pérez's run, Trina Robbins for two short miniseries, and best-selling novelist Jodi Picoult for a five-issue story arc.

Simone's politics and style are similar to Rucka's, emblematic of the Third Wave of feminism's use of pop culture as a means of pushing political change. Tonally, such work is often playful, campy, and ironic. Simone has a production company make a movie about Wonder Woman, portraying a scantily clad Hippolyta swooning over Hercules as Diana's father (rather than as the enslaver of the Amazons), and all of the Amazons chanting, "Kill the men!" because "They leave the toilet seat up!" Diana shakes her head at the movie, "Why is it that people feel that a belief in women equals a hatred of men?" (Simone and Bernard Chang 2008, *WW* Vol. 3 #25). Later, Simone has Diana and Dinah Lance, the Black Canary, team up. Dinah informs Diana that they have to go undercover, and that she has discovered in such situations, conforming to gendered expectations makes things easier, "the sexier the outfit, the fewer questions asked." Once dressed in her revealing undercover garb, Diana looks down at herself and asks, "Do we need to expose quite so much of . . . [my breasts]? And these boots seem completely impractical in a combat situation! I can't believe women are expected to wear these every day. The damage to the legs and spine!" (Simone and Aaron Lopresti 2009, *WW* Vol. 3 #34). An attractive female warrior noting her own objectification in a ridiculously tight, shiny, and revealing outfit both adheres to the familiar form of the superhero genre while delivering a feminist message about that form, couched in humor (Brown 2004; Madrid 2009; Pender 2002, 2003 and Taylor 2007). Such plotting and dialogue, along with playful art, wittily critiques misunderstandings of both Wonder Woman and feminism.

There were no letter columns in Rucka's or Simone's runs, apparently due to more fans commenting online on boards rather than with letters to the editor. DC began to use the letters' space for promotion. But Simone launched a "Wonder Woman" thread on *Comic Book Resources'* boards in September 2009 when the above-referenced issue came out. When all of the boards were shut down in April 2014, due to some fans' harassment of other fans who had critiqued sexualized portrayals of female comic characters, the Wonder Woman thread had over 6,000 sub-threads. A number of posters addressed the character's juxtaposition of strength and beauty: "As long as they portray WW as being strong and smart, the eye candy is just a bonus" (Wonder Watcher September 15, 2009, 1:25 p.m.). "Wonder Woman is supposed to be feminine. That's what's so amazing about her. She is 'girly.' And can kick your ass when diplomacy fails" (Meek, September 16, 2009, 12:15 p.m.).[18] Simone responded to many posts, some of which were pointed and negative, to enter into conversation with readers. Former writer/artist Jimenez posted as well.

Simone wrote on the boards about her biggest regret: that she had intended for Diana's mother, Hippolyta, to propose marriage to Phillipus, but that tentative editorial approval was rescinded (Simone 2010). This may have been about gender and sexuality if editors feared receiving more letters accusing them of being anti-Christian, as in the letters to Jimenez above. It may have also been about race as Phillipus is black and Hippolyta white, in an echo of, again, letters to Jimenez about Trevor Barnes and Diana. The result was similar—almost all fans who expressed an opinion expressed a positive one, but they would not get to see the story. In the cases of Diana having sex with Trevor Barnes and Hippolyta proposing to Phillipus, the subtext can be (and according to fans, has been) read as supporting such stories. The writers of the 2000s implied that Diana and/or the other Amazons were queer. But while Jimenez, Rucka, and Simone were able to disrupt traditional boundaries of gender in certain ways, it is clear that at least twice, struggles over feminist ideas at the intersections of race, gender, and sexuality led to nonfeminist outcomes. *Wonder Woman's* text and online spaces about the character were the arenas for these struggles.

Feminist ideas are at the heart of some of the animated versions of Wonder Woman in the 2000s as well, with mixed results. The *Justice League* series, beginning in 2001 and running over ninety episodes, built on the success of *Batman: The Animated Series* and *Superman: the Animated Series*, which ran through the 1990s. Although almost thirty years later than the *Super Friends*, which had no female writers, producers, or directors, only one episode of *Justice League* was written by a woman: comics writer Gail Simone. The creators, producers, and directors were all male as well. In general, the animated versions of Diana in the 2000s, like the *Super Friends* cartoon of the 1970s and some of her more conservative comics stories, would show a woman who was predominantly a lone fierce warrior who spoke little about compassion and peace. Diana is drawn to be the same height as Batman and Superman but much slimmer. She is curvy, but not spilling out of her top or bottom or posed in sexualized ways. The emphasis is on her physical strength. This conforms with the studies of animated series of the 2000s referenced in the Introduction, which found not only a smaller number of female characters, but also found that amid gender stereotyping of both male and female characters, the level of physical aggression displayed by them was about the same (Leaper et al. 2002; Baker and Raney 2007).

Along with Hawkgirl, Wonder Woman is one of two women out of the seven members of the League in the early seasons. In later seasons, others such as Black Canary, Vixen, and Huntress make sporadic appearances. Wonder Woman's sharp mind and physical prowess are unquestioned on the show, and in one episode she defeats these four superheroines all at the same time (Matt Wayne and J.M. DeMatteis 2006, "Grudge Match"). "For the Man Who Has Everything" (adapted by J.M. DeMatteis 2004) showcases Wonder Woman as well, when Superman requires rescue from the "black mercy," a plant that puts a person into a coma while they dream their "heart's desire." In the 1985 comic by Alan Moore and Dave Gibbons, Wonder Woman doesn't do much but get defeated. In the *Justice League* episode, though, notes writer and producer (and cofounder of Milestone Comics) Dwayne McDuffie, Diana's role

**Figure 1.3** Wonder Woman in the *Justice League* animated series, which highlighted her superstrength ("The Savage Time, Part Two," S01E25, 2002).

is pivotal as she pulls the plant off of Batman with brute force, and not only battles Mongul but throws the plant onto him (Siuntres 2007). Her strength is further on display in a three-part episode called "The Savage Time" (by Stan Berkowitz 2002). She throws a truck, takes down a number of soldiers, lassoes a motorcycle, punches through a wall, and survives after a building explodes onto her. Due to time travel, she rescues Steve Trevor, and as in the Marston comics, he calls her "Angel." Steve is not "manselled" here; he is confident, brave, kind, and capable. They kiss. In later episodes, it is implied that Diana and Batman are interested in each other, although neither acknowledges it openly to the other ("Maid of Honor," "Brave and the Bold Part 2," "Kids Stuff," "This Little Piggy"). This is also the case in the contemporaneous *Justice League of America* comic series by Joe Kelly and Doug Mahnke. Linking her romantically with male characters normalizes her, making her seem less of an "outsider" in terms of gender and sexuality. It softens an earlier portrayal in the episode "Fury," in which Hawkgirl repeatedly criticizes the "precious Amazon code" of "hatred" of men, which no Amazon character refutes (Stan Berkowitz 2002).

The 2009 *Wonder Woman* direct-to-DVD animated film (directed by Lauren Montgomery) is similar to the *Justice League* animated series in its displays of Wonder Woman's strength, its linking of the main character to a man, and its caricaturing of Amazons. It delivers some pointed commentary about gender with humor as well. Gail Simone, known for the latter technique, drafted the film first but was heavily rewritten by Michael Jelenic. She says the difference between their drafts was that "the gender issue stuff in my drafts was more subtle . . . the feminist discussions they're having [in the final film] felt very early 70s to me" (AfterEllen.com staff 2009a). At the time Jelenic knew little about the character, but would later write a well-received Wonder Woman comic issue (*Sensation Comics* #6, 2015). The film presents the classic "made from clay" origin story, her initial rescue of Steve in which he calls her "Angel," and the contest that she wins to return him to Man's World. The God of War (Ares), as per decades of Wonder Woman history, is the main villain. Jelenic retained Simone's basic plot outline and says he "tried to find a balance to create a character that doesn't lose her femininity by being a strong action hero" (Fritz 2009). This description implies that "femininity" and "action hero" are not compatible, and for many viewers, they may not be. The stress on "action hero" is exaggerated to the extent that this is an action-packed and often violent film. The stress on "femininity," too, has problematic moments. Ares escapes from Paradise Island with help from the Amazon Persephone, who is jealous and angry that Hippolyta has had a daughter in Diana while other Amazons were not able to. When Hippolyta confronts her with the words, "You were given a life of peace and beauty," Persephone responds, "And denied one of families and children. Amazons are warriors but we are women too." This definition of family and children and women is quite heteronormative, in that the queer potential of an all-female, close-knit, forged family on Paradise Island is dismissed, and the idea that all women want children is presented as a universal truth.

Where *Wonder Woman* (2009) is more nuanced is its presentation of all of the characters as having something to learn. Jelenic says, "If there is a message to the film, it's basically that men and women are not perfect [and] are actually stronger and better when they work together to overcome these problems" (Fritz 2009). In other words, it wasn't that only the Amazons had something to learn, as with the *Justice League* episode, "Fury." Steve can be seen as a chauvinist but also as admitting that some things men do are prejudicial against women. Diana can be seen as inflexible but also as defending herself from an angry womanizer. Later, Steve admits, "I am a pig . . . this macho bravado is a façade," and Diana learns that his "macho bravado" is learned and is just as confining as the ways women in the United States are "raised from birth to believe they're not strong enough to compete with boys and as adults taught to trade on their femininity." His initial vulgarity and her initial mistrust fall away as each protects the other and they see each other's heroism. The film ends with the two of them together, until Diana has to go stop a villain. Steve yells after her, "Call if you're going to be late! I don't want dinner getting cold!" The film is heteronormative in its coupling of her and Steve, but subversive in his acceptance of their nonnormative roles in their relationship.

The combination was financially successful, as viewers could take away the elements of their choosing. Yet James Tucker, supervising producer for Warner Brothers DC animated features, responded when asked about another Wonder Woman movie, "We'll probably do a Wonder Woman-centered *Justice League* movie. We'll use the Justice League as an umbrella to focus on characters who might not be able to support DVDs of their own. That's not my judgment, that's based on sales" (Nicholson 2013 (October 24)). This statement cannot be based on sales. There were twenty-four DC animated movies up to 2015. Wonder Woman ranks eighth in sales, above five movies with "Justice League" in the title, above four with "Superman" in the title, and above six with "Batman" in the title (http://www.the-numbers.com). Wonder Woman can clearly "support DVDs of [her] own" and is a marketable commodity, regardless of conventional wisdom that "female characters don't sell." The conventional wisdom is wrong.

This animated Wonder Woman of the 2000s—the superstrong warrior princess, quick to use violence and mistaken in her prejudicial beliefs about men—was rather different from the comics' Wonder Woman of the 2000s. In the comics, as written by Jimenez, Rucka, and Simone in particular, she remained a warrior as a last resort but was predominantly a diplomat, surrounded by friends whom she inspired due to her modeling of compassion and love, and with whom she formed supportive functional families. Her feminist beliefs about men, women, and inequality were threaded through these portrayals, usually in a humorous, quick, and easily palatable form. It would be Wonder Woman's animated version, assumed to be less threatening to the "traditional" fan base of older, male, white comic readers, which would be embodied in the comics and animated films of the early 2010s.

## New origin and new directions for *Wonder Woman* in the 2010s

Wonder Woman's portrayals would shift yet again in the 2010s, as a new creative team in some ways continued and in other ways upended her characterization of the

2000s, and more changes in distribution affected the ways in which the character was portrayed. In 2011 (as in 1987), DC Comics relaunched their line of superheroes to increase sales, calling the initiative the "New 52" because it encompassed fifty-two titles. "New 52" *Wonder Woman*, written by Brian Azzarello and drawn by Cliff Chiang from 2011–14, was initially roundly praised for the quality of its spare, suspenseful writing, its plot about Diana dealing with the politics of the Greek gods in order to protect a young pregnant woman, and its art depicting a strong and sexy but non-sexualized and non-objectified Diana. Artist Chiang, like an increasing number of vocal fans calling for changes to hypersexual female characters in the 2010s, says,

> We've gotten really used to the dial turned up to way too sexy. We do have to speak out about it. It's not like if I'm drawing, my hand slips and suddenly it's too sexy! [It is] a conscious choice. . . . People come up to me and say they really like the way I draw her. They appreciate that she's not oversexualized. (Weiland 2014)

Wonder Woman co-headlines a second book, *Superman/Wonder Woman*, and also appears in the *Justice League* title. In 2012–2015, these two books and the eponymous title are intertwined such that Wonder Woman presents as a similar character in all three in terms of her personality as well as her non-primary status.

Critiques of these 2010s portrayals of Wonder Woman have focused on its revision of her origin and background, its violence, and its portrayal of her as more of a secondary character not infrequently depicted as naïve and mistaken. The origin has been changed such that after seventy years, Diana is no longer born of clay in a nonaggressive matriarchal society. Rather, she is the product of her mother's affair with king of the Gods, Zeus. All of the Amazons know this except Diana, who believes she is made from clay. The Amazons are no longer peace-loving and immortal. Rather, they reproduce by having sex with (and then killing) passing sailors, selling any resultant male offspring into slavery in exchange for weapons. Diana does not know this either. She is no longer shown as the daughter of all Amazons who raised and trained her. Rather, God of War Ares, who had been her arch-enemy for decades of stories, is her mentor. She is quicker to use force in general, and she kills Ares and becomes the God of War herself. With such different and violent foundations for the character, with male gods replacing female Amazons as parents and mentors, her decades-old unique mission to teach Amazonian "lessons of peace and equality" with an open heart, mind, and hand seems to have fallen away. Former writer Phil Jimenez is concerned that this version of the character "plays into the fantasies and culturally sanctioned fears of anything overtly feminine of the predominantly straight male audience the comic industry serves instead of reshaping them. She . . . buttresses the conventional wisdom as opposed to bucking it. Her otherness, her queerness, is all but erased. And money is made" (2013).[19]

She is portrayed as honorable, compassionate, strong, and loving, and these values triumph at the end of the thirty-five-issue run even as they seem dismissed along the way. Writer Brian Azzarello says, "We've made her a very powerful woman" and "we've definitely de-sexualized her" (Kennedy 2013). These are feminist moves. Diana's nonobjectified performance of "male" and "female" qualities in and of itself shows that they are not bound by gender and perhaps opens up new gender possibilities for some readers. But if such a story embodies stereotypes of feminism in its violently anti-male Amazons and is unaccompanied by broader structural critique of inequalities, readers may not move toward the value that has been at the character's core from the start: equality.

Fans were initially on both sides of the "New 52" comic. Multiple podcasts discussed it at least once; some, several times. On seven of them, seventeen men and four women described the book as one of the best of all of the 2011 reboots. Some noted that they were not that familiar with the older stories of the character, and had never before bought the title but now did. Overall, this group found her a strong character, surrounded by an interesting supporting cast.[20] But 3 Chicks Review Comics and Comic Book Queers (CBQs), all of whom had more history with reading the character, liked only the first issue. The 3 Chicks disliked the new backstory for the Amazons and found Diana to be a weaker and too violent character, with a mostly male supporting cast leading her around (3 Chicks Review Comics 2012). Some of the Talking Comics podcasters and CBQs agreed, with one CBQ summing up, "I'm happy it's selling, but this character is not Wonder Woman" (CBQs 2012). The *Wonder Woman* boards online (now closed down, as noted) reflected a similar split, with partisans on both sides using the same arguments as the podcasters. Unlike Jimenez or Simone, Azzarello said he did not read or post to such sites, and there were no letter columns. This cut off two avenues of negotiation with readers, who will of course continue to make their own meanings of his work, alone or with each other.

Viewers have had two more *Justice League* animated movies with this "warrior" version of Wonder Woman, who may be more palatable to segments of the audience more accustomed to the norms of war and violence rather than a norm of equality. If she is just like Batman or Superman, then she's no longer anti-normative as she was at her origin; she's not critiquing our assumptions about gender, but rather, conforming to a male norm. The "New 52" animated movies *Justice League: War* and *Justice League: Throne of Atlantis*, are based on the first several issues in the 2010s *Justice League* comic, in which Wonder Woman is the lone female superhero—the Smurfette, again— among seven. These films and the 2009 *Wonder Woman* film each sold close to the same number of units in their first week (http://www.the-numbers.com). At this point, the *Wonder Woman* DVD has made much more money than the two new films, at least in part because people have had several more years to buy it, but also perhaps because of its different depiction of the character. In all three films (as in a failed television pilot for a live-action show in 2011), she is young, impulsive, mostly humorless, quick to violence. Similar to all of her other animated appearances, she is not sexualized in these films.

Unlike her appearance under artist Cliff Chiang's pen in the main title, in the "New 52" *Justice League* comic and in some *Superman/Wonder Woman* comics, Diana's face is drawn younger and sexier, her body is spilling out of her top and bottom, and that top and bottom are often emphasized in panels. The male superheroes are drawn with chiseled biceps, chests, and thighs. They are athletically objectified but not sexually objectified in the same way as the female character. She is positioned in both the comic and films as Superman's girlfriend. This is similar to the portrayals in *Wonder Woman* in 2015, with artist David and writer Meredith Finch. The former has drawn many of the *Justice League* covers, and his more objectifying art style is similar for both books.

Wonder Woman's portrayals change due to the complex interplay of broader political movements, comics distribution, and changing creative teams. Her more feminist, more queer, and less sexualized portrayals (as in the 1940s, late 1980s, and 2000s) have been followed by more heteronormative, more warlike and "just one of the guys," and more sexualized ones (as in the 1950s–60s, 1990s, and 2010s). Wonder Woman's debut on the big screen in *Batman v. Superman: Dawn of Justice* is similar to the latter portrayals. The film's costume designer Michael Wilkinson has said that director Zach Snyder wants Wonder Woman "to be a fierce and intimidating warrior—gritty, battle-scarred, and immortal" (Scharf 2015). Whether this carries over to her eponymous film, directed by Patty Jenkins, remains to be seen at this writing. "Gritty" and "battle-scarred" describe a version of the character that is quite recent and little like most of her history.

But critiques of these portrayals were sufficiently high among "nontraditional" comics reading groups more prone to buy digitally rather than from stores, and sales of and enthusiasm for these print titles was sufficiently high, that DC launched four digital-first titles. *Sensation Comics Featuring Wonder Woman* had weekly stand-alone stories unbound by the "New 52" characterization. It was edited by a woman, Kristy Quinn, run out of a different office than the print titles, and featured mostly female writers and artists: over twenty before the end of 2015 and its last issue by Trina Robbins. In this series, Wonder Woman has officiated at the marriage of a same-sex

**Figure 1.4** Wonder Woman, the "battle-scarred" and "intimidating warrior," played by Gal Gadot in *Batman v Superman: Dawn of Justice* (2016).

couple, treated Gotham City's villains and her own with compassion and trust rather than Batman's intimidation and force, pushed for diplomacy instead of war, taught girls to be confident in their own strength, and inspired other women, including villains, to live up to her example. The miniseries *Wonder Woman '77* by Mark Andreyko and multiple artists is based on the live-action television show, the miniseries *The Legend of Wonder Woman* that portrays a young Diana and the Amazons is written and drawn by Renae de Liz, and *DC Bombshells* by Marguerite Bennett and Marguerite Sauvage is set in an alternate world, the Second World War era. The creative teams on these books are clearly different from those across most of Wonder Woman's history. In terms of art, in none of the four is Wonder Woman sexualized or a mere passive object of the action. Rather, she is an active agent of her own stories. In 2016, this type of portrayal bled back into the main title, written again by Greg Rucka and drawn alternately by Nicola Scott and Liam Sharp.

Not since the 1940s has Wonder Woman starred in so many titles. In this time of diversifying comics fan base, some fans will buy one of the digital-first books, some will buy *Wonder Woman*, some will see the films and/or read *Justice League*, and others may consume all or none of these. The technology and the willingness to use it to reach a different audience from that driving print comics production and distribution for the last two decades disrupts the cycles in Wonder Woman's portrayals by broadening the ways in which she is portrayed.

## Conclusion: The "trickiness" of the female superhero

So often, the iconography of Wonder Woman—a female character assumed to embody power, compassion, capability, equality, and heroism—has not matched up with her actual portrayals in the comics or on television. There is a sense among some writers and fans that her corporate owner DC is not exactly sure how to deal with her. Certainly, there have been many different representations of her over her seventy-five years, at some times broadly appealing but at other times, appealing to some and alienating others. There have been many Wonder Womans. So often, she has been described as "tricky" to write, even by DC Comics president Diane Nelson, hence changes in her portrayals and her lack of representation on the big screen.

It's not Wonder Woman that's tricky, though. Her origin and her powers and her core values can be summed up in a sentence: "Superstrong Amazon, born of clay and given life by goddesses, goes to man's world to teach peace, love, and equality." On its face this is no stranger than "flying heat-visioned superstrong alien from a dying planet rockets to earth, grows up in Kansas, and fights for justice." What's tricky is that we live in an unequal world, in which girls and women are devalued, and in which the word "girl" is delivered as an insult to boys, who are admonished from a young age not to "cry like a girl" or "run like a girl." It's cute when little girls dress "up" in Daddy's clothes, but it's anxiety-producing when little boys dress "down" in Mommy's clothes. Many assume that girls and women will consume media with white male main characters, because they are aspirational figures with power in our society. Many assume that boys and men wouldn't, or shouldn't, consume media with female main characters. Why would they identify with someone less powerful than they, with someone they have seen represented only infrequently or with stereotypes, with someone that they are told not to be like? If people were seen as equal, a female superhero wouldn't be tricky, because she wouldn't be threatening or challenging to the social order through her very existence. She'd just be a superhero. But like Ginger Rogers dancing with Fred Astaire, Wonder Woman has to do everything that the male superheroes do, "backwards and in high heels." Everything is more difficult for the character because she is the only one of her kind.[21] And because she is the only one of her kind, she carries impossibly heavy representational weight.

We just haven't seen enough female superheroes in terms of either numbers or of different nationalities and sexualities and abilities, through whom we could more easily imagine that "anyone can be a hero." As noted in the Introduction, women have been historically underrepresented as characters in fiction across media. When they are represented, they are more likely to be shown as interested in romance and more likely to be sexualized, while they are less likely to be represented as leaders or mentors, or as having a high-status profession. Women have been underrepresented across Wonder Woman's history as creators as well, although the number has increased over time. We need more female creators and more female heroes across media, depicting and circulating more diverse representations that open up the infinite possibilities of what heroism can look like. Wonder Woman doesn't have to be either a severe "man-like" warrior or a relationship-oriented "woman-like" diplomat. She can be both at the same time. Rather than being alone, she can be surrounded by friends and allies and villains, drawn and written to be different from her and from one another. She can be drawn to be attractive without looking like she's posed for immediate sexual activity with the reader. She can convey strength, heroism, leadership, and humanity in a female body. She can be a hero to a variety of readers.

Different *Wonder Woman* audiences have pushed for more binary readings of gender as well as more fluid ones, sometimes in concert with authors and editors, sometimes in conflict with them and with each other. These negotiations have been framed by the distributions methods of comics and the political culture of the times: the 1940s newsstand and its broad accessibility during a time of acceptance of more flexibility in gender roles, the 1990s direct market and its narrow focus on certain fans during a time of backlash to feminism, and the 2010s digitization and downloading that has opened the medium to previously marginalized groups more empowered by the gains of various civil rights movements. It is clear that audiences do have power—with their pocketbooks, with letter columns and blogs and podcasts, and with their readings, reworkings and reinventions of what they see. This does not mean that there are no power differentials between different parts of the audiences, between producers and consumers, and between writers and editors. But as reader and creator demographics change, as conventions expand and diversify, as social media is used by more and more people, as outlets and technologies for consuming the medium change, and as the characters continue to cross different types of media, there are more opportunities for fans to pressure producers on how important representation is, and how everyone benefits from media that bring to life a variety of heroes.

The next chapter examines a different set of negotiations between and among readers and writers and artists from the last fifty years, through the character of Barbara Gordon, Batgirl and Oracle. Like Wonder Woman, there are debates over gender and sexuality, but there are differences as well, having to do with the resonance of disability and age to the character's audiences.

# Notes

1 Gail Simone (w) and Aaron Lopresti (p), *Wonder Woman* [hereafter, *WW*] Vol. 3 #34 (2009). Portions of this chapter appeared in Cocca 2013, 2014b. Reprinted with permission.

2 See, e.g., Brown 2011, Daniels 2000, Emad 2006, Fleisher 1976, Greenberger 2010, Madrid 2009, Peters 2003, Robinson 2004, Stanley 2005, Taylor 2007.

3 This begins with *Sensation Comics* #17 and *WW* #5, 1943.

4 Not only did villains get tied up, but Wonder Woman and her friends did as well, frequently. The images, like all others, can be received in a number of ways. Three recent books focus on this time period: Lepore 2015, Berlatsky 2015, and Hanley 2014. The first is more focused on Marston's life and its impact on the comics (including the bondage iconography); the latter two on the early comics with a particular interest in their scenes of bondage.

5 Lepore 2015: 373 citing a contemporaneous *Forbes* article. Berlatsky 2015: 10 comes to similar conclusions.

6 See, e.g., Costello 2009: 19 and Robinson 2004: 62 on the importance of costume changes vis-à-vis cultural changes.

7 Hollon 2012: 89. These features appeared in 27 out of 31 issues from 1962 to 1971. See also Hanley 2014: 79, 80, 85.

8 On the use of the wave metaphor to describe feminist activism, see note 18 in the Introduction.

9 Jan Duursema was first, as one of many artists on *WW* #300 in 1983. But in terms of a full issue, the first was Trina Robbins on *The Legend of Wonder Woman* miniseries in 1986.

10 The "postal service statement of ownership, management and circulation" in the back of the comics shows that the average number of copies sold through "dealers, carriers, street vendors, and counter sales" was about 150,000 in 1976 (*WW* #231) and about 158,000 in 1977 (#243). By comparison's, *X-Men* sales at the same time were about 135,000. The same statement in 1981 showed *WW* sales of about 80,000 (*WW* #291), whereas *X-Men*'s sales had shot up to 274,000. See Chapter 4 on *X-Men*.

11 See, e.g., *WW* #219, 1975; #230, 1977; #250–53, 1978–79; #263–64, 1980; #275, 1981; #288–90, 1982; #318, 1984; see also Robinson 2004 and Madrid 2009.

12 The average number of copies sold through "dealers, carriers, street vendors, and counter sales" after Pérez took over was about 120,000 in 1987 (*WW* Vol. 2 #15), as compared to about 52,000 in 1984 (#325), 80,000 in 1981 (#291) and 158,000 in 1977 (#243; see also note 10). By 1987, perhaps about 10–15 percent of sales were through the direct market. John Jackson Miller at Comichron computes this figure for 1986–87s *Watchmen* (http://www.comichron.com/special/watchmensales.html.) Therefore, Pérez's *Wonder Woman*'s initial average sales per month were probably about 135,000 or so.

13  Asking for more diversity, e.g., were Bill Campbell in *WW* Vol. 2 #5 and Corian in #32 (on race), Floyd McGee in *WW* Vol. 2 #18 (on sexuality), Kevin Harrington in #21 (on disability); see also, Darlene Dralus in #28 and Matt Gersper and Ernest Black's letters in *WW* Vol. 2 #35.

14  See the Introduction, as well as Brooker 2000, Emad 2006, Gabilliet 2010, Krensky 2008, Lopes 2009, Wright 2001 for more details on why the fan base became concentrated in this way.

15  See also Brown 2000, Cocca 2014a, Daniels 2000, Madrid 2009, Morrison 2011, Stanley 2005.

16  Along with conservative criticisms of such ideas, there are feminist ones as well. First, that embracing an individuality that affirms all women's choices can foster nonfeminist ideals. Second, that taking pleasure in dressing sexily or in images of sexiness to reclaim portrayals of women can lead to a lack of interrogation of the social inequalities manifest in such dress and such images and how different audiences may receive them. Third, that some of the cultural work reliant on individual storytelling fails to contextualize those stories with critiques of social structures (see, e.g., Kelly 2005, Kinser 2004, Snyder 2008, Showden 2009).

17  See Robbins 2008, Simone 2008, Comic Book Queers podcasts #49, 2007, and #125, 2010; see also Kaveney 2008 and Peters 2003 on the resonance to queer youth of a secret identity.

18  This board was housed at http://forums.comicbookresources.com/forumdisplay. php?69-Wonder-Woman, but the link is no longer active.

19  Former *WW* writers Trina Robbins and Greg Rucka have expressed similar sentiments about the early 2010s portrayal of the character (Talking Comics 2013b).

20  This includes twenty-four episodes of nine podcasts: Comic Book Queers (6 episodes), Comic Geek Speak (3), Crazy Sexy Geeks (1), IFanboy (2), Matt and Brett Love Comics (1), Modern Myth Media (2), The Stack (1), Talking Comics (6, one of which included this author), and 3 Chicks Review Comics (2).

21  Joan Hilty, comics writer and artist and former DC Comics editor, drew this connection at the "Wonder Woman" Panel at the Queers and Comics Conference, May 7–8, 2015, sponsored by the City University of New York Center for Lesbian and Gay Studies.

# 2

# "When You Go Out At Night, You Won't Be Alone": Batgirl(s) and Birds of Prey[1]

Debuting in 1967 as Batgirl, the character of Barbara Gordon originated as a brilliant librarian by day and costumed member of the Bat-family by night. Like Wonder Woman, she is privileged in terms of her white, middle-class heterosexuality. But in contrast to the superpowered Amazon princess who can function as a model of aspiration, Barbara is a non-superpowered hero grounded in the "real" world, such that she may be more a point of identification or relatability for some readers. She was famously and graphically injured and paralyzed in 1988, then relaunched in 1989 as Oracle: computer expert, information broker, tactical leader of various superhero teams, mentor to the new Batgirls, and wheelchair user. This change engendered fan and creator negotiations over mainstream superhero comics' portrayals of women, particularly having to do with "depowering" a female character (like Wonder Woman in 1968), with sexualized violence against female but not male characters, and with stories that center male characters versus those centering female characters. In 2011, a "cured" Barbara resumed the role of Batgirl, bringing a new wave of struggles over her story between her writers, artists, and fans about depictions of disabled and nondisabled bodies in the superhero genre.

Over her fifty years, Barbara Gordon's "origin story" was rewritten numerous times. Changes in the distribution methods of comics play a role in such alterations, as do corporate assumptions about consumers of different media. Interacting with these forces, the creative teams behind each revision have been embedded in but not completely bound by shifts in ideas about women and about the assumed marketability of female heroes. This chapter explores the changes to Barbara Gordon and how and why they were made, by examining her portrayals in comics and on television since 1967. It analyzes her early comics and television years as Batgirl in the 1960s–80s, during which time her femininity was stressed simultaneously with her accomplishments. These portrayals of her have some similarities and some differences to those of 1990s–2000s animated series as well as the comic miniseries *Batgirl: Year One*, which represent the character as younger and "girlier" and thereby perhaps less threatening, but no less determined, skilled, and courageous. Running concurrently to these younger, nondisabled, and mostly animated versions of Barbara Gordon as Batgirl was an older, disabled print version of Barbara Gordon as Oracle, also shown briefly on live-action television as well. The same person yet not, these two portrayals allowed creators and corporate interests to diversify slightly without creating a brand-new and therefore unfamiliar (and thus, less marketable) character. As with Wonder Woman, Barbara in print has been more nuanced than Barbara on screen.

This chapter considers the ways in which the production and reception of Barbara Gordon's earliest portrayals personify both the promises of the Second Wave of feminism as well as its limits at the time. Examining her portrayals in the 1990s–2000s as a younger Batgirl in some media and an older Oracle in others, it focuses on the ways in which these portrayals embody Third Wave feminism's emphasis on youth and on diversity, as played out through a profit-minded company mindful both of feminism and its backlash. Lastly, the chapter analyzes the debates over Barbara's "cure" of her disability in the *Batgirl* comics of the early 2010s as well as those over her less curve-hugging costume and representations of her "fridging." All of these incarnations, and the ways in which they were produced and received, are part of larger conversations about the importance of diverse representations in comics.

## From Barbara to Batgirl to retirement: Femininity, fashion, and crimefighting, 1960s–80s

By 1967, the live-action television show *Batman* was beginning to decline in the ratings, and so, says Batgirl actress Yvonne Craig, "They were adding Batgirl to the show because they needed someone who could encourage an over-40 male audience and a prepubescent female audience" and "they were right. Whenever I did public appearances, it was the little girls who came up to me" (Jankiewicz 2002 and Eisner 2011,

**Figure 2.1** Yvonne Craig as the petite, balletic, purple-clad Batgirl on *Batman*'s third season ("Enter Batgirl, Exit Penguin," S03E01, 1967).

respectively). In other words, these two audiences were assumed to be those who would watch a pretty female hero—in a tight costume. Craig wore a shiny purple catsuit, cape, cowl, and skinny-heeled boots with a yellow utility belt. Basically, the outfit was just like Batman's, setting the character up immediately as just a female version of Batman.

The outfit and the character were designed not by the TV show's executive producer William Dozier or by producer Howie Horwitz, but rather, at DC Comics. Executive editor Julius Schwartz spoke with Dozier about it and artist (later executive editor after Schwartz) Carmine Infantino designed it. Indeed, the comic Batgirl debuted months before her television counterpart. Her first stories would be written by Gardner Fox, who had angered *Wonder Woman* creator William Moulton Marston by making that character the secretary of the superhero team, the Justice Society, and having her stay behind as the male superheroes went on adventures (Lepore 2015: 210–11).

At her first comic appearance in January 1967 (Fox and Infantino, *Detective Comics* #359), Barbara Gordon is a librarian in her early twenties, light-skinned and red-haired, tall, fit, strong, pretty, funny, bright, independent, and capable. The daughter of the Gotham City Police Commissioner Jim Gordon, she makes her Batgirl costume—black, with a yellow bat, and yellow gloves and heeled boots, and a little red purse hooked to her yellow utility belt—to tweak her father at a policeman's masquerade ball. Despite her "PhD and brown belt in judo," she says, the masquerade ball "will be the highlight of my life!" But along the way, she sees Bruce Wayne being kidnapped. Calling herself Batgirl despite her age, she fights Killer Moth and loses, but she "is having the time of her life." Killer Moth calls her a "dame" and Batman and Robin discourage her, saying, "No, Batgirl! . . . you must understand that we can't worry ourselves about a girl." She then rescues Batman and Robin and locates Killer Moth so that the three can capture him. Batman protests they could have rescued themselves, but tells Commissioner Gordon that he'll "welcome her aid . . . she doesn't have to take a back seat to anybody." Gordon later says to Barbara, who is demurely reading a book in her glasses and cinnamon bun hairstyle, "That Batgirl is sure tops. . . . Too bad you couldn't be a little more like her, Babs!" She continues on as Batgirl, not because she has undergone some tragedy like Batman and Robin, but because she likes the excitement, has the skills, and wants to fight crime. She does not want to be around them for romance, telling Catwoman, "I don't consider myself a rival of yours! I have absolutely no romantic interest in Batman" (Fox and Frank Springer 1967, *Batman* #197). Her independence, capability, and drive are established immediately.

Batgirl is the only consistently speaking female role on the TV show and usually in the Batman comics as well. Like the 1950s and 1960s Wonder Woman, as written and drawn only by men, she exemplifies the "Smurfette principle" by being quite alone in terms of female peers, centering the male characters and highlighting her own exceptionality. And other than Catwoman as played by Eartha Kitt in the series' last season, just about everyone in both media is white. When Batgirl's not alone, her earliest stories have her and another female superhero plotted out in relation to men. In *World's Finest* #169 (Cary Bates and Curt Swan 1967), Batgirl and Supergirl scheme against Batman and Superman, tired of the latter stealing the spotlight. It turns out the "girls" have been kidnapped and replaced by doubles. In *Brave and the Bold* #78

(Bob Haney and Bob Brown 1968), Batgirl and Wonder Woman both pretend to be in love with Batman as part of a plan related to a villain, but then they both seem to really fall for him. Many early Batgirl stories fail the "Bechdel test": either there isn't more than one woman, or there is but she and the other one are talking about a man.

Plots of her early stories have to do with stereotypically female concerns such as appearance and fashion and dating. If Barbara were not the only female, this would not be problematic: there could be one character concerned with these things, and other characters with other things. But because she is the only one, these elements become tightly tied into her gender. While she is shown to be quite bright and even have a photographic memory, her resourcefulness is consistently grounded in her being a librarian, an historically feminized profession and one that at the time was probably almost entirely white. A number of both the early comics and early television episodes have her foiling villains' plots due to her work at the library and familiarity with books and book research (e.g., Fox and Infantino 1967, *Detective Comics* #363 and #369; Frank Robbins and Gil Kane 1970, *Detective Comics* #396–97; "The Unkindest Tut of All" [S03E06] by Stanley Ralph Ross, 1967). That her somewhat stereotypical femininity is coexistent with her strength and resourcefulness may have eased acceptance of that strength for some viewers.

Femininity was a stated concern for the TV show and for the early comics' issues. On *Batman*, not unlike Wonder Woman in her later TV show, Batgirl doesn't punch or get punched but tends to execute graceful high kicks, hit villains with objects, or employ useful items from her utility belt. Explains Craig,

> [Producer Howie Horwitz] . . . had a wife and three daughters, and he wanted them all to be very feminine. So, he specifically said that Batgirl was not to do any karate, kung fu, any sort of martial arts-type stuff. That wasn't ladylike to him. I was allowed to kick the bad guys in a sort of high-kick, ballet manner . . . or spin into them and waste them, but I was supposed to be able to sneak out of their grasp before any punches were thrown. (Eisner 2011)

Barbara's more "ladylike" in other ways on the TV show. She's younger than in the comic, having just graduated college, so she does not have a PhD. Barbara in the comic is 5'11", while the actress portraying Barbara on the TV show was a petite 5'3". The character debuted at the beginning of the third season in September 1967. Bruce Wayne is going to the opera and says, "Commissioner Gordon is bringing his daughter Barbara along as my date" (Stanford Sherman 1967, "Enter Batgirl, Exit Penguin" [S01E01]). This immediately positions Barbara as a daughter and a love interest, rather than as her own person.

The first episode displays Barbara's femininity, her strength, and her knowing that she must downplay the latter and highlight the former. The Penguin kidnaps her, but she escapes to her apartment, where she pushes a revolving wall behind her vanity that hides her bright purple costume. Batman is impressed by her graceful kicking of a villain, "I don't know who you are, young lady, but you certainly know how to handle yourself well." She says she knows they could have handled it themselves, but she just wanted to "join in the fun." Batgirl rescues them, but the tables turn and they must rescue her. She changes back into her street clothes and lets them think they've rescued Barbara. Playing into what she assumes is their view of women, she says as Barbara, "I'm sorry to be so helpless." The men take this in stride, and Batman says of Batgirl, "Whoever she is behind that mask of hers, she helped us out of a dire dilemma." They do not see that "Barbara" is in some ways the mask; that her female body is, in this time period, hiding her heroism.

The show calls attention to her being female in dialogue as well. Batman asks her, "How did you know that Robin and I might be in trouble with Penguin in this glue-factory?" She replies, "Through the one thing you couldn't possibly have in your utility belt, Batman . . . a woman's intuition" (Charles Hoffman 1967, "The Sport of Penguins" [S03E04]). In another, she exclaims, "I may just have figured out Tut's entire plot. It was a mistake only an Egyptian bibliophile would have noticed. Lucky I'm an Egyptian bibliophile." The narrator then chimes in, "And even luckier for us she's Batgirl! The supremely feminine scourge of all that is criminal!" (Stanley Ralph Ross 1967, "The Unkindest Tut of All" [S03E06]). She is also the first recipient of a new award, presented by Gotham's top couturier: "A new designation for the best dressed crimefightress in Gotham City, the first annual 'Batty' is hereby presented to Batgirl" (Stanley Ralph Ross 1967, "Catwoman's Dressed to Kill" [S03E14]).

A number of plots in the comics had to do with fashion as well, even into the 1970s (e.g., Frank Robbins and Gil Kane 1970, #406; Robbins and Don Heck 1970–71, #410–14). The fashion-oriented issue that deserves the most attention, though, dates from January 1968 (#371) and is written by Gardner Fox, who wrote her origin issue. The cover has Batman pleading, "Batgirl! Get over here—Help us! We've got a problem!" and Batgirl responding, "I have a bigger one—a run in my tights!" The cover is drawn by Carmine Infantino and Murphy Anderson, and the panels by Gil Kane. On the title page, she's looking at her face in her compact mirror while the men fight behind her. The story begins with Batgirl stopping in the middle of a fight when her "headpiece" gets misaligned, and "as any girl would" she stops to straighten it. She laments that this was "an instinctive feminine reaction!" Later, when she stops fighting criminals due to the aforementioned run in her tights, the villains also stop fighting so they can look at her legs, "What a pair of gams!" Apparently, as it is women's instinct to care about their appearance, it is men's to look at female legs even if it results in going to jail. Batman praises her, "You see, Batgirl? That was one time where you turned a feminine trait to your advantage—and the disadvantage of the criminals!" Barbara thinks to herself, "I just didn't have the heart to tell Batman and Robin that I tore my tights deliberately—to give me an excuse for showing off my legs and distracting those crooks! The fact that my feminine weakness betrayed me so often in the past—I just had to prove it has its strong points too!" Her "feminine weakness" or her complete lack of ability to turn any "feminine trait" to her advantage do not seem to have been in evidence when she fought alongside Batman and Robin before this point either in comics or on TV. Fox's story, its language, and its assumptions are indicative of a "traditional" 1960s view of womanhood and femininity, and manhood and masculinity, that many took for granted and that the Second Wave of feminism had just begun to challenge. One might even assume that the story was meant to be complimentary to Batgirl at the time, as she strategically uses her "feminine traits." But when DC Comics chose in 2007—forty years later—to collect 500 pages of early Batgirl stories from the 1960s and early 1970s into one volume (*Showcase Presents: Batgirl*), they chose for its cover the image of Batgirl looking into her compact as Batman and Robin fight behind her. Clearly, some still feel that that one image is indicative of who the character of Batgirl is, or what a female superhero is.

Barbara's adventures continued, by a different creative team, in shorter stories in the back of *Detective Comics*. At first, they were quite similar to the show, which ended in March 1968. She is a smart career woman and "dominoed daredoll" particularly concerned with fashion and dating. This was the same year that Wonder Woman was depowered, becoming a boutique owner and martial arts-based crimefighter interested in fashion and dating. Barbara goes out with a few different men, the most long term being Jason Bard. She also uses a computer dating service to find a criminal (Robbins and Kane 1970, #396–97). Generally, Batgirl's two-part stories had almost entirely male and white casts, with a first part ending with Batgirl in peril and a second part showing her defeating said peril.

In the early 1970s, her stories begin to engage with the student movement and with causes of criminality, and gets overtly political when Barbara reveals her identity to her father and asks him to let her run for the Congressional seat that he's being pressured to run for (Robbins and Heck 1972, #422–24). Having turned in a former boyfriend who doesn't then stay away from a life of crime, she says that being a lawmaker is "the only way I can really fight crime—prevent it—through prison reform. Legislation—law that creates order—not disorder!" Indeed, TV's Batgirl supported legislation at this time as well, as actor Yvonne Craig put her purple suit back on for a televised PSA in which she not only refuses to rescue Batman and Robin in protest over the former's paying Robin more than her for the "same job," but also directly urges viewers to contact the U.S. Department of Labor if they are subject to violations of the federal Equal Pay Law. Comic Barbara's 1972 campaign slogan is to "boot the rascals out," noting that the boot is a symbol of Batgirl as well as a call to vote out incumbents. She wins, and stays in office until 1980 when she loses her bid for reelection (Jack Harris and Dick Giordano, #487). The House of Representatives during this time had between 16 and 19 women, an average of 4 percent of its members, such that Barbara shows readers' possibilities while also foreclosing them with her exceptionality.

During her time as a Congresswoman, she continued to fight crime in the twenty-issue *Batman Family* comic, and to think about romance. With sort-of-boyfriend Jason Bard back in Gotham, she works with Robin and in one issue, kisses him to get him to stop talking down to her. Letter writers were mixed on this, with some liking the kiss and others protesting due to their age difference. The editor noted the age difference and wrote, "There are no plans to develop a romance between the two. That kiss, as correctly viewed by most of our readers, was Babs' way of putting Robin down for trying to come on like a father figure and/or male chauvinist" (Gardner Fox and Sheldon Moldoff 1975, #1). Despite this start, their relationship would be hinted at in this comic, as well as other comics and animated series for years after this.

Babs-and-Dick were definitely "off" in the concurrent sixteen-episode animated series *New Adventures of Batman*. While her personality and the way others received her in the two 1970s comics were quite similar, in that no longer was her womanhood assumed to be any barrier to her crimefighting or legislating, the cartoon was more similar to the comics of ten years before. It showed a more soft-spoken fashion-conscious librarian having to prove women could fight crime alongside men. Barbara wears cateye glasses and her hair in a bun, along with a skirt, blouse, vest, and pumps. Her Batgirl outfit is colored like Batman's, except her boots had skinny heels. In both guises she speaks in a light girlish voice. There is no budding relationship between her and Robin. Rather, little green imp Batmite moons over her in every episode. Babs tells her father, "I know someone who can unravel this mystery." He replies, "Of course, Batman and Robin." When Babs says, "I was thinking of Batgirl," Jim guffaws loudly, then says, "No. This is far too big for her." Barbara says "Oh, come on dad. Batgirl can do anything Batman can" (Chuck Menville and Len Janson 1977, "Curses, Oiled Again" [E12]). This exchange is ten years after Batgirl's debut in the comics in which her father says that Batgirl is "tops" and he wishes Barbara were more like her. Although Batgirl rescues Batman and Robin, and captures Catwoman by roping her plane, climbing up into it, and piloting it, her father does not see this but the viewer knows that she has done it. Assumptions behind these kinds of portrayals may have been in line with those from the live-action TV show in 1967, that a more "feminine" portrayal of Batgirl with some subversion of supposedly feminine weaknesses would be better received by a broader audience.

Barbara's portrayal in the comics shifted in the early 1980s, when she was written by Cary Burkett as having some new insecurities after her reelection loss. She continued to fight crime as Barbara at the Humanities Research and Development Center, "dedicated to solving urban problems and encouraging cultural development" (Burkett and Don Newton 1980, #492), and as Batgirl combating gangs. She begins to question whether she'd like to continue as Batgirl, particularly after surviving a shooting and after a villain manipulates those around her in ways that tax her emotionally. She teams up with Supergirl but she feels "a little overshadowed" by her. Barbara's appearances after this point dwindle, the most high-profile being that in DC Comics' universe-crashing event, 1985's *Crisis on Infinite Earths*. As noted in Chapter 1, this miniseries resulted in a reboot of the DC superhero universe. A still-insecure and newly afraid Barbara tells Supergirl, "I-I don't think I was ever cut out for playing hero." Supergirl reminds her she can make a difference like "police, firemen, soldiers . . . ordinary people trying their best." As Supergirl flies off to her death, Barbara thinks, "She's a hero through and through . . . what *have* I become?" On the one hand, this was similar to newer "imperfect" characters who would sometimes doubt themselves, such as the X-Men (see Chapter 4). On the other, since Barbara is usually the sole woman in her stories, her insecurities seem entwined with her womanhood. She later eulogizes Supergirl: "A hero is not measured by what her power may be, but by the courage she shows in living, and the warmth she holds in her heart" (Marv Wolfman and [future *Wonder Woman* writer and artist] George Pérez 1985, #7). Regardless of her own and Supergirl's inspiring words, Batgirl would retire. More accurately, she would be retired by DC Comics in order to help market a forthcoming graphic novel in which they had great confidence.

## Sexualized violence: The retirement of Batgirl and the "fridging" of Barbara Gordon

Barbara Gordon's Batgirl career would come to an abrupt and seemingly irreversible end in a story emblematic of the violence against female characters in comics that has no male equivalent. Such violence tends to have longer-lasting repercussions for the female character, tends to be used as a plot device that affects the story arc of male characters more than that of the female character who was hurt, and tends to be sexualized in its art. Barbara retired from her life as Batgirl in 1988, after appearing less in comics in general during the 1980s. The writer responsible for this story would be her first female writer. Barbara Randall Kesel had famously written DC Comics a lengthy letter about how their female characters could be written better, and they called on her to write Barbara Gordon's stories in *Detective Comics* #518 and #519 (1982). In that story, Kesel has Batgirl go after a female computer hacker codenamed Velvet Tiger, foreshadowing Barbara's future technology-based crimefighting, "To aid her, she has a phenomenal memory and analytic mind, and a set of finely honed athletic skills. No flashy superpowers. But then, she doesn't need any" (#518). When Kesel was asked about how she was approached to write Batgirl's last story (drawn by Barry Kitson), she recalled, "[They said] 'She's getting her spine blown out in *The Killing Joke*, so try to make people care'" (*DCWKA* 2011). Indeed, immediately opposite the last page of the retirement story is a full-page ad for the then-forthcoming graphic novel *The Killing Joke*.

*The Killing Joke* (1988) was written by Alan Moore, whose critically praised and high-selling 1986–87 *Watchmen* had been seen as inaugurating the new "grim and gritty" tone that comics would take, as well as showing the potential success of the "graphic novel" format. In this Batman and Joker-centric story, drawn by Brian Bolland, the Joker shoots Barbara, paralyzing her from the waist down, and then takes pictures of her in various states of undress while she is writhing in pain. The original art shows her nude breasts and buttocks along with her strained face and bloody torso, but this was changed in the final version as Bolland says he was asked to "tone it down a bit" (2013). It is implied that the Joker has sexually assaulted her as well. The whole point of the Joker's actions, as Moore has the character himself state, was to drive Barbara's father mad to prove "there's no difference between me and everyone else. All it takes is one bad day to reduce the sanest man alive to lunacy" (Moore and Bolland 1988).

This story prompted future *Birds of Prey/Batgirl/Wonder Woman* writer Gail Simone to create the "Women in Refrigerators" website, an accounting of the number of times in comics that female characters were victims of violence—particularly, sexualized violence—solely to show the violence's effect on male characters (Pantozzi 2011). The violence done to Barbara was a classic "fridging" in that no one in the story ever asks her how she's feeling after it happens, nor does the story follow her and her recovery. The whole point of what is done to Barbara is to explore how her father and Batman react to it and feel about it. Those at DC Comics were not so concerned about her character. Writer Alan Moore recalls,

> I asked DC if they had any problems with me crippling Barbara Gordon—who was Batgirl at the time—and if I remember correctly, I spoke to Len Wein, who was our editor on the project, and he said "Hold on to the phone, I'm just going to walk down the hall and I'm going to ask [former DC Executive Editorial Director] Dick Giordano if it's alright," and there was a brief period where I was put on hold and then, as I remember it, Len got back onto the phone and said "Yeah, okay, cripple the bitch." It was probably one of the areas where they should've reined me in, but they didn't. (Cotton 2004)

*The Killing Joke* was a huge success at the time. Its twenty-fifth anniversary prompted a new wave of sales such that it frequently topped the *New York Times* hardcover graphic novels best-seller list in the mid-2010s, and an animated version was scheduled for 2016. It was not intended to be a canonical story. But its crippling of Barbara has remained even as many elements of other superheroes have been rebooted. More than a few were and remain rankled by its treatment of Barbara. As José Alaniz writes, "Fan and critical discourses have established [*The Killing Joke*] as a pre-cursor to the ultra-violent spectacles of the 1990s, and later, Barbara's victimization representing both the revealed misogynist underbelly of superhero narratives as well as the start to her journey as Oracle, the genre's most developed disabled hero" (2014: 292).

# From Batgirl to Oracle:
# Hacker, mother, leader, friend, 1988–2011

Comic writers John Ostrander and Kim Yale almost immediately created the idea of Barbara as having a new identity, a new mask: "Oracle." Barbara's last story author Kesel spoke to Yale, and said the latter was "passionate about Barbara not sitting on the sidelines" (DCWKA 2011). Ostrander recalled, "Kim and I . . . felt the action should have repercussions. Barbara Gordon should be crippled as a result. However, it should make her no less of a 'hero' so we armed her with a mess of very high-end computers and made her the research person for the [DC Universe]" (2008). As Ostrander and Yale wrote later in the origin story "Oracle: Year One" (1996, drawn by Brian Stelfreeze), Barbara works through depression and self-doubt to truly come into her own and move beyond being a "distaff" or "second-hand version of someone else," that is, Batman. She embraces her new life, using a wheelchair as well as her exceptional intelligence, photographic memory, and facility with information sciences. These were skills that she had always had. But now, instead of using those skills occasionally as Batgirl, she would use them full time for her fellow superheroes as Oracle.

Barbara is a unique character among disabled superheroes. Some of the more prominent disabled superhero comic characters are Charles Xavier/Professor X, Matt Murdock/Daredevil, Victor Stone/Cyborg, and Misty Knight. But even in this small group there are some differences in their portrayals, in terms of race and gender. For instance, white male professor Charles Xavier uses a wheelchair and yet also has telepathic and psionic abilities; white male lawyer Matt Murdock is blind and yet "sees" even more with his radioactively mutated "vision." Both are privileged men, made more privileged through their mental superpowers. By contrast, Cyborg and Misty Knight are African American superheroes with sci-fi-prostheses much stronger than their replaced human limbs. Their superpowers are physical, rather than mental, such that their dark disabled bodies are made more fearsome and more exotic with technology. All four of them have some extraordinary power that so overcompensates for disability that the reader almost forgets what would have been labeled a disability in the first place. It is almost as if disabilities are not represented through these four characters.

Barbara Gordon has no superpowers and uses a wheelchair. She succeeds as a superhero not in spite of or because of her disability, but while living with it. This not only better represents the daily lives of people with disabilities, but can lead all readers to "reimagine disability" as a common human experience and work to be more inclusive of people with disabilities (Garland-Thomson 2005: 524). On the other hand, the idea that "disabilities are the gateway to special abilities" is a pop culture trope (Siebers 2010: 318) which can just as easily lead us to unrealistic expectations of people with disabilities.

Oracle became instrumental to DC superhero successes in a number of titles beginning in 1989, such as *Azrael, Batgirl, Batman, Black Canary, Catwoman, Detective Comics, Green Arrow, Hawk and Dove, Hacker Files, JLA, Manhunter, Nightwing, Robin,* and *Suicide Squad.* In John Ostrander's *Suicide Squad,* in which she was initially featured the most and in which her new identity was revealed, she was usually drawn frumpier than she had been as Batgirl, with formless suits, oversized glasses, and her hair in a bun. The first time we see her, she's crying due to the loss of one of the Squad (#38). The next time we see her, she's crying while talking to a psychologist about having been shot by the Joker (#48). These first appearances fall squarely into stereotypes of people with disabilities: she is portrayed as sad, lonely, pitiable, unable to "move on" (Davidson 2010; Linton 2010; Longmore 2003; Siebers 2010). She worries that her shooting has pushed her outside of norms of able-bodiedness *and* gender *and* sexuality, as she thinks, "I can't ever walk again, or have kids, or probably ever marry"(Ostrander, Yale, and Geof Isherwood 1990, *Suicide Squad* #48). After these first establishing appearances, she is portrayed as a stronger character and valued member of the team, albeit still rather dowdy in appearance.

Where Oracle really comes into her own is in *Birds of Prey.* The title, starring Barbara, launched in 1996 and ran for over 150 issues with only a few short gaps until 2011. Almost half of these issues were written by Chuck Dixon (Vol. 1, several one-shots and #1–46) and almost half by Gail Simone (Vol. 1, #56–108 and Vol. 2 #1–15). There were various artists. Barbara is written by both as young, attractive, intelligent, healthy, white, cisgender, heterosexual, wealthy, independent, and disabled. The series showcases her as a brilliant, caring, funny, thoughtful master tactician, computer hacker, and team leader for the various superheroes (mostly female) whom she runs on missions and with whom she forms a family. She isn't perfect, sometimes doubting her abilities and sometimes making personal and professional mistakes. But she keeps trying. Because Barbara is not the only woman in the series, her self-doubt and her mistakes are not associated with her being a woman. While we are never allowed to forget that she is a person who uses a wheelchair, her mobility does not totally define her character as is often the case for characters with disabilities (Mitchell and Snyder 2010: 276).

The title's initial pairing of Oracle and Black Canary was conceived by editor Jordan Gorfinkle, who asked Chuck Dixon (who had written Oracle in *Detective Comics*) to write it. Their approach was quite different from the mid-1990s hyperviolent and hypersexual "Bad Girl" trend that was geared toward the core fans buying through local comic shops: as noted, mostly older, white, heterosexual males. Dixon recalls, "I didn't want to do a cheesecake book and I wanted to do a straight-up superhero adventure. . . . We were very surprised by the response to the book, since it flew in the face of the conventional wisdom that for a book starring females to sell it had to be something close to costumed porn" (Bowman 2011). The book did sell, in the neighborhood of about 25,000–30,000 copies per month in the late 1990s and early 2000s. By point of comparison, at the time, both *Batman* and *Detective Comics* were selling only in the 40,000s (comichron.com). The two main characters complemented one another, with Oracle as the cool methodical planner in front of computers at their headquarters, and Canary as the warmer, more impulsive, and fishnet-clad "boots on the ground."

Fans reacted positively to Oracle's characterization.[2] One wrote, "The insights we got into a strong, determined, and attractive Barbara who has moved beyond the crippling tragedy was a treat" (Jake Rose, *Birds of Prey: Manhunt* #2, 1996). Another said, "Oracle is such a strongly written character—smart, principled, quick at analysis and so often on the mark in her judgment—that it's a very human touch that she hasn't got it all quite right" (Sarah Beach, *Birds of Prey: Wolves*, 1997). One even found her "the most fascinating character in comics today" (Joseph Stivers, *Birds of Prey* #31, 2001).

Many explicitly contrasted Batgirl to Oracle and found the latter more compelling. "I've felt sick about Batgirl ever since the Joker shot her. However, there was no pity in this story. Oracle is a wonderful character" (Jeff Mitchell, *Birds of Prey: Manhunt* #4, 1996). "Barbara Gordon's transformation from Batgirl to Oracle was, if you'll pardon the morbidity of the statement, the best thing that ever happened to her. She's a strong, intelligent woman who happens to be handicapped" (Beau Yarbrough, *Birds of Prey: Black Canary/Batgirl* #1, 1998). "The truth is that Oracle is way cooler than Batgirl ever was, not to mention an integral part of the entire DCU. I would never want to lose Oracle to regain Batgirl. And it is pretty darn great having a 'superhero' who is wheelchair-bound" (Chuck McKinney, *Birds of Prey* #6, 1999). "Oracle [is] the heart and soul of the DC Universe. I must admit that I miss Barbara as Batgirl, but I prefer her as Oracle" (Robert Acquaruto, *Birds of Prey* #17, 2000).

The praise for her "moving on" from her "tragedy" of being "wheelchair-bound," and admiration for her "strength of will" are common reactions to the pop culture trope of the "supercrip." The supercrip is the disabled hero who "accomplishes things that are unusual even for the able-bodied" due to unusually high levels of resources, and who "may give the able-bodied the false impression that anyone can 'overcome' a disability" (Wendell 2010: 346; see also Garland-Thomson 2005b: 1568, Alaniz 2014: 31–33).

Unremarked upon are Barbara's economic, racial, and sexual privilege, in the comic itself or in any letters.[3] She has a PhD, and later acquires an online J.D. and then an LL.M. from Harvard. She taps into villains' bank accounts and transfers money to her own. She gets grants from the Wayne Foundation (i.e., from Bruce Wayne/ Batman) for expensive and difficult-to-acquire technology. The weight machines she uses and the pool she swims in and the hot tub she soaks in seem to be in her own gigantic apartment. But in the real world, "by all estimates the majority of people with disabilities are poor, unemployed, and undereducated" (Davis 2010b: 312; see also Charlton 2010 and Schur 2004). Total independence is simply not a reality for many people with (or without) disabilities. Were Barbara to need assistance, she could afford it without difficulty, unlike most people with disabilities. But we never see another character assist Barbara with daily life tasks. Indeed, a number of times, she draws attention to the fact that there are no push handles on her wheelchair because she neither wants nor needs anyone's help.

When a number of letters in response to the first *Birds of Prey* special issue critiqued the design of Barbara's wheelchair, it was modified. Editor Jordan Gorfinkel wrote, "Because of your letters, we gathered reference on wheelchairs from the National Spinal Cord Association of America. . . . Please let us know if we're on the right track; we're trying hard to get it right" (*Birds of Prey: Manhunt* #2, 1996). In 1997, he wrote in response to a letter praising the redesigned chair, "I received a lot of feedback from paras which led us to do some homework . . . a simple standard applies: the less chair, the better (i.e., no handlebars or armrests) and keep the wheels as close to the body as possible" (*Birds of Prey: Revolution* #1, 1997). Fan input, specifically from those Gorfinkle describes as "athletic chairbound paraplegics," was incorporated directly into the book.

Barbara's athleticism, along with her privileges, further enables her to push away assistance. She is neither helpless nor weak nor dependent as stereotypes of disability would have us assume (Garland-Thomson 2002; Linton 2010; Longmore 2003; Mintz 2007). We see her working out, and defending herself physically with her escrima sticks and her fists. She was already a judo expert when she met Batman and Robin, who trained her further. Not long after her shooting, Batman sets her up with one of the best martial artists in the DC Universe, Richard Dragon, so that she can learn how to fight and defend herself from her chair (Ostrander, Yale, and Stelfreeze 1996). Indeed, her martial arts skills are comparable to those of the other "Birds." Coupled with her brilliance and ingenuity, this mostly keeps her safe from her foes. Almost every time we see her face a foe with her sticks, about twenty times, she wins.[4] This includes when she faces the Joker for the first time since he shot her. When he says,

"I took your legs, your future," she tells him, "You took nothing from me" (Tony Bedard and Claude St. Aubin 2009, *Birds of Prey* #124).[5] Such situations subvert a common plot point in which a "character's disability and femininity serve to indicate a terrifying or defeated situation" (Smith 2004: 4).

She is privileged in another way as well: because the nature of her work is in large part through computing, Barbara's gender and her disability are not visible. Usually, both the female body and the disabled body are objects to be looked at, albeit in different ways: "Women are objects of the evaluative male 'gaze' [but] the disabled body is the object of the 'stare'" (Garland-Thomson 1997: 26). But characters who know of Oracle only online or by reputation assume that someone with such intelligence and resources must be male.[6] Because Barbara not infrequently escapes both the "gaze" and the "stare," she can pass as a "normal" male (Garland-Thomson 2002: 22; Linton 2010: 229) and is treated with a respect and deference that someone who was face to face with her might not use.

Barbara is neither dependent nor isolated as stereotypes of people with disabilities would have us expect (Garland-Thomson 2002; Linton 2010; Longmore 2003; Schur 2004). Indeed, she is the leader of the superhero team, the Birds of Prey, and the Birds make a loyal circle of friends as well. This is the case in both the comic and the short-lived TV show from the early 2000s. The comic team's rotating roster, expanded greatly by future *Wonder Woman* writer Gail Simone, assures that she is surrounded by superhero women such as Black Canary, Huntress, Manhunter, Big Barda, Lady Blackhawk, Judomaster, Gypsy, Hawkgirl, Ice, Power Girl, Vixen, Katana, Dove, Misfit, and the two Batgirls who succeeded Barbara in that role. The sheer number of female characters guarantees that neither she nor any of the others has to represent "all"

**Figure 2.2** The short-lived *Birds of Prey* TV show, starring (left to right) Ashley Scott as Helena/Huntress, Rachel Skarsten as Dinah (here, the daughter of the Black Canary), and Dina Meyer as Barbara/Oracle ("Pilot," S01E01, 2002).

women. Rather, each can be different from one another and represent a spectrum of womanhood and of gender. It also means that the series always passes the "Bechdel test." There are plenty of female characters, and they talk about many topics other than (and including) men. Her reach extends to many male characters in the DC Universe as well, as we see her interact with Batman, Robin, Nightwing, Superman, Green Arrow, Wildcat, and Blue Beetle, as well as with her father, Police Commissioner Jim Gordon. She is sometimes shown posed similarly with the other Birds, usually sitting and talking, rather than having them standing around her.

In contrast to the 1990 *Suicide Squad* issue in which she laments that she will probably never have children, Barbara in *Birds of Prey* and other titles chooses to be a maternal figure. She acts as a mentor and sometimes as a guardian to the new Batgirls, the Asian-American speech-impaired Cassandra Cain (1999–2008) and the white working-class college student Stephanie Brown (2009–11), as well as to white orphan teen Charlotte Gage-Radcliffe (Misfit: 2006–11) and white villain's daughter and wheelchair user Wendy Harris (Proxy: 2010–11). Cassandra Cain was brought up to be an assassin, like her parents, David Cain and Lady Shiva. Cain had trained his daughter not to read, write, or talk, but to use those parts of her brain to be able to "read" people. At a young age, Cassandra assassinates someone for her father, but due to her "reading" skills realizes how painful the death is. She turns on her father, standing in between his gun and Commissioner Gordon, and becomes Oracle's ward while training to be the new Batgirl. Barbara helps her learn to communicate, and she later tells Barbara that she has been "like a mother" to her (Kelley Puckett and Damion Scott 2002, *Batgirl* Vol. 2 #25). As arguably the world's greatest fighter, Cassandra falls into the stereotype of Asian women as experts in martial arts, but her artists subverted some racial stereotypes as well by not sexualizing her depiction. Cassandra then helped train Stephanie Brown, the purple-clad "Spoiler" who sought to spoil her father's villainous schemes. In turn, Stephanie becomes the formerly isolated Cassandra's first friend. Stephanie dates Robin (Tim Drake, not Dick Grayson) on and off. She also becomes Robin herself, briefly, and suffered, like Barbara, a "fridging." Stephanie Brown's hyperviolent and hypersexualized torture and death was a storyline mandated by editors and protested by the *Batgirl* and *Nightwing* writers.[7] Due to fan outrage and the apparent continuing marketability of the character, she was brought back to be Spoiler, and then Batgirl, the title handed to her by Cassandra who then goes by Black Bat. Completely unlike Cassandra except in their motivation to be different from their fathers and fight crime, Stephanie as Batgirl is like a combination of Buffy the Vampire Slayer and Batgirl with her blonde hair, quippy and perky demeanor, and "can-do devil-may-care Pollyanna" determination (Brian Q. Miller and Ramon Bachs 2011, *Batgirl* Vol. 3 #19).

Barbara's role with Stephanie, like that of her past role with Cassandra and future one with Charlie and Wendy, is that of caring mentor. Barbara worries that Stephanie is not serious enough for the job and will get killed (again). But when Stephanie works to prove herself and is willing to listen to Barbara's guidance, the latter gives her a new purple-and-black costume with a yellow thigh pouch and they work together: "I pledge to you, Stephanie Brown . . . when you go out at night, you won't be alone." Stephanie replies, "I've got your back too. Neither of us is alone in this" (Miller, Lee Garbett, and Trevor Scott 2009, *Batgirl* Vol. 3 #3). Barbara's role with Charlie/Misfit is similar to that of both Cassandra and Stephanie, with Barbara opening her home to the young orphan and training her directly as a Batgirl-esque figure. And while Barbara sees her young Batgirl self in Stephanie and Charlie, she sees her young Oracle self in Wendy. Wendy, the same character as on the *Super Friends* cartoon in the early 1970s and in the *Teen Titans* comic in the 2000s, helps with information gathering, with working with Stephanie, and with opposing her computer-tech-based father. But all four of these young characters disappeared when DC Comics rebooted its superhero universe in 2011, to the consternation of their fans and Barbara's fans as well.[8] Not physically reproducing but still mothering as Oracle, Barbara subverts a stereotype of women with disabilities as unable to care for children or young people, yet falls into a stereotype of women as intergenerational nurturers. Her giving four young women the female guide they otherwise would not have challenges female characters' underrepresentation as mentors across media. She both embraces her role and finds it burdensome, complicating rather than stereotyping their relationships.

Despite her fears immediately following her shooting, Barbara has romantic and sexual relationships. A few men show interest in her, but the most long-term (albeit on-and-off) relationship is with the Robin to her Batgirl, Dick Grayson. This is in contrast to "cultural stereotypes [that] imagine disabled women as asexual, unfit to reproduce, overly dependent, unattractive" (Garland-Thomson 2002: 17; see also Clare 2009, Coleman-Brown 2010, Garland-Thomson 1997 and 2005, Siebers 2010, Wendell 2010). They kiss a number of times over the course of the run of the series and in other titles as well; once they are drawn naked and lying in a bed.[9] In most, but not all, of these panels, Barbara's chair is visible, making clear that one does not have to be either disabled or sexual but rather can be both. But she also pushes Dick Grayson away a number of times due to her wanting to remain independent. A letter writer noted, "She blames it on her disability and her eagerness to prove she doesn't need any help" (Wesley Porras, *Birds of Prey* #12, 1999). This is another trope,

> Disabled characters . . . spurn opportunities for romance because of a lack of self-acceptance, a disbelief that anyone could love them with their "imperfections." Nondisabled characters . . . have no difficulty in accepting [disabled characters] with their disabilities. . . . These depictions fly in the face of the real-life experiences of many handicapped men and women who find that even the most minor impairments result in romantic rejection. (Longmore 2003: 142)

At the same time, her heterosexuality works to "normalize" her (McRuer 2006: 41). That is, her disability takes a backseat to her heterosexuality. When she's kissing a man, or lying in bed with him, she seems more "normal." Barbara has a romantic life from the first issues of *Birds of Prey*, and in the television series from 2002 to 2003 as well. But she is not defined by it. Writer Gail Simone says she purposely had little romance in her run because she wanted to write about female friendship and to resist "constant pressure to have heroines have a romantic subplot, always" (Simone 2015). When Barbara is shown with a partner, she is on equal footing in the way they're drawn, in their language to one another, and in who is initiating the contact with whom. This allays feminist concerns about women being portrayed solely as objects; it upends the "assumption that disabled people cannot be sexual beings" (Hall 2011: 4).

"While feminism quite legitimately decries the sexual objectification of women, disabled women often encounter . . . 'asexual objectification'" (Garland-Thomson 1997: 25). In other words, while nondisabled women are portrayed suggestively as sexually available in terms of posing and clothing and behavior, disabled women are portrayed as lacking sexuality. Many *Birds of Prey* covers don't have Barbara on them at all, but have an action shot and/or a highly sexualized shot of the other Birds: Black Canary, Huntress, Lady Blackhawk, Misfit, Manhunter, Big Barda, etc.

Barbara—the main character of the series—was on only one-third of its covers, and her whole body was depicted on those covers only half of that time. In the first sixty-four issues of *Birds of Prey*, she was on twenty-six covers; on fourteen of them, she was depicted as a head in contrast to another Bird's full body.[10] In the next seventy-two issues, she was on twenty-seven covers; on twelve of them, she was depicted as a head in contrast to another's body.[11] In Volume 2 of the series, she was on four of the fifteen covers, each of which depicted most or all of her body.[12]

This non-sexualization of Barbara as Oracle is welcome, particularly as the sexualization of female characters was rampant in comics at the time, and particularly because it leads to evaluating the character on other bases. But her absence from the covers falls into a stereotype of people with disabilities as asexual and unattractive, and hides her body as if it should be unseen—or as if there is nothing to see. Showing only her head half of the time she is on the covers seems to indicate that various artists were not sure how to portray her body in a medium in which women are sexualized even more often on covers than they are in panels (Cocca 2014a). In a genre focused so closely on an idealized body, it is as if artists' inability to draw her as an able-bodied woman made it too difficult to imagine how to draw her at all, hence her omission from two-thirds of the covers.

In terms of how she has appeared in panels, as noted, as Oracle in *Suicide Squad* she looks like a stereotype of "old maid librarian," with her hair in a bun, unstylish glasses, and frumpy suits and blouses. Readers noticed that she was drawn differently in *Birds of Prey*. One wrote, "It was nice to see her drawn in a flattering manner for a change. So often she is drawn to look so dowdy" (Oracle 359, *Manhunt* #3, 1996). Editor Jordan Gorfinkle responded, "Thanks for noticing the efforts [we] put into showing Oracle as the attractive woman that we Batguys have always known her to be." Another letter writer thanked the writer and artist for having "strong female characters that aren't costumed like they work for a [strip club, and that] come off like real people" (Dave Rossi, *Birds of Prey* #4, 1999). A third noted about two years later, "[Artist Greg Land] brought back Barbara's beauty, grace, and dignity unlike so many other artists. Until Greg, most artists rendered her as a bitter old geek girl who rarely bathed." This writer also said that the next artist, Butch Guice, drew her like a "geek girl" again (ashndavd99@webtv.com, *Birds of Prey* #27, 2001). In many of the early *Birds of Prey* issues, Barbara's hair is bobbed to the shoulder, hanging lankly, and she often wears shapeless sweaters and pants, in contrast with the long-haired, curved-body, more sexualized drawings of the other Birds.

Later in the run, Barbara would be portrayed in a more sexualized manner. Particularly with Gail Simone's run as writer and Ed Benes' as artist (2003–05), Barbara was drawn as very attractive, with a shapely upper-body made strong by martial arts and swimming, large curvy breasts pushing out of her shirts, a small waist, and tousled longer hair. He drew the other main "Birds," Black Canary and Huntress, in this manner as well, and continued his style with Wonder Woman, Black Canary, and Vixen in the *Justice League of America* (*JLA*) title the following year. *JLA* writer Brad Meltzer recalled asking Benes to draw Wonder Woman's breasts "smaller" more than once, and Benes laughed, "Ahahah! . . . What can I say? I've drawn women like that for years and years and old habits die hard!" (Meltzer and Benes 2007: n.p.). Benes' Barbara is a sexualized object like so many other female superheroes, enmeshed in Euro-American standards of beauty. But at other times, and sometimes at the same time, Benes draws Barbara to be as sexy as she was when she was Batgirl, and as sexy as the other Birds, subverting the stereotype of people with disabilities as "asexual undesirables." Nicola Scott was the last artist on Simone's *Birds of Prey*, as well as the title's first female artist and the first woman to draw Barbara Gordon in an ongoing title. She drew Barbara as sexy but not sexualized. While we can and should critique sexualized portrayals, we can and should also note portrayals of a character who is disabled and beautiful and an agent of her own sexuality. Yet another complication in Barbara's appearance was that she was portrayed entirely differently on television and in film at exactly the same time.

## Batgirl on television and in *Year One*: Girl power, 1993–2007

Concurrently to Barbara Gordon's commercially successful and beloved portrayal as Oracle in the comics, she was de-aged and portrayed as Batgirl in a number of animated series, younger and slighter than she had ever been in the comics. This began in the critically acclaimed *Batman: The Animated Series* (1993–94) and its tie-in comic *Gotham Adventures*, and continued in *The New Batman Adventures* (1997–99) and *The Batman* (2005–07). In this way, DC could capitalize on two very different characterizations at once. In the comics, for a presumably narrower audience familiar with the character, there was an older, disabled Barbara, a leader surrounded by nondisabled and usually sexualized women. On TV, for a broader audience, there was a younger, nondisabled Barbara, often the only female and generally secondary to Batman and Robin. As with Barbara's portrayal in comics since 1967 (except for a few *Batgirl* issues written by Barbara Kesel and the *Birds of Prey* run by Gail Simone), the animated episodes were generally written by men.

Batgirl's first animated appearance is a retelling of her origin story (Dennis O'Flaherty, Tom Ruegger, and Gavin Wolf 1993, "Shadow of the Bat Part 1" [E57]).

Coming off of the success of the Tim Burton-directed Batman films of 1989 and 1992, this show began airing weekday afternoons on Fox in 1993. Barbara is similar to two characters that debuted on the big and small screen in 1992, Buffy the Vampire Slayer and Sailor Moon—teens whose size and frivolity masked their inner strength. In this version, Barbara is a petite gymnast rather than a statuesque brown belt in judo, shorter rather than taller than Robin. Like Wonder Woman would be a few years later on *Justice League*, her waist is drawn to be about the same size as her head. She is a college student rather than having already earned a PhD. And she is romantically interested in both Batman and Robin. Barbara does make her own costume, but here, to pose as Batman. When there's trouble, she jumps in the fray and stops it. Robin tears her mask and is taken aback, "A *girl?*" and a villain describes her as "like Batman, only a dame." As in the original comics version, Batman and Robin try to dissuade her, but she saves both Robin and her father and captures the main villain. Her father, echoing his praise for her at the close of her 1967 comics debut, says, "She's as welcome in this city as the Batman." At her next appearance the following year (Michael Reaves and Brynne Stephens 1994, "Batgirl Returns" [E85]), she's daydreaming that she saves Batman and that he leans in for a kiss. Robin/Dick Grayson arrives and wakes her, but she says she has to study, "Math. Why did it have to be math?" Calling attention to her female-ness was done in the early comics as well, highlighting the supposed disconnect between being female and being a superhero. But having her so physically small, stereotypically unconfident in math when in the comics she is a genius, and swooning over Batman while dating Robin position her as less capable and more a romantic adjunct to a male character.

Batgirl appears much more in the follow-up series, *The New Batman Adventures*, because, explained producer Paul Dini "Kenner wants to do a line of toys [and] we're taking advantage of the publicity from her being in *Batman and Robin*" (Allstetter 1997).

**Figure 2.3** The younger and slighter Barbara as Batgirl in *The New Batman Adventures* ("Old Wounds," S01E18, 1998).

This show aired on the WB after Fox' license ran out in 1997. Producer Bruce Timm added,

> The consumer products division and the people at the WB wanted to make sure kids would watch the show, so they strongly suggested we include Batgirl and Robin as a way of courting young girl audiences as well as young boys. At first we were a little reluctant to do it, but then we started thinking, why not? We liked the Batgirl character. (Nolen-Weathington 2004: 58)

In short, those higher up than the creative team basically mandated Batgirl's inclusion to make money from a younger target audience through higher ratings and toy sales. Such a mandate, along with the success of contemporaneous TV shows with young female stars, probably account for her youth and her girlish figure.

Batgirl's increased exposure was in 1997's *Batman and Robin* (written by Akiva Goldman and directed by Joel Schumacher). The film's Barbara is not Barbara Gordon but Barbara Wilson, butler Alfred's orphaned niece for whom he has made a leather costume with thigh-high high-heeled boots. Played by Alicia Silverstone after her star turn in 1995's *Clueless*, the character is a caricature of woman-resenting and man-judging "feminism." She dresses down villain Poison Ivy: "Using feminine wiles to get what you want. Trading on your looks. Read a book, sister. That passive-aggressive number went out long ago. Chicks like you give women a bad name." And she dismisses Robin's plan, "Men. Always doing things the hard way." She introduces herself as Batgirl, and Batman responds, "That's not very PC. What about Batwoman, or Batperson?" She doesn't answer. The character is little like her comics predecessor except for her willingness to fight crime and ride a motorcycle, little like her counterpart in *Batman: The Animated Series* except for her youth, and little like her Oracle counterpart in *Birds of Prey* except for briefly using a computer.

The publicity from the movie probably did increase Batgirl's profile, and she was indeed a strong recurring character in the animated series from 1997 to 1999, in some of its best episodes. One concerns her worst nightmares, as she has ingested the Scarecrow's fear gas: that she has died and her father blames Batman and Robin for it (Paul Dini 1998, "Over the Edge" [S01E12]). A second has Dick Grayson upset upon finding out Barbara is Batgirl (Rich Fogel 1998, "Old Wounds" [S01E17]). In both cases, she makes clear that she was not manipulated into fighting crime by anyone else, but chose it for herself. Rather than a librarian, she is a systems and data analyst for the police. As she had briefly in the comics, she teams up with Supergirl (Hilary Bader 1998, "Girls Night Out" [S01E20]). As apparently younger versions of themselves, they are at first easily overcome but then triumph, ending the episode by rather stereotypically eating ice cream and watching TV in little bathrobes and slippers. Barbara was also the featured hero in the (Paul Dini-written) 2002 animated web series *Gotham Girls*, among a number of female characters such as Poison Ivy, Harley Quinn, Catwoman, Zatanna, Renee Montoya, and Selma Reesedale. Like the *Birds of Prey* comic, the ensemble of female characters meant that Batgirl did not have to stand-in for "all" women. A range of female characters were portrayed, with the Latina Montoya and the transgender Reesedale furthering the diversity.

At the same time as the Oracle-starring *Birds of Prey* comic was adapted into a short-lived live-action TV series in 2002–03,[13] DC Comics released *Batgirl: Year One* by Scott Beatty and Chuck Dixon. The latter, as noted, had written *Birds of Prey* in its first years, steering it away from "cheesecake" and toward "superhero adventure." Beatty and Dixon had pitched *Robin: Year One* as a follow-up to the very successful *Batman: Year One*. When the *Robin* book did well, they pitched the same for *Batgirl*. The authors intended her origin to comport with that of her 1967 self, in that she makes her costume for a masquerade ball to annoy her father, winds up fighting crime on the way, and decides to continue doing so. When Batman asks why, she says, "Because I can" and because she is concerned for Gotham's future (#4). But unlike her first incarnation and more like the animated series and film, she is younger and smaller, not yet in graduate school, and wants to be a police detective. Her father resists, "My little girl, a cop?" (#1). She is so petite that she is rejected from the police and from the FBI for her height. Drawn by Marcos Martin, there is no hint of sexualization, and her slight look is similar to her animated TV appearance. She has a yellow belt in jujitsu rather than her original incarnation's brown belt in judo, using her male Sensei's low expectations of her against him and pinning him to the ground. She does the same with Robin, who dismisses her as "just a girl" (#3) although he is romantically interested in her once they get to know each other. "I'd have preferred Bat*woman*," she thinks when Killer Moth labels her Batgirl, but she does not protest aloud (#3). She looks up to Black Canary as a model, and is positioned in the book as younger and less experienced than her when they work together, reversing the relationship from *Birds of Prey* where Oracle is more of a mentor to Canary. She is as exhilarated by crimefighting as her other incarnations, and it is she who performs a seemingly foolish but mathematically calculated stunt in the last issue, delivering the villain to Batman and Robin. At that point, they welcome her to the team, complete with a gauntlet including a cardboard cutout of the Joker pointing a gun at her. "If this is my future, I'm not afraid of it," she says as she kicks the "Joker" in the face (#9).

The origin was retold yet again just two years later, on the WB animated series *The Batman*. Because the character of Robin was in the *Teen Titans* cartoon, Batgirl became Batman's first sidekick here. She is even younger and physically smaller this time, a junior in high school yet much shorter than the Batman and just a hair taller than Robin. This depiction was in line with other "girl power" cartoons of the time, such as *Powerpuff Girls, Kim Possible,* and *Totally Spies* (Hains 2012). Very stylized and not at all sexualized, Barbara sports a short lavender dress and leggings with high black boots. As in *Batman: The Animated Series*, she is a gymnast. As in *Batgirl: Year One*, she would prefer to be called "Batwoman." Indeed, she repeats the request four times, until her father calls her Batgirl and she gives in ([future *Wonder Woman* animated film writer] Michael Jelenic 2005, "Batgirl Begins" [S03E01]). Combining the origins from the two, her father tries to dissuade her from becoming a detective. She makes her costume from her purple gymnastic unitard, narrating to herself, "Mild mannered Olympic hero by day. Butt-kicking Batwoman by night." With a couple of mishaps, as in her other origin stories, she rescues both Batman and her father. When Robin arrives (after the end of the *Teen Titans* series), their banter is like that of siblings. In the final episode, written by *Buffy the Vampire Slayer* scribes Jane Espenson and Doug Petrie, they both "quit" being Batman's partners because he has ordered them to stay behind. Barbara says, "You picked us because you knew we were strong" and he relents (2007, "The Joining" Part 1 and 2 [S04E12]). This Batgirl is just as talented as her other animated versions, but her small stature and young age makes her request to be called "Batwoman" more of a joke than a social comment.

The worlds of Batgirl and Oracle are brought together in a later episode of this series set 1,000 years in the future (Greg Weisman 2007, "Artifacts" [S04E07]). The bulk of the show is a flashback from that perspective, but a flash-forward to the show's viewers. Barbara is called Oracle from the beginning, shown in a chair in front of computer equipment feeding an older Batman information, controlling the Batmobile and Batwing remotely, rerouting planes and contacting the police with orders to evacuate an airport. Barbara's chair is revealed partway through the show to be a wheelchair. Not dissimilar to her usual *Birds of Prey* portrayals, and cluing in the viewer who has never read that comic or seen its TV counterpart that she was Batgirl, she is wearing a white blouse under a lavender vest, a gold "bat" necklace, lavender gloves, and glasses, with a blanket on her lap. In this, Oracle's first animated portrayal, she is just as heroic as her Batgirl persona. But the character of Oracle was about to be erased from the DC superhero universe.

**Figure 2.4** Oracle's sole appearance in animated form: 2007's *The Batman* ("Artifacts," S04E07).

# From Oracle to Batgirl:
# Barbara Gordon rebooted, 2011–present

After fifteen years, *Birds of Prey* ended in 2011 as part of DC's "New 52" rebooting and relaunching of fifty-two of their superhero titles, wiping out some elements of long-standing continuity but not others. The character of Oracle disappeared, and Volume 3 of *Birds of Prey* was launched without her. A nonphysically disabled Barbara Gordon instead headlined her own *Batgirl* comic for the first time.

Written by longtime *Birds of Prey* writer Gail Simone from issues 1–34, *Batgirl* made mention of her having been paralyzed by the Joker and then having been "cured." "Three years after a savage attack that nearly ended her life, the brilliant Barbara Gordon returns to the streets as both survivor and avenger" (#3). Readers reacted passionately in a variety of spaces. As Simone put it, some readers were "thrilled and delighted" at her being "healed" and others felt "a punch in the heart" at losing a portrayal of a strong superhero who flew in the face of ableism and sexism (Pantozzi 2011).

In the early days of the *Birds of Prey* series, two printed letters asked for Barbara to be cured, but DC editors refused. In 1996, editor Jordan Gorfinkle wrote, "While it is true that the scientific community is coming tantalizingly closer to a breakthrough on such research. . . I feel that it would be a great injustice to allow [Barbara] to take a leap that her brethren cannot" (*Birds of Prey: Manhunt* #4, 1996). In 2001, associate editor Michael Wright rebuffed a call to "get her out of the chair already" with, "We think she's a unique and important hero just as she is" (*Birds of Prey* #26, 2001). "Cure" narratives have been criticized for their ubiquity and their emphases on changing bodies rather than on changing societal barriers (e.g., Clare 2009: 120–24, Mintz 2007: 130, Russell 2011: 183, Snyder and Mitchell 2005: 175). When such critiques were fused with concerns about the underrepresentation of people with disabilities and of strong female characters in mainstream superhero comics, the mix was explosive as soon as the new title was announced—well before it was published.

The most comments came from those who lamented the change, protesting that Oracle was a more interesting character than Batgirl, and that the politics of the change were problematic. Almost all of them focused on the real-world implications of Barbara's representation, for both disabled and nondisabled readers. For instance:

> Barbara Gordon is a beacon for the chronically ill, mobility impaired and disabled. . . . Even more importantly, Oracle has developed deep friendships with able-bodied people of all types, some of which were even romantic and presumably sexual, demonstrating that people like her don't have to be segregated to the unseen fringes of society. (Andy Khouri at *Comics Alliance*, 6/6/11: http://comicsalliance.com/batgirl-barbara-gordon-disabled/)

> Do you not see how ableist this is? Do you not see that while Barbara was fridged and victimized, Kim Yale and John Ostrander came and turned her into something amazing and empowering? A role model that people love and adore? (Benicio127 on the [now-defunct] *Comic Book Resources* message boards, 6/7/11, 7:17am)

Seeing a disabled person in a comic [can] ease the discomfort someone might feel when seeing someone in a wheelchair. . . . Disabled people can look at [Barbara] and see their own struggles for respect, for equality, for simple *dignity* reflected back at them. (Puckett101 on his tumblr: http://puckett101.tumblr.com/ post/6188747591/on-disability-and-visibility)

My dad was a paraplegic . . . [Oracle] eased the stigma and gave people like my dad and I representation. She made me hope for a day when discussions like this would be unnecessary because disabled people could be seen as individuals, not monsters. (MJ on her blog, http://comic-relief.tumblr.com/post/6279927548/the-musings-of-a-failed-black-woman-on-disability-and)

Barbara Gordon deserves to be Oracle. She deserves to be the symbol she's become. . . . Giving Oracle back the use of her legs to bring her back to her iconic role is a travesty. (Jill Pantozzi, at *Newsarama,* 6/6/11, http://www.newsarama.com/7749-op-ed-oracle-is-stronger-than-batgirl-will-ever-be.html)

Other fans, smaller in number, supported the idea of the new title:

I think it's a good thing that Babs finally gets to recover from her fridging. (Ziral on the *Comic Book Resources* message boards, 6/6/11, 5:40pm)

THIS disabled person is happy to see Babs healed because I never will be. (Tori Pagac on the *Comic Book Resources* message boards, 6/6/11, 6:08pm)

It never made sense to keep Babs in a chair for 20 years when the resources to heal her existed within the DCU. (Badou on the *Comic Book Resources* message boards, 6/6/11, 8:51pm)

Writer Gail Simone herself entered the fray on the *Comic Book Resources* message boards, responding to a number of posts. But it was Jill Pantozzi's column (the last one in the first set of comments, above) that led Simone to ask her for space to address people's concerns. In their conversation, Simone said, "It's been sort of simply accepted that there's this block of disabled folks who are against this idea, en masse [but] there has always been a vocal minority of people with disabilities who wanted to see Babs healed and out of the chair." She noted that Oracle as a character made storytelling difficult because she could solve any problem, that her continued disability made no sense when other injured superheroes had been healed from grave injury,[14] and that the most iconic Batgirl should finally headline her own *Batgirl* title. She also made clear that she was not completely sure about the change, but that DC was planning to go ahead with it, and if she did not write it, someone else would (Pantozzi 2011).

Simone incorporated content about disabilities into the *Batgirl* title to address the types of comments listed above. She establishes that Barbara was Batgirl for about a year, was shot, and after about three years of using a wheelchair visited a clinic in South Africa that restored her mobility. Barbara has survivor's guilt over this "cure," and is also living with post-traumatic stress disorder over the home invasion and shooting by the Joker.[15] In other words, Barbara as Batgirl could be considered disabled. She vacillates between confidence and fear, noting that she is "rusty" and that her "condition could deteriorate." Her body is drawn to look athletic, and she is only infrequently posed in a sexualized manner. This run also marked the first time that Barbara as Batgirl was drawn by a female artist, Alitha Martinez (on parts of #7 and 8, and on #10). The first villain Batgirl faces is "Mirror," who kills people somehow saved by "miracles" from certain death, a reference to Barbara's feelings about her cure as she thinks, "Why do you get a miracle when so many others never will?" (*Batgirl* Vol. 4 #4, drawn by Ardian Syaf).

Stereotypes of people with disabilities would have us expect their portrayals to show isolation. The character of Oracle, though, was surrounded by close companions. This Batgirl is not. She pushes away Dick Grayson (as Oracle did initially as well), worried that he pities her rather than respecting her. She does become friendly with her transgender roommate Alysia Yeoh and has the beginnings of a romance with a young man named Ricky Gutierrez, two new characters created by Gail Simone to bring more diversity to the title.[16] But her mother, father, and brother are a source of stress in contrast to the way in which Barbara as Oracle was supported through a close relationship with her father. And because Barbara has been de-aged and the characters of Cassandra, Stephanie, Charlie, and Wendy are not present, she has no mentoring role as she did in Volume 1 and 2 of *Birds of Prey* and Volumes 1–3 of the previous *Batgirl* titles. Simone said that she had "wanted to add lighter stories and more personal stuff, and that just was not allowed" by the editor (Simone 2014b).

Simone's *Batgirl*, which ran thirty-four issues up until August 2014, received mostly positive reviews and for over two years was usually the highest-selling female-headed comic title in any given month.[17] But resentment over the loss of the Oracle character remained, questions about her return persisted, and while some readers found Barbara's PTSD resonant, others didn't view her as disabled. Reflecting the feelings of many online about the difference between Barbara in this *Batgirl* series versus in *Birds of Prey*, one woman wrote,

> Disabled people are told that their bodies are wrong and that they should seek to be "cured," . . . that they are foolish and selfish if they are proud of the way they are. . . . In Oracle, we had this disabled woman who was one of the most powerful people on the planet. Who flipped ableist and sexist narratives on their heads and said, "I am here, and I am not broken." In the reboot, we lost all of that. (Amy B 2013)

This last comment highlights just how the character of Barbara Gordon/Oracle disrupts cultural assumptions about gender and disability, albeit in complicated ways.

## Conclusion: The Batgirl of Burnside

A "soft reboot" of Batgirl was at the forefront of the mid-2010s trend of redesigning female superheroes' costumes to be less sexualized, and a growing sense that the "Oracle" parts of Barbara's personality could and should be incorporated into her book. As Gail Simone's run came to a close, the new team of Brenden Fletcher, Cameron

Stewart, and Babs Tarr again had Barbara make her own costume, as she had been doing since 1967. This time, though, she doesn't sew spandex, but paints a bat on a leather jacket, which creates a more subtle curve that tapers at the waist rather than clinging to her breasts individually as most female superhero costumes do. She pairs this with leggings and Doc Marten boots.

In a number of ways, this new Batgirl combines the *Batgirl: Year One*/animated Batgirl with the characterization of Oracle.[18] She is petite and smart like the younger versions of her own Batgirl, with a little bit of Stephanie Brown in her (attempts at a) more sunny and spunky demeanor, as well as the leg pouch and purple-inflected notes of Barbara's TV and Stephanie's comic costume. And similar to Oracle in *Birds of Prey*, she shows her detective skills and eidetic memory, is extremely computer-savvy, and is working on her master's thesis with an innovative and complex algorithm for mapping potential criminal activity. The algorithm is based on a scan of Barbara's brain, and is like a technological encapsulation of her Oracle persona. Also more akin to characterizations of Oracle rather than Batgirl, she is not the lone female. Black Canary is present at first, with Barbara saying as they high-five, "The Birds are back!" (#39). Alysia, the Asian transgender character created by Gail Simone, is present as well. Further, Barbara has a new circle of friends around her: her disabled friend Frankie (who is being positioned as the new Oracle), her school friends Nadimah and Qadir and Sevin, and love interest Luke Fox. Each of these new characters is a person of color as well, reflecting the increasing prominence of fan and creator concerns about diversity.

The de-aging of characters, particularly female characters, can make them appear as less dangerous but their characterization is crucial. When a young female character is made consistently secondary to older male ones, both her age and gender become entwined with her lack of power. But she can also be the star and can subvert the status quo. With Batgirl, both have occurred. She might be produced and received as "just a girl" or as a serious threat to gendered inequalities. As *Batgirl* and *Birds of Prey* writer Gail Simone commented (on both tumblr and twitter) on creators and fans' approach to female characters:

> Here is the thing. The old guard in comics are comfortable with feminism mostly under very strict guidelines. It has to be palatable to them. They are VERY comfortable with characters who spout faux female empowerment slogans while wearing skin-tight rubber bands or whatever. They are comfortable with characters who say GIRL POWER loudly, as long as they don't actually accomplish anything or overshadow the hero. And now they are comfortable with super adorable little pixie heroines, because they wrongly believe they pose no threat to the status quo. But when female characters actually act with agency and are immune to being tut-tutted, there is still a lot of pushback. HOWEVER! I think the audience has moved past this, mostly. I think the audience is ahead of the industry.[19]

Indeed, when female characters such as the new Batgirl were launched in the mid-2010s, they were generally well received.

There were controversies over Batgirl's 2014 redesign and relaunch, however, two of which were emblematic of today's changing comic fandom. Writer and artist Cameron Stewart says that he was asked to be on the book due to his drawings of Stephanie Brown as Batgirl (in *Batman Incorporated*), and that his acceptance of the book was "conditional" on his being able to "redesign the costume to be upbeat and fun . . . assembled out of real world fashion items . . . and it was also important to me that it wasn't sexualized" (Talking Comics 2014 [August 27]). He brought in Babs Tarr, a fashion-conscious artist who draws in a stylized rather than sexualized manner. She became the first woman to draw Barbara Gordon/Batgirl as an ongoing artist. In July 2014, the new team was announced with a drawing of a smiling, non-sexualized, leather- and boot-clad Barbara. Within twenty-four hours, dozens of pieces of fan art had been tweeted and posted on tumblrs, many of which the creative team reposted on their own tumblr.[20] Within two weeks, there were several hundred pieces of fan art, and yellow Doc Martens became difficult to find due to the number of cosplayers and fans ordering them online. Print orders for their first issue doubled the sales from the previous issue. Criticism, again within the first twenty-four hours and well before the book came out, came mostly from Stephanie Brown fans who felt that that character should be returned and that this character sounded too much like her; others protested that Barbara looked too much younger and too much like a hipster.

The second debate about this Batgirl title, in the spring of 2015, also pointed up the heated debates between newer and older fans, and between more diverse and more homogenous fans. A variant cover by Rafael Albuquerque was commissioned by DC for their themed month of covers referencing the Joker. It was not the main cover to the issue, but was targeted toward collectors and would be on a smaller number of the issues. Barbara Gordon has had many run-ins with the Joker, a number of them triumphant, but the most famous being the oft-referenced *The Killing Joke*—the story in which the Joker shoots, paralyzes, and possibly sexually assaults and takes pictures of a helpless, crying, naked, unable-to-move Barbara in order to torment Barbara's father and Batman. Albuquerque's cover shows the Joker holding Barbara motionless with a gun pointed down at her waist, as he draws a bloody smile on her face. Her eyes look terrified, and one of them leaks a tear. Reaction was immediate from those who felt uncomfortable or triggered by the cover and were offended by its marketization of violence against women in general. They specifically protested the enshrinement of the victimization and "fridging" so unfortunately common to female characters and not to male characters. They wanted the cover to be pulled and petitioned DC through twitter to do so. The creative team wanted it pulled as well. They had not been consulted on the illustration, and they felt the cover was the antithesis of what they wanted their book to be. On the other side were those who felt that the cover was a well-drawn homage to a famous story and that Albuquerque should be allowed to draw what he likes. Some in this group harassed those who found the cover distasteful, accusing "social justice warriors" of being oversensitive and politically correct and accusing the creative team of lacking integrity and being pro-censorship for caving in to a hysterical "vocal minority." Some of these were plain-spoken, some were rude, some were cruel, some were menacing, and some included rape and death threats. Albuquerque then said publicly that the art was not appropriate for the new *Batgirl* book even though he was asked by DC's marketing department to make the illustration dark, that he realized it touched a nerve for many people due to the industry's sexism, and that freedom of expression was important but also required responsibility at this moment of "an opening in the industry." He asked DC Comics to pull the cover, and the company acquiesced, more concerned in this case about losing new and/or concerned fans rather than losing old and/or angry ones (who had seen and could print out the art anyway), and bringing more rounds of both praise and criticism.[21]

This representation of Barbara Gordon has been a hot button for current debates over representations of women in comics since the day it was announced. Her mid-2010s portrayal, and those of the new characters around her, encompass the types of changes to comics that the "newer" and more diverse fan base has been clamoring for without losing her historically action-oriented characterization New title *Batgirl and the Birds of Prey* launched in 2016, written by sisters Shawna and Julie Benson and drawn by Claire Roe. Both this new title and *Batgirl* combine numerous features of her many incarnations in print and on television, potentially maximizing her marketability. Still, the character of Barbara Gordon as Oracle, the superhero with disabilities, is lost. Barbara's Batgirl is a young, white, nondisabled, heterosexual woman—a point of identification or a role model for some, a nonthreatening "girl" for others, and a representation of narrow privilege for still others. The next chapter, on *Star Wars*, likewise deals with these complications, but on a much broader scale given its monumental recognizability and popularity.

# Notes

1   Brian Q. Miller (w), Lee Garbett (p), and Trevor Scott (p) 2009, *Batgirl* Vol. 3 #3. Portions of this chapter appeared in Cocca 2014d.

2   From *Birds of Prey* #4–46, there were twenty letters about her. In seven unnumbered one-shots, there were twelve such letters. There were only four critical ones. Two suggested she be "cured," one criticized the design of her wheelchair, and one said that a particular artist drew her too much like a "geek girl" and preferred Batgirl. The rest of the run had no letter columns.

3   To be fair, there are other comics characters with such privileges. Bruce Wayne/Batman, Tony Stark/Iron Man, and Oliver Queen/Green Arrow, for instance, are all young, attractive, brilliant, healthy, white, cisgender, heterosexual, wealthy, independent, and nondisabled men.

4   See, e.g., *Black Canary/Batgirl* #1; "Oracle: Year One" in *Batman Chronicles* #5; "Oracle" in *Showcase '94*; *Birds of Prey* #1, 6, 15, 19, 28, 61, 63, 73, 75, 99, 111, 124; *Oracle: The Cure* #3; *Batgirl* Vol. 3 #10.

5   Contrast the depictions of the Joker's mental disability with Barbara's physical disability: the former is mad and villainous and the latter is his innocent victim, then hero. See Alaniz 2014: 123 comparing their situation to that of the Green Goblin and Gwen Stacy from *Spider-Man*.

6   See, e.g., issues by five different writers: *Birds of Prey* #20, 34, 111, 117, 123; *Oracle: The Cure* #1; *Batgirl* Vol. 3 #1.

7   *Batgirl* writer Dylan Horrocks remembers,

> They planned this big long torture scene, I said I don't want to really have anything to do with that . . . . I wrote my comic out of the key events in the story. . . . So when there was that big online debate about Stephanie Brown's death I felt kind of really pleased and vindicated, and the other person who I think was probably happy about that . . . was Devin Grayson who was writing *Nightwing*. . . . She raised several issues during this meeting [like] how come we're always killing off the girls, and also how come we're killing off the ethnic characters. . . . There are these kind of commercial expectations on where the stories are going to go and we do get these directives from the head editorial office. (Auckland Writers and Readers Festival, July 2011): http://www.bleedingcool. com/2011/07/15/%E2%80%9Csome-kind-of-gang-war-in-gotham%E2%80%9D-and-%E2%80%9Cspoiler-was-gonna-die%E2%80%9D/

8   After a three-year absence, Stephanie did return as Spoiler; after four years, Cassandra returned as Black Bat.

9   See, e.g., *Birds of Prey* #8, 35, 54; various issues of *Nightwing* between #38 and 117. The bed scene is in *Nightwing Annual* #2.

10  These fourteen are from writer Chuck Dixon's lengthy run: *Black Canary/Oracle: Birds of Prey, Manhunt* #3 (covers by Gary Frank), and *Birds of Prey* Vol. 1 #1, 2, 4, 9, 10, 12 (Greg Land), 32, 33, 39, and 41 (Phil Noto). Interior art was by Greg Land and Butch Guice. *Birds of Prey* Vol. 1 #52 and 55 were written by Gilbert Hernandez with covers by Phil Noto and interior art by Casey Jones.

11  These nine are from writer Gail Simone's equally lengthy run: *Birds of Prey* Vol. 1 #61 (cover by Ed Benes), 65 (Greg Land), 66 (Phil Noto), 67, 72 (Greg Land), 86 (Adriana Melo), 91 (Jesus Saiz), 99 (Jerry Ordway), and 101 (Stephane Roux). Tony Bedard wrote #110 and 123 and Sean McKeever, 115; the cover artist on these three was Stephane Roux. Interior art was by Ed Benes, Joe Bennett, Paolo Siquiera, and Nicola Scott.

12  These four were written by Gail Simone: *Birds of Prey* Vol. 2 #1 (cover by Ed Benes), 8, 10, and 12 (Stanley Lau).

13  In the TV show, a flashback to the Joker shooting Barbara establishes why she is using a wheelchair, and she works to train a version of the Huntress and a sort-of-version of Black Canary as her partners. In two of the thirteen episodes, she uses some technology to fight as Batgirl as well. In general, the show represented Barbara as a heroic (but not a flawless "supercrip") person with disabilities who was a tech-savvy leader, a caring friend, and an equal romantic partner with a male character. The plots, the stereotypes of gender, and the characterizations of others, unfortunately, lacked the nuance of its comic counterpart, and the series was not successful. Gail Simone wrote on her tumblr in 2015 (July 13) that,

> I am friends with the person who developed the show, and she wanted to make it more like the book, but the network insisted on so many ridiculous changes that she left the show. . . . [If] they had just gone with the classic BoP formula, it could have been great . . . it could have been a game changer in the way that the *BoP* COMIC was a game changer (not just my run, the whole thing). http://gailsimone.tumblr.com/ post/123973111145/hey-i-know-youve-said-you-dont-watch-much-tv-but?utm_ campaign=SharedPost&utm_medium=Email&utm_source=TumblriOS

14  Most famously within the Bat-universe, Batman's back is broken by the villain Bane in the story arc "Knightfall" (along with "Knightquest" and "KnightsEnd"), in 1993–94. He recovers from paraplegia within that arc.

15  Note that Barbara's shooting by the Joker is referenced frequently. See, e.g., "Oracle: Year One" in *Batman Chronicles #5*, *Black Canary/Oracle: Birds of Prey*, *Birds of Prey* #1, 8, 16, 50, 61, 72, 84, 123, 124, 127; *Oracle: The Cure #3*; *Batman: Gotham Knights #6*; *Nightwing #45*; *Batgirl* Vol. 3 #11; *Batgirl* Vol. 4 #0, 1, 3, 6, 14, 15, 19, 22, 24, 27, 31, 49; and the *Birds of Prey* TV series pilot.

16  Simone said that she wanted Barbara to deal with post-traumatic stress disorder and to have a transgender roommate (Alysia). DC Comics copublisher Dan DiDio approved the character upon Simone's promise that Alysia would not be a token. She noted that positive emails from readers far outnumbered the negative ones. Further, "DC insisted" that Alysia continue on after the creative team changed in 2014 ("Secret Identities: Transgender Themes in Comics Books" Panel at NYCC, October 2014).

17  For such reviews, see, e.g., *The Mary Sue*: http://www.themarysue.com/review-batgirl-1/, and *Comics Alliance*: http://comicsalliance.com/new-batgirl-comic/. For sales figures, see http://www.comichron.com/monthlycomicssales.html. *Batgirl* was generally the highest-selling female-headed title (in terms of orders by comic shops) from its debut in September 2011 until the launch of *Harley Quinn* in December 2013.

18  In 2014, in the animated *Beware the Bat*, Barbara is quite young and adept with computers. She does not "become" Batgirl, but rather, a nondisabled Oracle. This is the first Bat-universe animated series following DC's reboot, which wiped away the character of Oracle. I am not discussing it in depth because its premature cancellation meant that the episodes with Oracle were all shown in one block on one day after the cancellation, curtailing its visibility sharply. In the *Batman Beyond* cartoon (1999–2001), by contrast, Barbara is much older, and the new "Commissioner" Gordon. She was apparently Batgirl for a number of years, even after Dick Grayson left Gotham City. But she was tired of the life (and of a romantic relationship with Bruce Wayne) and decided to fight crime in a different way. In the *Batman Beyond Unlimited* comic she plays the same role, and in one arc encounters a young woman of color dressing as Batgirl and fighting crime, Nissa (created by Scott Peterson and Annie Wu; collected in Adam Beechen, Scott Peterson, Adam Archer, and Annie Wu's *Batgirl Beyond*, 2014).

19  On tumblr: http://gailsimone.tumblr.com/post/126599477605/here-is-the-thing-the-old-guard-in-comics-are?utm_campaign=SharedPost&utm_medium=Email&utm_source=TumblriOS, on twitter: https://twitter.com/GailSimone/status/6318460867 10132736.

20  See, for instance, http://comicsalliance.com/best-batgirl-art-ever-this-week-babs-tarr-cameron-stewart-brenden-fletcher-fan-art/, and http://batgirlofburnside.tumblr.com/.

21  See, for instance, http://www.comicbookresources.com/article/dc-comics-cancels-batgirl-joker-variant-at-artists-request, http://www.dailydot.com/geek/rafael-albuquerque-batgirl-joker-cover-interview/, and http://www.bleedingcool.com/2015/03/18/albuquerque-was-asked-to-make-batgirl-cover-more-extreme/, summarizing the story and reprinting Albuquerque's statement and interview. See also, Cameron Stewart's twitter as he engaged fans who both criticized and supported the creative team's asking the cover to be pulled: https://twitter.com/cameronmstewart/status/577656291839119362. See also, the twitter hashtags #changethecover and #don'tchangethecover as well.

# 3

# "Somebody Has To Save Our Skins!": Padmé Amidala, Leia Organa, and Jaina Solo in *Star Wars*[1]

To an extent unparalleled by any other characters and stories in this book, *Star Wars* is an exceedingly well-known, beloved, and lucrative global transmedia franchise. It is best known for its films, but it also includes animated series, a holiday special, approximately three hundred novels, fifty reference books, and well over a thousand comic books. The novels include more than seventy *New York Times* best sellers and the 180 or so video games are the best-selling of all movie-based video games (Taylor 2014: 286; Scott 2013: 13). Its merchandising and theme parks, widening and deepening the reach of its iconic characters, are legendary. The franchise had sold over $20 billion of products as of 2014 (Scott 2013: 12; Taylor 2014: 202), with several billion more expected from *Episode VII: The Force Awakens* (2015)—a film that has shattered numerous box-office records. None of these dollar figures includes fan-generated content, which is long-standing and plentiful and has been encouraged with few limits from the release of the first film in 1977. *Star Wars*' producer Lucasfilm has a full-time head of fan relations and a dozen employees who converse with fans daily through snail mail, email, and several social networks. It also holds a convention every other year that attracts tens of thousands (Barnes 2015; see also Gray, Sandvoss, and Harrington 2007: 4, Jenkins 2007).

Princess Leia Organa, her mother Padmé Amidala, and her daughter Jaina Solo are all central characters in what was called the "Expanded Universe" (or EU) of *Star Wars*, rebranded in 2014 as its "Legends" universe. One can trace certain through-lines in their portrayals, in terms of the ways in which they embody numerous feminist ideals while simultaneously undermining them in a variety of ways. All three characters subvert binary gender roles and stereotypes in that they act not as damsels in distress, but rather as independent, competent, shrewd, and respected leaders and warriors from a young age. All three characters provide heroic representations of women, who have been historically underrepresented in a variety of media in terms of numbers, and particularly as leaders, mentors, professionals, heroes, and superheroes.

But at the same time, the characters also embody discomfort with both the Second and Third Waves of feminism. For instance, all three characters are exceptionally privileged in terms of race, ethnicity, class, ability, and sexuality, and face no discrimination in their seemingly postfeminist and colorblind universes. All may further reception of women and men as equal, but given that in most *Star Wars* media the numerical imbalance between the numbers of female and male characters is extreme, the implication is that these particular women must be exceptional. All, in different degrees, are oriented toward heterosexual romance and in some measure "completed" by marriage to men. The two portrayed on screen are both (briefly) sexualized while their male counterparts are not.

Padmé, Leia, and Jaina embody heroism while being embedded in heteronormative assumptions and gendered and raced stereotypes, similar to Wonder Woman and Batgirl. But dissimilarly from Wonder Woman and Batgirl, the portrayals of Padmé and Leia in terms of their physical appearance remain relatively consistent across time and across media. This is likely due to their grounding in the likenesses of the films' actors and to their creator George Lucas's vision and guidance.

This chapter focuses on the production, representation, and receptions of Padmé, Leia, and Jaina, drawing from the first two trilogies of the franchise (1977–2005), the second *Clone Wars* animated series (2008–14), various novels from 1978 to 2015, and multiple comic series published by Marvel and Dark Horse from 1977 to 2015. In short, it finds that the novels have the most, and most diverse and nuanced, female characters; the comics and animated series less so but both have improved over time; and the first six films have the least number, least nuanced, and most stereotypical portrayals of female characters even as they portray them as variably heroic. The seventh film, *The Force Awakens*, and the ways in which it both conforms to and disrupts these trends are discussed in the conclusion. These portrayals are a function of the nexus of feminisms and their backlash in particular time periods, of varying authorship and varying levels of centralized creative control, of the assumptions made about the audience for and profitability of female characters vis-à-vis different media, and of fan-creator interactions that push and pull at the female characters' representations.

## Hero, leader, warrior, and diplomat in the Second Wave of feminism

As the first *Star Wars* film began in 1977, its crawl read, "Princess Leia races home aboard her starship, custodian of the stolen plans that can save her people and restore freedom to the galaxy." Most theatergoers at the time probably thought this petite princess would shrink before the tall, menacing, murderous Darth Vader. But she looks up at him, leans in with her Mexican revolution-era hair buns and confronts him sharply, "Darth Vader, only you could be so bold!" She is taken away and "her resistance to the mind probe is considerable." In her next scene, she is lifting her chin defiantly to insult both Vader and Governor Tarkin.

*Star Wars: A New Hope* is not a movie built around the rescue of a damsel in distress—in that respect alone it was new and different in 1977. The main male characters (Jedi Master Obi-Wan Kenobi, farm boy Luke Skywalker, scoundrel Han Solo, and Wookiee Chewbacca) did not know that Leia was on the Death Star when they, too, were captured. They break her out of her cell, and then she takes control of

**Figure 3.1** Princess Leia (Carrie Fisher) is a rebel leader positioned between the two main male characters, Han (Harrison Ford) and Luke (Mark Hamill). (*Star Wars: A New Hope*, 1977).

her own rescue and that of the others: "This is some rescue . . . . Somebody has to save our skins! Into the garbage chute, flyboy!" She figures out that the Imperials let them go and are tracking them. She is in the control room during the final battle sequence, and she awards the other main characters medals. Creator George Lucas says on the 2004 commentary track to this film, "The story is ultimately about Princess Leia and her attempts to destroy the Death Star, as a rebel leader. And the boys kind of just tag along on her adventure." Granted, this may not have been the way he envisioned the film thirty years earlier.[2] His earlier drafts had Leia variously as a passive damsel in distress and as not present at all (Taylor 2014). The Leia of Lucas' final draft was simply groundbreaking in 1977, in her prominence, her confidence, her independence, her passion, and her impact on viewers. She showed that women could be leaders, that men and women could be equals if treated as such, that courage and conviction were not only male traits but human traits.[3]

*A New Hope* was released at a time at which Second Wave feminism had made many political and social gains, and the liberal Lucas's strong portrayal of Leia occurred within that context. But high-level visibility for women in general at that time remained elusive except for a small number, and that small number was mostly white. The number of superwomen characters did increase during this time, slightly, with Ms. Marvel, Storm, Spider-Woman, and Power Girl in comics, and Wonder Woman, Isis, and the Bionic Woman on television. Leia fit into their mold in terms of being capable, confident, independent, strong, and caring. But she did not conform to the sexualization of the female superheroes. She was not clad in revealing or skintight clothing, nor was she posed or framed in ways that called attention to specific parts of her body rather than to her character as a whole. She was not written as weaker than the male characters of the story. And the main male characters are not stereotypical either. They are not physically imposing lone wolfs, unwaveringly strong, coldly calculating and lacking compassion, or prone to use violence before words. Rather, only the villains are, in itself a critique of hypermasculinity. She requires rescue but so do the male characters, not dissimilarly to the Wonder Woman-Steve Trevor dynamic discussed in Chapter 1 and the Batgirl-Batman/Robin dynamic in Chapter 2.

Quantitatively, Leia is quite alone in a sea of men. All three *Star Wars* original trilogy movies, like most episodes of the contemporaneous *Wonder Woman, Super Friends*, and *New Adventures of Batman* TV shows, exemplify the "Smurfette principle" and fail the "Bechdel test." Two of the films have more than one female character, but they do not speak to each other at all (Leia and Aunt Beru in *A New Hope*, and Leia and Mon Mothma in *Episode VI: Return of the Jedi, 1983*). In *Episode V: The Empire Strikes Back* (1980), Leia is the only named female character who speaks. In *A New Hope*, there are split seconds of a female alien in the cantina and a couple of white women walking around Mos Eisley. Otherwise, there is not one woman, not even in the background. And except for a couple of men walking around Mos Eisely, all of the men are white too. There are a handful of female extras in *The Empire Strikes Back* and one woman says four words. In *Return of the Jedi* there are two alien women in Jabba the Hutt's place, the dancing slave girl and the puppet/computer-generated singer. Every line spoken by a woman other than Leia across these three movies totals sixty-three seconds across six hours of film (Vulture 2015). Lucas assumed that the audience for his science fiction space opera would be of his same demographic back when he was watching *Flash Gordon* serials. Indeed, he has said that "*Star Wars* was designed for twelve-year-old boys" (Roper 2015).

Alongside this "cinematic negation" of women, particularly, of women of color, is a striking level of "cinematic racism" (hooks 1992: 109). The films are about empire and rebellion and were written in the shadow of the Vietnam War and of various independence movements and civil rights movements, but they play out their themes between English-accented white men and American-accented white men. Indeed, a fan noted in 1978, referring to the first film as well as the comics, "There's one complaint I keep hearing about *Star Wars* and that's the absence of Blacks and other non-white humans. I agree that's one major fault" (Julie Cesari, *Star Wars* #17, archived at http://starwarscomics.5u.com/whats_new.html). In *A New Hope*, the extremely small number of women and all of the men are white. In *The Empire Strikes Back*, there is one prominent person of color, Billy Dee Williams as Lando Calrissian. In *Return of the Jedi* there are two male pilots of color, who carry forth the trope of introducing characters of color only to kill them off, as they are shown for a few seconds when their fighters explode. Both Leia and Lando play key action and leadership roles and that cannot and should not be understated. But while those characters, and the actors who played them, may have been points of identification and perhaps pride for groups previously unrepresented or previously represented with negative stereotypes, the singular nature of their representations undercuts a broader depiction of gender and racial equality as well as undercutting diversity within identity categories.[4]

**Figure 3.2** The sole woman in a sea of white men, Leia (Carrie Fisher) explains the plan they are to follow (*The Empire Strikes Back*, 1980).

Qualitatively, Leia's character in her second and third films follows the same basic pattern set out in the first in that she is a capable and respected leader. She manifests hints of Force ability when she hears Luke calling her, and when she knows that he survived the explosion of the second Death Star. She disguises herself as a bounty hunter to rescue Han, kills her captor, and zooms around on a speeder bike. Her qualifications for these actions are not questioned. Her character is fleshed out further through her deepened bonds with the rest of the main characters and her kindness to and trust of the teddy bear Ewoks. She calls Han a "laser brain" and a "nerf herder" not long before she confesses her love for him and he responds that he knows. She deals calmly with the news that Luke is her brother and Darth Vader is her father. After she herself has been shot, she shows Han her hidden blaster and he says he loves her. She responds that she knows, and she blasts some stormtroopers.

A 1982 article in the fanzine *Jundland Wastes* notes that not only does Leia not play the role of a "prize" to be won by the stories' (male) heroes, but rather, she is a "hero of the hero" herself (Nowakowska 1989: 21). Indeed, it is only Leia who remains physically unscathed as Han is captured and frozen due to his past mistakes with Jabba, and as Luke faces Vader and loses his hand due to his impatience with his training. In *Return of the Jedi* when she tells Luke that she wishes she could run away with him to avoid Vader, he responds, "No, you don't. You've always been strong." In the film's comic adaptation, Luke's reply is extended, "No, you don't. You've never faltered, Leia. When Han and others doubted, you've always been strong . . . never turned away from responsibility. I can't say the same" (Goodwin, Al Williamson, and Carlos Garzón 1983, *Return of the Jedi* #3).

Only about two dozen issues of comics have sold over a million copies since 1960, and *Star Wars* #1 from 1977 is one of them. *Star Wars* #1 from 2015 is another

(Miller 2014).[5] Both the novelization and the comic adaptation of the first film sold out their print runs (Taylor 2013: 162). Indeed, it has been claimed that *Star Wars* "saved" Marvel Comics (see, e.g., Shooter 2011a, Veronese 2011, Jennings 2014, Casey 2015). The first two issues were on newsstands before the film and the rest after, at which point sales really took off. For the first five issues, Marvel paid no licensing fees and paid royalties only after the first 100,000 issues sold. After that, *Star Wars* was licensed to Marvel (Lippincott 2015), and the creative teams were given relatively free rein in their stories, as long as they did not conflict with what was in the films. This allowed more room for fleshing out the characters.

Leia in the comics is viewed "both as a leader and as a symbol" of the rebellion (Roy Thomas and Howard Chaykin 1977, #8). She goes on risky undercover missions to show that the rebellion's leaders "survive and continue to fight [and] to give hope" to worlds under the Empire's thumb (Archie Goodwin and Carmine Infantino 1979, #30). She flies with mechanical wings, blasting a stormtrooper and rescuing Han and Chewbacca (Annual #1). She matches wits with and holds a blaster on Darth Vader, gleefully foiling his attempt to kill her (#48). Burdened by the loss of Alderaan and her roles as "princess, senator, rebel leader, warrior," she withstands torture and defuses a bomb (Chris Claremont, Carmine Infantino, and Walt Simonson 1981, #53–54). She leads survey teams to find a new base, leads the rebel fleet, destroys an imperial base, and leads a band of aliens against their enemies (#55, #58, #65, #106). To find (the frozen) Han Solo, she deals with bounty hunters and slavers (#68–69), and defeats, at least temporarily, the part-Cyborg Sith Lumiya (#88). While she is sometimes captured and requires rescue, so do the male characters. In general, she tends to save herself and others (e.g., #15, #21, #36, #48, #51, #86, #93, #106). Her actions and her leadership skills, along with her deepening characterization, were praised by readers (see, e.g., letter columns in #59 and #86). In the newspaper strip from 1981 to 1984 (Goodwin and Williamson 1996), her personality is about the same as in the films as she spars with Han, is kind to Luke, and is part of or leads their missions. Altogether, Leia is on about one-third of the 107 early Marvel *Star Wars* comics covers, about 90 percent of which were drawn by men.

Unlike the contemporaneous *Wonder Woman* and *Detective Comics'* Batgirl stories, and the later *Star Wars* comics from the 1990s to 2010s, far more issues of the 1980s *Star Wars* comics had a female writer and/or artist and/or editor. New female characters Dani and Lumiya were brought in toward the end of the run, and Mon Mothma from the third film was featured, by a female writer and artist, Mary Jo Duffy (#70–107) and Cynthia Martin (#93–107), respectively. Their editor was Ann Nocenti (#84–107) and the colorist often Glynis Wein (#70, 75–86, 89, 91–92).[6] This all-female team was certainly unusual for the mid-1980s. It remains unusual in the mid-2010s. Still, even adding in a few nonrecurrent female characters, their numbers would not match the number of new male characters. Indeed, most issues of the comic, particularly earlier ones, would fail the "Bechdel test." But even this small number of female characters is more than that of the original trilogy films. That number would be increased in the novels of the 1990s–2010s.

# Heroes, leaders, warriors, and diplomats in the Third Wave of feminism: In print

Leia's characterization in the novels is that of a diplomat, pilot, mother, fighter, strategist, and sister, as well as a "superhero" user of the Force. From the first novels and in some of the most prominent comic stories, she trains in the Force, communicating telepathically with Luke, and using a lightsaber (e.g., *Splinter of the Mind's Eye* 1978, *Heir to the Empire* 1991, *Dark Empire* 1991–92). Not until the books of the early 2000s, set thirty-five years after *A New Hope*, is she written as leaving her high-level political positions entirely to become a Jedi in training and copilot of the Millennium Falcon. When Luke asks her if she is ready to assume her place in the New Jedi Order, she counters with, "No, I want to *earn* my place in the Order" (Denning 2005: 442). From this point, Leia's Jedi skills are on full display: lightsaber wielding, telekinesis, mind tricks, and mindmelds. She is trained by female Jedi Master Saba Sebatyne, and is close to her sister-in-law, Jedi Mara Jade Skywalker and to her childhood friend Winter Celchu. These 2000s book series are similar to the contemporaneous *Wonder Woman* and *Birds of Prey* and particularly to *X-Men* and *Buffy the Vampire Slayer* in their ensemble nature, their mix of grand action and small relationship dramas, and their settings in which there are other characters who alternately rely on the superwomen while sometimes not trusting or fearing their powers (see Chapters 1, 2, 4, and 5).

Indeed, this Leia is surrounded by other female characters of different ages and races whose personalities are different from hers. The most important is her daughter with Han Solo, Jaina. From the time Jaina is a young child her personality and her Jedi skills are manifest as she rescues herself and others from kidnappers (*The Crystal Star*, 1994). She becomes a Jedi Knight at sixteen, along with the other "Young Jedi Knights" of the 1995–98 novels: another girl, three boys, and a male Wookiee. These characters continue in the novels through the 2010s. Asked about Jaina's characterization, Kevin Anderson, coauthor of the series with his wife Rebecca Moesta, said, "Rebecca and I didn't want her to be a typical 'girl' character, but intended to make her more of a tomboy . . . while her brother [twin Jacen] is the goof-off" (Wookieepedia 2008). The novelists of the 1990s were given the freedom by Lucasfilm for this subversion of gender roles because none of the book series' main characters were in the original films or set for the forthcoming ones.

Jaina Solo is much like both of her parents: brash, rebellious, confident, capable, and more thoughtful as she ages. Adept with machinery and a skilled pilot like her father (and like her grandfather Anakin Skywalker), she is also a duty-bound and perseverant peacekeeper like her mother: "It was the sight of Jaina, the fire in her brown eyes, the determined set of her jaw, the sheer concentration. At that moment, Leia knew. Her daughter was a woman now, and with all of the grit of her father and mother combined" (Salvatore 1999: 1–2.) But being a daughter of those two particular parents can be stressful: "With my parents I could be a smuggler who saved the galaxy or a diplomat who saved the galaxy. [Being a Jedi is] something neither of my parents became, so it let me have something to myself . . . .I'm getting tired of being my mother's daughter and my father's daughter" (Stackpole 2000: 133). She is not the perfect daughter, sister, or Jedi, chafing against parts of these roles at various times. Nor was there meta-pressure on her to be so, because she was one among many characters rather than being the sole female character like her mother in the films and the early comics.

Jaina does not need to be a stand-in for all women because she is surrounded by family such as her mother and her aunt Mara Jade, as well as other female Jedi such as Cilghal, Tionne Solusar, Tenel Ka Djo, Tahiri Veila, Jysella Horn, and Saba Sebatyne. There are also numerous female non-Jedi, some of whom are villainous, such as Natasi Daala, Viqi Shesh, Lumiya, Vergere, Alema Rar, Aurra Sing, Vestara Khai, Ailyn Vel, and Mirta Gev. Having female characters who are representing not just a spectrum of heroism but also a spectrum of villainy is another way in which Jaina's and Leia's stories in the novels encompass more diversity. Still, quantitatively, even the most recent Expanded Universe/Legends novels do not have the same number of female versus male characters. There are still at least twice as many male characters as female, or several times as many depending on how they are counted, varying by title (Morrison 2012; LaVorgna 2013).

Of the eighty or so authors contributing to the three hundred or so EU novels, only about one-quarter have been women. Of the forty books in the four series of the 2000s–10s, in which Jaina is a starring member of the ensemble cast, eight were written by women, all of whom are white (Elaine Cunningham, Christie Golden, Karen Traviss, and Kathy Tyers). This is not to say that women should only write women and men should only write men. But having more demographically representative creators brings a diversity of experience, fomenting more authentic storytelling from still-underrepresented groups. This is a disproportionately small number of female authors. However, it is many more than in the forty years of comics and films, which were scripted, drawn, edited, directed, and produced almost entirely by men except for the aforementioned comics by Jo Duffy, Cynthia Martin, Glynis Wein, and Ann Nocenti in the mid-1980s and the comics issues (without the female characters focused on in this chapter) drawn by Jan Duursema in the 2000s.

The novel series published by Del Rey from the late 1990s to 2010s, as opposed to their stand-alone or trilogy-bound predecessors from Bantam, were conceptualized by a group. These series, starring Jaina and Leia along with the other characters noted above, ranged from nine to nineteen books each. The committee consisted of a few of the authors, along with Sue Rostoni of Lucasfilm Licensing, Shelly Shapiro of publisher Del Rey, and representatives of Dark Horse Comics. Authors were then assigned to the books to carry out the story arcs. Rostoni described Lucas's involvement thus: "Our job is to try to mesh the EU as closely as possible with George's galaxy so that it can appear as one continuous history. There are times when we ask for his input and permission—generally when we have questions about his main characters and what we can do with (and to) them" (EUCantina.net 2013). Lucas, then, allowed the novel writers some leeway to flesh out "his" characters, but maintained the final say on them up to his retirement in 2012.

Novels cost less to produce than do films, such that the story committees could take more risks in introducing new characters and new plot points while keeping to the highly popular *Star Wars* mix of action, adventure, and relationship drama. Jaina Solo in the novels is a teenage member of the prestigious Rogue Squadron of fighter pilots as well as a Jedi Knight. She and her brothers can meld their minds in battle, giving them an edge over invading forces of the New Jedi Order series. But that does not prevent her younger brother Anakin from being killed. Jaina's reaction is not like that of her stoic mother, but rather, she skirts close to the dark side of the Force, taking out enemies with black Force lightning and becoming distant from others as she focuses on revenge (*Star by Star*, 2001). She steps back, though, coming back around to her usual self (*Dark Journey*, 2002). Luke Skywalker says to her, "I name you the Sword of the Jedi . . . . Always you shall be in the front rank, a burning brand to your enemies, a brilliant fire to your friends. Yours is a restless life, and never shall you know peace, though you shall be blessed for the peace that you bring to others" (Williams 2002: 311). This is somewhat similar to the conception of the lone hero, or the more "warrior" versions of Wonder Woman, perhaps more palatable because it is more traditionally "masculine." Part of Jaina's being the Sword of the Jedi means that she must kill her twin brother, who has turned to the dark side of the Force and is responsible for increasing fascism along with torture and death ("Legacy of the Force" series). She trains relentlessly, decimating a piece of material just by touching it in one spot with the Force. Her father comments on it with a callback to *Return of the Jedi*: "I haven't seen anything that impressive since your mother wrapped a chain around Jabba's throat" (Denning 2008: 200). She does fight and kill her brother Jacen, tearfully cradling his dead body.[7] In this series and that following ("Fate of the Jedi" series), she remains a strategic thinker and warrior in the thick of the action, mostly putting duty before her personal desires but also parrying with a romantic interest as had her mother before her. Like Leia, she is not defined by this relationship. Jaina and her partner initially demur so as to put duty first, but then both integrate that love interest with the other parts of their lives.

Along with featuring Leia in the record-selling *Star Wars* comic and miniseries *Shattered Empire*, two new comics series starring her launched in the 2010s, as new Lucasfilm owner Disney geared up for *The Force Awakens* film. Both featured more central female characters than any *Star Wars* comic before them. The first was a *Star Wars* series from Dark Horse comics written by Brian Wood (who was also writing an all-female *X-Men* title) and penciled mostly by Carlos D'Anda. These 2013–14 comics basically had Leia as the main character, and centered a number of other female characters as well, such as rebellion leader Mon Mothma. At a time of increased fan attention to and media coverage about the sexualization and marginalization of female characters, this comic indulges in neither. "Whether it be in an INCOMT-65 snub fighter or in the grand chamber of the former Senate, [Leia] is anyone's equal" (#3). Leia leads a squadron of the rebellion's best X-wing pilots: four white men, two white women, a blue alien woman, and an alien Chalactan woman named Prithi, whose appearance could be described as South Asian. This was the most even distribution of male and female characters in the Expanded Universe, albeit not very diverse in terms of race and ethnicity. Leia seeks a new base for the rebels, considers marriage to a prince in order to deliver his world to the rebellion, and blasts her way out of trouble— all plot points that were explored in the earlier EU/Legends novels and comics, but this time, with more female characters. Similarly, not unlike some 1970s comics, as well as the novels *Rebel Force: Hostage* (2008) and *Razor's Edge* (2013), the 2015 comic miniseries *Princess Leia* explores how Leia is both a source of hope to the rebellion as well as resented for having brought destruction to her home planet. Written by Mark Waid and drawn by Terry Dodson, it features Leia and the tall blonde Evaan as well as Tace, Tula, Jora, and Uwa, who are not as pale, petite, and young as the main characters. Writer Waid acknowledges, "I wanted as many roles to be filled by women in this story as possible and anytime I had a choice, I would rather it be a woman in that role" (LaVorgna 2015).

Across thousands of pages and multiple book covers, neither Leia nor Jaina is objectified in dress, framing, posing, or description. This is the case even as both have been written and drawn mostly by men, and even through the 1990s "Bad Girl" era of comic art. Leia is usually wearing a full white dress, or a jumpsuit with boots, in the Marvel Comics from 1977 to 1986; the newspaper strip from 1981 to 1984; the novels from 1978 to present; prominent Dark Horse comics *Dark Empire*, the *Thrawn Trilogy, Splinter of the Mind's Eye, Shadows of the Empire*, and *Star Wars* from 1991 to 2014; and Marvel Comics' *Star Wars*, *Princess Leia*, and *Shattered Empire* from 2015. Jaina probably doesn't own a dress, and is almost always in a flight suit or a jumpsuit, occasionally with a Jedi robe: "I'm a pilot. Appearances aren't important to what I do" (Cunningham 2002: 151). This lack of sexualization from the 1970s to 2010s, in particular, makes these characters' representations different from almost every other female superhero discussed in this book. Creator Lucas had directed that the comics and novels could not conflict with the canon of the films, and that canon included a Leia that was played by a specific actress whose look was replicated in print media. Jaina's look, in turn, was based on Leia's. Further, that *Star Wars* was highly popular across media meant that its producers felt no corporate pressure to cater to the presumably narrow fan base of 1990s–2000s superhero comics.

In short, then, Leia in the novels and comics (1977–2015) is depicted as having the same smart, spunky, capable but not infallible personality as in the original trilogy films (1977–1983). She is not a stereotypical sexualized damsel in distress, but rather a leader who moves forward strategically with both grit and compassion, and later, with the superpower of using the Force. Her daughter, Jaina Solo, is depicted similarly in several *Star Wars* novel series (1994–2012). In the later novels and comics, neither is a token female and neither is perfect, but is surrounded by a number of female characters of differing personalities and sometimes, races and ethnicities, similarly to 1940s and 2000s *Wonder Woman* comics as well as the 1990s–2000s *Birds of Prey* and the 2010s *Batgirl* comics. However, Leia is virtually the only female character in the first film trilogy and the early comics and as such she carries tremendous representational weight along with her relative privilege.

# Heroes, leaders, warriors, and diplomats in the Third Wave of feminism: On screen

Representations of Leia and Jaina have some similarities to those of their ancestor, Padmé Naberrie, also known as Padmé Amidala and Queen/Senator Amidala. Padmé's story was written entirely by George Lucas, while Jaina's stories were conceived by committee and written mostly by men with a few exceptions. Both characters were centered in their stories and depicted as being in their teens in the late 1990s and in their twenties in the early 2000s, Padmé on film and Jaina in print. While Leia's early portrayals from the late 1970s are somewhat time-bound, embedded in both gains of and backlash to Second Wave feminism, one might expect that these characters of the late 1990s would be different from Leia and more similar to each other.

Padmé and Jaina were both written during the Third Wave of feminism, which as noted is self-described as more diverse, more mindful of intersectionality, more embracing of traditional signs of femininity, and more prone to produce humorous pop culture artifacts critiquing sex discrimination. Their characterizations came after blockbuster films with female protagonists such as the *Terminator* films, the *Alien* films, and the first *Star Wars* trilogy; after the first few seasons of popular cult classics centering powerful young women and with more female supporting characters, such as *Buffy the Vampire Slayer* and *Xena: Warrior Princess*; and at the same time as other similar TV shows such as *Dark Angel* and *Alias,* among others (see Chapter 5). Jaina Solo seems to fit in well with the TV characters: young, smart, strong and headstrong, imperfect, sometimes working alone but often working as a team with other women and men. But her portrayal does not employ any reclamation of femininity, nor much irony to carry feminist critiques of the world around her. It is a "postfeminist" future in which people are supposed to be equal, but are not by either numbers or prominence.

Padmé fits in with these Third Wave feminist characters from the 1990s to 2000s, in some ways. In *The Phantom Menace* (1999), she is heroic in word, strategy, and action. She was elected queen of Naboo at fourteen and in that capacity wears elaborate, feminine, royal garb with smooth and intricate hairstyles. Her stilted speech and formal bearing in her queenly appearance indicate how performative such a role is. She's described by the Sith Lord Darth Sidious/Senator Palpatine as "young and naïve." But when he tries to manipulate her into calling for a vote of "no confidence" against the Chancellor, into going to the courts, and into surrendering to the Trade Federation, she resists all three suggestions. Her curiosity about and her affinity for ordinary people are on display when she goes in disguise to explore Tatooine and when she asserts that "my fate will be no different from that of my people." She sets out a military plan, which she then leads, to retake the capital city and the palace from the Trade Federation. This sequence shows her out in front with a blaster, the Jedis slightly behind and on either side of her, followed by her handmaidens and guards. At a later point, she is the only woman in a group of about fifteen, and is leading them, alone and exceptional like Leia in the original films.

**Figure 3.3** Queen Padmé Amidala (Natalie Portman), mother of Princess Leia, in her elaborate royal garb and white makeup (*The Phantom Menace*, 1999).

In general, twenty years later, Padmé in the first prequel trilogy film is portrayed quite similarly to Leia in the first original trilogy film: they are young, independent, royal, petite, light-skinned, politically savvy, physically active, and except for a few minutes, the only women on screen. Padmé is even younger, more royal, and more light-skinned than Leia in her queen's finery and chalk-white makeup. For both, their privilege enables their breaking of traditional gendered boundaries (Helford 2000: 2; Inness 2004: 8) In terms of female characters with speaking roles, they were both virtually alone. In addition to Padmé, there is only Shmi, Anakin Skywalker's mother. Unlike Leia and Beru never meeting in *A New Hope*, however, Padmé and Shmi do meet and exchange a few sentences. Padmé's handmaidens don't speak to one another or to her. There are quick flashes of an old woman and a couple of Anakin's female friends on Tatooine. All of these females are white. There is some racial and ethnic diversity among male characters with Captain Panaka and Mace Windu. Women of color are subject to erasure, again.[8] Given the passage of over twenty years, given the success of films and television shows with female leads and ensemble casts, and given the clear efforts in the novels to increase female representation and diversity, the increase in female roles in the *Star Wars* film universe from its first to its second trilogy is painfully incremental. Like the first *Star Wars* film, this one was perhaps also written for the assumed desires of twelve-year-old boys.

In contrast to the second film in the original trilogy in which Leia is basically the only female character who speaks, the second film in the prequel trilogy (*Attack of the Clones*, 2002) has several female characters who speak, although most say very little: Shmi, bounty hunter Zam, handmaidens Dormé and Cordé, Naboo Queen Jamillia, Beru, Jedi librarian Jocasta Nu, a Jedi youngling, and diner waiter Hermione. All but two of these women are white, and the British-Indian actor playing Queen Jamillia is in chalk-white makeup. A few female Jedi appear very briefly, uncredited and silent in the background: Aayla Secura, who is blue; Luminara Unduli, played by a Kenyan woman who appeared much lighter-skinned due to thick makeup; Shaak Ti, played by an Israeli woman under heavy dark makeup; and Depa Billaba, played by a Turkish-Indian woman. In other words, almost all of the "diversity" among the film's women is due to its alien characters rather than its human characters. Similar to the first film, there is more diversity among the male speaking characters with Captain Typho, Mace Windu, Jango Fett, and Bail Organa. Both this film and the first film "pass" the "Bechdel test" of two women talking to each other about something other than a man—the first film due to a couple of sentences between Padmé and Shmi, and the second film due to a few sentences between Padmé and her handmaidens and between Padmé and the Queen. In each case, these conversations were a minute or two of screen time, out of over four hours of film.

Most of Padmé's screen time in *Attack of the Clones* is spent in building the romance between her and Anakin. She is no longer queen but rather a senator, and she is removed from political action to be protected by Anakin from an assassination attempt. Displaying her will and her strength, it is she who decides to defy the Jedi Council to help Obi-Wan, and it is she who escapes capture first, riding a large animal and firing a blaster. In deleted scenes, she speaks out at the Senate and stands up to Count Dooku. But even with the deleted scenes, she is mostly surrounded by men.

The way Padmé is portrayed in the *Clone Wars* animated television series (2008–14) is similar to *The Phantom Menace* and these more action-oriented and diplomacy-oriented parts of *Attack of the Clones*. This series is set after the events of *Attack of the Clones* and before the third prequel film, *Revenge of the Sith*, but was created and aired three years after *Revenge of the Sith*. Padmé in *Clone Wars* is a seemingly fearless action-oriented young woman who is capable of defending herself in difficult situations, as well as a strategic politician trying to end war through diplomacy. She blasts droids and sets her own ship to blow up inside an enemy one ("Destroy Malevolence" [S01E04]); she rescues herself from a dungeon ("Bombad Jedi" [S01E08]); she spies on a fellow senator for the Jedi Council ("Senate Spy" [S02E04]); and she uses her blaster skills to help capture the villainous General Grievous, as well as her political ones to trade him for Anakin ("Shadow Warrior" [S04E04]). In terms of diplomacy, she speaks out to cut military spending and against bank deregulation ("Senate Murders" [S02E15]), and against diverting money away from education, health, and infrastructure programs to fund war ("Heroes on Both Sides" and "Pursuit of Peace" [S03E10–11]).

Twenty-three episodes of *Clone Wars* (out of 121) were written by women. About half of them were by George Lucas' daughter Katie, and several of hers star female villain Asajj Ventress. Most of the twenty-three episodes written by women do not center on Padmé. Of the twenty-seven *Clone Wars* episodes that Padmé is in, she interacts with other women in some of those: mostly the alien Jedi Padawan Ahsoka Tano, and the human Duchess Satine Krayze, Mon Mothma, and Mina Bonteri. That the brown Ahsoka is much more scantily clad than the white Satine, Mon, Mina, and

Padmé unfortunately replicates the ways in which darker-skinned women have been represented in more sexualized ways than lighter-skinned ones (see Brown 2013, Gray 1975, hooks 1992, Tyree 2013, West 2008).

There are more female characters in the *Clone Wars* than in the films. Producer Dave Filoni noted that "34% of viewers are girls" and that he sought to increase that figure with a variety of strong female characters ("Clone Wars Panel," Celebration VI, 2012). Padmé supports Duchess Satine and Senator Riyo Chuchi when their planets are having war-related difficulties and investigates corruption with Satine ("Duchess of Mandalore" [S02E14]; "Corruption" [S03E05]; "Sphere of Influence" [S03E04], respectively). When Ahsoka has a vision of an assassination attempt on Padmé, Padmé proceeds to go to a conference on refugees that she has organized and she herself shoots the assassin ("Assassin" [S03E07]). Ahsoka, in turn, has Padmé as a mentor, as well as alien female Jedi Masters Luminara Unduli and Aayla Secura, subverting the historic lack of women appearing in mentorship roles. Padmé's relationship with Ahsoka and her respect for process are at the heart of her defending the wrongly accused Ahsoka in court ("The Wrong Jedi" [S05E20]). Most often in *Clone Wars*, though, and in the small number of novels in which Padmé makes an appearance, she is just with Anakin, or with Bail Organa, or with Chancellor Palpatine, or with a group of mostly male senators.

To keep Padmé's fate in *Revenge of the Sith* tightly under wraps, Lucasfilm editors restricted authors from using her character in novels such that unlike Leia and Jaina, Padmé is featured in very few print media pieces (Hidalgo 2012: 88). In the books *Clone Wars Gambit: Stealth* and *Clone Wars Gambit: Siege* (2010), she interacts only with Anakin, Obi-Wan, and Bail. She works long hours at the Senate, and it is she who comes up with a plan that aids the rescue of Anakin and Obi-Wan as well as saving thousands of lives. Bail thinks to himself, "She'd make a brilliant Supreme Chancellor one day" (Miller 2010: 339). Her characterization in the novels is similar to that of the first two films and the *Clone Wars* animated series: alternating between her Senate duties and her secret relationship with Anakin.

**Figure 3.4** Senator Padmé Amidala in the *Clone Wars* series, in which she engaged in action, diplomacy, and romance ("Destroy Malevolence," S01E04, 2008).

Increasingly, Padmé's characterization is narrowed as her story is given over to her relationship with Anakin. Only briefly is she shown in a political capacity in *Revenge of the Sith*, remarking in the Senate Chamber that "this is how liberty dies, to thunderous applause," when Chancellor Palpatine is becoming emperor (Cavelos 2008: 316). This gives the impression that she has done nothing, in terms of the political world in which she was so fully engaged in the first two films, as the Republic crumbled around her. Three scenes that would have displayed Padmé's political life were filmed but edited out. They are accessible on YouTube or on DVDs, and are also in the novelization of the film. Padmé, Mon Mothma, Bail Organa, and a diverse group of senators talk about forming an alliance to save the Republic from the Chancellor's increasing power grabs. She speaks for them with Palpatine, saying they want no further amendments to the Constitution, pushing him to say he's pursuing a diplomatic solution to the war, and thanking him "on behalf of the delegation of 2000" which implies that she and others have worked behind the scenes to forge this alliance of their fellow senators. She says all of this even with her husband Anakin standing behind the Chancellor. While these three scenes' political maneuvering and strategic diplomacy were cut, numerous scenes of her alone in her apartment, looking out the window or sitting and/or crying, were left intact and thereby give viewers the impression that "no longer a convincing heroine or politician . . . the domesticated Padmé is now merely the object of Anakin's possessive need" (Wilson 2007: 140). The heteronormative romances of Leia, Jaina, and Padmé both add to and undercut their characterizations as independent and self-assured women.

## Love triangles and sexualization in the Second Wave of feminism

Along with all three being strong and capable leaders, all three of these characters are also embedded in love triangles with men: Leia between Han and Luke, Padmé between Anakin and Obi-Wan/Clovis/Bail (in Anakin's mind, that is), and Jaina between Zekk and Jag. This continues forth the tired trope of women being defined by their romantic interests. Of course, many if not most people are looking for love. The problem is when it is only the female characters who are discussed or fought over as if they are possessions or prizes. While it appears that it is the female characters who appear to be the ones making choices between the men, this is really not the case. Luke is removed from Leia's choices because he is her brother, Jaina does not choose because Zekk chooses someone else, and Padmé did not have feelings for other men that competed with her feelings for Anakin. The points on all three of these triangles are white, heterosexual, nondisabled, and middle class. This goes unnamed and unmarked in a way that renders it somewhat invisible (Jowett 2005: 13).

Also within the positioning of these women as leaders was another type of backlash to feminist ideas, as explained by actor Carrie Fisher in 1983, "There are a lot of people who don't like my character in the movies; they think I'm some kind of space bitch.... The only way they knew to make the character strong was to make her angry." This is next to a picture of her in a metal bikini with the caption, "Princess Leia: A feminist from the fourth dimension" (Caldwell 1983: 10). That anger, while carrying stereotypes of feminism also carried with it a level of privilege in that Leia's petite whiteness eased the threatening nature of her anger (see, e.g., Helford 2002, Jowett 2005). Letters in late 1970s fanzines such as *Alderaan* and *Jundland Wastes* show that some letter writers did see her as "unfeminine and bossy" (Nowakowska 1989: 3), just as letter writers of the late 1970s found Wonder Woman "anti-male" (see Chapter 1). Jaina, too, can be perceived in this way: brusque, no-nonsense, independent, always in a "non-feminine" flight suit. Their heterosexuality serves to "normalize" these female characters, such that they present less of a challenge to gender roles.

Lucas says on the 2004 commentary to *A New Hope* that Leia is

> young, nineteen, the same age as what Luke was supposed to be, but instead of being kind of an idealistic naïve farm boy from the far reaches of the netherlands, she's like a very sophisticated, urbanized ruler, a Senator, so she's a politician, she's accomplished, she's graduated, got her PhD at nineteen and she rules people and is in charge. [I needed an actress] who could be young and play with a lot of authority ... and push these guys around.

In a nutshell, this embodies feminism and its backlash. The idea that there could be an accomplished young woman is certainly feminist, and that Lucas assumes this must go hand in hand with "pushing guys around" plays to fears that feminism means not equality, but man-hating female superiority. What some saw as strong defiance (to Vader, Tarkin, Chewbacca, and Han), others saw as rude and antimale. What some saw as Barbara Gordon-esque accomplishments, others saw as Wonder Woman-esque "hatred" of men.

Leia is a princess rescued by male characters even as she assists that rescue. She is a rebel leader who does the work of smuggling the Death Star's schematics but receives no medal for her part in destroying it. Her female-ness is marked through her dress, through Han's insistence on calling her "sister," and through his dismissal of her "female advice" (Ellis 2003). And except for a few minutes of Aunt Beru, she is as noted the only woman in the movie. This encompasses the feminist goal of showing a woman is on a level playing field with men, but it also implies that this one particular (white, royal, heterosexual, nondisabled) woman is exceptional in its lack of other female characters. All of the male characters grow while she does not. Han and Lando become generals, Luke becomes a Jedi, and she is captured in all three films as they lead the action against the Empire (Cavelos 2008: 308, 310).

Her sole status means that Leia must be all things to all people, a burden that none of the male characters must bear. This is why her "space bitchiness" and her being embedded in a love triangle are problematic. If there were several female characters, and one was bitchy and one had to be rescued and one was brave and one was in a love triangle, the situation would be quite different.

Han's offscreen shout in *The Empire Strikes Back* of "You could use a good kiss!" underlines discomfort with a woman in a non-sexualized role. In the extended version of this scene, deleted, Han goes on: "You've been so busy being a princess, you haven't learned how to be a woman . . . . You're as cold as this planet!" She is the ice princess, "trembling" on the Millennium Falcon when Han is close to her, melted by the charm of a scoundrel. She is the purported feminist who really just needed a man to stop being humorless and uptight. Lucas wrote in his original treatment of this film, "She rejects Han, though she is excited by him [and eventually he lands] an Errol Flynn kiss that knocks her off her feet" (Taylor 2014: 236). The implication is there's one way to be a woman: being open to romance with men.

In *Return of the Jedi*, Leia is enslaved by Jabba the Hutt and clad in a skimpy metal bikini. This is particularly jarring because she had worn practical clothing for the first two films and for six years in the comics. In the aforementioned 1983 interview in *Rolling Stone*, which was accompanied by several photographs of her in said bikini, Carrie Fisher said of her character, "In *Return of the Jedi*, she gets to be more feminine, more supportive, more affectionate. But let's not forget that these movies are basically boys' fantasies. So the other way they made her more female in this one was to have her take off her clothes." Unlike the impractical and revealing clothes that are often drawn on female superheroes in comics, the "slave bikini" did have a purpose in the plot: to show how a (male) villain tries to degrade a (female) slave, not just with a chain around her neck but with near nudity for his amusement. She shows no pleasure at the situation. Further, the film fulfills a revenge fantasy, as the narrator says in the *Return of the Jedi* comic (#2), "She turns the tether that keeps her captive into a weapon!" (Goodwin, Williamson, and Garzon; see also Dominguez 2007, Travis 2013, Barr 2011). As a much-older Leia remembers it in a novel, "Jabba put me in that slave outfit, and I strangled him with my own chain" (Denning 2013: 356).

Reception of the metal bikini is complicated. Some see it as sexy and as a symbol of power. There is Facebook page called "Leia's Metal Bikini," on which women upload pictures of themselves in the bikini, and organize meet-ups at conventions and elsewhere. But it is also an object of gaze that other fans are uncomfortable with, particularly in action figure form. Indeed, if one looks at *Star Wars* action figures of the last thirty years—marketed toward boys—one will find that most Leia figures are clad in the bikini, even though she only wears it for a few minutes over the course of the three films. This is similar to the ways in which other female superheroes have been marketed as eye candy for (presumably) young males, undermining their strength as subjects by presenting their bodies as objects. Noting that the only female *Star Wars* figure on the shelves at ToysRUs for the previous two years had been Leia in a bikini with a chain around her neck, and hearing no plans from Hasbro at the New York Toy Fair in 2015 for more and different figures, fans pushed for more diversity in Leia figures via social media (Whitbrook 2015a). One week later, Hasbro introduced a Leia figure clothed in her bounty hunter disguise from the same film (Whitbrook 2015b). Similarly, upon discovering that Disney not only had no Leia merchandise in its stores, but also stated that they had "no plans" for such merchandise, incensed fans took to social media (Faircloth 2014a). One week later, Disney announced plans for "several items" of Leia

**Figure 3.5** Jabba the Hutt forces Leia (Carrie Fisher) to wear a metal bikini and puts a chain around her neck. She later strangles him with that same chain (*Return of the Jedi*, 1983).

merchandise (Faircloth 2014b). On the one hand, this seems to show the power of individuals to direct a company to diversify its ideas and its merchandise. On the other, this is a company that sees new profit in those fans, and reaches for that new source of profit by marketizing diversity—putting a price tag on diversity such that people must pay to see it, and companies make money from it while also generating goodwill.

The small number of other female characters in the early Marvel Comics are sexualized. The first is Amaiza, former dancer and current gang leader and hired gun, who wears a bikini and thigh-high high-heeled boots (Roy Thomas and Howard Chaykin, 1977–78, #8–11). The second is Jolli, who wears hot pants and a tiny shirt that barely holds in her breasts. She has been a "man-hater" (#15) since her father abandoned her, but Han stirs up uncomfortable feelings for her such that she sacrifices her life to help him get away from their pirate friends (Archie Goodwin and Carmine Infantino 1978, #11–15). Leia, by contrast, is sometimes drawn curvier but as noted is almost never objectified in terms of dress or pose (for exceptions: see e.g., #68, #81). The sexualized and stereotypical renderings of Amaiza and Jolli shore up Leia's usual non-sexualized dress and non-stereotypicality.

Leia is objectified in a different way: through the love triangle between her, Han, and Luke. Comic artists and writers in the late 1970s and early 1980s did not know that Leia and Luke would be revealed as siblings in 1983's *Return of the Jedi*, nor did the author of the first *Star Wars* novel, *Splinter of the Mind's Eye* (1978). There are two kisses between Luke and Leia and both are framed rather romantically even in the comic adaptation of *A New Hope* (#4 and #5). While most comic letter writers wanted Leia with Han, objecting to her sort-of-romances with others while Han was frozen in carbonite (#49 and #53; see Miller 1997), there was one that definitely wanted her with Luke,

> I feel that one of the most charming aspects of the original movie's ending was the sweet affection between Luke and Princess Leia. However, in your comic series they act more like young brother and sister than sweethearts ... since it has already been clearly established that Luke and Leia are in love, I don't think it would spoil anything that will be shown in the sequel if you gave a little more emphasis to the romance between them. (Reina Greene, #24)

Editor Archie Goodwin replied,

> We haven't forgotten the romance between Luke and Princess Leia [but] we might be tempted to argue just how *clearly* the original film establishes them as being in love. It seems to us, the film leaves open the possibility that the lady *might* be interested in Han Solo. Plus, there's the added aspect of Leia's role in the Rebel Alliance ... Stay tuned. (Ryan 2015)

In a comic issue months after this letter, Luke asks Leia about an old female friend of Han, "She's a nice looking lady, princess. Are you jealous?" The narrator continues, "For the umpteenth time Luke Skywalker thinks of his attraction to her, and wonders how she truly feels about him" (Chris Claremont and Mike Vosburg 1979, *Annual* #1). Like the man-hating scantily clad Jolli, this friend of Han is more sexualized than Leia. Like Jolli, she dies. Unlike Jolli and unlike almost every other character in these comics, she is black and has natural hair. In the adaptation of *The Empire Strikes Back*, there is a scene early on in which Luke and Leia are tilting their heads at one another, "Leia ... you're the only one I ... I ..." The narrator tells us, "Uncertain, but drawn by the moment, the princess leans close to the young rebel hero" and they are interrupted by C-3PO (Archie Goodwin, Al Williamson, and Carlos Garzón 1980, #40). A similar scene was filmed and deleted from the film. The love triangle was in the 1981–84 newspaper strip as well, with Leia's deferrals of Han's overtures similar to those of early Wonder Woman with Steve Trevor (Goodwin and Williamson 1996: n.p.). Leia says, "Han, I'm a rebel leader. I can't afford time from our struggle to romance you—or anyone else!" He counters with, "Look, Leia, I didn't ask you to give up the rebellion ... just give into your feelings!" Luke thinks to himself, "*I wish I had his nerve. I can never seem to tell her how I feel.*" Later, Luke kisses another woman, and Leia sees. He asks her, "You're not jealous, are you?" She replies, not with "no," but rather, "A rebel leader can't afford to be jealous."

The triangle-making in the early comics and the comic strip ends after the 1983 theatrical release of *Return of the Jedi* due to the reveal of Luke and Leia's siblinghood. In the fanzine *Southern Enclave*, which succeeded *Jundland Wastes*, most 1983–84 letter writers discussing this plot point were not impressed. A few noted that Luke's sister pretty much had to be Leia since she was almost the only woman in all three films (archived at http://www.trektales.com/SEArchive.html). Luke and Leia's strong feelings for one another are noted by other characters in the 2013 *Star Wars* comic (by Brian Wood and Carlos D'Anda) from Dark Horse as well as the 2015 *Princess Leia* comic from Marvel (by Mark Waid and Terry Dodson), both set before the events of *Return of the Jedi*. There is, however, no kissing or even leaning in. Rather, Leia and Han banter in these comic series and in the 2015 *Star Wars* comic series, alternately with care and with sarcasm, as they do in the films. When the duty-bound Leia is willing to marry a prince in order to cement an alliance with his resource-rich world, Luke "can't believe it!" and Han says, "If she thinks this'll make me jealous, she's dreaming" (Wood and D'Anda #12).

This plot point of Leia as romantic object or prize—shoring up her femininity and heterosexuality as well as the male characters' masculinity and heterosexuality—is not an anomaly. In several books and comics as well, stories revolve around men falling for Leia (e.g., *Star Wars* #18–23 (1979), #53–54 (1981)), or trying to seduce or marry her through kidnapping or deception (e.g., *Queen of the Empire*, 1993; *Shadows of the Empire*, 1996). Others show Leia considering marriage with a royal to forge alliances for the New Republic or the rebellion (*The Courtship of Princess Leia*, 1994; *Star Wars* #12, 15–18 (2013–14)). This is not to say that love is not or should not be important in the *Star Wars* universe. Indeed, love of various types propels the action in all of the films. It is to say, however, that the male characters of the original trilogy do not have similar plot points to Leia's. Luke is shown romantically interested in Shira very briefly in the early Marvel Comics, paired similarly briefly with Callista and then long term with Mara Jade in the novels. All three of these female characters are killed, their deaths serving to advance Luke's character development and reduce the number of female characters in the comics and novels. Han is never shown as interested in someone other than Leia, to the point of kidnapping her to convince her of his love and dissuade her from marrying a prince, in the novel *The Courtship of Princess Leia*. There is no hint of nonheterosexual romance for any of these characters.

## Love triangles and sexualization in the Third Wave of feminism

There was no "official" nonheterosexual romance as a possibility for anyone in Lucasfilm's *Star Wars* universe until April 2015 when Del Rey publishing announced that the first-ever LGBTQ character had entered the *Star Wars* canon. Many readers missed that there was a same-sex married couple in the mid-2000s "Legacy of the Force" series books. This does not mean that fans weren't interested in such relationships. From the first organized fandoms in the late 1970s, people were writing same-sex relationships between main characters and secondary characters into their fiction. Those involving the main characters were seen by other fans "underground" but not submitted to fanzines, while those involving secondary characters were published in fanzines (Nowakowski 1989). Lucasfilm was tolerant of fanfiction and even encouraged it, unless they considered it "obscene or pornographic." Neither hetero- nor homoerotic "slash" fiction were tolerated and Lucasfilm threatened legal action against fans who wrote it (Nowakowski 1989: 13, 15; Taylor 2014: 186). The month after the 2015 Del Rey announcement, the most prominent home for *Star Wars* message boards and fanfiction since the mid-1990s, TheForce.net, ended its ban on fanfiction with same-sex relationships.

Like Leia, Jaina Solo is written as heterosexual. And like Leia, Jaina is positioned between two white men: her friend-that's-more-like-a-brother Zekk and the possibly-not-trustworthy-but-ultimately-honorable Jag. Both are light-skinned with black hair and green eyes. Zekk is like a parallel to Luke, and Jag in some ways to Han. For several years on the boards at TheForce.net, fans debated who was a better match for Jaina, with the weight on the side of Jag. In the "New Jedi Order" novel series, sixteen-year-old Jaina seems to look at Zekk as more of a brother, and her relationship with Jag grows. He asks her to meet his family. But similar to her mother before her she says she needs to focus on her duties and sort out her feelings (*Unifying Force*, 2003).

Things get complicated between the three in the "Dark Nest Trilogy" (2005), and the number of pages spent on their triangle increases. Now in their mid-twenties, Jaina and Zekk get absorbed into a hive-like-mind of a species called Killiks, such that they communicate telepathically and feel each other's feelings. When they say goodbye to Jag, their bond is such that both Jaina and Zekk are sad, "the same crestfallen expression on both their faces" (Denning 2005: 440). At the close of that war (brought about by a diplomatic solution of Leia's), Jaina and Zekk undergo some reconditioning so as not to be so enmeshed in the hive mind, but their mental link remains, weakened. Zekk and Jag argue over her to such an extent she tells them she wants to be with neither of them and they both needed to leave her alone (*Inferno*, 2007). The three of them become friends.

> Then Jag caught her looking at him, and his grim frown was replaced by a passably warm smile. Jaina glanced away without returning the gesture, telling herself that she had only been looking in Jag's direction because Zekk wasn't present, that she wasn't ready to think about choosing anyone until she was finished with [stopping her villainous twin brother] Jacen. (Denning 2008: 29)

When Zekk disappears for several months and returns with a girlfriend, he is removed from the equation just as news of Luke and Leia's family relationship did with Luke. Jaina and Jag are then a couple in the "Fate of the Jedi" series (2009–12), although both tend to put duty first. The last novel with these characters ends with Jag and Jaina's wedding: "The darkness was eternal, all-powerful, unchangeable. She had stared into it for too many years, alone and unblinking, determined that it would not take her. Now it never would. Now she was lighting a candle" (Denning 2012: 445).

Both Leia and Jaina's relationships with men are in sharp contrast to that of Jaina's grandmother and Leia's mother, Padmé. In the case of Leia and Jaina, both balance their own identities, friendships, and professions with their imperfect romantic relationships. Both work together with their significant others toward similar goals, and both are admired and supported by that person personally and professionally. These relationships display humor and concern and love, through stressful times and through misunderstandings and forgiveness. In the case of Padmé, these nuances are not present.

Padmé and Anakin's story follows the arc of an abusive relationship and ends with her death. In *Attack of the Clones*, many of her scenes are only with him. He is obsessed with her, having thought about her every day since he was a child and watching her through security cameras. He blames her for his turmoil, saying he's "in agony" and "can't breathe" because she is in his "very soul" and "tormenting" him. At first, she tells him he makes her "uncomfortable," but she softens. This may have been meant by George Lucas to parallel the ways in which Han stirred feelings in Leia. In both cases, harmful stereotypes abound: that women are uptight, that they don't mean it when they say they are uncomfortable and uninterested, and that if men persist they will be rewarded. Padmé does not seem to see any of Anakin's words and behaviors as warning signs. Actor Natalie Portman felt that Padmé found his darkness "intriguing" ("Love" featurette, Attack of the Clones DVD, 2002). Padmé comforts Anakin when he reveals that he "slaughtered" the Tusken raiders "like animals," and she soothes him with platitudes when he vows he will someday be all-powerful.

Padmé is increasingly objectified in the second and third films, which contributes to the discomfiting nature of the love scenes in *Attack of the Clones*.[9] As Padmé tells Anakin they can't be together, she is wearing a strapless leather corset with her breasts popping out of the top. It is unlike anything she wears otherwise in the films or animated series. Veronica Wilson comments, "In this rather confusing and clumsy scene, Padmé Amidala, the clean-cut responsible heroine is suddenly crossed with a worldly seductress out of film noir" (2007: 138). Padmé's costuming in this film was dictated by Lucas to Trisha Biggar as Portman needing something "sultry in nature" so as to appear "sexy, gorgeous, and young in skimpy clothes" (Lucas and Biggar, respectively, "Love" featurette, *Attack of the Clones* DVD, 2002). Portman called the overall effect a "sexed-up version of the queen." Women, of course, should be able to wear whatever they like and not be judged for it. Indeed, reclamation of femininity and sexiness was foregrounded by Third Wave feminists. But some might interpret such a look as her teasing him with his responding appropriately to her seductive outfit. She confesses her love for him when they are captured. In the following scene, her shirt (unlike anyone else's) gets torn, exposing her midriff for the remainder of the extended sequence and giving birth to the most commonly found Padmé action figure, "Ripped shirt Padmé." As one *Star Wars* blogger, author, and podcaster notes, "It's simply gratuitous—it adds nothing to the story or to her characterization. Instead, it falls right into the typical pattern of marginalizing female characters by showing their skin" (Barr 2012). The film ends with Padmé and Anakin's wedding, in a melancholy frame echoing the last scene of *The Empire Strikes Back*.

In the second film in both *Star Wars* trilogies, then, as well as in the middle of the novel series arcs of the 2000s, the main female character's devotion to duty and outward reserve is "melted" by her male counterpart: Leia with Han, Padmé with Anakin, Jaina with Jag. In each case, they take risks for that love. However, in the

**Figure 3.6** Padmé (Natalie Portman) wears a "sultry" outfit while protesting Anakin (Hayden Christensen)'s affections in *Attack of the Clones* (2002).

original trilogy and in the novels, the relationship of Leia and Han and the relationship of Jaina and Jag do not overtake the rest of the story as in the prequel trilogy, nor are they abusive. They are merely parts of those stories, deepening the characterizations of the women and men and also underlining the privilege of the main characters: all white and all heterosexual.

If there were a number of diverse female lead characters in the film, Padmé's overarching arc would be a cautionary tale among many other types of women and types of relationships. But her story exemplifies Jeffrey Brown's concerns about young female action heroes of the 1990s,

> As girls, the heroines can play out the most extreme fantasies of heroism in a liminal realm, and yet they may put aside such behavior as simply youthful. . . . [Such young heroines present] challenging images of powerful girls without challenging cultural expectations of women that are still bound up with notions of nurturing mothers and sexual availability for men" (2011: 167)

Padmé transitions from a strong and self-assured ruler and fighter at fourteen to a frightened pregnant girlfriend/wife in her twenties.

Padmé is not the only female in the *Clone Wars* animated series, which broadens the portrayal of Padmé as well as those of the women with whom she interacts personally and professionally. Her relationship with Anakin is part of the plot throughout its six seasons, but she is also engaged in other activities. The events of the series take place after those of the second film and before the third. In terms of production, though, the show was made a few years after the third film, and thus could take into account fan reactions to her dramatic confrontation with Anakin and her subsequent death in that film. There are some scenes in *Clone Wars* in which they do act like a couple, and/or work together, in positive ways. Anakin is also demanding, isolates her with their secrecy, and acts annoyed whenever she has to work in the Senate rather than be with him. When she is asked to spy on an ex-boyfriend, Clovis, and does so, Anakin becomes jealous and angry, although he saves her from poison in the end. Rather than him apologizing for his lack of trust in her, she apologizes to him for "making" him doubt her. He responds, "Never" (Melinda Hsu, Drew Z. Greenberg, and Brian Larsen 2009, "Senate Spy" [S02E04]). Clovis later returns and she gives him another chance through a mission the Chancellor has asked her to undertake. She asks Anakin to trust her and he responds, "As your husband, I demand that you tell the Chancellor you are stepping down." She refuses and again asks him to trust her (Christian Taylor 2014, "An Old Friend" [S06E05]). In the next episode, Anakin walks in on Clovis trying to kiss Padmé as she is saying "Clovis, no!" Anakin beats Clovis at length, ignoring Padmé's pleas to stop. When he does stop, she says "Stay away from me." Anakin admits, "I know I went too far. It's just that something inside me snapped." She responds, "I don't know who's in there sometimes. I just know that I'm not happy anymore. I don't feel safe. I think it's best if we don't see each other anymore. At least not for a while. I'm sorry, Anakin." He says he's sorry too (Christian Taylor 2014, "Rise of Clovis" [S06E06]). But they do see each other again, and she tells him twice that she's sorry. This is her last appearance in the *Clone Wars* series (Christian Taylor 2014, "Crisis at the Heart" [S06E07]).

There are a number of ways to receive Padmé and Anakin's relationship. It follows an unfortunately common pattern of abusive relationships in which an abused person is made to feel like they are at fault for the other's anger and violence, and apologizes to smooth things over. Similarly, an abused person may accept the abuser's passionate declarations and sometimes positive actions as love, however unsafe the overall relationship feels. These first two reactions would probably be more likely among those with some knowledge of the workings of abusive relationships, either personally or academically. This relationship, then, can be viewed as a set of warning signs indicating a negative dynamic between these two people. Those who have seen the film *Revenge of the Sith* before the *Clone Wars* know that it all ends in tragedy, caused by Anakin's violence. But at least two other reactions are certainly possible. One, seeing his heroism throughout the series and being willing to interpret his actions as sad insecurities requiring reassurance that she was not providing, some may have felt that she actually had something to apologize for. Two, that his "snapping" was a one-time situation brought about by his great love for her, and she should just give him another chance. This type of reaction might be more common among young people with romantic notions about the level of drama in relationships, or among those more accustomed to gendered inequalities within relationships. Adding pregnancy into such a relationship increases its danger.

## Family and motherhood

Pregnancy for Padmé and for Leia are portrayed very differently. In the best-selling and most well-reviewed *Star Wars* Expanded Universe/Legends books published to date, the three books of the "Thrawn Trilogy" by Timothy Zahn (1991–93), Leia is very pregnant with the twins Jaina and Jacen. This does not stop her from carrying out the mission, nor does anyone try to stop her from doing so. This was also true when she was pregnant with Han's and her third child, Anakin (comic series *Dark Empire*, 1991–92). Leia's status as a parent is key in dozens of books from 1991 to 2012, as her Jedi children and their friends and allies are integral parts of the novels' ensemble casts. But parenting for Leia carries heartbreak with it, as she loses her two sons: Anakin due to sacrificing himself in war (*Star by Star*, 2001), and Jacen due to Jaina's having to kill him because of his turn to the dark side of the Force (*Invincible*, 2008). As in the original films, Leia is buoyed by her fighting for a cause, along with her strong relationships that give her strength, with Luke, Han, her daughter, her granddaughter, and her friends. The importance of community to the character, many of whose members are female, is similar to early and 2000s *Wonder Woman* and to Barbara Gordon/Oracle in 2000s *Birds of Prey*. It is also a mark, as noted, of numerous contemporaneous television series in the 1990s–2000s starring women (see Chapter 5; Inness 2004, Jowett 2005, Knight 2010, Payne-Mulliken and Renegar 2009, Ross 2004, Stuller 2010).

In contrast to the similar characters of Leia and Jaina, and in contrast to this spate of 1990s–2000s TV shows, Padmé is completely isolated during her pregnancy. There are deleted scenes from *Attack of the Clones* in which she interacts with her family, and deleted scenes from *Revenge of the Sith* in which she takes a number of actions as a senator while very pregnant. But what is actually in the films is someone who seems to have only one relationship, and it is her destructive one with Anakin. Pregnant Leia in the novels is surrounded by people and acting exactly the same in terms of her political responsibilities and in putting herself in danger. Pregnant Padmé on film is alone, tearfully looking out windows.

In *Revenge of the Sith*, as written and directed by George Lucas, Padmé has no role but to be Anakin's pregnant wife. Against a backdrop of galactic war, there is only one female character in this film that viewers could identify with or empathize with, and she is a young pregnant white woman sitting in a large apartment and crying. She has no conversations with other women. She is in one scene in the Senate, in which she says one sentence to no one in particular. Except for a short but important conversation with Obi-Wan in which he tells her of Anakin's turn to the dark side and his killing of younglings, all of her scenes are with Anakin. She says they'll go back to Naboo to raise the baby, since she doubts the queen will allow her to continue to serve in the Senate. This implies that women with young children are expected to stay at home with said children and also can be received as providing explanation for why Padmé has not been shown working for the length of the film. Even after Obi-Wan informs Padmé of Anakin's murderous turn to the dark side, she runs to Anakin. He doesn't deny he has murdered, but explains that everything he is doing is for her. She tells him she loves him and just wants to raise their baby with him, but she begins to see he has changed. When he warns her not to turn against him, she says, "I don't know you anymore. Anakin . . . you're breaking my heart . . . . You're going down a path I can't follow. . . . Stop now. . . . I love you!" But Anakin doesn't believe her, assuming she had brought Obi-Wan there to kill him. He chokes her with the Force, and she clutches her throat and falls to the ground. Anakin doesn't look at Padmé again once she's on the ground, nor does he check on her as Obi-Wan does. Padmé and Anakin's story ends with her death. "Ultimately, rather than a [female] role model to try to emulate, the prequel trilogy's audiences are given a character that sends a depressing message: love can be deadly, but you should want it at any costs" (Dominguez 2007: 129).

Padmé dies. If she were not the only female character in the film, she would not have to stand-in for all women. But since she is and she does, her story became much-debated among fans, particularly the circumstances surrounding her death. She is diagnosed by a medical droid: "Medically, she's completely healthy. For reasons we can't explain, we are losing her. We don't know why. She has lost the will to live." The last things Padmé says are, on the ship, "Is Anakin all right?" and in the medical bay, "Luke," "Leia," and "Obi-Wan, there's good in him, I know. I know there's still . . ." Most of Padmé's last words are for Anakin, not her just-born children. These words mirror Luke's insistence that there is still good in Anakin, in the original trilogy. In the novelization of the film and in the comic adaptation, the line about her losing the will to live is not present. The novel reads, "'All organic damage has been repaired.' The droid checked another readout. 'This systemic failure cannot be explained.' *Not physically*, Obi-Wan thought . . . 'Padmé, you *have* to hold on'" (Stover 2005: 410). Obi-Wan reflects on how his own love for Anakin, and his willingness to overlook danger signs and make excuses for him, has brought them to this point. These few sentences make quite a bit of difference to Padmé's character. She is not the only one blinded by love for Anakin into having made bad decisions, and her heroism is not subverted by her unwillingness to go on. Love in this rendering is not a "feminine" weakness, but a source of strength, motivating Padmé to birth the children, Obi-Wan to dedicate his life to watching over Luke, and Bail to adopt Leia. Love and compassion motivate the male and female characters in the original trilogy films as well, not always leading them to the safest decisions in the short term, but leading to the overthrow of the Empire in the end. Of course, millions more people saw the film than read the book. Wilson writes of the film version, "Instead of working to help educate the galaxy about and to save it from Palpatine's evil designs, Padme chooses her personal pain over her political duty . . . she also opts out of motherhood entirely. . . . The Padmé we see in the first two films would have scoffed at the mere notion of such a fate" (2007: 142; see also Travis 2013).

Some fans accept that she died of a broken heart and lost the will to live, finding the end of the film Shakespearean in its melodrama and doomed romance in which both Padmé and (metaphorically) Anakin die. Dominguez writes that some young fans commenting on forums saw the movie's end as romantic. "Young girls with little to no experience with relationships (like Padme, it must be assumed) consider dramatic, excessive emotions on the part of a boyfriend (like jealousy or an obsessive desire to always be in touch or protect her) to be expressions of his overwhelming, consuming love for her" (2007: 125). His remorse in later media support those who see the story as tragic and romantic. In the *Revenge of the Sith* novelization, Anakin thinks to himself, "It was all you . . . . You killed her" (Stover 2005: 417). Similarly in the 2011 comic, *Darth Vader and the Lost Command*, Vader has visions of Padmé that are alternately

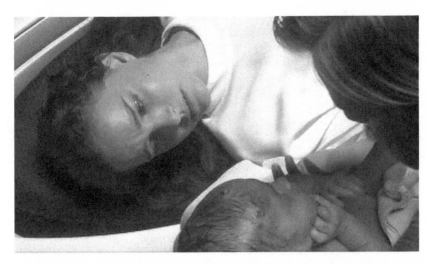

**Figure 3.7** The broken-hearted Padmé (Natalie Portman) tells Obi-Wan (Ewan MacGregor) that there is still "good" in Anakin even after he has murdered many and strangled her. She dies after birthing Luke and Leia (*Revenge of the Sith*, 2005).

romantic and accusatory. He says, "You died" and she replies, "You killed me. You." He kneels before her, "Yes . . . . And I hate myself for all I have done." (Haden Blackman and Rick Leonardi, #6). In the suit that keeps him alive and enables his mobility, Vader's state of mind here conforms to stereotypical depictions of disability as correlating with malevolence and bitterness (see Alaniz 2014, Longmore 2003, Davis 2010, Siebers 2010). Such regret can further add to the melodramatic romance. Some viewers might feel saddened for him in this situation, with the vision of Padmé making it feel as if she is alive so she does not require a reader's grief as much as Vader does. Indeed, like so many "women in refrigerators," Padmé's death serves Anakin/Darth Vader's character development much more than her own.

Other fans heavily criticize the turn of events, with some providing their own explanations: Padmé dies as a result of residual effects of being choked by Anakin but the medical droid doesn't recognize the Force. The emperor siphoned life from Padmé and fed it into Anakin through the Force. Padmé is dying because of Anakin's choking, but she fights death off long enough to give birth to Luke and Leia. Padmé wills herself to die because Luke and Leia will be safe from Vader that way; he'll assume her child died with her.[10] Such discussions speak to the need for fans to integrate the characterization of Padmé in *Revenge of the Sith* with the characterization they felt they saw in *The Phantom Menace* (and to some extent, *Attack of the Clones*). Viewers negotiated. They accepted some elements, rejected others, and struggled to rework what they saw so as to fit it with their own view of the characters.[11] Writers other than Lucas would flesh out Padmé's character and add other female characters in the *Clone Wars* animated series, which began airing three years after the film was in theaters.

## Conclusion: Legends, Lucasfilm, and *The Force Awakens*

Viewers of the first two *Star Wars* film trilogies are quite limited in terms of the female characters with whom they can identify or in whom they find qualities to which they can aspire. Across six films that were more or less authored by one white, male, heterosexual person, there are exactly two plot-central female characters, Padmé and Leia. Even when one counts the hundreds of extras, they are still quite alone. Burdened with being all things to all people, particularly female viewers, these characters in different ways embody active heroism, political strategizing, and romantic and familial love and caring. Their flaws, so to speak, are in high relief because of the numerical imbalance.

In the equally financially successful comics and novels of the "Legends/Expanded Universe," there are more female characters and they are more diverse, but none as central as Leia and Jaina. Early on, writers of the novels and comics had more freedom to create new characters and plot points as long as they did not conflict with the films, and they consulted Lucas first on major developments with the main characters. Later, Lucasfilm formed committees to hash out major plot points and assign writers to the novels, giving them a certain amount of leeway but with Lucas retaining the final say. Since Lucasfilm's acquisition by Disney and Kathleen Kennedy stepping into Lucas' former position, a "Story Group" of six women and two men from Lucasfilm, DK Publishing, Del Rey, and Marvel has had a more "vertical" chain of command for storytelling rather than the more "horizontal" version in place during the writing of many of the EU novels up to that point (Tosche Station 2015a).[12] In all three versions of creative control, across decades and across media, the main female characters have not been sexualized except for a few moments in two of the films. The comics and novels have emulated the likenesses of the actresses who played the characters in the films, in terms of their body types and usual attire. The number of female characters in the *Star Wars* universe has increased over time but has never been at parity with the number of male characters. Many fans have been calling for more while a smaller number of others have pushed back.

In what *Star Wars* fandom took to calling "The Great Gender Kerfuffle of 2012," a column on EUCantina.net called "Let's Stop Thinking about Gender" berated female fans (although not male fans) asking for more and better written female characters in the EU novels, "You know what I *never* see? Guys discussing the need for *Star Wars* stories that focus on strong male characters. Because if we did, it'd be sexist. . . . So why do women readers cry out for stories that focus on strong female characters?" (Chris, http://www.eucantina.net/archives/11915, May 4, 2012). The simple answer, of course, is that pretty much every *Star Wars* story—thousands of them—already focuses on strong male characters and the number of strong female characters is disproportionately small. Responses and comments filled other fansites such as Roqoodepot.com, ClubJade.net, Tosche-Station.net, TheGalacticDrift.com, and FanGirlBlog.com, emblematic of the debate taking place across media about representations of women. Similarly, fans irate that author Chuck Wendig had gay and lesbian characters in the *Star Wars* novel *Aftermath* (2015) accused him on their own blogs, on his blog, and in numerous reviews of the book on Amazon.com of using "social justice warrior propaganda." Wendig responded, "If you can imagine a world where Luke Skywalker would be irritated that there were gay people around him, you completely missed the point of *Star Wars*. . . . Stop being the Empire. Join the Rebel Alliance. We have love and inclusion" (Wendig 2015).

The number of *Star Wars* fan websites, discussion forums, podcasts, and convention meet-ups in which fans can voice their opinions on this subject is a sea change in the fandom community from the print zine-based culture of when the original trilogy first appeared on screens. On StarWars.com itself, under the "community" tab, there are links to fan organizations, fan news and blog sites, fan collector sites, and podcasts, as well as fan films given awards by Lucasfilm. Lucasfilm has strategically cultivated this fandom, particularly in the run-up to its third trilogy of films.

*Star Wars: The Force Awakens* (directed by J.J. Abrams; written by Abrams, Lawrence Kasdan, and Michael Arndt) initially did not look as if it would deviate much from the pattern of the first two film trilogies. The three main characters from the original trilogy are in the film, with the one female, Leia, in a reduced role. Daisy Ridley (Rey) is young, light-skinned and dark-haired—like Carrie Fisher and Natalie Portman before her—and at first was the only woman announced as cast. A cast photo of the table read showed Ridley, Carrie Fisher, and John Boyega (Finn) as the only non-males or nonwhites out of fifteen people. This was apparently followed by a visit from Geena Davis (representing her Institute on Gender in Media) and a social media outcry that Lucasfilm was replicating the lack of female representation in its first six films. Not long after, Gwendoline Christie was cast in a role that was originally written for a male actor, with some fans assuming responsibility for that change (see Faraci 2014; Fangirl Blog 2014; Tosche Station podcasts, April 4, 2015 and May 4, 2015). These three white actresses were then joined by Lupita Nyong'o, as a motion-captured CGI alien. Initial joy by some fans led to their questioning why the one prominent woman of color in the cast would not actually be represented on screen, and so would replicate the ways in which women of color had been masked as aliens in the prequel trilogy. Nyong'o countered some of this criticism herself by stating that because her body was so central to her role to her performance in *Twelve Years a Slave*, she embraced the "challenge" and the "liberation" of a CGI role in which her body would not be focused upon (Carter 2015). These four represent, to date, the largest number of women starring in any *Star Wars* film.

Quantitatively, if one were to go by crowd scenes, *The Force Awakens* has by far the largest number of women, period, in any *Star Wars* film. Countless reviews and fan posts and podcasts have noted this. But a closer look at the numbers reveals more. Of 109 characters listed on IMDB, 88 are male (81 percent) and 21 are female (19 percent). Seventy-five characters are credited and 34 are uncredited. Males are 57 of the 75 credited characters (76 percent), and 31 of the 34 uncredited characters (91 percent). Females are 18 of the 75 credited characters (24 percent), and 3 of the 34 uncredited characters (9 percent). Of the 58 characters who speak, some with names and some without, 44 are male (76 percent), and 14 are female (24 percent). Four of the fourteen women who speak have at least a few minutes of screen time: Ridley, Fisher, Nyong'o, and Christie. The other women who speak say between one word and two sentences. These kinds of figures are right in line with the disproportionately low percentages of female characters in films, as noted in the Introduction. Yet even this low level of diversity, along with the centering of the characters of Rey and Finn, brought out anger among a small number of fans who boycotted the film due to its "über-SJW [social justice warrior] . . . non-white and female agenda" (Brown 2015). Given the film's record-breaking ticket sales, it is clear that far more moviegoers embraced the new cast, plotting, and themes.

Qualitatively, the film indeed centers on Ridley's character, Rey, which cannot be understated within the context of either *Star Wars* films or all Hollywood films. She is resourceful, vulnerable, smart, lonely, humble, skilled at piloting and fighting, and quickly and increasingly strong in the Force. For much of her on-screen time she is accompanied by Finn, who at first goes to rescue her but then sees she does not need that help. They forge a deep and seemingly non-romantic bond as they each undertake their own hero's journey, and the two spend most of the film with Han Solo and Chewbacca. Fisher's General Organa (listed as Princess Leia in the credits) is the leader of the Resistance, conversing with many male military characters as well as with her husband, Han Solo. Her strained but caring banter with Han builds from their prior relationship in the films and the offscreen tragedy of losing their son to the dark side of the Force. It is clear that Leia has Force sensitivity in her reaction to Han's death. Nyong'o's Maz Kanata plays a key role as well, particularly in speaking with Rey about the Force. Rey, Leia, Maz are not mere one-note "strong female characters" nor caricatures of feminist ideals. They are each multifaceted. Christie, as Phasma, however, is on screen little and her face is unseen.

**Figure 3.8** Leia (Carrie Fisher) and Rey (Daisy Ridley) embrace, sharing their grief in *The Force Awakens* (2015).

Numerous reviews of the film proclaimed that it "passed," passed "with flying colors," and even "smashed" and "busted" the "Bechdel test." However, there is only one conversation between two women in the film, when Ridley's Rey and Nyong'o's Maz speak a few sentences to each another. Despite the film's focus on a young woman, despite the larger number of named female characters who speak as well as women in the background, most of the movie consists of men speaking to one another and women speaking to men. Leia says one sentence to Rey and Rey does not reply. Two white women say one sentence to Leia and one woman of color says one word to her; Leia does not reply. The other women who speak, most of whom are white, each say between one and several sentences to male characters. Except for Captain Phasma, their names are not stated aloud in the film. In a critical scene, when the heroes are arrayed around a large schematic planning how to defeat the enemy, there are nine people contributing: eight men, and Leia.

*The Force Awakens*, then, is quite different from previous *Star Wars* films in its centering of a female character and her journey to heroism, but it is not so different in that it barely passes the low bar of having two named female characters have a conversation about something other than a man. In the film's #1 *New York Times* best-seller novelization by Alan Dean Foster, Leia and Rey have a short conversation, Rey and a female doctor have a short conversation about Finn, and Leia and her female envoy (who is seen for a brief moment in the film but does not speak) also have a conversation. Leia's role is larger in the book as well, as she speaks more not only to Rey, but to other characters as well in ways that make clear not only her feelings about various events but also her leadership role. Her thoughts open and frame the book. This work conforms to the rest of *Star Wars* printed media with its more detailed portrayals of female characters, but far more people will see the box office-busting film than will read the novel.

Male characters in the film are more diverse, both in background shots and with speaking roles. John Boyega's Finn and Oscar Isaac's Poe (who some fans are reading as queer) are central characters, and Ken Leung's Admiral Statura has a prominent leadership role as well. And *Rogue One: A Star Wars Story* (2016)'s first cast photo shows one white woman and eight men of diverse backgrounds. These two films, like the previous six, look like they can be described by the title of a foundational work in black women's studies from 1982: "All the women are white, all the blacks are men" (Hull, Bell-Scott, and Smith 1982). In other words, women of color were not then and are still not reaping as much of the gains of antisexist and antiracist movements as white women and men of color.

Gross receipts of the first seven *Star Wars* films show that about half of each film's receipts are from outside the United States (http://www.boxofficemojo.com/franchises/chart/?id=starwars.htm). Movies and television shows with more diverse casts are more financially successful than those which are more homogenous, with the notably diverse *Furious 7* breaking the Guinness Book record for the fastest billion-dollar gross worldwide in mid-2015 (Hunt, Ramon, and Price 2014; Lynch 2015), and then having its record broken by *The Force Awakens* in late 2015. Lucasfilm president Kathleen Kennedy has hired a number of women executives and has indicated in more than one venue that more female characters are forthcoming. Another way in which the franchise is reaching out to more diverse fans is by making all of its Marvel and Dark Horse comics from 1977 onward available in digital form on Marvel.com, either by subscription or a pay-per-comic model. As noted, comic fans who buy digitally tend to be a more diverse group than those going in to local comic shops. Albeit late in the game, now would be an opportune time for *Star Wars* owners and producers to look to their own Expanded Universe and beyond to incorporate more diversity, of a variety of kinds, into their stable of creators and characters.

While this chapter analyzed a set of blockbuster movies coincident in time with comics and novels, the next chapter will similarly cross media but look more closely at the transition from print to screen. Specifically, it focuses on certain *X-Men* comics and the television series and films that were based on those comics. Marvel has published both *Star Wars* and *X-Men*, and both Lucasfilm and Marvel are now owned by Disney, a corporation known for synergizing its products across media. Both franchises were remarkably successful beginning in the 1970s, even while Marvel's prevailing wisdom at the time was that neither science fiction nor female characters would sell well (Shooter 2011a). The female X-Men are discussed in the next chapter.

# Notes

1   Princess Leia Organa in *Star Wars: A New Hope*, written and directed by George Lucas, 1977.

2   See Denison 2007 on how DVD commentaries can shape or reshape perceptions of a film or television show, "DVD becomes an opportunity in which the makers can put back in or re-emphasize missed or missing genre parts," and can even "re-inscribe our memories" (63).

3   See, for instance, Emily Asher-Perrin's (2012) "Can We Talk About Why We Really Love Princess Leia?" on *Tor.com*: http://www.tor.com/2012/08/10/can-we-talk-about-why-we-really-love-princess-leia/; Megan Kearns' (2012) "Women in Science Fiction Week: Princess Leia: Feminist Icon or Sexist Trope?" on *bitchflicks.com*: http://www.btchflcks.com/2012/08/women-in-science-fiction-week-princess-leia-feminist-icon-or-sexist-trope.html#.VeR4AflViko; Alyssa Rosenberg's (2015) "Princess Leia, Political Icon" in the *Chicago Tribune*: http://www.chicagotribune.com/entertainment/movies/ct-princess-leia-political-icon-20150505-story.html; Cher Martinetti's (2015) "Why Princes Leia is My Hero and the One All Girls Deserve" on *blastr.com*: http://www.blastr.com/2015-5-4/star-wars-day-why-princess-leia-my-hero-and-one-all-girls-deserve; "What Princess Leia Means to Me" panel at Star Wars Celebration 2015 (April 19) on *Tosche Station*: http://tosche-station.net/tosche-station-radio-at-celebration-what-leia-means-to-me/.

4   Lando's nuanced depiction and character growth across two films is unlike those of a number of black male superheroes in comics at the time, who Svitavsky notes were usually exoticized, had "black" in their name, or were weak imitations of blaxploitation characters (2013: 154). See also, Brown 2000 on "subtly counter-hegemonic" depictions of black male characters in Milestone Comics (166).

5   *Princess Leia* #1 and *Darth Vader* #1 both sold over 250,000, a rare occurrence in the 2010s (http://www.comichron.com/monthlycomicssales). At the same time, Marvel put hundreds of *Star Wars* comics on its website and app, Marvel Unlimited. Digital comics are accessed by a more diverse audience base than are willing or able to go to a local comic shop, some if not many of which are masculinized unwelcoming spaces. Marvel was anticipating sales of 250,000 for a trade paperback collecting the first six issues of the 2015 *Star Wars* comic. Their usual trade paperback sales are more like 30,000–50,000 (Burlingame 2015).

6   Other than these two, one issue of the comic was written by Ann Nocenti (#89), and one penciled by Jan Duursema (#92).

7   *The Force Awakens* has incorporated some of this plotting: a son of Han and Leia, named Ben rather than Jacen, turns to the dark side of the Force. Whether the main female character of the film, Rey, becomes an analogue of Jaina who must be the one to stop him remains to be seen at this writing.

8   There are elements of this film that have been received as racist. The Neimodians have been viewed as Chinese or Japanese stereotypes, Watto as a caricature of Jews or Arabs, Jar Jar as African American and/or Caribbean minstrelsy. This is in stark contrast to the mostly white Jedi and their clipped Anglo-American diction. See Brooker 2001, Deis 2007, and Williams 1999. Lucas envisioned Jar Jar as a physical comedian like Buster Keaton or Charlie Chaplin, mixed with Jimmy Stewart or Danny Kaye; Neimodians as having a "soft Transylvanian accent"; and Watto as a "gruff Italian shopkeeper" (Taylor 2014: 306). Lucas has also said that Disney's Goofy was an inspiration for Jar Jar (https://www.youtube.com/watch?v=pRtVGjgii4U).

9   See, e.g., Brooker 2002's epilogue; Taylor 2014; "Can You Defend *Attack of the Clones?*" thread at *TheForce.net*: http://boards.theforce.net/threads/can-you-defend-attack-of-the-clones.50024368/and "Attack of the Clones is a Masterpiece" thread at *TheForce.net*: http://boards.theforce.net/threads/attack-of-the-clones-is-a-masterpiece.25120297/; "Anakin/Padmé vs. Han/Leia" thread at *Rebelscum.net*: http://forum.rebelscum.com/t882817/and "The Love Scenes" in *AOTC*: thread at *Rebelscum.net*: http://forum.rebelscum.com/t1086073/. See also mainstream reviews of the film, in the *New York Times, USA Today, Chicago Sun-Times*, etc.

10  See, e.g., the "Death of Padmé" thread at *Lucasforums*: http://www.lucasforums.com/showthread.php?t=182872; the "The Reason of Padmé's Death is Stupid" thread: http://www.swtor.com/community/showthread.php?t=389995; the "What Was the Original Idea for Padmé's Death" thread at *TheForce.net*: http://boards.theforce.net/threads/what-was-the-original-idea-for-padmes-death.50004632/); "Fan theory on Padmé's Actual Cause of Death" thread at *Rebelscum.com*: http://forum.rebelscum.com/t1117145/; "Padmé Didn't Die of a Broken Heart" by Joseph Tavano: http://www.retrozap.com/padme-didnt-die-of-a-broken-heart/; "The Power to Save Padmé" by Tricia Barr: http://fangirlblog.com/2012/02/the-power-to-save-padme/; podcasts such as *Fangirls Going Rogue, Full of Sith, Rebel Force Radio,* and *Tosche Station Radio*.

11  See, e.g., Brooker 2000, Brown 2000, Duggan 2000, Fiske 2002 [1989], Hall 2003 [1997], Hall ed. 2003 [1997], Jenkins 2007, Johnson 2007a, Kellner and Durham 2012, Smith 1994 on reception, resistance, and constraints. Edited works with a variety of points of view on this subject include Brooker and Jermyn 2002; Gray, Sandvoss, and Harrington 2007; Durham and Kellner 2012. Those focusing more on gender include Jones 2010 and Milestone and Meyer 2012.

12   Marvel comics editor Heather Antos says,

> We go to Lucasfilm and we sit down with the Story Group. . . . We talk with them about what we want to do, they tell us what they have going on. . . . When we get scripts in at our end, we look at them and add our notes, it gets sent to Story Group . . . they'll come back to us with "oh no, you can't do that because this contradicts something going on [on tv or in upcoming films], but you can do this instead." (Tosche Station 2015b)

# 4

# "No Such Things as Limits": The X-Women[1]

Created by Stan Lee and Jack Kirby, *X-Men* #1 and its team of teenage "mutants" with special powers hit the newsstands in 1963. It was not much of a hit, unlike its "Silver Age" sister publications at Marvel Comics: *Fantastic Four, Incredible Hulk, Spider-Man, Thor,* and *Avengers.* While the seeds of *X-Men*'s future success were sown in that original version, its low sales resulted in its cancellation in 1970. The title's relaunch in spring 1975 occurred as George Lucas was writing *Star Wars,* a few months before the launch of *Batman Family* featuring Congresswoman Barbara Gordon, and not long before Lynda Carter would come to personify Wonder Woman on television. The X-Men's re-debut—as with *Star Wars, Batman Family,* and *Wonder Woman*—would at first have one main female character surrounded by men, just as it did in 1963.

Over time, though, the various *X-Men* comic series would come to be widely touted for their diversity, for their teams of forged families, and for their "mutant metaphor" that employs prejudice against mutants as a stand-in for all types of discrimination and alienation. This metaphor, imperfect as it is, has been resonant across diverse audiences. Further, it offers the notion that the outcast can find her or his own identity, strength, and community among a group of outcast "others," who have one trait in common but perhaps not others. Male and female characters of various backgrounds have been added to the X-Men rosters such that there are at least one hundred X-Men.

Quantitatively, though, despite perceptions about the racial, ethnic, and gender diversity of the main cast over time, teams of X-Men have been dominated by white males (Darowski 2014b: 2). On the one hand, this may make the themes of non-discrimination and civil rights more palatable to some. On the other, these themes are more legible when grounded in the realities of racial, ethnic, and gender discrimination.

Qualitatively, there have been prominent female characters and characters of color in the franchise. This chapter focuses on the most popular and longest-running transmedia X-Women—Jean Grey, Storm, Kitty Pryde, Rogue, and Mystique—and the ways in which their portrayals differ over time and across media, particularly through comics stories that were then adapted for television and film. Launched to increasing sales via newsstands in the 1970s and 1980s and written by the same person (Chris Claremont) for almost seventeen years, these characters' looks, powers, motivations, and personalities display a range of characterizations of girls and women whose centrality and diversity can provide points of entry, identification, and empathy for a wide spectrum of comic readers. Representations of the X-Women from the late 1980s to the 2000s, with new artists and writers and editors, were much different. They were strongly affected by the mutually reinforcing growth of the direct market of comics distribution to local comic shops, the narrowing of the superhero comic audience to a more homogenous group of older males, and the industry's emphasis on "star" artists known for their hypermuscular male and hypersexualized female characters. While opposition to such portrayals made inroads in the mid-2010s comics, the X-Women's transitions to animated series and to films have been emblematic of the underrepresentation and stereotyping of female characters in superhero media.

## "Second Genesis:" The X-Women in the 1970s and 1980s

In a world that "hated and feared" them and their mutations—the X-Factor in their genetic makeup giving them special powers—the 1963 X-Men as written by Stan Lee and drawn by Jack Kirby could generally "pass" as nonmutant, or, "normal." They were all white. Scott Summers/Cyclops wore special glasses to contain his eye blasts, Warren Worthington hid his Angel wings under his clothes, brilliant Henry McCoy just seemed to be oversized and agile rather than a Beast, Bobby Drake the Iceman could change his form back and forth, and pretty redhead Jean Grey's telekinesis and telepathy were entirely invisible dis/abilities. Their wheelchair-using leader, Professor Charles Xavier, could likewise hide his own extensive mental powers as he trained the teenagers to use theirs for good and for defense against prejudiced humans. Creator Stan Lee originally pitched the gender-neutral name "The Mutants" for the team, but was told by his superiors that the word would not be resonant enough to bring sales. His second idea, the non-gender-neutral but assumed to be inclusive "X-Men," was approved (Darowski 2014b: 15–16). This chapter will alternately refer to the female characters under study as X-Men and X-Women.

Like depictions of Wonder Woman in the 1950s and 1960s, a time of emphasis on binary gender roles and on female inferiority and domesticity, lone female Jean Grey conformed to traditional stereotypes of women. She tended to faint when she overtaxed herself by using her powers (as did her contemporary Susan Storm in Stan Lee and Jack Kirby's *Fantastic Four*). She cooked (1964, #6), acted as nurse to injured teammates (1965, #13), redesigned the team's new individualized uniforms (1967, #39), and went undercover as a model (1968, #46–48). Just about all of the male characters seemed to flirt with her and/or have feelings for her from the first issue, including her much-older mentor Xavier, and her at-first-unspoken love for teammate Scott Summers would come to define her character for years. Her telepathic abilities were at first somewhat blocked by Xavier because he assumed she could not control them. Each of these elements highlighted her femininity and the traits assumed to go along with that femininity—fashion-oriented, positioned in relation to men, assumed to be unable to control her power.

At the same time, though, it was clear that Jean was, or had the potential to be, the strongest of the team. Xavier did eventually unblock her telepathic powers and teach her how to use them. She was the only one on the team whom Xavier trusted with information about an upcoming alien invasion, and with the knowledge that he had not in fact died while the others thought that he had (1968–70, #41–65). But this incarnation of the series was canceled. It would be relaunched shortly due to a top-down corporate idea on how Marvel comics might increase their profits.

Marvel's then-editor-in-chief Roy Thomas says that given declining domestic sales, "the idea of a revived 'international' X-Men was my idea in 1974, after the company's president, Al Landau, suggested that it would be good to create a group of heroes from different countries we sold comic[s] to" (Darowski 2014a: 39). The narrative premise was that the original team of five was captured and required rescue, so Professor Xavier would recruit new members from around the world. Thomas stepped down as editor-in-chief not long after, and initial writer Len Wein and artist Dave Cockrum's new characters did not really represent the countries to which Landau referred.

The new international cast would bring diversity to the franchise: Ororo Munroe/ Storm, from Kenya; Logan/Wolverine, from Canada; Kurt Wagner/Nightcrawler, from Germany; Piotr Rasputin/Colossus, from the Soviet Union; Sean Cassidy/Banshee, from Ireland; Shiro Yoshida/Sunfire, from Japan; and John Proudstar/Thunderbird, from an Apache reservation in Arizona. Because these last two left the team immediately (one through choice, the other through death), and Scott Summers/Cyclops from the old team joined the new team, the new X-Men remained mostly male, white, and unmarked by their mutations. Even Nightcrawler, who was blue, could use an "image inducer" to appear as he chose, and he often chose Errol Flynn. In some ways, Storm's status as the only black character in an environment in which her race is rarely called out puts her in the camp of "white heroes in black face" who "have little or no reference to a sustaining black family, a viable black community, continuity within black history or black culture, and the character is represented as black in color only while operating in an all-white cultural context or world view" (Ghee 2013: 232).

In other ways, Storm's blackness being unmentioned was groundbreaking, standing in for hope for a "postracial" future society in which such categories are immaterial. This black woman, in 1975, is a core member and sometimes leader of a team of superheroes. Under writer Chris Claremont, who would helm the series and its first spin-offs for the next sixteen years to come, the new team was grounded in noting its differences from "mainstream" American society. This was happening elsewhere in comics at the time through such characters as Sam Wilson/Falcon, Luke Cage/ Power Man, Misty Knight, Colleen Wing, and John Stewart/Green Lantern, as well as through new storylines that were more socially relevant and engaged with civil rights movements of the times (Fawaz 2011: 355–56). Claremont and artist Dave Cockrum, as well as later artists John Byrne, Paul Smith, John Romita, Jr., and Barry Windsor-Smith (all white males), presented "radical identities and radical bodies." Together, the African American female leader Storm, the muscular and gentle Russian-accented Colossus, the animalistic short and hairy Wolverine, and the blue and staunchly Catholic Nightcrawler were a "punkish evolution from the milquetoast first class, and a rebellious rejection to conformity. To read an X-Men comic after 1975 was to read about empowerment through otherness" (Wheeler 2014a).

A few early letter writers specifically praised the "international" and "multi-ethnic" nature of the new cast; others focused on race and gender. Such letters are generally chosen by the editors and sometimes by the writers, and those chosen and the editorial responses to them may also serve to shore up or defend a creative team's vision (see, e.g., Pustz 1999, McAllister, Sewell, and Gordon 2001, Gordon 2012). Claremont has said that each issue netted about 100–150 letters which he indeed read, and described his approach to them as, "If they liked it, that's wonderful, if they don't like it, why don't they like it, tell me why, and I try to take that and use it and find a way to tell the story better" (MIT 2009). One fan wrote,

> I thought it highly unlikely that all the "good" mutants were Caucasians. . . . An international and interracial team is a great step forward. As a young black woman, I am particularly interested in Ororo. I wonder how Chris [Claremont] will handle her relationship with a group of white males. . . . I hope Chris avoids the cliché of domineering and super-strong black women. (Marilyn Brogdon, #103)

Others were concerned the comic wasn't feminist enough: "By far the most dynamic member of the new X-Men is the sensational Storm. . . . I'm all in favor of your continuing to put this powerful lady in a more dominant position." This same letter writer also criticized the treatment of another female character, Lorna Dane/Polaris, whom he felt was written as too dependent on her male partner. He went so far as to ask if the writer "had ever heard of the women's movement?" (Daniel Raskio, #99). Editor Marv Wolfman responded,

> Claremont has indeed heard of the women's movement and he believes in many of their goals. But where in their manifesto does it say that a woman cannot feel complete or fulfilled by being with a man she loves. . . . Isn't that the ultimate goal of all these People Liberation movements: to give every person—regardless of race, creed, or sex—the right to be whatever he or she wants to be, and not play a role imposed on them by the society around them?

The new creative team on *X-Men* apparently saw itself as grounded in civil rights movements of the time and sought to cultivate a similar readership.

Over time, the new characters and the soon-to-be-introduced Kitty Pryde and Rogue (among others) would forge alliances grounded at first in the shared nature of their mutant outsider status. Later, these bonds would deepen into friendships, family ties, and romantic relationships as well. Not unlike *Wonder Woman, Batgirl* and *Birds of Prey,* and *Star Wars,* the stories are strongest when they have more than one woman, and when they focused on the characters' love, compassion, and care as enmeshed with their heroism. The characters do disagree, but clearly support and love one another in a variety of ordinary and extraordinary situations. Indeed, many letter writers note the friendships and noncompetitiveness of the female characters in particular as strong points. One wrote, "This seems to be the only Marvel comic that is free of sexual stereotype or bias. The women do not act like men. They are not aggressively, or defensively, feminist. They are not sex objects, or cowards, or perpetual hostages. Instead, you have made them individuals, and I heartily approve" (Elizabeth Holden, #136). The main female characters are characterized in the comics as powerful, smart, and independent albeit imperfect agents who, each in her own way, is feminist and queer. Each is also somewhat bound by stereotypes of gender, race, sexuality, and class.

## Storm and Jean: The sisterhood of the Wind-Rider and the Phoenix

Ororo Munroe/Storm is not only the first female team leader in superhero comics, but also the first black team leader (Darowski 2014b: 78). She was born in the United States to a Kenyan witch-priestess-princess mother and an African American photojournalist father, and grew up in Egypt. Professor Xavier finds her in midair, with her hair swirling around her and over her breasts, her only clothing a flowing loincloth, "She soars aloft like an ebon bird. . . . She is happy here—only truly happy here among the elements" (Len Wein and Dave Cockrum 1975, Giant Size X-Men #1). She is a beautiful, powerful, black African woman using her powers to end drought in Kenya, unbound by Western norms of clothing. The scene becomes unnerving when the white male American Xavier disabuses her of the notion that she is a goddess and informs her that she is a mutant who should leave her cause and her country to help his cause in his country: "I offer you a world—and people who may fear you, hate you—but who need you nonetheless." She is presented as exotic, but also conforms to Anglo-European "ideal" beauty in a combination both rare and associated with whites: blue eyes and a thin nose; long, full, straight white hair which can be read as platinum blonde; a small waist and hourglassed figure (see Patton 2006). Stromberg notes that in black-and-white reproduction one might not recognize the character as "black" (2003: 171). Indeed, in the large black-and-white reprint series called "Marvel Essentials," this is the case.

While Storm is the first major black superheroine, she and those to come such as Vixen, Pantha, and the Black Panther Shuri are "explicitly associated with exoticized notions of Africa, nature, noble savagery and a variety of dark continent themes" (Brown 2013: 134; see also Fawaz 2011: 371). Her emotional control is closely linked to her weather control. If she's upset, the weather gets more extreme. This positions her as yet another female for whom both emotion and power control are issues. Likewise, her body is accentuated by her costume, designed by Xavier, which is like a cross between a one piece bathing suit and a bikini, a cape, and thigh-high boots with holes cut out across the top. To be fair, Colossus' costume, unusual for a male character, is very similar in shape to Storm's and shows a similar amount of skin. But his form emphasizes his musculature while hers emphasizes her curves. The serial nature and long-term run of *X-Men* comics has allowed for Storm's character to be individualized and made complex, but her introduction is highly stereotyped. Her gender and race are highlighted, and would be more accentuated on covers than in the interior panels.

Storm does not, however, suffer from many of the "recurring formulas" applied to black superheroes: "weak emulation of Blaxploitation film formula, names that proclaim race as identity, costumes that disguise it, and conceptual ties to established white heroes calculated to achieve the legitimacy of second best" (Svitavsky 2013: 154). She doesn't embody other common stereotypes of black women, such as the asexual caretaking mammy, the hypersexualized jezebel, the emasculating Sapphire, or other variants of angry (and/or sassy) black woman (Gray 1975; hooks 1992; Tyree 2013;

West 2008). True, her costume was taken from a design by artist Dave Cockrum for a discarded superhero idea of a black woman named the Black Cat who wore a bell around her neck and could indeed turn into a cat. That idea relied much more on stereotypical animalistic notions of black women and their sexuality, not uncommon with other female superheroes such as Vixen and Pantha mentioned above. But here, the Black Cat costume was merged with another discarded idea of a male character who could manipulate the weather, named Typhoon (Claremont et al. 2013). Storm's power set, in other words, was not originally conceived as "female."

The centrality of Storm's character and the high visibility of her race and gender challenge notions of who can be a superhero. The white male Scott refers to the black female Storm as his equal (#154), an idea no doubt still uncomfortable for many readers in the early 1980s, but welcome to many others as well. The two are shown as supportive of one another, and not infrequently hugging, even as they are something of rivals for leadership of the team. Somewhat similar to Wonder Woman, Storm's particular variety of character traits constructs her as a figure of aspiration for those totally unlike her in terms of demographics, who could admire her for a number of reasons while recognizing her difference (see, e.g., Brown 2013, Stuller 2010, Inness 1998, Gibson 2015). The character provides a point of representation and identification not only to women and girls (particularly women and girls of color), but also to others who feel or are forced to feel marginalized due to gender, race, sexuality, etc.

Storm and Jean Grey's close friendship challenges racial boundaries as well. Shortly after Storm's arrival, original X-Man Jean returned, this time with much more power—the power of the "Phoenix Force." Despite their outward differences, the two characters become very close. Jean volunteers to pilot a space shuttle back to earth while keeping the others safe from deadly radiation that will kill her. All of the men try to talk her out of it by berating her, making her feel worse. Upon Jean's request ("Not you too, Ororo, I couldn't bear it"), Storm says merely, "May the gods protect you" as the two cry and hug, and Jean thanks her (Claremont and Cockrum 1976, #100). When the shuttle crash-lands in water and Jean does not immediately emerge, the team assumes that she has given her life to save them. But then, she flies up out of the water, "Hear me, X-Men! No longer am I the woman you knew! I am fire! And life incarnate! Now and forever—I am PHOENIX!" (Claremont and Cockrum 1976, #101). At the time it seemed an interstellar force had merged with Jean, or had possessed her in some way.

But even the Phoenix Force is not all-powerful, as Jean discovers. She needs her friends to save the universe. A scene similar to that in issue #100 encapsulates both characters:

Jean:    I don't have the strength!
Storm:   You need an anchor in this cosmic maelstrom, Jean. I will be that anchor.
Jean:    No, Storm, the "anchor" you offer is your life force!
Storm:   It is my life to give my friend.

Storm holds out her brown hand and Jean takes it with her white one. The hands dominate the panel (Claremont and John Byrne 1977, #108). With the love of Storm and the other X-Men, with teamwork across demographic "boundaries," worlds are saved. This type of power-sharing and support, common in this era of *X-Men*, subverts a more stereotypically "masculine" lone-wolf style of heroism and is similar to that in some *Wonder Woman* comics, in *Birds of Prey*, in some *Star Wars* novels, and in *Buffy the Vampire Slayer* (see Chapter 5), in particular.

Jean is again the focus of perhaps the most beloved *X-Men* story, Chris Claremont and John Byrne's "Dark Phoenix Saga" (1980, #129–38). The combination of her merging with/possession by the Phoenix Force and her manipulation by telepathic villains causes her to lose control and alternately fight against and revel in her newfound power. Her struggle for emotional control can be read as grounded in stereotypical femininity and intimately tied to her sexual awakening, through her revealing villain-influenced dress and through her finally consummating her relationship with Scott Summers/Cyclops (#132).[2] It is not until a 2010s comic series (*Avengers vs. X-Men*) that men possessed by the Phoenix Force become similarly corrupted by its absolute power, removing gender as a variable.[3] Jean's love for Scott and her friends help her to fight against it, but she commits genocide by eating a star and thereby wipes out the lives of millions. Here the "mutant metaphor" for civil rights struggles does not work well. Socially marginalized and discriminated against groups may feel "threatening" to those in power, but their real-life "threat" does not tend to involve the power to wipe out a planet in one stroke. Scott pleads with Jean, "You can't kill us because you love us and we love you" (#136). All of the X-Men stand with her as she is put on trial for her crimes. Storm laments that Jean is "beloved sister [she] never had and the X-Men her family" (#137). Jean wants them to kill her but they won't, so after professing her love for Scott, she makes the decision again to sacrifice herself to save the universe from her power. Unlike the last time she did this, in 1976–77s "Phoenix Saga," this time she does not come back to life within the story arc.

Jean's death was mandated by Marvel editor-in-chief Jim Shooter, who felt Jean's genocide required consequences. Editor Jim Salicrup and artist John Byrne did not want the character to die because they thought of her as possessed and therefore not at fault. Writer Chris Claremont wrote and Byrne drew a draft in which Jean got depowered like so many female characters before and after her. He had planned for a future issue in which Magneto would kidnap Jean and offer her the power of the Phoenix, which she would refuse and thus "prove her own heroism." *Phoenix: The Untold Story* from April 1984 contains the first draft of the story (as well as a conversation about it between the four men noted above), in which the X-Men lose the battle and Jean undergoes a "psychic lobotomy" to "excise those parts of her brain which relate to her mutant abilities." Wolverine protests. Cyclops allows it. The process occurs and Jean collapses. But this version wasn't published. Jean's death at the end of the published story was dictated from the top-down by Shooter.

The number of letters received for issue #137 was, according to the creators, more than for any other issue. A few full letter columns were devoted to "Dark Phoenix." Some letters had poetry, some said the issue made them cry, and a few said "thank you." Some echoed concerns that had been voiced about twenty issues previous, when after Jean/Phoenix saved the universe, her powers seemed to be curtailed. Fan Brenda Robnett had written (in #117),

> I was SO EXCITED by the creation of Phoenix. At long last a POWERFUL super hero and a *woman* at that! . . . Her magnificent powers saved the entire universe! . . . And then it started. The gradual deterioration of Phoenix's power . . . . Why can't Marvel have at least *one* super heroine worthy of the name??? . . . They are what *you* make them.

The editors asked readers for their responses to this letter. Some agreed with it and some did not. Editor Roger Stern responded to all of them, "Would we have chopped Phoenix's powers if she was a man. . . . The answer is yes!" A letter writer similarly accused the "Dark Phoenix" authors,

> I bet if Phoenix had been a man, you guys would have wrote in the story that he was emotionally strong enough to control his power. However, since Jean was a woman, you guys killed her off! Dr. Don Blake didn't become mad with power when he became Thor, so I don't see why Jean couldn't handle her power boost! (April Curry, #139)

Granted, these fans did not know of "the untold story." But their sensitivity to the stereotype of female characters being depowered or characterized as more emotional and weaker than male characters is not unwarranted. Overall, most letter writers were passionately positive about the story, showing how invested they had become in the character of Jean.

As the first writer (and later editor) after the 1975 relaunch Len Wein recounted this pivotal moment in *X-Men* publication history, "The circulation of *X-Men* #137 tripled. . . . Suddenly, the *X-Men* went from a solid mid-level title to the bestselling title in the line, outstripping even such stalwarts as *Spider-Man*" (2006: 4–5). Available figures bear out these assertions. In 1980, before the "Dark Phoenix Saga," the number of single issues sold through "dealers, carriers, street vendors, and counter sales" nearest to the company's date of filing this paperwork was 163,000 (#131). Months after the "Dark Phoenix Saga," in 1981, the number was 274,000 (#156); by 1983, it was 337,000 (#182); by 1985, 445,000 (#205). These figures do not include the burgeoning direct market sales, which were probably about 10–15 percent of these figures at the time in the mid-1980s.[4] To be clear, *X-Men*'s sales increased via the first type of distribution method for comics: newsstands that were accessible to a wide range of people. The high sales generally allowed creators leeway in plotting and characterization. Claremont introduced new characters and for the most part, expanded upon and pushed the limits of the X-Men's "otherness." His two female editors during this time period, first Louise Simonson and then Ann Nocenti (who was also editing *Star Wars*), were both influential in and supportive of the writer and his strong female characters.

## Storm and Kitty, Mystique and Rogue: Queer families, fluid sexuality, and team leadership

In short order, Storm would lead the team and two new and long-running female characters would join, Kitty and Rogue. A new female villain would become similarly prominent and popular as well, Mystique. The team at this point was more or less balanced in terms of gender, a subversive rarity then and still in the 2010s. A letter writer comments on Storm's new leadership role, as well as on the creative team's approach to its female characters, "Storm is the logical candidate for team leader, partly because she's the coolest and brightest X-Man left . . . but mostly because of your history of feminism" (Dr. Phillip Kott, #143). Storm's leadership role, as noted, made her the first African American team leader and the first female team leader (and by extension, the first African American female team leader) in comics. Her only peer on the team is the white male Wolverine and she does not hesitate to pull rank on him: "I am leader of the X-Men. While that is so you will use your claws as I command. No other time." When he responds, "I wouldn't take that from Cyclops," she counters, "You will take it from me." He gives in, "All right, Storm" (Claremont and Byrne 1981, #142). Years later, Scott returns and fights her for leadership. Wolverine merely says, "My money's on the lady" (Claremont and Rick Leonardi 1986, #201). Even though she has no powers at that time, Storm still defeats him and her role as leader is cemented.

Storm's lack of a close female friend in this time period shifts her role more to that of a mother. One of the strengths of the X-Men universe is in its queer families: its diverse characters who are not related through a "traditional" and nuclear patriarchal structure, but rather, who choose each other as family based on mutual love and support. Storm refers to Nightcrawler and Colossus as her little brothers, and her matriarchy extends when they recruit Kitty Pryde, a petite Jewish brunette teen who can make herself intangible to "phase" through solid objects. Many letter writers praised the new character, particularly her awkwardness, ordinariness, innocence, intelligence, passion, and spunk. To one of them, writer Chris Claremont responded, "You were one of the many—heck, why be modest—the multitude of fans who applauded the debut of Ms. Katherine "Kitty" Pryde of Deerfield, IL. [Artist John Byrne] and I figured we were creating a pretty nifty character, but we never counted on the incredible—completely favorable—response she generated. Whew!!" (#135). Her coloring and body type are much closer to the contemporaneous Princess Leia than that of any of the adult superwomen, such that she "extends the field of what powerful superheroines look and act like" (Galvan 2014: 47). She was a precursor to the younger and more petite Batgirl and Buffy the Vampire Slayer of the 1990s–2000s (see Chapters 2 and 5). Her frequent costume changes are a source of comic relief and underscore her youth. When Xavier tries to put her on a team (the New Mutants) with those closer to her age, a full-page panel of Kitty points at the reader yelling, "Professor Xavier is a jerk!" (Claremont and Paul Smith 1983, #168). Her bravery, passion, and cunning in the face of danger puts her on an equal footing with the other X-Men and Xavier relents, in a move applauded by multiple letter writers.

Kitty, as a young, headstrong, but physically unthreatening female character is often used by Claremont (and later writers) to state subtext in a seemingly "innocent" way. At their first conversation, Kitty says, "We got black kids in my school, Ororo, but none of them look like you. I mean, you know, white hair an' blue eyes??" Storm smiles, "So far as I know Kitty, I am one of a kind" (Claremont and Byrne 1980, #129). This not only establishes Kitty's curiosity and bluntness, but also calls attention to Storm's appearance, reminding us that a dark-skinned, Anglo-European-featured black woman leads the generally white X-Men. Another set of panels calls attention to Storm's race as well, in the "Dark Phoenix Saga." At this time, Storm's nose is generally drawn to appear thin, similar to Jean's, with two smudged dots rather close together just above her lips. Her long straight hair flows down around her cape. But when Jean, manipulated by others, sees the world as it was in the eighteenth century, she sees Storm as her "slave": Storm's nose is wider, with more of a horizontal wavy line for nostrils and some definition on the sides. Her hair is bound in a scarf and her neck and shoulders are exposed rather than caped. The differences are clear in John Byrne (penciler) and Terry Austin (inker)'s adjacent panels (1980, #133). The change in features could conform to some readers' associations with blackness, or could confront them. Here, too, the "mutant metaphor" as an analogue to other civil rights concerns cannot cover the ways in which intersectional discrimination occurs: Storm is perceived by Jean much differently from three white males, even though all four are mutants.

Race comes up directly in the dialogue, again with Kitty, in 1982's graphic novel, *God Loves Man Kills* by Chris Claremont and Brent Anderson. Kitty is immediately and unreservedly close not only to Storm but also to her dance teacher Stevie Hunter, again displaying skin color as no barrier to the relationships. Stevie, who is dark-skinned and has her hair in small cornrows, chides Kitty for having punched a kid who called her a "mutie-lover." The furious Kitty responds, "Suppose he'd called me a nigger-lover, Stevie?! Would you be so damn tolerant then?!!" The question positions mutation as a civil rights issue akin to that of the struggle against racial discrimination, although as noted the parallels are not perfect. Indeed, Kitty not infrequently speechifies about discrimination, often using blacks and Jews as examples.[5] She dresses down the anti-mutant crusader in *God Loves Man Kills* who points at blue, tailed Nightcrawler and asks, "You dare call that thing human?!" Kitty responds, praising the mutant around whom she herself initially felt uncomfortable due to his appearance, "More human than you! Nightcrawler's generous and kind and decent! . . . I hope I can be half the person he is, and if I have to choose between caring for my friend and believing in your god, then I choose my friend!" She is almost shot for these words, but saved by a policeman. Claremont has been clear that this story was grounded in 1980s backlash, much of it constructed as "Christian" and "heartland," to the civil rights movements of the 1960s and 1970s (Claremont et al. 2011). The story plays out, more directly than most X-Men stories, the clash between tolerance and intolerance and the costs of the latter.

The "mutant metaphor" was resonant with readers. One wrote,

I am a gay white male . . . the mutant-hatred that is becoming so prevalent in the Marvel Universe has existed in our own world in various guises. . . . To say that I identified is extreme understatement. I'm sure that . . . a black, an Italian American or Asian-American could have read the same thing and had the same reaction. . . . The issues you deal with in your stories are important ones. (name withheld, #214)

Another wrote about Nightcrawler,

Because my hands and feet are mis-shaped and I wear an artificial limb I can no more pass for "normal" than Kurt. . . . Like Kurt, and sometimes with or through him, I discover that it truly is better to be a whole "me" than "normal." . . . He's a terrific reminder of the ultimate truth [that] "freaks" and "normals" share at heart one common human experience. . . . There aren't too many characters—in books, comics, movies, or elsewhere—that us real-life "misfits" can look onto to form or celebrate positive images of ourselves. . . . Thank you [for] your terrific example that different can be good—excellent, in fact! (Carolyn Amos, #149)

Editor Louise Simonson responded, "If ever we at Marvel . . . need a reason for doing what we do . . . this letter is it." Rising sales, coupled with a supportive editor, allowed the creative team to keep doing what they were doing.

The story "Days of Future Past" (Claremont and Byrne 1981, #141–42)[6] also plays out the mutant metaphor, and like the "Phoenix Saga," the "Dark Phoenix Saga," and *God Loves Man Kills* would be adapted to film. The future Kitty is sent back in time into her present self in order to prevent an assassination of a political figure that results in a dystopian future. Her older self is married to Colossus and working with Storm, Wolverine, and the heretofore unseen Rachel Summers in a fascistic future brought about by humans' fear of (and politicians' capitalization on the fear of) mutants. "In [Kitty's] hands lies the fate of mutantkind, of humanity, of the earth itself. Failure is unthinkable, yet success may well be impossible, for she seeks to change history" (#141).[7] This story also introduces the blue shapeshifter Mystique who leads the Brotherhood of Evil Mutants, consisting of her female partner Destiny as well as male mutants Pyro, Avalanche, and the Blob. They square off against the Storm-led X-Men, with Kitty pushing Destiny's bullet off course such that the assassination is averted. The female characters are the leaders and the stars of this story, as is true of the two Phoenix story arcs. When the four stories mentioned above were adapted into the 2000s–10s *X-Men* films, in each case, the centrality and nuance of the all of the female characters as written in the late 1970s-early 1980s—notable in comparison to all of the other superwomen discussed thus far from the same time period—would be lost.

Mystique is like Storm in a number of ways. Both are team leaders, both are nonwhite although Mystique can appear with any skin tone and features she chooses, both are queer mother figures, and both have been written and read as interested in male as well as female partners. Mystique's long-term partner in the comics is Destiny, a precognitive and blind mutant also known as Irene Adler, the nemesis of Sherlock Holmes. It is made clear that the two together adopt future X-Man Rogue as a young girl and raise her. Rogue refers to them later as "my mothers" (Marjorie Liu and Mike

Perkins 2012, *Astonishing X-Men* #51). Destiny describes Mystique as, "my dearest friend [whom] I have loved from the moment we've met" (Claremont and Marc Silvestri 1989, *Uncanny X-Men* #254). But she was not Mystique's only partner and Rogue was not Mystique's only child. At one point she was married to a man and had an affair with a male demon, and the X-Man Nightcrawler was the result. This is hinted at early on when he first sees her and says, "Your skin—your eyes . . . we are so alike!" (Claremont and Byrne 1981, #142). Given that Mystique is a shape shifter who can and has taken on female and male forms, longtime X-Men writer Chris Claremont had plans to make her Nightcrawler's father and Destiny his mother, but this did not happen due to his leaving the title (Byrne 2005). Still, in the comics "she is a transgressive character, a villain/woman/lesbian/mother/shapeshifter who destabilizes the binary oppositions of the superhero universe" (Murray 2011: 59).

Unlike Storm, Mystique's mothering is usually portrayed as suspect, intertwining her transgressiveness with her "bad" parenting. She apparently threw Nightcrawler over a waterfall to save herself (and, perhaps, him) from fearful and angry townspeople. And although she clearly loves Rogue, she groomed her to be ruthless and villainous and cannot accept that Rogue leaves her and goes to the X-Men. Rogue does so mainly because she feels she is losing her mind, having absorbed Carol Danvers/Ms. Marvel's powers and some of her personality as well (Claremont and Michael Golden 1981, *Avengers Annual* #10, discussed in more detail in Chapter 6). The experience was "a physical and psychic trauma that scarred both women" that left Carol for dead and Rogue feeling "crazy" (Claremont and Cockrum 1982, #158). These first glimpses of Rogue show her with angry eyebrows along with white-streaked, short, sharp hair. She initially fights the X-Men, but goes to them for help when she feels Carol's personality is taking over her own, "Ah tried t'make Mystique understand . . . . Ah love her, Professor—she's been like a mom to me—but ah knew she was wrong. . . . You're my only hope" (Claremont and Walt Simonson 1983, #171). None of the X-Men trust Rogue. Carol, who had been with the X-Men for a short time, punches her into outer space and leaves angrily. But Xavier is willing to give Rogue a chance. In short order, she proves herself by saving Wolverine's fiancée and Storm, thinking "Too bad you ain't awake t' see this rescue, Storm. If ah was the evil mutant you still believe me t' be, ah'd'a let you go splat all over the floor" (Claremont, Smith, and John Romita Jr. 1983, #175). She becomes a mainstay of the book, as do Mystique's not infrequent and usually misguided attempts to win back Rogue's primary loyalty. By this point drawn by Walt Simonson (husband of editor Louise Simonson), Paul Smith, and John Romita Jr. as a hero, the angles of Rogue's facial features and her hair are softer. She looks younger and friendlier. By the 1990s, she will be a fan favorite, drawn with huge hair and an ultra-curvy body.

While Mystique's gender fluidity is quite literal, as she is a shape shifter who can take on the form of any human, Storm's can be read through her dress and relationships and behaviors. Storm's romantic life is multifaceted and complicated in the comics. The first time she really seems to be taken with someone is with female Japanese ronin Yukio. Fans have certainly read into the relationship between Storm and Yukio since the 1980s, with some asserting their meeting merely inspired Storm to change her style, others saying that Storm admires Yukio in a kind of romantic friendship, and still others assuming that they are engaged in a loving and/or sexual relationship (see, e.g., Wheeler 2014a, Edidin and Stokes 2015). The Storm who met Yukio was already somewhat different from when she joined the team. The level-headed and duty-bound leader had begun to question her vow never to kill, particularly when the X-Men's lives were at stake, and she had begun to find it more difficult to hold her emotions in check to keep her powers under control. She not only ruminated on her changing feelings but also began to change her behavior. Fans were as concerned as the comic's characters, but interested as well, "What's this? Ororo stabbing [mutant Morlock leader Callisto] in the heart? . . . Kudos" (Philip Cohen, #178). Storm thinks:

> I feel as though I stand at a crossroads. To remain an X-Man—especially as leader—I must sacrifice the beliefs that give my life meaning. Yet the alternative means leaving those I love, forever. . . . And Xavier told me, the day we met, that my powers should be used for the benefit of all humanity. Was I wrong to listen? Can I deny that responsibility? . . . Whatever I choose, I will no longer be the woman I was—but what will I become? Ororo or Storm, which is it to be? (Claremont and Simonson 1983, #171)

It would be both, as Storm allows herself to change outwardly and inwardly, in ways that make her a more strategic and hardnosed leader, while also allowing herself to feel her own emotions more than in the past.

> Storm's transformation from elemental goddess to mohawk leather punk is one of the queerest stories ever told in comics, because it's a story about liberating oneself from other people's expectations and finding a greater strength through letting go. . . . Though the character's bisexuality has never been more than hinted at, it's clear that Storm's relationship with the female ronin Yukio was the trigger for her awakening. (Wheeler 2014a)

Following Yukio, with her short punk hair, willingness to use force, and zest for life, Storm at first says, "I envy you your madness, Yukio. It is a luxury denied me ever since my powers first appeared. My safety, and that of those around me, requires an inner serenity . . . I have lately lost" (Claremont and Smith 1983, #172). Later, she gives in, "This madness of yours has infected me—I welcome it!" In a combination of Yukio and Callisto's clothes and hairstyles, the "new" Storm appears. Proposed as a joke by artist Paul Smith as a way to restyle Storm's hair after she had lost some of it in the story, and approved by editor Louise Simonson, Storm wore her hair in a Mohawk, with a collar necklace, bicep bracelet, tank top and sleeveless vest, and tight black pants and boots (Cronin 2011; Claremont and Smith 1983, #173). Kitty is upset, fearing a change in her mother figure. Wolverine thinks, "Storm's change is more'n cosmetic. She's wilder, tougher. Walkin' mine and Yukio's road. Wish I could be sure that's right for her" (Claremont, Michael Golden and Bret Blevins 1983, Annual #7). Four years later, when the team members are tricked into having dreams of their heart's desires,

Storm's dream is of a smiling Yukio, "I never knew how to laugh before I met Yukio. In many ways, I have never been as happy since. I want to join her." But she defers to her duty to lead the X-Men, as usual (Claremont and Alan Davis 1987, Annual #11).

The editor framed the initial letter column about Storm's changes in her voice: "I am Storm, leader of the X-Men. As many of you noted in the many letters received, I am not the woman I was. Whether my metamorphosis is for good or ill remains to be seen." Mostly, they were positive: "She's awesome! Leather pants! Mohawk! Eye makeup! She's great! . . . I love it!" (Anthony Rosso, #182). Another letter writer felt rather differently, "Why is pretty-nice Storm in an ugly punker suit?!? It looks UUUGGGLLLY!!!" (Sean Gonsalves, #182). "Storm" (editor Ann Nocenti) responded,

> Perhaps, Sean, because I was never as "pretty-nice" as you would like to believe. I cannot live my life as a mirror, reflecting images of how others see me and pretending that these are my real selves. I must be what I am. I must discover who—what—I am. And live with that. It may not be pleasant. It may not be what others would prefer me to be, but at least it will be the truth.

Others split the difference: "Just wanted to register my vote of approval for the change in Ororo. It shocks me still, and I don't particularly like it, but I think it's a necessary step in the evolution of the character" (Rand Lee, #189).

Storm also has a fraught romantic relationship with disabled Native American male mutant Forge, who is able to conceive of and mold complex machinery with ease. He develops a weapon for the government to neutralize mutants' powers, to be used on the formerly villainous Rogue. Storm, however, bears the brunt of its blast to protect Rogue and loses her powers. Her depowerment remains the state of affairs for almost forty issues (1984–88, #185–227), not unlike Wonder Woman from 1968 to 1972, or, some might argue, Barbara Gordon from 1988 to 2011. As noted, this is a trope that affects female superheroes more often and for longer periods than male ones—a part of the recurrent storytelling device called "women in refrigerators." Forge nurses Storm back to health and helps her deal with the loss of her powers, calling attention to his own disabilities. She realizes she no longer has to fear her emotions' effects on the weather, and they fall in love . . . until she finds out it is he who created the depowering weapon. The duology "Lifedeath" I and II finds Storm saddened by her loss of "oneness with the world," and emerging stronger yet again, "Is this the mountain I was meant to climb, the purpose—the destiny I have so long sought? A bridge, not simply between old ways and new, but races as well—between humanity and its mutant children!" (Claremont and Barry Windsor-Smith 1985, #198). Artist Barry Windsor-Smith's expressive, detailed, active Storm is not posed in an objectified manner; she is not sexualized even when she is nude or barely dressed. It is this depowered but powerful Storm, rejecting Forge because she cannot forgive him although she still loves him, who battles Cyclops to remain leader of the X-Men and emerges victorious. "'Lifedeath' has to be one of the most well-crafted stories of the year and definitely the best X-Men comic to date. Jean Grey's death does not even touch it" (Mark Gentry, #196). Most letter writers echoed his praise.

As the 1980s wound down, a number of changes took place in the X-universe. More mutants, particularly female ones, were added to the X-roster such as Betsy Braddock/ Psylocke and Rachel Summers/Phoenix. Soon, Jubilation Lee/Jubilee and Alison Blaire/Dazzler would join them and Storm, Kitty, and Rogue. Indeed, Claremont has a young male character comment, "Team used to be so boss! Now they're all a bunch of girls! They need more boy mutants!" (Claremont and Silvestri 1988, #225). Team books such as the *Justice League*, or *Avengers*, were not then and are not now nearly as close to gender parity as were the X-Men at this time. Despite the "complaint" in this panel, the title remained high-selling and popular.

## Changing roles for the female characters in a Darker-Toned X-Universe

The main title, over time, would add more male mutants, and would change in style and tone. In part, this was in keeping with the darker-themed comics and graphic novels that began to take center stage in the mid-to-late 1980s, such as *Watchmen* and *Batman: The Dark Knight Returns*, as well as *The Killing Joke* (see Chapter 2). The X-Men story *God Loves Man Kills* from 1982 was something of a precursor to this development (Clarke 2011: 203). New mutants arrived and core team members left. The X-Men, having sacrificed themselves to save the world yet again (with Forge's help as he and Storm reconcile and she regains her powers, as a number of letter writers hoped she would), would pretend to be dead to the rest of the world. Kitty, Rachel, and Nightcrawler would go to the spinoff series *Excalibur*, written by Claremont and drawn by Alan Davis. This title was more continuous with the style and tone of the early 1980s X-Men—action was intermixed with relationship drama, queer relationships (particularly, with Kitty),[8] serious moments amalgamated with comic ones, and art more similar to the *X-Men* from 1975 to 1985. Most of the letters across the first ten years of this title are quite complimentary, and most of the letters that talked about specific characters were about Kitty. *Excalibur*, like *Wonder Woman* and *Star Wars* comics in the late 1980s and early 1990s, were among the few that did not (yet) follow a trend that would only accelerate in the coming years, of increasingly violent and muscled male characters, and increasingly sexualized female characters. The cover of *Excalibur* #4 would comment on the trend, showing no heroes or villains but a nightwatchman sweeping up, asking presumably about his own place on the cover, "Cover? You mean with huge muscular heroic males and beautifully erotic females engaging in gratuitous violence . . .?" (Chris Claremont and Alan Davis 1988; cover by Davis and Paul Neary).

Artist Marc Silvestri began a three-year run on *Uncanny X-Men*. He then left to become one of the founders of Image Comics, known in the early 1990s for hypermuscular and hypersexualized characters and artist-driven titles. While his first arc, "Fall of the Mutants" (1988) is not far removed from the previous comics, the next prominent arc called "Inferno" (1988–89) would be. The relaxation of the Comics Code's guidelines on portrayals of female characters in 1989 allowed the "Bad

Girl" trend with no fear of repercussion. "Inferno" features markedly sexualized and tough versions of the female characters, as well as females typecast as weak-minded, sexualized, and out of control. Rogue is battling the split between her own and Carol Danvers/Ms. Marvel's personalities in her head. Madelyne Pryor, the Goblin Queen, is a barely dressed and violent clone of Jean Grey who tries to kill (the resurrected) Jean and then kills herself. Jean absorbs her memories and is written as having a split personality. Darowski notes that the "The Dark Phoenix [Jean] and the Goblin Queen [Madelyne] were both killed to balance the scales of justice" but when Professor Xavier became the villain known as Onslaught, he was "simply arrested" (2014b: 115). These women as well as Storm have big hair, big breasts, angry faces, supertight or revealing tattered clothing, and very arched backs accentuating their curves regardless of context. Except for one panel in which Storm finds that Jean is alive and the two women hug (1989, #242), there is little warmth or understanding within the X-family here. This arc foreshadows both the style and substance of the 1990s blockbuster and transmedia *X-Men* franchise.

## The best-selling comic of all time, bad girls, and transitions to television in the 1990s

With X-Men specifically, the increase in sexualization and action-driven plots were intimately tied to changes in the production and distribution of comics in the early 1990s, particularly having to do with the rise of star artists and the rise of the direct market. As noted in the Introduction, in 1972, there were only a couple dozen local comic shops constituting the direct market. By 1983, there were at least 2000. By 1993, there were about 10,000 (Beerbohm 2015; Smith and Duncan 2012; Stroup 2015). "The direct market changed whom comics were sold to and, subsequently, the content standards associated with this audience. Newsstand comics were produced for a mass, undifferentiated audience. But once the direct market takes over, the principal audience for comic books becomes, primarily, the specialty storeowners making the orders, and secondarily, the specialty store consumer" (Clarke 2011: 196). Due to the growth of the direct market and of local comic shops, a new market for spin-offs and variant covers and crossover events could be cultivated catering to the more hard-core fans, the "one niche market of reader-collectors" who frequented such shops (Smith and Duncan 2012: 149). They were mostly male, white, and older, and they were buying the X-books in large numbers. The main title *Uncanny X-Men* and its several spin-offs, *New Mutants, X-Factor, Excalibur, Alpha Flight,* and *Wolverine,* were high sellers. The books, being purchased at even higher numbers than in the early to mid-1980s, had shifted their art style as described above and therefore the art was assumed to play a part in driving the sales.

Marvel, now under the ownership of Revlon executive Ron Perelman, figured that they could further profit from their perceived demographically similar and dedicated audience with new books drawn by emerging "star" artists, at raised prices. The original X-Men, who had been in the spinoff series *X-Factor*, were merged back with the current X-Men. A new title called *X-Men* would have half of them (females Rogue, Psylocke, and Jubilee; males Cyclops, Wolverine, Beast, Gambit). *Uncanny X-Men* would have the other half (females Jean and Storm; males Colossus, Iceman, Archangel, and Bishop). They would be coequal headliners of the X-franchise. *Uncanny X-Men* in 1989–90 was drawn mostly by Marc Silvestri as mentioned, but also by Jim Lee. Going into the 1990s, *New Mutants* would be renamed *X-Force* and would be penciled by Rob Liefeld, *X-Men* by Jim Lee, and *Uncanny X-Men* by Whilce Portacio. These four men would be four of the seven star artists who would found Image Comics in 1992.

What would come to be called their "Image House Style" or "Bad Girl" style would be copied, in hopes of also copying their sales, by many artists. At a time when "non-event" top issues sold maybe 125,000 copies per month, the initial sales of the new X-books were record-breaking. *X-Force* #1 (1991) sold about five million copies to shops. A few months later, the new *X-Men* #1 (1991) and its five different "collectible" covers became and remains the best-selling comic of all time—at least in terms of direct market sales to an overexpanded number of comics shops, which ordered over eight million copies. Only about three million of those were sold to readers and/ or collectors. The rest were held back by dealers and speculators hoping to cash in on the issue. Unfortunately, in retrospect, *X-Men* #1 relied on "a mix of sexualized women and classic superhero adventure" such that it "is neither memorable nor rare; instead it's more like the comics' equivalent of a Michael Bay film—fun, attractive, sexy, bombastic, and ultimately, hollow" (Elliott and Watkins 2014: 112, 108). Longtime writer Chris Claremont left *X-Men* after only the first three issue arc of the new series. He said, "It was not a happy time . . . .They're not very good issues. . . . .That book at that point was in the process of being defined by the editor [Bob Harras, who followed Ann Nocenti and Louise Simonson] and the new writers and artists the way they wanted it and has been so ever since" (Andersen 2013, quoting Tue Srensen and Ulrik Kristiansen's interview of Claremont that appeared in 1995 in *seriejournalen*).

Letter columns, ads, characters, and art (especially covers) reveal the ways in which the perceived audience had changed, and ways in which it was cultivated to change. In the late 1970s and early 1980s, 30–40 percent of the letters chosen for print in the main title *Uncanny X-Men* were from female writers. But from the late 1980s into the 2000s, those letters were almost entirely by male writers. One female letter writer would show up about once every several issues during this time. The ads changed as well, reflecting the collecting culture. Ads by large comic shops for readers to purchase back issues appeared, as well as those for football and baseball cards, video games, and statuettes of comic characters also sold in such shops. Comics began to be sold in stores selling other types of collectibles as well. Increasingly in the 1990s and into the 2000s, superhero comics niche-marketed to the assumed core audience of white heterosexual males, and the *X-Men* franchise was at the forefront of the trend.

The number of male characters and the number of white characters each increased during this time, by about 10 percentage points (Darowski 2014b: 137, 138). Female readers dropped off. A letter writer to *Excalibur* in 1995 noted, "I keep hearing about how comic companies are trying to think of ways to attract more women readers.

Well, it's capable, intelligent characters like Kitty (and Storm, and Jean Grey, and Amanda Sefton, and gee, most of the X-Women) who are going to attract and keep female readers. Hum, maybe that's why the X-books have so many female readers?" (Elizabeth Milford, *Excalibur* #88). Editor Suzanne Gaffney's response made clear the book's focus on the male characters: "X-Women are terrific--but you're sure hunks like Peter Rasputin, Logan, and Remy Lebeau have nothing to do with it, Elizabeth?"

Covers and panels in the 1990s are different from the comics of the 1970s and most of the 1980s as well. The late 1970s and early 1980s covers, not dissimilarly from today, did tend to focus on idealized bodies but those bodies were not unbelievably out-of-proportion. In the 1990s, the female characters on covers are impossibly long-legged, small-waisted, big-haired, and large-breasted. If facing front, they have their hips jutted out to the side. Sometimes they are in the "broke back" pose, with an arched and twisted back such that all of their curves in front and back are simultaneously visible. They are usually drawn from the side or the back, with exaggeratedly large breasts and upturned buttocks, partially closed or angrily narrowed eyes and open mouths, and posed in ways that indicated sexual receptivity, or readiness. Comics writer Christy Marx explains, "If an artist were to draw male characters with the same level of sexual receptivity, those characters would also be walking around with permanent erections" (Marx 2005: 177). But rather, the male characters of the 1990s are much more likely to be drawn facing front, hairy, angry, hugely muscled and with a stress on their physical strength and athleticism.

Many letter writers praised the new artists and their styles specifically. For instance, "Jim [Lee]'s art is the best I've seen and the way he draws Psylocke . . . hubba hubba" (Toby Neal, *Uncanny X-Men* #277). Another wrote, "Kudos to Jim Lee for that double page spread on 18 & 19. I thought Psylocke had looked good for the first couple of pages, but then I turned to these pages and all I could think of after that was the remarkable job he did on Ororo and Jean Grey. Yowza!" (Augie De Blieck, *X-Men* #9). The spread in question shows all of the male X-Men fully dressed, some in uniforms and some not. Psylocke is in the background in a bikini and small jacket with her hip jutted out to the side. Jean is seated, popping out of the top of a tiny strapless dress, with huge hair, and her head, waist, and each breast all about the same size. Storm is standing next to her, like Jean in a strapless dress with the same body type and hair-size, thrusting out her hip and buttocks. It is no doubt such praise that led Marvel to issue their "Swimsuit Issues" beginning in 1991, which like its *Sports Illustrated* namesake is full of posed women in bikinis (and a few men too). The "Swimsuit Issues" show the female characters posed in the same ways as in the concurrent comic titles, highlighting the artificiality and the lack of narrative reason for them to be posed like that in the comics.

A much smaller number of letter writers did not like aspects of the art, "Whilce [Portacio], I love the art, I have a question, though. Why does every woman have a 40 inch minimum breast size? And how can they possibly wear the clothes that they do if they really are that endowed. Other than this, I think you are redefining comic art" (Russell Johnsen, *Uncanny X-Men* #285). Editor Bob Harras replied, "Don't worry Russ, assistant editor Suzanne Gaffney is ever vigilant when it comes to our X-women."

This was the same Suzanne Gaffney noted above, who would edit *Excalibur* and ask the reader three years later in if female fandom wasn't based on male character "hunks." Another writer questioned the art style on the other main title, after Andy Kubert took over penciling from Jim Lee,

> [Psylocke and Storm] both seem to be ideal examples of women in the nineties— even though their costumes make them more like sex objects and less like heroes! The X-Men probably wouldn't have made it this far if it weren't for the female characters. I just feel that the women of the group should get more emphasis as good female role models—on abilities and personality, and less bathing suit posing. (Jane Han, *X-Men* #22)

As comic artist and writer Trina Robbins noted at the time,

> Using a circular kind of logic, editors at the major comic companies continue to produce sex object-heroines which appeal to a male audience. Their excuse for not adding strong female characters who might appeal to women is that "women don't read comics." Of course, as long as female comic characters are insulting to the average woman, she won't read comics. (1996: 166)

Male and genderqueer readers might similarly be turned off. On the one hand, such exaggeration of female bodies can draw attention to the fact that the superheroes are women. On the other, the emphasis on female sexuality undercuts that heroism (Brown 2011).

Race was addressed during this time period, albeit infrequently, by letter writers as well.

> For years I've been wanting to see someone of my race and gender included into one of my favorite books, and after almost thirty years on the stands, it's about time . . . . I would particularly like to thank Mr. Portacio for giving Bishop his distinctly African facial features. Too often, black comic book characters have European features and are just colored brown. (Kristopher Mosby, *Uncanny X-Men* #285)

Another felt the same artist was doing exactly that, with Storm,

> Dear Mr. Portacio . . . [you are] robbing Storm of any and all ethnic identity . . . the way she is drawn is not a black woman at all, but a white woman with brown skin . . . . Those images only reinforce the lie that American society tells in order to create unrealistic standards that few people could ever hope to achieve. (Bea McNeal, *Uncanny X-Men* #289)

Editor Harras noted that Storm from her creation was "a unique looking black character. Her features have always been set as unusual: white hair and blue eyes . . . . But if we offended you in any way Bea—we apologize, because, believe us, such was not our intent." He doesn't address one of the points of these two letters: that most black characters, Storm included, have rather Anglo-European features. Several letter writers thought that Storm and Bishop were being put together as a couple, or should be. Whether this was how they read the dialogue and art or whether they presumed such due to the characters' similar skin tones is not clear.

Marvel sought to capitalize on the franchise in other ways as well. *X-Men: The Animated Series* debuted in October 1992 on the Fox Network and ran for seventy-six episodes on Saturday mornings with high ratings.[9] The following year, Marvel licensed the movie rights for the characters to Fox. The animated series probably helped keep the sales of the various X-books relatively high through the mid-1990s, as well as providing comic readers a new medium for their fandom: "X-Men fans were surprised by the respect for the source material provided by the writers and artists working behind the scenes, who were themselves comics professionals and/or fans" (Skir 2005: 20). The core cast of the new cartoon was Storm, Jean, Rogue, Jubilee, Cyclops, Wolverine, Beast, and Gambit—an equal number of males and females, led by the male Professor Xavier. Their look matched that of the contemporaneous main titles, with uniforms as redesigned by artist Jim Lee. Storm, for instance, wore neither her original black bathing suit and cape nor her Mohawked hair with a vest and pants, but rather a full-coverage white catsuit with white cape and huge white hair.

Changes made to the female characters from comics to television had both negative and positive effects. The animated series versions of the male characters were not as hypermuscular as the comics, nor were the (still curvy) female characters as hypersexualized, due to the assumptions of a younger and more diverse target audience for cartoons. Broadcast standards and practices played a role as well, not only in clothing but also in language. For instance, the word "kill" could not be used on Saturday mornings. However, in terms of leadership and of power, the female characters are diminished in the animated series as compared to the comics. Storm does not lead the X-Men, and most of her lines have her narrating how she is using her powers. Teen Jubilee veers more toward annoying than spunky. Jean is sometimes weaker, even fainting as in her 1960s "Marvel Girl" days, and is often positioned as a love object between Cyclops and Wolverine. Indeed, the writer for one of the episodes that stressed this triangle remembers, "This is an element for which I personally lobbied and which was introduced in [the episode] 'Captive Hearts'. It was based on two panels from the Byrne/Claremont era wherein Wolverine lamented first the apparent death of Jean after a battle with Magneto and later her actual demise after the Dark Phoenix Saga" (Skir 2005: 23). Some of these elements would remain in the films of the 2000s. A number of the episodes in the animated series portrayed some of the "classic" stories noted above, such as the "Phoenix Saga," the "Dark Phoenix Saga," and "Days of Future Past" (as would the later films) as well as original stories and current comic arcs such as the 1995 "Age of Apocalypse," albeit somewhat differently.

The move from comics to television also impacted the representation of X-Women in terms of their numbers and their key storylines. Quantitatively, women were underrepresented in key roles. Qualitatively, the characters of Jean and Rogue generally

**Figure 4.1** Rogue, realizing the villainous Mystique is her adoptive mother, allows her to escape without punishment (*X-Men: The Animated Series*, "Days of Future Past, Part 2," S01E12, 1993).

benefited. For instance, in the "Days of Future Past" comic story (Claremont and Byrne 1981, #141–42), the main character who travels back in time and into a younger version of herself, in order to prevent a political assassination by Mystique that caused a dystopian future, is Kitty. She is sent back by Rachel. The climactic battle sequence takes place between the X-Men, led by Storm, and the Brotherhood of Evil Mutants, led by Mystique. Mystique's female partner, Destiny, fires the key gunshot but it misses its target due to Kitty's intervention. *All* of the key roles are played by women. In the corresponding animated series episodes (Julia Lane Lewald, Robert Skir, and Marty Isenberg 1993, S01E11–12), though, the main character who travels back in time is Bishop, as noted a male mutant of color. He is sent back by Forge, also a male mutant of color. White male Cyclops, rather than Storm, leads the X-Men. Mystique leads the Brotherhood, is fought by Cajun male mutant Gambit, and is allowed to escape by Rogue upon Rogue's realization that Mystique is her adoptive mother. Neither Kitty nor Destiny appears at all. Still a leader, Mystique is no longer portrayed with a female life partner. Storm is no longer portrayed as a leader. Such moves would occur at an even higher rate in the later Hollywood films. While some welcome diversity in terms of race, national origin, and disability is added in with the roles played by Bishop and Forge, these characters simply replaced female characters.

With the animated "Phoenix" and "Dark Phoenix" stories, the changes were smaller but significant for the character of Jean. In the animated "Phoenix" saga, Wolverine replaces Storm—who is not present—in wishing Jean luck in piloting the shuttle back to earth and sacrificing herself. Jean emerges from the water declaring that she is Phoenix, as in the comics. The Phoenix is clearly a separate entity from Jean in the cartoon, speaking through her and speaking of her in the third person (Mark Edward Edens and Michael Edens 1994, S03E29–33). This disentangles Jean's gender and her sexual awakening with the Phoenix's lust for killing. Second, while in the comics "Dark Phoenix" saga Jean commits genocide, in the animated series she does not. As Dark Phoenix, she still consumes a star, but there are no people around to suffer the consequences. Together, Xavier and Jean "bind" the power of the Phoenix, with him commenting that "the strength of her mind is truly awesome." As in the comics, Jean tells Scott she loves him and sacrifices herself for fear the Phoenix cannot be controlled. But then in the cartoon, the Phoenix takes a little bit of life force from each of her friends and resurrects her (Jan Strnad, Steven Levi, Larry Parr, and Brooks Wachtel 1994, S03E37–40). All of this has the effect of reinforcing the familial bonds of the team, as well as rehabilitating and strengthening the character of Jean.

Rogue generally fares well in the animated series, but one episode streamlines her past in ways that erase some of what made her character so distinctive. "A Rogue's Tale" (Robert Skir and Marty Isenberg 1994, S02E22) begins with Rogue having strange visions. Apparently, Xavier blocked Rogue's past out of her mind, such that she doesn't know that Mystique was her adoptive mother, nor why she is having visions of herself (reluctantly) absorbing Carol Danvers/Ms. Marvel's powers. Rogue discovers all of this, then accuses Mystique of using her as a mere weapon, ending with "I ain't your daughter." Jean enters Rogue's mind and sees Rogue and Ms. Marvel as two separate entities, and Rogue puts "Ms. Marvel" in a cage in her mind. Rogue then visits the actual comatose Carol in the hospital and touches her face, seemingly bringing her out of her coma. While these changes probably served to cement Rogue as a beloved central character, it deprives Mystique of nuance and erases Destiny such that Rogue's adoptive family is no longer queer, it deprives Mystique and Rogue's relationship of its

**Figure 4.2** Together (clockwise from left), Professor Xavier, Storm, Cyclops, Wolverine, Rogue, Beast, and Gambit give some of their "life force" to Jean Grey, center, in her old Marvel Girl uniform (*X-Men: The Animated Series*, "The Dark Phoenix Saga, Part 4," S03E17, 1995).

complexity, and it deprives Rogue of her chosen journey from villain to hero (1982–83, #158–71).

Rogue's journey and her character engendered very positive fan letters beginning in the late 1980s. Indeed, love for Rogue was a mainstay of the letter columns through the 1990s, with many citing her as their favorite character. For instance, "Things I like . . . Rogue going from the least trusted to one of the core members of the group" (Tom Quinn, *Uncanny X-Men* #230). Many letters expressed sadness for her plight of being unable to touch, and happiness at her burgeoning relationship with Gambit (although a few wanted her to be with a clone of Magneto, Joseph, instead). As noted, by this point the authorship and content of the letters had changed quite a bit. When once the letters were split between male and female writers, now they were almost all male. Also, when once the letters were split between rhapsodic love and occasional hate for characters and their relationships, now they centered mostly on plot points and on art. Sometimes there were questions about male characters such as Magneto, Xavier, Bishop, and Sabretooth, and only rarely was there mention of female characters other than Rogue. Rogue's sexualization and her inability to touch the men in her life, coupled with her brashness and sweetness, was a potent combination for 1990s comic readers. She was a mainstay of the animated series, which may have boosted her comic popularity as well.

Anecdotally, it appears that some X-Men comics fans came to the title through the animated series. Several letters in the mid- to late-1990s comics attest to this, such as, "When I first watched the cartoon, I was so happy that such a fantastic cartoon had finally come to Singapore. And then I started to collect X-Men comics" (Jill Chia, *X-Men* #44), and "I've been watching the X-Men cartoon series for almost three years now, but didn't really get into the comic books til last April, and now I'm hooked" (Amy Dayton, *X-Men* #58). That these two letters were from female readers made them outliers in the universe of printed letters at this time. These fans may have been within the target group for the animated series, but not for the comics which were still pitched toward the male, older, white demographic observed in comic shops.

In the late 1990s and into the 2000s, the art style of sexualized females and muscular males remained. There were twice as many male characters as female characters, and most of the characters were white (Darowski 2014b: 137–38). This artist-driven era would see more action-oriented plots and crossover events. A few letter writers noted that the feeling of family and character development in general seemed to be lacking. One asserted that it had been so "for about a hundred issues" (Darrell Walker, *Uncanny X-Men* #309). Such decisions were mutually reinforcing with the audience of readers frequenting local comic shops and thus still being marketed to by comics producers. The core female characters were cycling in and out of main teams. Jean and Scott were famously and finally married upon Jean's proposal to him, a move that elicited (according to the editors) "a ton" of positive letters from fans. They quit the X-Men, then returned, and Scott was "killed." Excalibur disbanded, and Kitty returned to and then left the X-Men. Rogue briefly led the field team, but had to step down due to her inability to control her powers (not unusual for female characters). She and Storm became "X-Treme X-Men" in a separate title of that name. Then she was depowered for a time (also not unusual for female characters) and could touch people. More new characters were introduced, some spinoff titles were canceled and new ones begun, such as the alternate-universe continuity-free *Ultimate X-Men* which initially outsold *Uncanny X-Men*.

The speculative bubbles of the early 1990s burst. The 10,000 comic shops of 1993 would decrease to about 4,000 by 1996 and about 2,300 by 2002 (Duncan and Smith 2009: 77; Gabilliet 2010: 152). X-books were still among the top ten sellers in the direct market in the late 1990s and early 2000s, but a smaller number of books selling a smaller number of copies. Marvel filed for bankruptcy in 1996, due in part to an internal power struggle and in part to having expanded too much before the crash.

X-Men fandom would be sustained in the 2000s through the narrowed audience for the comics who would support star writers' turns on the titles, through bookstore sales of trade paperbacks collecting comics issues, and also through the (re-)expansion of the potential audience through Hollywood films that differently characterized the X-Women. The female X-Men in the comics are smart, powerful, kind, independent, and nuanced. But in the films, these characters are more contained and domesticated, with their main plot points positioning them as adjuncts to white, male, heterosexual characters and their development.

## The 2000s: New and Astonishing X-Men, and transitions to film

The first five core *X-Men* films both conform to and exacerbate the gendered and raced lopsidedness of American-produced films in general: *X-Men* (2000), *X2: X-Men United* (2003), *X-Men: The Last Stand* (2006), *X-Men: First Class* (2011), and *X-Men: Days of Future Past* (2014).[10] Due to the 1993 agreement between Marvel and Fox, the latter has film rights to the characters. Three of the five films have some basis in six specific comic arcs. In each of these six arcs, the main characters and/or heroes of the stories are women: namely, Kitty, Rogue, Mystique, Jean, and Storm. The corresponding films, however, center both quantitatively and qualitatively on three male, white characters: Wolverine, Xavier, and Magneto. And one female character, Mystique, is nude without any apparent narrative justification. No film need be totally bound by its source material, but when the thrust of adaptation is the same five times—diverse female characters replaced by, or shunted aside by, white male ones—in an era in which we are perhaps more aware than ever of the inequalities of representation in various media, this should give us pause.

The first film, *X-Men* (David Hayter, Tom DeSanto, and Bryan Singer 2000) stars Scott, Jean, Logan, and Storm. They are wearing black leather uniforms rather than varying colors of spandex, in stark contrast (especially for the female characters) to their comic counterparts. This change would be mirrored in the 2001–04 comics, retitled *New X-Men* under writer Grant Morrison and artist Frank Quitely. They would retain the core characters Scott, Jean, Logan, and Hank/Beast, while adding scantily clad and possibly reformed villain Emma Frost as well as a host of new students. There are no female friendships to speak of in this book. One typical exchange between "good girl" Jean and "bad girl" Emma has the former ask, "What makes you such a bitch, Emma?" and the latter reply, "Breeding, darling." These two main female characters in this comic series, very different from one another in personality and dress and both compelling, are positioned in a love triangle with Scott such that their relationships to him foster their negative interactions with each other. Jean in the films is positioned in a triangle as well, between Scott and Wolverine such that they argue over her as if she is a prize. This latter triangle, as noted, existed in only "two panels" in the comics in the 1980s, was expanded in the animated series in the 1990s (Skir 2005: 23), and then was amplified in the films. The TV and film Wolverine is much less respectful of the Jean/Scott relationship, and Jean seems more uncertain about her choice to be with Scott. Most of Jean's scenes in the film are with Logan, Scott, or both.

There are elements of Jean's characterizations in the films that undermine historic stereotypes of women and the lack of female characters in high-powered occupations. For instance, Jean is introduced on film as a doctor, and seems to have taken on some research and medical work performed in the comics by Hank McCoy/Beast. She testifies before Congress about mutant registration, she contributes to giving the viewer some exposition along with Professor X, and she uses her telepathic and telekinetic powers. Yet Jean's powers in the films grow, as in the comics, to seemingly unstable levels. In the second film *X2: X-Men United* (Michael Dougherty, Dan Harris, David Hayter, Bryan Singer, and Zak Penn 2003), both Scott and Logan comment that Jean's power has increased, which worries them. Later, she tells Scott "something's wrong" as her eyes look fiery. By the end of the film, she looks fiery all over. In the movie's climax, a dam breaks and the X-Men's plane is in danger, so she sacrifices herself to hold back the water and lift the plane, as she seemingly disintegrates in the water. This is similar to the comic's and animated series' "Phoenix Saga." In the film, Scott and Logan cry and hug, and Kurt prays. Professor X tells them that they have to respect that "she made a choice." She is the hero, although one could also argue that her sacrifice was meant to further the development of male characters here more than her own.

*The Last Stand* (Simon Kinberg and Zak Penn 2006) undercuts Jean's heroism.[11] It seems at first to parallel the comics' and animated series' "Dark Phoenix Saga," in which she is possessed by the Phoenix and is manipulated by villains, pushing her toward increasing instability and violence. In both of these media, the X-Men stand with her, she professes her love for Scott, and kills herself to save the universe. The film, by contrast, has Professor X explain that the Phoenix is a dark part of Jean's own "dual personality," "a beast" that is "all desire and joy and rage," which he has worked to suppress since he met her as a child. The Jean of the last two films, it seems, was tightly controlled by Xavier, for which Logan berates him. But once she breaks those controls, she kills Scott and asks Logan to kill her but backpedals because she likes the way she is feeling. She then destroys her parents' house, kills Professor X, and joins Magneto against the X-Men. As Zingsheim says, "The narrative offers Jean space to explore and advance in her powers. [Yet] rather than suggesting the empowerment of femininities, this exploration demonstrates the risk of unsupervised sexual feminine subjects"

(2011: 234). At the end, Logan endures extreme physical pain to approach Jean and tell her he is willing to die "not for them" but for her. She asks him again to kill her, saying "Save me." He tells her he loves her, and kills her. This Jean Grey is not the agent of her own sacrifice, and she is not concerned about saving the world, but rather, herself. Further, her role and her agency in the previous two films are undermined, because this film tells us that Xavier has been controlling her powers and her personality for years (as in the 1960s comics). Logan rather than Jean takes center stage. The comic arc for which Jean is best known, in which she fights against an evil force possessing her in order to save her friends and everyone else, is turned on its head to become yet another stereotypical tale about how women are irrationally, destructively emotional and must be controlled by men.

Kitty and Rogue in the films are not dissimilar from Jean. On the one hand, they embody the kind of determination, physical strength, and care for others typical of a superhero. But they too are positioned in a love triangle, so the viewer tends to evaluate them on the basis of their heteronormative relationships rather than as individuals. Rogue is Mystique (and Destiny)'s sassy and headstrong adoptive daughter in the comics, who leaves behind a life of villainy to join the X-Men. In all media, she is haunted by the destructive power of her touch. In an episode of the animated series from 1993 ("The Cure" [S01E09] by Mark Edward Edens) and a comic issue from 1998 (*Uncanny X-Men* #359 by Stephen Seagle, Joe Kelly, Chris Bachalo, and Ryan Benjamin), she so longs to be able to touch freely that she strongly considers the mutant "cure." In the animated version, Wolverine and Storm both dismiss the idea of mutants becoming "normal." But Rogue approaches a doctor (Mystique in disguise), saying, "I don't want to live my whole life without knowing what it's like to touch another human being." Later, though, after using her powers to save Jean, she tells the doctor, "There ain't no cure for who you are. I am my powers and the good they can do, for my friends and the whole world. I reckon maybe I can live with that after all." In the

**Figure 4.3** *X-Men: The Last Stand* (2006)'s adaptation of the Dark Phoenix Saga foregrounds Wolverine (Hugh Jackman) and stereotypes Jean (Famke Janssen). By contrast, the animated series' "Dark Phoenix Saga" in Figure 4.2 emphasizes the X-Men family and Jean's heroism.

comic, the narration reads, "She's led a life of lonely isolation, denying herself life's most basic joys. But having kissed the love of her life [Gambit] . . . having convinced herself to give mouth-to-mouth to her fallen teammate Joseph [a clone of Magneto] . . . she knows how good it felt to touch. And God help her, she wants more." In this version too, Mystique tries to talk her out of it with reference to the mutant metaphor: "How could my own child come to be so filled with self-hatred as to try and change what she is? . . . If someone had invented a ray in the midst of the civil rights movement to turn black skin white, would you have championed its use as well?" Rogue tells her it is not the same thing, and seems to move forward with her plan. But thinking of how such a machine might be used on mutants against their will, she destroys the "cure" machine.

The films focus not on Rogue's transition to heroism, nor her triumph in her struggle to deal with her inability to touch loved ones, nor her self-sacrifice. Rather, her prominence decreases over the course of the films as her arc increasingly centers on her insecurities about her boyfriend, such that she seeks out and obtains, rather than refusing, the "cure" as she had in the animated series and in the comics. In part, she feels pushed to do this through the love triangle between Rogue, her boyfriend Bobby Drake/Iceman—that is, not Gambit, a relationship that comics and animated series fans had praised for years—and Kitty Pryde. This triangle had never occurred in the main comic series. It had, however, in the parallel "Ultimate" universe of comics. These comics, launched in 2001, were meant as an entry point for new (or returning) readers and were unburdened by continuity, so the characters had numerous differences from their usual incarnations. The writer who launched the series, Mark Millar, was not an *X-Men* reader and was hired in part because of that. He based the *Ultimate X-Men* comic characters on their incarnations in the *X-Men* film of 2000 (Lien-Cooper 2002). As written by Brian K. Vaughan and drawn by Brandon Peterson in 2004, "Ultimate" Bobby and Rogue are a couple; they go ice skating; Rogue is troubled by her inability to touch; Bobby kisses Kitty and Rogue sees; Rogue punches Kitty; Rogue goes off with Gambit (#46–50). The 2006 film *The Last Stand* filmed a scene (later deleted) with Bobby kissing Kitty while the two are ice skating, with Rogue watching. Even without the kiss, the film highlights the romantic tension between the three. Kitty and Rogue, two beloved characters and stars of the comic series in the 1980s and 1990s, are put in the same space not to be central characters who will work together heroically, but merely to become romantic rivals on opposite sides of a male character. As Madrid states, "The implication is that no matter how powerful a woman is, she needs the love of a man to complete her" (2009: 57).

Despite her prominent role in the comic stories on which the films are based, and despite her starring role in the concurrent animated series *X-Men Evolution*, Kitty's presence in the films of the 2000s is greatly diminished such that she is barely on screen at all. She was the main character in three of the six comic arcs from which the films draw: Claremont and Byrne's "Days of Future Past" (adapted into the film of the same name) in which she time travels and prevents an assassination in hopes of avoiding a dystopic future; Claremont and Anderson's *God Loves Man Kills* (adapted into *X2*) in which she questions the humanity of those who would discriminate against mutants; and part of Joss Whedon and John Cassaday's 2004–08 run on *Astonishing*

*X-Men* (adapted in part into *The Last Stand*) in which she opposes a mutant cure and later saves the earth through self-sacrifice. When Whedon was negotiating to write the comic, one of his demands was that he be able to use Kitty, his favorite X-character who had been out of the team for some time previous, and who was in large part his inspiration for Buffy the Vampire Slayer (see Chapter 5). It is clear that the influence went the other way as well. The portrayal of Kitty in the 2000–04 animated series, *X-Men: Evolution* feels quite similar to Whedon's 1997–2003 *Buffy the Vampire Slayer*. *Evolution* producer Boyd Kirkland said, "I plead guilty to being a big Buffy fan. . . . I always thought it had many similarities to what we were trying to do with this show" (Denaill 2004).[12] Mark Millar, speaking of the concurrent *Ultimate X-Men*, said the comic series was "competing with Buffy" as well (Lien-Cooper 2002).

Regardless of Buffy's popularity at the time and the similarities between them, Kitty's much-touted brilliance, bravery, martial arts skills, resourcefulness, talents with computers, strong female friendships, on-and-off romance with Piotr/Colossus, and her mother-daughter relationship with Storm are not part of her on-screen characterization. Neither are her initial fear of some mutants nor her teenage hotheadedness, both of which she works through in the comics. Rather, her most memorable moments involve her calling the character Juggernaut a "dickhead" after he calls her a "bitch," and her ice skating with Bobby in *The Last Stand*. Rather than holding "in her hands the fate of mutantkind, of humanity, of the earth itself" as in the "Days of Future Past" comic story in which she stars, the film version has her holding

**Figure 4.4** No longer the protagonist or hero of the story as in the comics' version of "Days of Future Past," Kitty Pryde (Ellen Page) holds her hands around Wolverine (Hugh Jackman)'s head in the film version of *Days of Future Past* (2014).

her hands shakily around Wolverine's head for a few minutes (*Days of Future Past* by Jane Goldman, Simon Kinberg, and Matthew Vaughn 2014).

These changes in personality and this sidelining in importance are also issues with Mystique and Storm. As noted, both in the comics are team leaders, both are mother figures, and both have been written and read as interested in male as well as female partners. While both characters take part in the films and carry weight in representing superheroic (and at some turns, villainous) women on screen for huge international audiences, both play much different roles from their comic counterparts. This conforms to the ways in which women are quantitatively underrepresented in the media, particularly as leaders and mentors, and are more often cast as supporting rather than central characters.

It is clear that neither Storm nor Mystique is a leader in any of the films. In the first one, *X-Men*, Storm says about twenty sentences, one of which is about how she can't control her power with precision. This is in contrast to the second comic issue in which she appears, saying, "I have total control over my abilities" (Claremont, Wein, and Cockrum 1975, #94). In *X2*, Storm's number of spoken lines is about the same. She teaches a class, ably pilots a plane, goes over a plan with the other X-Men, and plays a pivotal role in saving the day by freeing Professor X from mind control. In *The Last Stand,* perhaps because actor Halle Berry said that she would return "if they could give Storm a little bit more to do," (Superhero Hype 2003), Storm does have a more prominent role. She saves Wolverine in what turns out to be a battle simulation, she takes Professor X's place as headmistress of the School per his wishes, she pilots a plane, she fights hand-to-hand, and she uses her weather powers. She argues with Wolverine more than once, and strongly states that there's no reason to seek "a cure" for being a mutant because "there's nothing to cure." However, even though Cyclops is not present, she does not assume leadership of the X-Men as in the comics. Rather, Wolverine seems to be leading the team as well as the film.

Storm is not included at all in the fourth film, *First Class* (Ashley Miller, Zack Stentz, Jane Goldman, Matthew Vaughn, Sheldon Turner, and Brian Singer 2011) and her presence in the fifth film, *Days of Future Past*, is quite limited. In the comic version of "Days of Future Past," she leads the X-Men; in the animated series version, she is present but does not lead them; in the film version, she is basically silent cannon fodder. Worse, in the extended battle sequence in "the future" at the end of *Days of Future Past*, all of the nonwhite mutants outside die protecting all of the white mutants who are inside an armored room. Meanwhile, in "the past," every mutant is white. This trope, of characters of color being the first or only characters to die across many forms of media, feels particularly uncomfortable in a series grounded in the value of diversity and the wrongheadedness of prejudice. That Storm had been such a prominent character of color for forty years in the comics, and was featured in both animated series, makes her marginalization in this film all the more problematic.

Parallel to Storm, Mystique was shown in the films to have superpowers, to be able to fight, and to be a strategic thinker, but the elements from the comics that make her particularly special are just not translated to the big screen. Mystique in the films is the leader of neither the Brotherhood of Evil Mutants nor the Freedom Force, as in the comics. Rather, Magneto is the strategist and leader. In the first three films, she is framed as Magneto's partner in crime and romance. In the latter two, she is paired with Hank McCoy/Beast and then Magneto again. None of the films explores or even references the relationships between Mystique and Destiny, Mystique and Rogue, or Mystique and Nightcrawler. But she is also a capable, smart, and physically formidable subject.

However, both actresses who played the character were nude but for a few strategically placed scaly prosthetics, as opposed to the Mystique of the comics and the animated series, who usually wears a long, white, sleeveless dress. This cannot but position her as an object at the same time: something to look at, instead of someone to root for or identify with. The first film's special makeup designer, Gordon Smith, described how he was told to deal with the character: "The director slamm[ed] his fist down on the table screaming, 'I want her nude! I want her nude! I want her nude!'" (Metropolitan Museum of Art 2008). Perhaps because the actors could not possibly have the proportions and poses of their 1990s–2000s comics counterparts, Mystique's nudity was a way of sexing up the film and providing a counterpoint to the others' plain black leather uniforms. Perhaps discomfort with strong females prompted such a counter balance of exaggerated sexualization (see Brown 2004 and 2011, Cocca 2014a, Madrid 2009). In the case of Mystique, some viewers might identify with her strength, some might note that such strength coexists with posing in a sexually appealing way, and some might gaze at the female body with prurient interest and care little for the actual character; others might feel turned off and taken out of the story by the unnecessary nudity, and a last group might have all of these reactions at different points in the *X-Men* films (Cocca 2016).

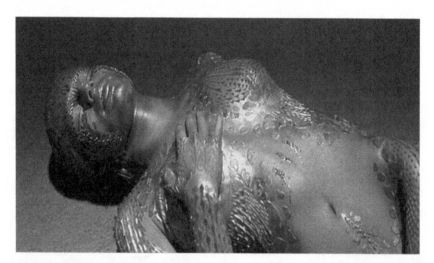

**Figure 4.5** Rebecca Romijn as Mystique, nude, in *X-Men* (2000). Compare to Figure 4.1, in which the animated Mystique wears the same long white dress as she does across years of comics.

In the first two movies, the nude Mystique capably carries out much of the villains' plans single-handedly, prompting Wolverine to observe, "She's good," and Magneto agrees, implying they are a couple, "You have no idea." This changes in the third film: she is "cured" when she throws herself in front of Magneto, and is then rejected by him because she is "no longer one of us . . . such a shame . . . she was so beautiful." There is only one other glimpse of her, turning over Magneto's location to the government because, as the white, male president notes, "Hell hath no fury like a woman scorned." Not only does she barely appear in the film, but reducing this multifaceted character to a "beautiful" woman "scorned" who would turn on another mutant underrepresents, diminishes, and stereotypes her (and to an extent, all women) at once. Like the character of Jean, Mystique is built up in the first two movies and taken down in the third.

In *First Class* and *Days of Future Past*, Mystique is de-aged, romantically interested in Hank, and positioned in the middle of the feud between Erik Lehnsherr/Magneto and Charles Xavier. Both of these men try to secure her affection and loyalty to their ideologies, and both treat her as a much younger and immature character even though the film credits state that Mystique is only two years younger than Xavier. The second of these films frames Mystique as a young, confused, emotional girl, caught between two men in a star-crossed bromance who mostly talk about her as if she is a mere object. This is in sharp contrast to the *Days of Future Past* comic, in which Mystique is the determined leader of the Brotherhood of Evil Mutants, who plans an assassination that is averted due to Kitty pushing Destiny's bullet off course. One could argue that in the movie version it is she who makes the "right" choice not to carry out the assassination, and that the story is focused on her as she comes to that choice. But it is also the case that the entire film is based around four white men (Xavier, Erik, Logan, and Hank) convincing her that her assumptions and actions are wrong. Her role is central, but at the same time carries forth the historical underrepresentation and stereotyping of female characters.

In short, female characters central to the original X-Men comic arcs have repeatedly had their parts (and in one case, her clothes) diminished in the films. This includes having two characters, Storm and Mystique, who were historically written as team leaders, no longer occupying those roles and being devoid of their comic characterizations as queer mothers. It also involves having four other female characters—Mystique, Jean, Rogue, and Kitty—positioned in love triangles, thus being characterized primarily in romantic relation to males. Rather than subjects of their own destinies as main characters, the women are constructed more as objects of control and as side characters. They also conform to stereotypes of race, gender, and sexuality, as race goes unacknowledged and each white woman is presented as interested in and an object of romance with white men.

However, given that most heroic figures of fiction have been written as male, it should not be understated that these female characters demonstrate for massive audiences that power and heroism are not gendered traits that can be performed only by males. Increasingly vocal, diverse, and organized fans would pressure comics companies for more.

## Conclusion: Rebooted comics, rebooted films

By the mid-to-late 2000s, the five most prominent female X-Men characters were not really in the core X-books. They would return in the 2010s. This was likely in response to the movement among groups of more diverse comics fans to push back against the hypermasculinization and hypersexualization lingering from the 1990s. Such preferences have been displayed through increased purchases of non-mainstream digital comics and trade paperbacks in bookstores, through direct contact with producers via social media, and through attendance and conversation at comics conventions. The large comics companies have increasingly sought to monetize that discontent by offering new portrayals of favorite characters as well as scaling down hyperbolic art-driven books in favor of more writer-driven ones. But they do so with caution and at the margins, not wanting to alienate their direct market fan base who had become accustomed to the status quo.

The main title, *X-Men*, was relaunched in 2013 with a new #1 and the first all-female team: Storm, Rogue, Jubilee, Kitty, Psylocke, and Rachel. Sales for this issue were up 400 percent not only from the previous issue but also from the previous year's average. It also outsold the previous *X-Men* #1 from 2010 by tens of thousands. The 2013 book by Brian Wood (who was also writing the Leia-centric *Star Wars* series for Dark Horse) and several different illustrators initially suffered from stereotyping its female characters. Namely, the women disagreed with each other quite a bit while protecting a baby. Kitty and Rogue were written out of the title and new and younger characters swapped in. Jean returned in 2012's *All New X-Men* by Brian Michael Bendis and Stuart Immonen, when she and the other four original teenage X-Men time traveled to the present. No longer close to being the youngest team member, "Professor" Kitty takes them under her wing. Storm is the Mohawked headmistress of the school and also starred in an eleven-issue eponymous solo title by Greg Pak and Victor Ibanez. These books centered the female characters as leaders, friends, and lovers, reminiscent of the 1970s–80s writer-driven era of the books that preceded both the artist-driven era of the 1990s and the women's non-centrality in the films of the 2000s and 2010s. Initial reactions to all of these were quite positive and stressed the importance of characterization.[13] The stories of these two books and the *Uncanny* title ended in late 2015 with *Uncanny X-Men* #600, as Marvel launched its "All-New All-Different" initiative.

"All-New All-Different" Marvel encompassed a launch or relaunch of about seventy books, including four X-titles and two others with X-Men in them. As has been the case since 1963, except for Marjorie Liu writing twenty issues of *Astonishing X-Men* in 2012–13 and G. Willow Wilson writing four issues of *X-Men* in 2015, the main ongoing X-titles are written and drawn solely by men.[14] Such creative teams on these books as well as others, along with a demographic accounting of the characters across titles, caused some fans to tweet that rather than "All-New All-Different" the titles should be branded as virtually "All-White All-Male." The female X-characters are highlighted, albeit mostly separated, in the relaunched titles.

The 2016 film, *X-Men: Apocalypse,* features Jean Grey and Storm as well as Psylocke and Jubilee, diversifying somewhat in terms of gender and race. Storm and Psylocke are two of Apocalypse's "Four Horsemen" along with white males Angel and Magneto. Director Brian Singer (the same director who demanded that Mystique be nude in the first film) describes why he chose these four to act as members of Apocalypse's "cult," saying,

> a cult has traditionally four factions to it . . . a political faction, and I'd always felt Magneto could fill those shoes . . . a military faction, so Archangel could fill those shoes . . . a youth faction, those that you're trying to seduce and grow into your cult . . . [and a] sexual component because cult leaders tend to sexualize their position and have sex with half the people in their cult. (Dyce 2016)

Magneto and Angel are political and military leaders, while Storm and Psylocke's roles are to "seduce" and "have sex" with others. The dividing line of gender in *X-Men* films remains a prominent one.

Longtime X-Writer Chris Claremont notes that the structure of the company has changed since he was writing *X-Men* stories in the 1970s, when he was "left alone" by editors and corporate management. Now, rather, "a group of creators and editors [plan out] what will happen for the next two years" and those "editors are not only caretakers of a creative arc that runs back forty-five years, but are also responsible to the management structure of a multibillion dollar corporation, Marvel and by extension Disney, to influences that didn't exist while I was doing the series" (Comic Shenanigans 2015). Film licensee Fox is in the mix as well. As has been true since the first *X-Men* film, "Marvels' plan is to maximize box-office marketing and predictability by making the central characters as commercial as possible, which may not be critically aligned with character complexity" and also has an eye toward "long-term licensing potential" (McAllister, Gordon, and Jancovich 2006: 111, 114). Their current definition of "commercial" seems to be, as it was with their previous films, tilting the X-universe quantitatively and qualitatively toward its white and male characters without taking into account that in the 2010s television shows and movies with more diverse casts are earning more at the box office and are higher in the ratings so important to advertisers (Hunt and Ramon 2015). The push and pull over the X-Women characters across decades and across media has yielded representations of them both as clever, compassionate, powerful leaders as well as domesticated, diminished, and sexualized objects of male desire.

The "mutant metaphor," though, is quite malleable. It could easily be used on the big screen and on the small page to center the outsiders—in terms of race, gender, ethnicity, sexuality, religion, etc.—it claims to represent. This formula has sold a large number of comics on newsstands to a diverse mass audience, in local comic book shops to a more narrow one, and in digital and trade paperback form to a more diverse audience again. Fans can support diversity among creators and characters by communicating such to film producers and by using their dollars as well, as they have done in the comics sphere to varying degrees of success. The next chapter analyzes another example of outsiders with broad appeal, but one that started on the big screen and transitioned to the small screen and to comics: *Buffy the Vampire Slayer* and her friends.

# Notes

1   "My name is Ororo Munroe. My name is Ororo Iqadi T'Challa. I am a woman, a mutant, a thief, an X-Man, a lover, a wife, a queen. I am all these things. I am Storm, and for me, there are no such things as limits" (Christopher Yost (w) and Diogenes Neves (p) 2009, *X-Men: Worlds Apart* #4). Portions of this chapter appeared in Cocca 2016. Reprinted with permission.

2   Darowski is an example of this, "to the reader at the time the Dark Phoenix was a morality tale . . . with implications that sexual awakening in women has dire consequences unless removed" (2014b: 82). Fawaz offers an alternate reading, "The Dark Phoenix Saga is better understood as a frustrated lament over the failures of left world-making and alternative kinship projects in the 1970s rather than a conservative critique of feminist politics" (2011: 387).

3   The Phoenix splits into five parts, possessing three men and two women. Scott Summers is one, and thinks, "This is what Jean felt like" (Brian Michael Bendis and Olivier Coipel 2012, *Avengers vs. X-Men* #11).

4   John Jackson Miller at Comichron computes this figure for 1986–87s *Watchmen*. The higher end of this percentage probably holds for *Uncanny X-Men*. In seven of the twelve months of Capital City distributor numbers versus postal service numbers that Miller tallies for *Watchmen*, an *X-Men* title outsold it in the direct market (with the "Mutant Massacre"-"Fall of the Mutants" era stories). http://www.comichron. com/special/watchmensales.html. He says that *Watchmen* #12 had orders of 34,000 through Capital City and *Uncanny X-Men* had about double that, so around 70,000. Postal service numbers indicate that *Uncanny X-Men* at that time printed about 600,000 and sold through about 400,000.

5   See, for instance, decades apart, *New Mutants* #45 in 1986, *All New X-Men* #13 in 2013.

6   *X-Men* was renamed *Uncanny X-Men* with issue #142.

7   She doesn't change history; she creates an alternate timeline. Much later in *Excalibur*, Rachel Summers and Kitty will end that dystopian future ("Days of Futures Yet to Come," 1993, #67). Still later, Kitty and Piotr's daughter in the future, Christina Pryde, stars in another sequel, the miniseries "Years of Future Past" (2015).

8   On Kitty, see, for instance, #19 and #24's subplot with the alien Sat Yr 9 impersonating Courtney Ross. Penciler Alan Davis said, "Although I knew Chris had some plan for Sat Yr 9 to corrupt Kitty and that the various cross-time versions of Saturnyne were attracted to Kitty, I had no idea what, if any, the goal of this relationship was to be. I just played it as a lesbian affair" (Posted January 7, 2006 at: http://www.alandavis-forum.com/viewtopic.php?f=3&t=59). Some fans read into Kitty and (Piotr's sister) Illyana Rasputin/Magik's strong bond as well, with some calling it "Katyana," particularly because of Kitty's ability to house and wield the weapon that manifests Illyana's soul and magical power, the Soulsword.

9   This was the second attempt at an animated series: the first, *Pryde of the X-Men*, focused on Kitty, Storm, Dazzler, Colossus, Nightcrawler, Wolverine, and Cyclops, but did not get past the pilot stage.

10   *X-Men* (2000) and *X-Men: First Class* (2011) are not closely based on specific comic
stories, with both serving as origin stories for the X-Men and the latter going further
afield from comic portrayals. *X2: X-Men United* (2003) is based on the graphic novel
*God Loves, Man Kills* (1982), with a dash of the "Phoenix Saga" (*X-Men* #101–08,
1976–77). *X-Men: The Last Stand* (2006) is based on the "Gifted" arc (*Astonishing
X-Men* Vol. 3 #1–6, 2004), as well as on the "Dark Phoenix Saga" (*X-Men* #129–38,
1980) with a little bit of "Power Play" (*Uncanny X-Men* #359, 1998). *X-Men: Days of
Future Past* (2014) is based on the story of the same name (*X-Men* #141 and *Uncanny
X-Men* #142, 1981).

11   For examples of negative reviews and comments, see almost 1,900 of them at: http://
www.imdb.com/title/tt0376994/reviews. Comic Vine hosts a forum thread entitled,
"Why did you hate *X-Men: The Last Stand*?" at http://www.comicvine.com/x-men/
4060-3173/forums/why-did-you-hate-x-men-the-last-stand-1463157/ and another
entitled "Why does everyone hate *X-Men: The Last Stand*?" at http://www.comicvine.
com/x-men/4060-3173/forums/why-does-everyone-hate-x-men-the-last-stand-555062/.
See IFanboy's podcast review and fan comments from 2006: http://ifanboy.com/
podcasts/x-men-the-last-stand/. Jason Adams' 2014 review, "Awfully Good: *X-Men:
The Last Stand*," and the comments at http://www.joblo.com/movie-news/awfully-
good-x-men-the-last-stand, show that even several years later, fan ire had not cooled
much. For a more academic critique, see Zingsheim 2011: 234–35.

12   The *Evolution* series is not discussed at length here due to this chapter's focus on
storylines that crossed comics, television, and film.

13   See, e.g., *Comic Book Resources* Forum at: http://community.comicbookresources.
com/showthread.php?43263-All-New-X-men-Worth-Picking-Up, and a roundup of
reviews at http://comicbookroundup.com/comic-books/reviews/marvel-comics/all-
new-x-men/1.

14   Marie Severin drew several covers of the main title in the early 1970s, Jan Duursema
drew a number of issues of *X-Factor* in the mid-1990s, and Marguerite Bennett wrote
the five-issue miniseries *Years of Future Past* in 2015, but they did not write or draw
the interiors of the main title.

# 5

# "Slayers. Every One of Us": Buffy the Vampire Slayer[1]

*Buffy the Vampire Slayer's* creator Joss Whedon has described her origin as follows,

> The first thing I ever thought of when I thought of 'Buffy: The Movie' was the little blonde girl who goes into a dark alley and gets killed in every horror movie. The idea of Buffy was to subvert that idea, that image, and create someone who was a hero where she had always been a victim. That element of surprise, of genre-busting, is very much at the heart of both the movie and the series. ("Welcome to the Hellmouth" [S01E01] episode commentary, DVD)

The heart of *Buffy* was that its main character was "just a girl" who was also a superheroic and supernaturally strong vampire slayer, and would be portrayed as both ordinary and extraordinary.

*Buffy's* 1997–2003 television run would pave the way not only for a comic series that continued from where the show left off, but also for an explosion of other quippy young heroines on television, in film, and in comics. In terms of the other characters in this book, during Buffy's television and comics run, *Batgirl: Year One* and a few animated series portrayed Barbara as a petite teen Batgirl, and the very Buffy-like Stephanie Brown would become Robin in 2004 and then Batgirl in 2009. A TV series called *Amazon*, in development but not picked up, would have starred a teen Wonder Woman. Dozens of *Star Wars* novels starred teen Jaina Solo as the universe-saving "Sword of the Jedi." The *X-Men: Evolution* animated series centered on the heroes' high school years, with its producer admitting to its similarities to *Buffy*, and the writer of the *Ultimate X-Men* comic would say that his main competition was *Buffy*. And Kamala Khan would become the new ordinary and extraordinary teen Ms. Marvel in the number one digital selling comic for Marvel in the mid-2010s (see Chapter 6).

As Wonder Woman, Barbara Gordon/Batgirl, and Princess Leia, in particular, were associated closely with Second Wave feminism, Buffy was grounded in the Third Wave of feminism. Like these Second Wave predecessors, Buffy unsettles gendered boundaries as a "woman warrior" who displays strength and capability equal to any male hero. Like them, she embodies white, heterosexual, and middle (to upper) class privilege. Like them, she was created by and mostly written by men. What is different about Buffy is her origination during a time in the 1990s when her comic counterparts, as noted, were hypersexualized and hyperviolent. Even when those characters were well written, the stylized art rendered them as angry yet seductive pin-ups. That she was not written or drawn that way makes her similar to Princess Leia in that comic art for both was based on likenesses of the actresses who portrayed them on screen, and storylines for both were more tightly controlled by their creators. Buffy represented a shift in film, television, and comics culture that centered "girls-next-door" employing irony and humor in their feminist heroism, and employing their friends as allies as they dispatched their nemeses. She was, in short, written as more nuanced than most of her predecessors and contemporaries, who tended to be presented as one-dimensionally "strong" and alone in their strength.

This chapter examines *Buffy's* Third Wave feminism, its emphasis on forged families and redemption, its treatment of bodies and sexuality, and its diversity. The characters' various privileges, in terms of race, class, and sexuality, both enable their challenges to cultural norms as well as curtailing them. To illustrate these points, the chapter draws from Seasons 1–7 of the *Buffy* television show (Fox, via WB and UPN, 1997–2003) and Seasons 8–10 of the comics (Dark Horse, 2007–15).[2] It focuses mostly on the comics, because although there were at least 1,500 scholarly pieces about Buffy written between 1992 and 2012, almost all of that attention was on the seven seasons of the television show (Comeford, Klein, and Rambo 2012). The chapter also analyzes fan blogs and letter columns in order to analyze receptions of a set of characters that simultaneously embody, parody, and subvert "traditional" articulations of gender. Embodying these seeming contradictions broadens the character's potential audiences as well as widening the possibilities for different receptions by those audiences.

## Third wave feminist sensibilities in pop culture and in *Buffy*

Joss Whedon had specific feminist goals when he created Buffy, stating, "If I can make teenage boys comfortable with a girl who takes charge of a situation without their knowing that's what's happening, it's better than sitting down and selling them on feminism" (Bellafante 2001). This is not dissimilar from Wonder Woman's creator, William Moulton Marston, who thought war would not end "until women control men" but he was optimistic this would occur because "if they go crazy over Wonder Woman, it means they're longing for a beautiful, exciting girl who's stronger than they are" (Richard 1942). Whedon would write numerous episodes of the TV series and issues of the comics, as well as polishing other writers' dialogue and giving notes to artists. Not like George Lucas with *Star Wars*, he was the final say in the show's writers' room and at writers and editors' summits that plotted out the directions of each of the comics' seasons, such that his vision is deployed throughout both media.

The vehicle for this message, petite white blonde California Valley girl Buffy Summers, is "the chosen one," the "one girl in all the world" who has the "strength and skill" to battle the "forces of darkness," the latest in a long line of young women destined to slay vampires and other demons. She at first resists but then shoulders the weight of responsibility. She slays not only vampires but other types of monsters, many of them acting as metaphors for high school problems and then increasingly adult problems. When her mother dies and when her "Watcher" Giles leaves town, adulthood itself becomes the enemy as Buffy struggles to come into her own. The most metaphorical "Big Bads" were five of the seven on the TV series: her former boyfriend and love-of-her-life, a corrupt politician allied with another slayer, the military and its experimental cyborg technology, casually misogynistic young male nerds, and a superpowered overtly misogynistic priest. With the last two especially, Whedon said, "I want[ed] to come down against the patriarchy" (Miller 2003).

Buffy launched not in the 1940s, 1960s, or 1970s, or 1980s like the characters discussed thus far in this book, but in the 1990s. At this time, the "Third Wave" of feminism became more prominent, organized in part by young women who had benefited from the 1960s to 1980s Second Wave of feminism but who felt its advances were not enough and also were not distributed equally. Equality remains the central organizing principle, but it is more attentive to intersectionality than the Second Wave may have been—the idea that while "women" may have some things in common, certain women are going to be hit by other types of discrimination at the same time, and such differences must be taken into account. The Third Wave is also more open to both an ironic use of and a celebration of "femininity" and "girliness."[3] This has led to its being conflated with the phrase "girl power" and also with the concept of "post-feminism." The latter is anathema to feminists because it is grounded in the idea that feminism isn't necessary because equality has been achieved. "Girl power" was exemplified in the 1990s by riot grrrl bands like Bikini Kill who used the slogan on an early one of their zines to push for antisexist, pro-community ideals, for the reclamation of the word "girl" from its connotations of subordination and weakness, and for media production that would exemplify these traits. These women, and other activists using the term, were grounded in protest to conservative policies of the 1980s and early 1990s, particularly those curtailing reproductive rights. The phrase became associated with the wildly successful Spice Girls and was mainstreamed and commodified as a less threatening message on merchandise purchased by the individual dollars of young women, rather than a description of a collective political movement by young women. However, capitalizing on the lucrative marketization of the "girl power" term probably enabled shows such as *Buffy* to get on the air on the WB network (rather than on one of the main three). *Buffy* then paved the way for other shows with powerful young women such as *Alias, Dark Angel, La Femme Nikita, Charmed,* and even *Birds of Prey.*

Whedon recognized the power of pop culture and sought to transform it, saying, "The one thing I had hoped to take part in was a shift in popular culture in the sense of people accepting the idea of the female hero" ("The Last Sundown," Season 7 [hereafter, S7] DVD featurette). Third Wave media generally foregrounds personal narrative and tonally is often playful, campy, and ironic. This is encompassed in the way in which Whedon begins with turning superhero tropes on their head—particularly, the types of storylines and gendered characterizations occurring in the 1990s. According to comics writer Grant Morrison, at the time "no story could pass without at least one sequence during which an unlikely innocent would find herself alone and vulnerable in some completely inappropriate inner-city back alley setting . . . a skimpily attired naïf penetrating the seedy underbelly of the urban nightmare." Threatened, she would always be rescued at the last minute by a superhero (Morrison 2011: 251.) Joss Whedon thought the hero should be the "skimpily attired naïf," saying, "There's the girl in the alley.... And then the monster attacks her and she kills it" (Robinson 2007). Buffy does indeed kill a vampire in an alley in her 1992 film debut. The coexisting femininity and strength in the small body subvert stereotypes of gender.

Buffy is a teenager concerned with clothes and boys and cracking jokes, and remains so after the awakening of her powers, her being informed about her mission as the sole protector of humans, and her training by her adult male "Watcher" in strategy, vampire and demon history, and martial arts (film 1992; Brereton and Golden's adaptation of Whedon's original screenplay, 1999). Asked what she wants to do, she replies, "Date and shop and hang out and go to school and save the world from unspeakable demons. You know, I wanna do girlie stuff!" (David Greenwalt 1998, "Faith, Hope, and Trick" [S03E03]). She conforms to expectations of "girls" in terms of her looks and her personality, both of which are tightly tied in with her race and class, while subverting them at the same time with her mission and power.

Buffy embodies an attractive female warrior while parodying it through her body and speech, criticizing the superhero and horror genres and gendered inequalities with humor.[4] This complicates the show's politics and makes it fodder for what is apparently the largest number of academic works written about a pop culture character. Scholars debated whether the show was feminist, whether it was just reinscribing "traditional" norms through a cast of pretty, white, stylish young women, whether Buffy's femininity disrupted assumptions about gender through campiness, whether the humor delivered critique well or merely deflected critique by making light of various serious situations, whether viewers could reconcile the strong female agency and community-building with the commercialized violence and the emphasis on individual consumer power through merchandizing.[5]

Whedon addressed *Buffy*'s adherence to traditional forms while delivering a subversive message about those forms,

> It's better to be a spy in the house of love.... If I made "Buffy the Lesbian Separatist," a series of lectures on PBS on why there should be feminism, no one would be coming to the party, and it would be boring. The idea of changing culture is important to me, and it can only be done in a popular medium. (Nussbaum 2002)

In other words, one will get a larger audience using popular tropes in popular culture that people are comfortable with, while simultaneously undermining them in an entertaining way.

Buffy's stories are grounded in the emotional realities of her high school world and the monsters that served as metaphors for the hell that is high school while learning how to deal with her powers and still have a "normal" life. Like Kitty Pryde, who Whedon has called the "proto-Buffy" (Grossman 2005; Edwards 2004), or like Spider-Man, Buffy is self-reflective and angst-ridden. All three loved and lost, and acted selfishly and selflessly. They were point-of-view characters for readers and viewers with their "real-ness." By contrast, characters such as Wonder Woman or Storm often spoke rather regally, formally, and earnestly, and both have at times been referred to as goddesses. This removes them somewhat from our everyday lives and concerns while Buffy is enmeshed in them. The content of *Buffy* always contained slangy, humor-laden, realistic talk about everyday life, laced with cultural critique. Such talk forges connections for viewers and readers while not alienating those who might tune out the critique if it was preached, but might hear the critique if it was ironically phrased. Like a more humorous version of the 1970s–80s *X-Men*, *Buffy* is a dramatic soap opera intermixed with suspense, horror, and superhero action.

This combination was definitely marketable. Generally, the TV series *Buffy the Vampire Slayer* had between 4 and 6 million viewers, according to its Nielsen ratings (Rohaly and Wohaske 2004). This viewership was about the same as those for the young Superman show on the same network, *Smallville,* demonstrating that viewers do not make distinctions between male leads and female leads when their stories are good. During the first season, female teens made up about half the audience, and adults between eighteen and thirty-four and male teens made up most of the other half. Within a few years, however, the audience was fairly evenly split between teens and adults aged eighteen to thirty-four, and between females and males (see Kociemba 2006). This was, in other words, a younger and broader audience than those assumed to be buying comics from local comic shops at the time, and to whom the new comics would be pitched. Having a comic series continue directly from the end of the TV series was a move virtually unprecedented at the time, but duplicated by a number of other TV series' since.

Sales of the *Buffy Season 8* #1 comic, from Dark Horse, were about 110,000 in its first month in 2007, with another 17,000 the following month. It was reprinted two more times in its first few months to total 150,000 copies sold. At that time, usually, only a handful of comics of the hundreds sold had sales over 100,000 in any given month, such as *Batman, Superman, Justice League, Spider-Man, Avengers,* or *X-Men*. All of these decades-old titles from DC and Marvel were supposedly dependent on the older, male, hard-core "Wednesday Warriors" who went to their local comic shops each week for muscular male characters surrounded by a smaller number of sexualized female characters. *Buffy,* certainly, did not fit this mold. Dark Horse editor Scott Allie says, "I think we've been really good about getting Joss Whedon fans to go into comic shops" (Siuntres 2013). Sales of *Season 8* about one year later were still at about 90,000, and after another year, they were about 80,000. They continued to decline over the course of the run, which is common. *Season 9* began in 2011 at only 43,000 in its first month, and also declined over the course of the run in terms of print sales (*Comichron.com,* various pages). This may have been due to waning interest in the story, but more likely it was due to splitting the cast of the one book into two with *Buffy Season 9* accompanied by *Angel and Faith Season 9,* to the success of sales in trade paperback form, and to Dark Horse at about that same time making *Buffy* available digitally. Judging by who was watching the series, the younger and/or female viewers would be more likely to be purchasing the comic in trade paperback form or digitally than by going to a comic shop each week. According to Dark Horse in 2009, by the time the third volume of the *Season 8* trade paperbacks was released, the first two had sold over 160,000 copies, and by the time the fifth volume of the *Season 8* trade paperbacks was released, the first three volumes had sold over 220,000 copies. As with the single comic issues, these sales are much higher than average. One would have to assume that both of these types of sales remained strong or Dark Horse would not have launched *Season 10* in 2014 (which debuted at about 28,000 in print sales), nor would they have put out hardcover special editions of each trade paperback. The *Season 8 Volume 1* hardcover edition, almost ten years after the comic collected in it began its run, remained a top seller on Amazon.com in its young adult graphic novel section, and the *Buffy* title remained the highest-ranked Dark Horse comic.

*Buffy* fandom is well established and vocal. Only months into the show they made the WB-hosted online space "The Bronze" (named after the local dance club on the TV show) one of the most popular fansites. Much of that activity spilled over into Whedonesque beginning in 2002, Buffyboards from 2002, and Slayalive from 2007,[6] not to mention individual tumblrs and other websites and podcasts that continue to archive, review, and provide information, entertainment, and community for fellow fans. Writers, producers, and some actors participated in posting on these boards while the TV show was on the air, and continue to be interviewed on them as well. While *Buffy*'s comics editor of sixteen years, Scott Allie, encouraged fans to communicate with creators through letter columns because he says that the comics creative teams do not go to the message boards (*Season 9* [hereafter *S9*] #4), those boards remain a place for others linked with the show to communicate with fans, and for fans to communicate with one another. Sometimes those communications have been a lovefest. Other times they have displayed what Derek Johnson (2007a) calls "fantagonism," which sees fans struggle over the meanings of the show and comics and struggle for their own meanings to become dominant.

The fantagonism stems from love, of course, and *Season 8* #10 reprints some of the thousands of entries solicited in a MySpace contest on how Buffy has affected one's life. Melissa from Roseville, CA wrote, "It showed me it's all right to be different . . . that you can still be strong, you can change the world if you just try." Rachel from Flower Mound, TX wrote that *Buffy* showed her that it is "okay to be gay, it is okay to be a nerd, and it is completely possible for a woman to do anything she sets her mind to and take control of her own life." Later, Tess Barao wrote,

> She does something better than anyone else: She keeps fighting. She can be beaten, and bloodied, and betrayed, but never broken. She keeps fighting. She can have everyone question her methods and actions and decisions, and still keeps fighting. . . . So thank you for keeping our girl and all of her incredible friends alive for us. You know what you all are, don't you. You're heroes. Heroes creating heroes. Thank you. (*S9* #24)

Not all of this is about Buffy herself. One of the most important aspects of the character is that while she is "the chosen one" who has and exerts particular powers, the premise is grounded in the idea that power can and should be shared, that everyone can make a unique contribution, that there is no need to go it alone, that working together and forgiving one another's flaws is preferable to competition and strife. Fans latched on not just to Buffy but to the female and male characters around her and the ways in which together, they represent a spectrum of different identities.

## Forging family

Buffy has an origin and mission that stresses her uniqueness. She is the "one girl in all the world" who has the "strength and skill" to battle the "forces of darkness," and she uses violence only as a last resort with humans. She repeatedly shows transgressors' compassion and allows them a path of redemption. Both before and after the death of her mother, she surrounds herself with love and relies on others. The empathy and the ways in which she encourages her chosen family to work with her make her unlike most other superheroes (Durand 2000; Early 2001; Inness 2004; Jowett 2005; Knight 2010; Payne-Mulliken and Renegar 2009; Robinson 2004; Ross 2004; Stuller 2010). It makes her particularly unlike numerous male heroes who maintain a gap between themselves and those close to them in order to protect them. Because of the large number of female characters, there is no single one that has to bear the weight of representing "all" women, nor are there two token women who only talk about men or are competitive with each other. A range of relationships is displayed within the group, changing over time.

This queer family consists of initially insecure computer hacker and witch, Willow; Buffy and Willow's other best friend who is always quietly helping to save the world, the bumbling and stalwart Xander; and Buffy's "watcher" and team father figure, Giles. Outside of the core four characters are Buffy's two on-and-off boyfriends, allies, and vampires with souls: the brooding and emotional Angel, and the sarcastic and sensitive Spike. Buffy's one-time boyfriend, chivalrous military man Riley; Buffy's younger sister Dawn; and the wisecracking rebellious slayer Faith would join as well. Buffy's kind and supportive mother is in the first half of the series until her death, and her father is not present. Other key figures are the three significant others of Willow: the quiet werewolf Oz, the sweet and shy witch Tara, and the brash bratty slayer Kennedy; and the two significant others of Xander, the tactless beauty queen Cordelia and the equally tactless vengeance demon Anya. The theme of family and the theme of redemption are intertwined. Every character in *Buffy*, at some point, makes terrible decisions that hurt the others. And every one of them, including almost all of the villains, is given a chance at redemption. The gender balance is generally either quantitatively or qualitatively even or tilted toward the female characters.

Both male and female characters are equally interested in and shaped by their romances, rather than only the female characters being defined by their relationships. Both the male and female characters display positive and negative emotions, strength and resolve, insecurity and doubt, and humor and sadness. Some of these characters are quite queer in terms of their challenges to normative roles of gender and sexuality, and others become increasingly so over the course of the TV and comic series. There is not,

**Figure 5.1** The "core four" of Buffy's chosen family (left to right): Giles (Anthony Stewart Head), Willow (Alyson Hannigan), Xander (Nicholas Brendon), and Buffy (Sarah Michelle Gellar). ("The Harvest," S01E02, 1997).

however, any kind of balance in terms of race and ability. Every one of these characters is white and nondisabled. This group, in various incarnations, works with and supports Buffy in her mission, becoming essential parts of both planning for it and carrying it out.

The "one girl in all the world" is not alone, she is not always the leader, and she seeks to share her burdens and her power. In this, she is similar to Diana in the 1940s exhorting the women around her to stand up and be strong. Like the Birds of Prey and the X-Men, Buffy saves the world with her friends, to whom she refers as family. It's clear the family is a queer forged one when it's juxtaposed against biological relatives. When Tara's father wants to take her away and all of the main characters stand in his way, he protests, "You people have no right to interfere with Tara's affairs. We . . . are her blood kin! Who the hell are you?" Buffy replies simply, with the others arrayed around her, "We're family" (Joss Whedon 2000, "Family" [S05E06]). Forging family and sisterhood, and sharing power, were themes throughout the series. Whedon intended these moves to bridge the genre's usual gap between the hero and those around him ("The Last Sundown" S7 featurette, DVD). Her leadership style is sort of a cross of X-Men leadership styles. She becomes a tactician and sometimes must remove herself from letting herself appear to care too much, like Scott Summers/Cyclops. She thinks, "Suck it up, Summers. You're a big girl now," drawing attention to the last name she shares with the X-Man (Whedon and Georges Jeanty 2007, *Season 8* [hereafter *S8*] #1). She also leads with her heart and is concerned for her teammates, and over time hesitates less to use extreme force, like Storm. Her approach highlights the instability of the categories of "masculine" and "feminine" by bridging the supposed gap between them.

These same themes, overtly stated, are the pivotal plot point at the end of the *Buffy* TV series. She discovers that while the line of slayers was indeed started by men who violated a young woman and made her take on that role, and that while the "Watcher Council" that she rejected was always all-male, there was always a group of women called "The Guardians" who were "watching the Watchers" and watching over the slayers. Over the course of the final season, Buffy and her friends gather potential slayers to train against a seemingly undefeatable foe. In the finale, Buffy has the idea that Willow can use her magic to share Buffy's strength with all of the potential slayers, through a scythe forged by the Guardians. She then gives the young women a choice as to whether or not they will use that strength. Whedon commented, "We got the opportunity to say what we've always subliminally said, which is 'We're all slayers' . . . . 'You've worshipped this one iconic character. Now find it in yourself. Everybody'" ("Full Circle" and "The Last Sundown" S7 featurettes, DVD). Buffy talks about her power and asks the potential slayers:

> What if you could have that power? Now. All of you. "In every generation one Slayer is born" because a bunch of guys that died thousands of years ago made up that rule. They were powerful men. [She points at Willow.] This woman is more powerful than all of them combined. So I say we change the rules. I say *my* power should be *our* power. Tomorrow, Willow will use the essence of the scythe to change our destiny. From now on, every girl in the world who *might* be a Slayer, *will* be a Slayer. Every girl who *could* have the power, *will* have the power. Who *can* stand up, *will* stand up. Every one of you, and girls we've never known, and generations to come . . . they will have strength they never dreamed of, and more than that, they will have each other. Slayers. Every one of us. Make your choice. Are you ready to be strong?" (Whedon 2003, "Chosen." [S07E22])

The *Buffy Season 8* comics continue from this point. "Once upon a time, I did something good. I didn't do it alone, of course—but that's the point. I found a way to share my power. Girls all over the world were given power—not just strength, though that does come in handy—but purpose, meaning, connection." (Whedon and Jeanty 2008, *S8* #11). It also ends on this point, with Buffy turning down a chance to live in paradise and looking at a vision of the core main characters, "That's what I need to fight for. Not happiness. Not humanity. Them. Those people . . . . My family" (Brad Meltzer and Jeanty 2010, *S8* #35).

While still retaining its humor and pathos, Buffy's adventures in this *Season 8* comics run became increasingly fantastical, with more monsters and demons, alternate dimensions, and large-scale battles—more akin to *Wonder Woman* and *X-Men*. Letter writers initially loved the comic and its grander scale and its wider cast, but turned negative about it toward the end as it got increasingly otherworldly and action-focused. In general, there were more male than female letter writers represented in the *Season 8* letter columns; like that of the TV series, the comic audience was neither just young women nor just young women. In this season's last issue in January 2011, Joss Whedon wrote,

> We've learned what you like, what you don't, how this tv show translated to the world of comics, and how it didn't quite . . . [In *Season 9*, we'll go] back, a bit, to

the everyday trials that made Buffy more than a superhero. That made her us . . . .
I changed [my plan for *Season 9*] for the reasons stated above. (*S8* #40)

Here and on message boards during the time of the TV series, both the tone and the content of posts by creators speak of listening to fans and caring about their feedback—whether because they agree with fans' point of view, whether they want to please them so that they are happy, or whether they are trying to just keep fans buying their product.

The *Season 9* comic backed away from the large-scale fantasy action and initially focused on Buffy, her friends, the dark-alley slaying of vampires, and the fallout from Buffy's having destroyed all magic in the world to save it at the end of *Season 8*. This elicited numerous positive letters. But after a few issues, the usual supporting cast disappeared: Willow, Xander, Dawn, Spike, Angel, Faith, and except for a couple of issues, all of the previous forty issues' supporting cast of Slayers. Multiple letters across this series decried that the core of Buffy, its community, was lacking. Within the story, she feels betrayed by her friends, but as usual, forgives them. Outside of the story, the other were absent because of their marketability: they were spun off into the ongoing *Angel and Faith*, a *Spike* miniseries, and a *Willow* miniseries. Indeed, many of the letters in the back of *Buffy Season 9* issues were not about *Buffy Season 9*, but about these other series. Editor Scott Allie finally replied that "you can look forward to the team being back together" in *Season 10*.

From the first issue of *Season 10*, the core cast was at the heart of the series—the original four: Buffy, Willow, Xander, and (resurrected tween) Giles, plus Spike, Dawn, and Andrew. They struggle through rewriting the rules of magic. This drew universal praise from letter writers, such as "finally, *Season 10* feels like it has been getting back to the basics of the show we all know and love" (Aaron Gies, *Season 10* [hereafter *S10*] #13). Buffy thanks the formerly villainous Faith "for everything" and Giles thanks her as well (Christos Gage and Rebekah Isaacs, *S10* #2). They call on the formerly villainous Angel for help, and he arrives immediately and is welcomed. The theme of family is back strongly and is embedded in several issues. Willow says, "That's what friends are for. The people who aren't in your life 'cause they're related, or hot for you. They just love you" (Gage, Nicholas Brendon, and Isaacs, *S10* #3). Spike tells Buffy, "We all have two families. The one we're born into, and the one we choose. Seems like you've picked a pretty good one" (Gage, Brendon, and Isaacs, *S10* #5). Threatened by a giant demon, the group stands together in a big splash panel that echoes the TV episode in which they faced down Tara's abusive father, with Buffy stating in no uncertain terms why they would defeat their foe, "We're family" (Gage and Isaacs, *S10* #15). That same demon, recalling *Star Wars*' early Jedis and the monastic lifestyle they were supposed to have, taunts Buffy, "The slayers of the past knew emotional attachments made them weak. A lesson you'll learn far too late." Willow swoops in and saves her, retorting to the demon, "Depends on who you're attached to, doesn't it?" (Gage and Isaacs, *S10* #18). This family supports one another even as it is not conflict-free. In particular, romantic relationships tend to strain the family ties, while incorporating many of the core characters' exes into the queer family structure. Love and sexuality are key components of the *Buffy* series, with the characters sexual but not sexualized.

## Embodiment, love, and sex

In contrast to Wonder Woman's, or (the original) Barbara Gordon's, or Storm's, near six-foot tall, solidly muscled, curvy, frames, Buffy Summers is nearer to five feet, slim, and bottle blonde. She is a young petite woman like Kitty Pryde, or Princess Leia or Queen Padmé Amidala, at first seemingly unthreatening due to their age, size, and gender. Indeed, *Buffy* actress Sarah Michelle Gellar became slimmer and flatter over the course of the series, such that her figure became even more girlish. Fuchs writes that "part of *Buffy's* genius lies in its ironic undermining of the status quo it appears to epitomize" (2007: 102) and Buffy's body is central to that. But Brown writes, "The overall girlishness of the contemporary action heroine allows these characters to be sexually appealing to male viewers without implicitly challenging patriarchal standards" (Brown 2011: 166). Both can be true, broadening the appeal of the character. This was intentional on Whedon's part to both subvert the genre and make a political point. The petite Valley girl, societally dismissed as frivolous, has superstrength and is critical to the world's safety. Whedon said, "One of the reasons I've always been attracted to female heroines is that I have always been interested in the people that nobody takes seriously, having been one the greater part of my life" (Ervin-Gore 2001).

Objectification of the characters was never considered. Whedon directed the comics away from that due to his aversion to the "Bad Girl" style: "Because of that stuff, I went away from comics for a long time. Everything seemed to be soft core and all of it was disguised as 'empowerment'" (Ervin-Gore 2001). Buffy, instead, just wears regular clothes that cover her curves. Only briefly in the first year of the *Buffy* show and original comic was there even a hint of Buffy's cleavage as she often wore a tank top under a cardigan sweater, and some leg as she wore skirts and boots. Comics editor Scott Allie writes, "When we first started the *Buffy* comics back in'98 . . . the one edict [from Joss Whedon] was to draw women that look like real women—not overtly sexualized, or robust, or unnaturally proportioned. I spent a lot of time on a top-selling title reinforcing that idea" (*S8* #7). Almost all of the "non-canon" 1998–2003 Dark Horse comics, most of which were drawn by Cliff Richards, do indeed uphold Whedon's edict, as do the "canon" *Seasons 8, 9,* and *10* that follow from the TV series. Allie clarified, "With *Buffy*, I've often had to push my most well-intentioned artists to play down the cheesecake. I remember once [the main artist throughout *Seasons 8* and *9*] Georges Jeanty (male) complaining to me that Jo Chen (female) had made Buffy's breasts too large on a cover, and I had to ask her to tone it down" (Pantozzi 2014). This sensibility in the comic art continues through *Season 10* in the mid-2010s, as drawn by Rebekah Isaacs.

While her body has always been more subject than object, her complicated love life and her sex life—in which she is portrayed as an active agent—are integral parts of her stories. Because Buffy is not the only central female character in the series, alongside the fact that love is clearly as important to the main male characters as it is to the females, the series does not fall into the problems of having female characters who exist only as adjuncts to males. At some point, every one of the main characters has, at least, one romantic and/or sexual relationship. During these times, the characters support each other as well as calling each other out on various hypocrisies and other lacks of self-reflection. They talk to each other about many topics other than romance, which is commented on in a meta way as Buffy brings up romance and Dawn protests, "Nuh-uh. No talking about boys. This is a Bechdel-test-approved spa day," When the conversation then turns to Buffy's love life, she demurs and says, "Respect the Bechdel test" (Gage, Brendon, and Isaacs 2014, *S10* #10).

Buffy's first major relationship, dramatic and star-crossed, was with the vampire Angel, a light-skinned, dark-haired man much older and much larger physically than her. The vampire slayer and vampire-with-a-soul had a steadily building relationship. On her seventeenth birthday, they confess their love for one another and have sex. Due to a curse put on him, his "true happiness" at all of this causes him to lose his soul and become a remorseless killer. He subsequently treats her quite cruelly, physically knocking her to the ground, "You know what the worst part was? Pretending that I loved you" (Whedon 1998, "Surprise"/"Innocence" [S02E13–14]). Over the next several episodes, he tortures Giles and kills a number of people. As she later describes her next actions, killing Angel to stop his evil plot to end the world, "I loved him more than I will ever love anything in this life and I put a sword through his heart because I had to" (Drew Goddard 2002, "Selfless" [S07E15]). Willow performs a powerful spell that restores his soul just before she does so, and he remembers nothing of his evil. Buffy kisses Angel and ostensibly kills him, sending him to a type of hell. But he comes back, in a scene that Whedon and artist John Cassaday would reproduce exactly with Kitty Pryde and Piotr Rasputin in his later run on *Astonishing X-Men*: the assumed-dead older man naked and on his knees, embracing the younger girl and softly saying her name. Although the others are wary of the returned Angel, warning Buffy that she "can't see straight" where he is concerned, he does work on the side of good. The last episode of *Season 7* of the *Buffy* TV series leaves the door open between Buffy and Angel, and the cataclysmic events of the *Season 8* comic hinge on their love and their having sex. Indeed, they have sex on more than half of one issue's pages, in a number of positions, much of it while floating or flying in the air as they are both temporarily superpowered (Meltzer and Jeanty 2010, *S8* #34). This apparently fulfills their destinies and balances her sharing of her power by creating a new idyllic world for them and allowing demons into this one. She then rejects it due to loyalty to her family of friends. Fan reaction to this season-end, as it was to the latter half of the season, was somewhat negative. Whedon knew it and hence his writing the open letter to fans mentioned above that the next season of the comic would be less fantastical. Angel, possessed, kills again, but remains an ally through the *Season 10* comics.

Buffy's next major—and similarly doomed—relationship was with traditional military man Riley, who asks his friends, "What kind of girl is gonna go out with a guy who's all Joe Normal by day and turns demon hunter at night?" In theory, someone like Buffy, who leads the same kind of life. But Riley causes her pain different from that caused by Angel. Before each knows of the other's work, Buffy asks him, "You think that boys can take care of themselves and girls can't?" and Riley answers, "Yeah" as if he finds the answer completely obvious (Petrie 1999, "The Initiative" [S04E07]). This is similar to the way in which, in disguise as Diana Prince, Wonder Woman seethes when

**Figure 5.2** The star-crossed Buffy the Vampire Slayer (Sarah Michelle Gellar) and Angel the vampire (David Boreanaz), just before they consummate their relationship and he loses his soul ("Surprise," S02E13, 1998).

military man Steve Trevor tells her, "Di, you'd better go home and rest. This is a man's job" (Marston and Peters unpub., 1971). Riley (and Steve Trevor's) black-and-white assumptions about gender and power feed into his feelings that she doesn't need him because she is the stronger and he is uncomfortable with that. His assumption is that she should need him and want to need him. This is problematic for many adolescent girls, as there may be some fear among boys about girls who compete with them, or even within society at large of such girls as threatening to an established "traditional" order. Again in a disruption of gender stereotypes, Riley feels like the weaker party in the relationship.

Joss Whedon confirms that the Buffy-Riley dynamic was intended to show the fears of, and the historical cost to, young women who compete with young men. On the show, he says, this manifests through a clash between the "feminine" mysticism of the slayer and the "masculine" military. Because the latter, and to some extent Riley, don't truly understand the value and complexity of the former, it will fail (Whedon commentary on Whedon 2000, "Restless" [S04E22]). The first day she tries to work with the military, Buffy stands out by wearing her usual delicate pastel garb and by being about a foot shorter than the large camouflage-clad soldiers around her. When she is advised to change, she says, "Oh, you mean the camo and stuff. I thought about it, but on me it's gonna look all Private Benjamin. Don't worry, I've patrolled in this halter many times" (David Fury 2000, "The 'I' in Team" [S04E13]). Riley does begin to question the military after Buffy is almost killed by his commanding officer, but he still remains loyal and in the end, goes back to it as Buffy feared he would. Not persuaded that she loves him, Riley leaves town just as Angel did before him, giving Buffy no say in the matter. While inside the relationship he felt that she had more power and was uncomfortable with that, it is he who exerts his power by ending it. He does later return, an ally in the large-scale battles of the *Season 8* comics. But the "masculine" government remains a problem for Buffy and all of the slayers she later empowers. Calling X-Men to mind yet again, a military officer tells her, "You've upset the balance, girl. Do you really think we were going to sit by and let you create a master race?" She replies, "This isn't about demons at all, is it? It's about women. It's about power and it's about women and you just hate those two words in the same sentence, don't you?" No, he says, "You think it's only men want to bring you down? You're not human . . . it's you against the world. You're at war with the human race" (Whedon and Jeanty 2007, *S8* #4).

Buffy's relationship with the initially soulless vampire Spike, for whom she puts humans at risk, displays yet a third type of problematic partnership. It is a main storyline in the last two seasons of the TV show and into the comics. After he realized he was in love with Buffy, he began to work mostly for good, seemingly just to get her attention. Different from Angel who was motivated by his soul and his guilt to fight against dark forces, Spike could be constructed as choosing, against his soulless vampire nature, to do good. Buffy felt that Spike was the only one who understood her alienation when she returned from the dead. At first, he is the only one she tells that she thinks she was in heaven and is miserable being back in this world. She is able to show him a darker side of herself, and for some moments, their physical connection overcomes her feelings of numbness. Although it is not named, she seems to have depression, or perhaps post-traumatic stress disorder. From the first of their apparently passionate, rough, and consensual sexual encounters, Buffy is disgusted with herself and takes much of it out on him. He puts up with her abuse with the assumption that he will prove himself worthy of her. He returns her verbal abuse in reminding her that she is not as good a person as her friends believe her to be but rather, she came back from the dead "wrong" and belongs in "the dark" with him. She finally breaks off their relationship, admitting that she wants him but that "I'm using you . . . . I can't love you . . . . And it's killing me . . . . I'm sorry" (Doug Petrie 2002, "As You Were" [S06E15]).

Spike attempts to rape Buffy after this, muttering to himself that he was going to make her love him through this act, a conflation of sex and power and violence. That he regretted it and was sorry are immaterial. As Buffy says tearfully, "Ask me again why I could never love you" (DeKnight 2002, "Seeing Red" [S06E19]). But after Spike goes through torturous trials to get his soul back, thinking that Buffy would then love him, he begins a redemptive journey that she is quick to support. Sometimes she is the only one to support him, as her friends have not forgiven him for the attempted rape. She feels that he had no soul when he tried to rape her, and now he does. Therefore, like Angel, Spike-with-a-soul is like an entirely different person. This undergirds the constant theme of redemption in the series, but also implies that such a serious violation should be forgiven when people say they have changed. Not long after this, it is obvious that he has been killing people (while mind-controlled), but she forgives him and keeps him close by. With her friends are increasingly uncomfortable with her behavior, Buffy feels that Spike is the "only one watching [her] back" (Greenberg 2003, "Empty Places"

[S07E19]). The potential slayers kick her out of the house in favor of Faith being their new leader, and Spike reaches her, telling her she is "the one" and holding her through the night (Rebecca Rand Kirshner 2003, "Touched" [S07E20]). She, in turn, tells him that he gave her the strength to go out and face a seemingly invulnerable villain. Spike contributes to saving the world in the series finale by wearing a magic amulet brought to them by Angel, which must be worn by a "champion." The implication is that if he were not such a champion, the amulet would not have its intended effect. She tells him just before he sacrifices his life that she loves him.

Some writers on the show were alarmed at many fans' positive reactions to Spike and Buffy's relationship, as they had intended for it to be viewed as abusive (See e.g., DeLullo 2003, Gottlieb 2002, interviewing four of the main writers). Spike actor James Marsters also felt that "what the final episode did very well was admit that Buffy really is in love with Angel. That the sexual relationship she had with Spike was unhealthy. That it was unwise . . . . Spike was evil" (Butler 2003). The positive fan reaction to Buffy and Spike as a couple recalls some fans' reactions to Anakin Skywalker's abusive behavior toward his wife Padmé. While many saw its problematic nature, a number of fans, particularly younger ones, seemed to see his possessiveness and aggressiveness as romantic (see Chapter 3). Here, with Buffy and Spike, fans were not judgmental of the heavily implied BDSM overtones in their physical acts, but they were perhaps not judgmental enough of the verbal abuse that both parties hurled at each other, and the way they isolated one another from others. The writers listened, and continued to grow his character, ambivalently, emphasizing through him in the last season of the TV series the themes of family, forgiveness, and redemption that undergird the show. *Season 9* of the comic portrays Buffy and Spike as continuing to strengthen their bond as awkward but trusting friends. When Buffy thinks she is pregnant (she isn't, because her brain has been put in a robot body), it is Spike that she asks to go with her to have an abortion (Chambliss and Moline, Jeanty, and Richards, *S9* #5–10). Letter writers mostly applauded Buffy's struggle to make her choice about what to do, but were not pleased with the "robot" turn. The story was discussed heavily in online forums as well, with roughly the same breakdown. In *Season 10*, it is clear that Buffy and Spike have become very close, but in a different way from before. He tries to apologize for the attempted rape, and she says, "You didn't have a soul. I can't hold what that guy did against you any more than I could blame Angel [for killing people when he didn't have a soul]. I'm not excusing what you—what he did, but it shouldn't matter now. You're a totally different person. In a lot of ways, so am I" (Gage, Isaacs, and Richard Corben, *S10* #8). Dawn says she should give him a chance now that he has a soul, and Willow says the same. Buffy and Spike confess their love for one another, different now from their younger selves, and begin a relationship generally praised by letter writers.

Across the seven seasons of the TV show, Buffy and most of the other female characters were portrayed as interested only in men, and all of the male characters on the show were portrayed as interested only in women. Each of these relationships had its own complexities in terms of gender and sexuality. Further, both the television show and the comics represented relationships between same-sex couples.

## Heterofluidity and homosexuality

While Buffy is based on Kitty Pryde in that she is an adolescent dealing with finding out she has powers, her best friend Willow also has a number of things in common with Kitty: her brilliance, her great computer skills, her Judaism, and her queer subtext, which in Willow's case became text. Part of why Willow and Oz broke up was Willow's budding relationship with fellow witch, Tara. The shorthand version of the Willow and Tara relationship sounds painfully trope-laden. Two witches fall in love and experiment with magic as a metaphor for their growing relationship, and then one becomes out of control and violent when the other dies (see Wilts 2009). But as Willow later says, "I'm as sensitive to profiling as the next gay Wiccan Jewess, but not every stereotype is untrue" (Vaughan and Jeanty 2007, *S8* #7). The story was written with nuance and care, nominated for a number of Gay and Lesbian Alliance Against Defamation (GLAAD) awards. Her friends are briefly taken aback by her coming out, but after that, none of the characters question the relationship, which is probably the longest and most stable one portrayed on the show. Both characters were not only loving to one another but also worked on the side of good and acted as parental figures to Buffy's younger sister while Buffy was dead. As with Buffy's challenge to gender roles, Willow and Tara's feminine dress and their whiteness probably eased their challenges to heteronormativity.

"The Bronze" message boards were ablaze as soon as Willow made clear that she was with Tara. Joss Whedon (2000) posted numerous times in response to the comments, such as,

> I realize the rabidly homophobic posting contingent represents a smaller percentage of Americans than the EVIL GAYS they were posting about. . . . But of course there were just as many voices raised in support of the arc as against [and] one post from a gay or questioning teen saying the show helped them is worth six hundred hate letters. . . . To me, having a character that is open to exploring their sexuality is about the same as having a girl hero—just something natural and cool.

Network censors would not at first allow Willow and Tara to be shown kissing, but allowed it in a later episode upon Whedon's threat to quit if they forced him to cut a filmed scene with the two of them (Ausiello 2008). Willow and Tara's relationship is derailed by Willow's addiction to magic, and just as they come back together, Tara is killed and cannot be brought back by any magic. This reverberates not only through the rest of that season as Willow becomes "Dark Willow," or "Darth Willow," an analogue of *X-Men*'s Dark Phoenix or *Star Wars*' Darth Vader, full of destructive power shot through with passion. She kills Tara's murderer and she threatens to end the world, but the love of her friends (particularly Xander) brings her back from the brink and she is forgiven. Everyone is still concerned that Willow could "go dark" again. By *Season 10*, with a few of the characters openly using the phrase "Dark Willow" to describe a former ally on a rampage, Willow objects, "Dark Willow? I'm a trope now?" with Andrew responding, "Embrace it. I'd kill to be a trope" (Gage, Brendon, and Isaacs 2014, *S10* #4). Willow does have other relationships after Tara's death, with the slayer

Kennedy and with a female demon, and she is shown with a couple of other female characters as well.

While on the television show there were no male same-sex couples, one was introduced in the comics[7]: Billy and his boyfriend, Devon. Billy wants to slay vampires in part to offset the bullying he has endured for identifying as gay, but he worries, "I'm not a real slayer. . . . They're special. They're called. They're strong. They punch really hard and run really fast and they're always, always girls." Devon compliments him by subverting the usually insulting connotations of the following phrases, "I think you can punch like a girl and run like a girl" (Espenson and Karl Moline 2012, *S9* #14). Buffy welcomes them to the team, saying, "You belong" (Greenberg, Moline, and Ben Dewey 2012, *S9* #15). In *Season 9* #17 and #18, six of the eight letters about the new characters were from gay men thanking them for having out gay male characters: "As a gay teen I dreamt of something bigger, caught myself fantasizing of being one of [Buffy's team] . . . . A motley crew to call family. A cause to fight for. A direction for my life to go. A cute, broody, boyfriend to teach me how to fight!" (Noah B). Another though, felt that "It's just one stereotype after another" and it was "borderline offensive that the first male Slayer is a guy who acts like a girl" (Brett). Two others also objected, saying it subverted the mythology that only girls could be slayers (*S9* #19). Some readers, aligning binaries of gender and sexuality, might feel that because Billy does not identify as heterosexual, he is less like a "boy" and more like a "girl." Other readers, though, might see Billy as simply heroic, his gender no barrier to his declaring his goals and making a difference in the world. One of the two comics writers, Drew Greenberg, addressed this in the team's announcement of the character, made exclusively to *Out* magazine:

> I have no problem telling a story about a boy who's always felt more comfortable identifying with what society tells him is more of a feminine role. So much crap gets heaped upon us as gay men [about how] your value is determined by your ability to fit into masculine norms. . . . And those attitudes are a reflection of not just our own internalized homophobia, but of our misogyny, too. . . . So if this is a story that causes people to examine traditional gender roles and think of them as something more fluid, I'm thrilled. (Portwood 2012)

Unfortunately, Billy was then barely present in *Season 10*, causing one letter writer to lament,

> People call Buffy a feminist role model for girls and young women, which is true, but she is also a role model for boys. It is important for boys and young men to have empowered females to look up to. People should be able to relate to characters across gender. . . . That Billy embodied the type of person who I am, a young male who looks up to strong women like Buffy, was fantastic . . . . I can only assume the backlash against Billy on sites like Whedonesque and SlayAlive played a role in his removal from the series. The comments against him have been homophobic and misandric. (Rion Chmura, *S10* #4)

Although the author doesn't mention it, Billy is darker skinned than many of the other main characters, and this characteristic heightens his importance given the underrepresentation of people of color across comics. Editor Allie responded, "We didn't do it because of anti-Billy sentiments. You should know by now that we're more moved by people like you, for whom we created Billy in the first place. But the book got crowded, and in twenty-two pages a month we can't do justice to a giant cast of characters" (*S10* #4). It may have been, but launching the character on the cover in a self-titled issue, with fanfare and interviews, and then scaling back his role makes it seem more like tokenism than integrating a new character into the story. It was the opposite of the way the character of Tara was launched on the TV series.

As Billy fades into the background, Andrew finally comes out. A bumbling villain in TV's Season 6 who then works for redemption, he drinks a potion that makes him like "golden age Superman." As his confidence soars and he kisses a man he is attracted to, Andrew finally realizes what the rest of the characters (and readers) have suspected: that he's gay (Gage, Brendon, and Megan Levens 2015, *S10* #11). Xander tells him it's a big deal and Buffy says it's not. Andrew counters that it's both, "Xander . . . I appreciated your reaction because to everyone else it wasn't a big thing at all. And I get that it shouldn't be, in the larger scheme of things. But whether it should be or not . . . it's a big deal to me" (Gage and Isaacs 2015, *S10* #14). One letter writer was effusive, "I absolutely loved and totally identified with Andrew's recent discovery of his sexuality" (Barry Williams, *S10* #15). Another thought it was handled poorly, and a third praised the creators for creating non-token diverse characters that are "multifaceted" and said Andrew's coming out had "credibility and depth" (Staff Sergeant JB, *S10* #15).

While numerous letters were sent in on the above two relationships, they were a drop in the bucket compared to those about Buffy and an Asian female slayer named Satsu. Wonder Woman, Barbara Gordon, Storm, and Kitty Pryde are portrayed as openly interested only in men, but in both text and art have been hinted at and/or received as queer. While Buffy's on-screen sexual relationships had all been with men, one could read homoeroticism between her and fellow slayer Faith. Buffy is increasingly sexual over the course of the TV series, and in the first *Season 8* comic, Buffy muses, "I miss my home. I miss the gang. And churros. And sex" (Whedon and Jeanty 2007, *S8* #1). Satsu is in love with Buffy and Buffy is attracted to Satsu. They have sex twice, with Buffy clear that she enjoyed it physically but that they would not have a relationship. After the first time, they are drawn in the act's aftermath, lying in sheets as one by one, all of the other main characters come into the room. The second time is portrayed in one panel with both of them nude, and one of them on top of the other. Willow and Kennedy both try to comfort Satsu—the three of them portraying a range of queer women—and remind her that Buffy does not identify as lesbian. Buffy herself does not announce that she is firmly heterosexual either. All of this together allows space for the idea of fixed sexual identity as well as that of fluid sexual identity (Frohard-Dourlent 2010: 44). Fans sent so many letters about these panels and this story that rather than printing their usual four or five letters in the back of an issue, Dark Horse printed forty-seven. More than half of the letters were positive, seeing the story as in-character and as expressing openness to varying sexualities. About fifteen said it was out-of-character, such as the one saying that Buffy is "100% heterosexual. Fans know that" (Sara, *S8* #24). About six were very negative, such as "Turning Buffy gay was a horrible mistake! She was a role model for young girls!" (unsigned, *S8* #24). Several more, like these, labeled Buffy gay or not gay, implying that she must be understood or that they could only understand her as one or the other, reflecting staunchly binary views of gender and sexuality. About an equal number of men and women were positive about the story. About twice as many men as women were negative.

Buffy's sexuality has been central to her story. None of her relationships is idealized and none is portrayed as being between a dominant male and passive female. Rather, they are all messy disruptions of a traditional narrative of heterosexuality: one in which she is much, much younger that is on and off for years; one with a military man who cannot abide that she is the more powerful party; one sadomasochistic and physically consensual but verbally abusive, and later, more equal and loving; one brief one with a woman who is a fellow hero. The first three of these were with white men, indicative of the series' initial lack of diversity in terms of race, ethnicity, and sexuality. The last was with an Asian woman, indicative of the attempts to address the TV series' whiteness in its last season and in the subsequent comics.

## Race and class

Buffy's cast includes a number of "others," human and demon, that serve to construct her, in her white, heterosexual, middle-class-ness, as a "normal" female. She also has a more violent foil that constructs her as a "proper" female warrior, Faith, in a relationship not dissimilar to that between Wonder Woman and Artemis (see Chapter 1).[8] When Buffy dies, and then her replacement dies, Faith is called to become the new "one girl in all the world" slayer. She retains the slayer's powers even though Buffy has been revived.

Faith is young and light-skinned, like Buffy, but is more muscular and voluptuous, dark-haired, and marked as working class in her language, tattoos, clothing, and behavior.[9] She often wears a tight tank top that shows some cleavage, a wide belt, and jeans and boots. She grew up with neglectful and abusive alcoholic parents, is guarded and arrogant and responds more quickly with violence, and is somewhat traumatized by seeing her Watcher get killed. She seems to be a young woman who enjoys sex, although she has had some "loser" boyfriends that have cemented her problems with trust. She doesn't care how she is judged by others for talking about and pursuing sex: "Isn't it weird how slaying always makes you hungry and horny?" (David Greenwalt 1998, "Faith, Hope, and Trick" [S03E03]). Briefly, Buffy does let down her hair with Faith, particularly in a very close dance between the two of them at a club (later homaged in the *X-Men: Evolution* cartoon episode "Spykecam" with Kitty as Buffy and Rogue as Faith). Xander loses his virginity to Faith, as she coaxes him, "A fight like that and no kill, I'm about ready to pop. . . . Just relax . . . I'll steer you around the curves." She is affectionate with Xander for a minute, then literally pushes him out the door, "That was great. I gotta shower" (Dan Vebber 1999, "The Zeppo" [S03E13]). Faith also is portrayed as a vulnerable young woman who has learned to use sex as a tool or weapon or her only means to closeness with someone. When Angel tells her he just wants to talk. She replies, "That's what they all say. Then it's, 'Just let me stay the night, I won't try anything'" (Marti Noxon 1999, "Consequences" [S03E15]). When the villainous mayor first shows her the apartment he has rented for her, she is overwhelmed. She then sidles up to him and purrs, "Thanks, sugar daddy" as she puts her arms around him. But he pushes her away, saying that he is a "family man" (Whedon 1999, "Doppelgangland" [S03E16]). She later reflects that he might have been a "snake" but he wasn't a "dog," like a lot of other guys she's dealt with in the past, and "it's still hard to look back at my time with that guy and feel anything but love" (Vaughan and Jeanty 2007, *S8* #9). In this apartment and in her hotel room, she is almost always alone, and lonely beneath her bravado. With this "parent" and this isolation, she is not only what Buffy could have been if brought up in different circumstances, but also somewhat akin to Rogue of the X-Men, set apart due to her powers and her struggle to be a hero.

Like Artemis resenting comparisons to Wonder Woman, Faith resents being constantly compared to Buffy: "I'm the Slayer. I do my job kicking ass better than anyone. What do I hear about everywhere I go? 'Buffy' . . . . Everybody always asks, why can't you be more like Buffy?" (Petrie 1999, "Enemies" [S03E17]). In anger, she unites with the mayor against Buffy and her friends. But Faith begins to change after Angel will not give up on her (Jim Kouf, Tim Minear, and Joss Whedon 2000, "Five by Five/ Sanctuary" [*Angel* S01E18–19]). She willingly goes to jail and accepts responsibility for her actions. Later, the potential slayers reject Buffy and choose Faith to lead them. Buffy learns from Faith that she must help them work through the experience, and Faith learns from Buffy and her friends to be more cautious, less impulsive, and more open to trust. She enters a seemingly healthy relationship with Robin Wood (the son of a previous slayer), although it is short lived. In the subsequent *Buffy* comic series and the *Angel and Faith* comic series, she, like Angel, is a hero working on the side of good to try to offset her past misdeeds.

But Faith can't entirely escape her past, and must work through her bitterness that Buffy is still the "golden girl." When Giles first comes to her she says, "I ain't your beloved Buffy, I'm the go-to-girl for dirty deeds done dirt cheap, right? So what do you need me to kill?" (Vaughan and Jeanty 2007, *S8* #6). But she and Giles continue to work together, in a "partnership of equals" (Vaughan and Jeanty 2007, *S8* #9), and she wants to be something of a "social worker to the slayers." Faith is the only one willing to help Angel after he kills Giles and, like her in the past, Angel is numb and self-hating. She tells Buffy, "[Your] empowerment trick . . . put a lot of girls through the meat grinder. I spent a lot of time trying to put some of them back together. Guess that training should come in handy now . . . . Everyone else wants [Angel's] head on a pike. Me . . . I'm all about forgiveness" (Whedon and Jeanty 2011, *S8* #40). She works not only with Angel but also with a new team of slayers. In the *Angel and Faith* comic, advertised as the two characters "Fighting for redemption," she helps Angel resurrect Giles, as she feels she owes both of them for believing in her when she didn't believe in herself. But she says, she needs to move on without either of them and she needs to be strong enough to do so on her own: "Or I'm gonna end up . . . like

**Figure 5.3** With Willow on the far left (Alyson Hannigan), Spike behind her (James Marsters), and Faith to the right in her usual tank top (Eliza Dushku), Buffy addresses her extended chosen family of new slayers ("Chosen," S07E22, 2003).

I used to be. Empty except for hate" (Gage and Isaacs 2013, *Angel and Faith S9* #25). She continues to work at vampire slaying, with occasional detours that further her redemptive journey.

The characterization of Faith can be read as condemning those outside a more "feminine" stereotype of heroism in which the core hero is morally certain, cares for everyone, and is surrounded by equally caring and privileged people—like Wonder Woman or Barbara Gordon or Princess Leia or Storm. But Buffy also follows Faith in embracing her mission and her sexuality. She begins to understand that people may not make the same decisions she makes if they have been brought up in more adverse circumstances. Readers and viewers have been clear that they love both characters.[10] As an unnamed slayer says in the comics, individual names of slayers are not so important; rather, "The real questions run deeper. Can I fight? Did I help? Did I do for my sisters?" (Whedon and Paul Lee 2007, *S8* #5). Fans showed that they knew that there's more than one way to be a female superhero, and writers listened by continuing to grow Faith's character.

The diversity the character of Faith provides, like Artemis to Wonder Woman, is grounded in class. Buffy as a TV show was overwhelmingly white. Due either to the viewpoints of its main writers who were all white, and/or due to assuming its consumers would be generally middle class and white, the show's portrayal of "difference" was centered more on gender and sexuality rather than race and class, highlighting the ways in which privilege can ease challenges of norms (Jowett 2005: 13, 42; Helford 2002). The first character of color was Kendra, a vampire slayer called into service when Buffy died: "They call me Kendra. I have no last name." Kendra's "they" sounds more like "dey." A dialogue coach taught the actress the accent of a particular Jamaican dialect, but to most viewers, it sounded like a stereotypical Jamaican accent (Marti Noxon episode commentary, "What's My Line" Parts 1 and 2 [S02E09–10]). Her lack of last name, her accent, and her sorrow over her "only shirt" being ruined are all played for laughs. Kendra is killed, causing Faith to be called to be the slayer. Brief views of three past slayers, two of whom are killed on screen, show them to be women of color: one during the Boxer Rebellion in China, one in 1970s New York (Nikki Wood, the mother of Robin Wood), and the "first" slayer whose dark skin and tattered clothing and dreadlocks are supposed to mark her as being from somewhere in Africa long ago. One male character of color, the villainous vampire Trick, comments, "Sunnydale . . . admittedly, it's not a haven for the brothers, you know, strictly the Caucasian persuasion here in the 'Dale. But [we could] have us some fun" (Greenwalt 1998, "Faith, Hope, and Trick" [S03E03]). After several episodes of Trick allying with the aforementioned mayor, Faith kills him when he is about to bite Buffy. Another black male character is Riley's friend and fellow military man Forrest, who doesn't trust Buffy and her friends. He too is killed. As Kent Ono sums up the first few seasons of Buffy on TV, "No person of color acknowledged as such on the series has been able to remain a significant character. All . . . have either died or have failed to reappear" (2000: 177).

## Conclusion: Diversity, privilege, and girl power

In the last season of the TV series and into the years of the comics, more characters of color were introduced. The graphic novel *Tales of the Slayers* features one story about Nikki (and her Asian boyfriend), one of the first slayer, and one of a Navajo slayer, all of which are written by the TV show's writers (Doug Petrie, Joss Whedon, and David Fury, respectively, 2002). On TV, when the two dozen or so potential slayers assemble in Season 7, the most prominent ones are Kennedy, played by a Mexican-American actress; Rona, played by an African American actress, Chao-ahn by a Chinese-American actress; and Amanda and Violet who were not played by women of color. Lastly, there is the son of the deceased slayer Nikki, Robin Wood, who appears throughout the season as the high school's principal who later enters a relationship with Faith. He tells Buffy that he had once threatened a bully when he was in high school, and he got suspended because "talk like that is taken pretty seriously where I come from." Buffy asks, "The hood?" and he responds, subverting stereotypes, "Beverly Hills . . . which is *a* hood" (Kirshner 2002, "Help" [S07E04]). Given the show's pattern and the larger trope of characters of color being killed first, viewers expected Robin to die, some going so far as to set up a website at LiveJournal.com called "DeadBroWalking" to track how long it took for the character to be killed off. The African American Rona even says in the show, when she has been knocked out in a training exercise, "The black chick always gets it first" (Kirshner 2003, "Potential" [S07E12]). Robin does appear dead for a split second in the series finale, but he opens his eyes and surprises Faith (and, presumably, many viewers). He appears briefly in the comics, speaking with Faith in *Season 8*, and also speaking with Buffy in *Season 9* when she thinks she is pregnant and seeks counsel about how Robin's mother balanced motherhood with being a slayer. With Faith and Robin, with Giles and his briefly seen girlfriend Olivia, and with Willow and Kennedy, the barrier-crossing nature of the relationships goes unmentioned, normalizing them.

There is some diversity in terms of race and ethnicity across the large number of slayers in the comics. Kennedy, who had become Willow's girlfriend on the TV series, remains so for a time in the comics. She later fights alongside the other new slayers and opens a lucrative bodyguard business. Satsu, as noted, has a short relationship with Buffy and later takes charge of a squad of slayers in Japan. Other slayers are clearly nonwhite also, such as Renee, Xander's girlfriend who gets killed, but many of these characters remain in the background. Oz's partner, Bay, is in a couple of issues that take place in Tibet, where she has taught Oz and is now teaching the slayers to let go of their power. Bay and Oz have the girls engage in meditation, doing chores by hand, and wearing traditional clothing. This stereotype of eastern mysticism is not infrequent in comics, for instance, in Wonder Woman's period with I-Ching (see Chapter 1).

While the new slayers are diverse in skin tone and in dress, they are not in body type. As noted, female characters are not sexualized in the Buffy comics. Two letters noted both tendencies: "[Artist Georges Jeanty's] female characters do look human, unlike [those] in superhero comics, but he has a tendency to draw all the new slayers as identical skinny hotties" (Philip Eagle, *S8* #18). Another lamented that all the girls are "size 0" and "it's not quite empowerment if only hot girls get the powers" (Kirk Anderson, *S8* #20). Assistant editor Sierra Hahn responded to a similar letter in the next issue, writing, "I agree that there are a lot of female comics characters that are gratuitously drawn—big eyes, big heads, big breasts, itty-bitty waists. I feel fortunate to work on a book that doesn't (in my opinion) rely on Buffy as a sex symbol to sell comics. Is she attractive? Stylish? Strong? Intelligent? Vulnerable? Yes, yes, yes." She goes on to say that slayers are thin-bodied because of their physical training, and that the characters are drawn as conventionally attractive because of the actors who were cast to play them on TV. The standard of attractiveness in the comics, while not a gratuitously sexually objectified one, is still an Anglo-European one grounded in whiteness.

There are some new characters of color in *Season 9* who are in several issues: police officer Miranda Cheung who gets killed, Buffy's roommate Anaheed who turns out to be a slayer protecting Buffy, and the aforementioned Billy the Vampire Slayer. Altogether, they have a moderate amount of character development. Willow appears briefly with a darker-skinned new girlfriend but later is interested in a white woman, Lake. Kennedy and two other slayers named Leah and Holly appear briefly, and Holly appears African American. Robin Wood is in one issue and so is Satsu. But this diversity is reduced in *Season 10* as Anaheed, Billy and his boyfriend Devon, and Faith, Kennedy, Leah, and Holly are only in the first issues and then recede. This was done in order to focus on the core cast of the TV series: Buffy, Willow, Xander, and Giles, along with Dawn, Spike, and Andrew, with appearances by Faith, Angel, Anya, and Harmony. While this is welcome to many fans of the series who particularly love these characters and expressed to the creative team that they wanted them to be back together, it means that there is no representation of people of color in the *Season 10* comic. This brings the comic full circle to the beginning of the TV series, in that it is diverse in terms of gender, but not in terms of race, ethnicity, or ability. This not only limits its reach but reinforces the idea that "girl power" is more accessible to those already privileged.

As Jeffrey Brown describes the girl power genre and its limits, "It can depict challenging images of powerful girls without challenging cultural expectations of women" (2011: 167). This certainly may be the case. But it may also be pessimistic. Girls who felt empowered watching the young female hero could bring that empowerment into their adulthood, and boys who respected that hero could bring that respect into adulthood as well. *Buffy* film director and coproducer of the TV series, Fran Rubel Kazui, notes, "You can educate your daughters to be Slayers, but you have to educate your sons to be Xanders" (Jowett 2005: 119).[11]

What can be seen as apolitical, postfeminist, commodified girl power can also be seen as thoroughly political and thoroughly feminist activism, so there is potential for innovative, intersectional, and inclusive reworkings of gender and power in comics and TV. As *Buffy* has shown across media, the boundaries of representations of gender can be pushed through while in some ways still relying on them. Anna Marie Smith theorizes about changes to cultural ideas about gender: "The effectiveness of new articulations depends on two basic factors: the extent to which traditional articulations have become increasingly weakened . . . and the extent to which new articulations borrow from and rework various traditional frameworks so that they already appear somewhat familiar" (1994: 6). In other words, familiarity can help smooth the path to change. Part of Buffy's appeal is in the mix of her being more "real" than, for instance, a goddess-like Wonder Woman or a Storm, more like a Kitty Pryde or a Barbara Gordon in her mix of youth, heroism, fears, mistakes, and growth. The new teen Ms. Marvel, discussed in the next chapter, follows not only from the 1970s adult Ms. Marvel but is also an heir to Buffy the Vampire Slayer in a number of ways—both relying on and subverting traditional portrayals of heroes.

## Notes

1   Buffy says this to a host of "potential" slayers, about girls all over the world (Joss Whedon 2003, "Chosen," [S07E22]). Portions of this chapter appeared in Cocca 2003, 2014b. Reprinted with permission.
2   The "Buffyverse" also includes the 1992 film that launched the series, the 1997–2004 noncanon comics from Dark Horse, and the noncanon novels from Simon and Schuster's Pocket Books. Whedon disavows the film: "My original idea was . . . a much more serious action horror movie with the funny . . . I wanted it dark" (Ervin-Gore 2001; Robinson 2001). His script was heavily rewritten. The other comics and the novels do not depart dramatically from the "canon" material of Seasons 1–10 of the TV show and comics.

3   See Chapter 1. See also hooks 1981, Lorde 1984, Moraga and Anzaldúa 1981, Baumgartner and Richards 2000, Heywood and Drake 1997, Walker 1992 and 1995; see also Kinser 2004, Purvis 2004, Snyder 2008.

4   See, e.g., Brown 2004, Camron 2007, Inness 2004, Jowett 2005, Mikosz and Och 2002, Pender 2002, Peters 2003, Playden 2001, Spicer 2002, Symonds 2004, Wilcox and Lavery 2002. See also Butler 1990 on parody as destabilizing.

5   See, e.g., Brown 2004 and 2011, Camron 2007, Early 2001, Early and Kennedy 2003, Helford 2002, Inness 2004, Jowett 2005, Magoulick 2006, Pender 2002, Robinson 2004, Tung 2004, Wilcox and Lavery 2002.

6   The (original) Bronze is archived at: http://web.archive.org/web/19981206153347/ buffy.com/slow/index_bronze.html. An archive of "Bronze VIP" postings by Whedon, writers, producers, and actors, is archived at http://www.cise.ufl.edu/~hsiao/ media/tv/buffy/bronze/. The Bronze was later retitled Bronze.beta when show went to UPN: http://www.bronzebeta.com/. Whedonesque is at: http://whedonesque.com/, BuffyBoards at http://buffy-boards.com/, and SlayAlive at: http://slayalive.com/ forum.php.

7   One could argue that one is implied with Xander and Dracula. See Marti Noxon 2000, "Buffy vs. Dracula" (S05E01); Drew Goddard and Jeanty 2008, *S8* #12–15; Gage, Brendon, and Isaacs 2014, *S10* #3–5. These last issues were cowritten by Nicholas Brendon, the actor who played Xander in the TV series.

8   For an exploration of the parallels between Buffy and Faith as compared to Wonder Woman and Artemis, see Cocca 2014b.

9   A number of Buffy scholars have written about Faith in varying levels of detail. See, e.g., Early 2001, Helford 2002, Kaveney 2001, Wilcox 2002.

10  See e.g., letters about Faith in *Buffy Season 8*, particularly after she featured prominently in a four-issue arc by Brian K. Vaughan and Georges Jeanty (#6–9); see also slayalive.com/showthread.php/2806-Buffy-amp-Faith, or faithlehane.com. If one googles "Faith Lehane" or "Faith and Buffy," there are about one million results. The character has spun off into the well-received comic, *Angel and Faith,* with letters praising her not only in that series' letter columns but also in those of *Buffy Seasons 9* and *10.*

11  Quoting Christopher Golden and Nancy Holder (1998), *Buffy the Vampire Slayer: The Watcher's Guide*, Pocket Books: 248.

# 6

# "Part of Something Bigger":
# Captain Marvel(s) and Ms. Marvel(s)[1]

The current Captain Marvel and Ms. Marvel are emblematic not only of the changing faces of superhero characters, but also of the changing faces of superhero comics authorship and fandom. While not as well known as many other licensed characters, Captain Marvel is the only female Marvel Comics character with a solo film in development. Carol Danvers as Captain Marvel may not seem all that different from other superheroes: white, blond, heterosexual, tall, attractive, strong, smart, and determined. But in the 2010s, something about her characterization resonated with female and male fans looking for a hero. This "Carol Corps" of fans has been encouraged by writers, artists, and editors to discuss and write about the characters, provide one another moral and material support, share digital download comic codes with fans who can't afford to buy, conduct fundraisers for various causes, and lobby for more diverse representations of superheroes.

Captain Marvel's fans, many of whom are purchasing the book digitally, enabled the 2014 relaunch of the *Ms. Marvel* title starring Pakistani-American Muslim teenage girl Kamala Khan. *Ms. Marvel* sells much more digitally than in stores, has at times been Marvel's top digital seller overall, and is Marvel's top-selling book internationally. Both books—along with concurrent mid-2010s title like *Buffy, Extraordinary X-Men* and *All-New X-Men, Princess Leia, Batgirl*, and *Sensation Comics featuring Wonder Woman*—upend conventional wisdom that most, if not all, comic fans are older, white males who buy male-character-centric superhero titles with sexualized female side characters in brick-and-mortar stores. The years of repetition of only one type of portrayal of female bodies and female characters made it seem as if such portrayals were "natural" or had always been that way when such repetition was also suppressing alternatives and circulating gendered and raced inequalities (see, e.g., Butler 1990, Smith 1994, Hall 2003). *Captain Marvel* and *Ms. Marvel* both sought to subvert that status quo.

This chapter analyzes the production, representations, and reception of Captain Marvel (called Ms. Marvel from 1977 to 2012), examining the numerous changes in her portrayals in various comics and animated series. Like 1940s Wonder Woman and 1970s X-Women, the character was launched as a strong feminist role model. But also like 1990s Wonder Woman and the X-Women, changing methods of comics distribution and the intertwining of the distribution method with the makeup of the fan base pulled the character in a more sexualized direction at the turn of the century, and a less sexualized and more nuanced one in the 2010s. It includes analysis of the new Ms. Marvel, Kamala Khan, as well as of the first female Captain Marvel, Monica

Rambeau. More than most other superheroes in this book, even Wonder Woman, fan letters and social media have engaged specifically with the meanings of gender roles and feminism, both with comic creators and with each other. And more than most other superheroes in this book, debates over race, ethnicity, religion, gender, and heroism through *Captain Marvel* and *Ms. Marvel* expose the nexus of the politics of representation and the politics of production and distribution.

## "This Female Fights Back": Ms. Marvel, the "Female Fury" of Second Wave feminism

*Ms. Marvel* debuted in January 1977, with multiple cultural, political, and economic motivations behind it. *Wonder Woman* was on television alongside the *Bionic Woman* and *Charlie's Angels*. Princess Leia and *Star Wars* were coming that spring. X-Woman Jean Grey had just become the powerful Phoenix, and Storm was at the title's forefront with her. *Newsweek* magazine would, in short order, declare that "Superwomen Fight Back!" (Shah 1978). In other words, attractive, superpowered, heterosexual, non-disabled white women were increasingly prominent and profitable, their privilege making their challenges to the status quo more palatable (Helford 2000 and 2002; Tung 2004; Jowett 2005). Madrid says Ms. Marvel was meant to be an "iconic female superhero that could headline her own title" (2009: 175). Howe says the character was more "an empty gesture toward feminism" and that she, along with Spider-Woman, was conceived as a "trademark strategy" for "shoring up copyrights and brand names" (2012: 193, 221). All of these factors may have been in play at the same time.

The comic was certainly pitched to readers as having a politically progressive and feminist mission, like *Wonder Woman* under the pen of William Moulton Marston and (later) *Buffy* under the pen of Joss Whedon. Editor and initial writer Gerry Conway, who on the first page of the first issue thanks Carla Conway for her assistance,[2] wrote a full-page column in the back: "Ms. Marvel, because of her name if nothing else, is influenced, to a great extent, by the move toward women's liberation. She is not a Marvel Girl; she's a woman, not a Miss or a Mrs.—a Ms. Her own person." The way in which the all-white-male creative team went about creating and fleshing out this superhero was enmeshed both in the triumphs of and the backlash to Second Wave feminism. This tension ran through both the comic itself in terms of its plot, text, and art, as well as through its letter columns. Readers, writers, and editors worked through the comic's representation of gender, as well as their own ideas about gender roles, sometimes reconciling the two and sometimes not. Except for one character who appears in a handful of panels, every character in the comic is white. Race is not mentioned once in the letters. Just under half of the letters printed over the course of the twenty-three issues were from women, not dissimilar to the *X-Men* at this time. Most of the letters and responses in *Ms. Marvel* engaged directly with stereotypes of gender and with ideas about feminism, an unusual percentage compared to the letter columns of other comic titles analyzed in this book.

Readers may have approached this new comic knowing the character Carol Danvers from her appearances in the *Captain Marvel* comic beginning in 1968. That titular Captain Marvel was a male alien warrior named Mar-Vell, a Kree sent to Earth working to reconcile his warrior ways with his growing care for Earth's people.[3] Carol, with her long, straight, blonde hair was a romantic interest for him. The base commander calls attention to the apparent disconnect between her job and her gender but is confident in her, "This is Miss Danvers! Man or woman, she's the finest head of security a missile base could want!" (Gary Friedrich and Frank Singer 1969, *Captain Marvel* Vol. 1 #13). Carol gets caught between Captain Marvel and another Kree, Yon-Rogg. As Captain Marvel is rescuing her, a machine called the "psyche-magnitron" blows up and its radiation floods through her body (Roy Thomas, Gil Kane, John Buscema, and John Romita 1969, *Captain Marvel* Vol. 1 #18).

Years later, the cover of *Ms. Marvel* #1 showed an unknown short-feathered-hair white woman (Carol) in a much-reduced version of Captain Marvel's uniform. His, like almost all male superhero characters, is full coverage. He wears black "undies" and black gloves and black boots over a long-sleeve and long-legged red suit, a yellow "Hala" star on the chest, and a black domino mask framed by blonde hair. Ms. Marvel wears the same black undies, black gloves, black boots, yellow Hala star, and a black domino mask framed by blonde hair. But her midriff and back were bare and her legs were bare where all those parts on Captain Marvel were covered, and she wore a long red scarf around her neck that villains would later grab. This sets her up immediately as a distaff and half-clothed version of Captain Marvel. An early letter writer said that this launched her as a secondary character, and concluded, "Any super-heroine who has to bare her navel isn't my type" (Roger Klorese, #6). A second asked rhetorically, "Where is a woman who wears long sleeves, gloves, high boots and a scarf (winter wear), and at the same time has a bare back, belly, and legs? The Arctic equator?" (Debbie Lipp, #8). Another wrote, "Ms. Marvel's costume is a little too blatantly sexy" (Mrs. Mary Lou Mayfield, #11). The costume would be one among many gendered elements of her portrayal in the original run of the comic, which would become more blatant during a time of increasing dependence on the direct market method of comics distribution to local shops frequented by older males, and then would lessen as the distribution methods and fan base diversified.

At the same time, with a similar name and costume to Captain Marvel, Ms. Marvel is set up as a female superhero just as strong as a male, with the potential sales of the new character boosted by positioning her as related to current characters. Word balloons on the first cover say "fabulous first issue" and "all-out action" and "At last! A bold new super-heroine in the senses-stunning tradition of Spider-Man! Featuring the most mysterious woman warrior since Madame Medusa!" Ms. Marvel's powers are the same as Captain Marvel's: superstrength, flight, and a "seventh sense"—foreknowledge of threatening events akin to Captain Marvel's "cosmic awareness" or Spider-Man's "Spider Sense." At no point in the original series is a "sixth sense" mentioned. It could be that the authors thought that a sixth sense was a generalized intuitive feeling by anyone, or it could be that they associated it only with women only; that is, "women's intuition." The renaming of it may have been meant to refer to Ms. Marvel's adventures as being more Earthbound than his "cosmic" ones, or it may have been meant to specifically call attention to her being a woman.

Her "woman-ness" and her strength as Ms. Marvel are highlighted in just about every issue. The early ones had the words above the cover logo on the left, "This female fights back!" One letter writer called this "stupid" and a second called it "sexist," saying "it implies that other females don't fight back—that it is, in fact, unusual and somewhat entertaining that a female should fight back. You wouldn't consider putting 'this male fights back!' on the cover of Spider-Man; it would be degrading" (Jana Hollingsworth in #5 and Debbie Lipp in #8 respectively). That was dropped quickly, to be replaced by cover references to Ms. Marvel as a "female fury." Invariably, villains address her as "woman" or "female" or "broad." In the first issue, a villain refers to her as "some dame in a costume" while one onlooker comments, "That little lady makes Lynda Carter [TV's Wonder Woman] look like Olive Oyl!" and a girl says to her mother, "When I grow up, I wanna be just like her!" (Gerry Conway and John Buscema 1977, #1).

Her woman-ness and her strength as Carol Danvers are highlighted in most issues as well, starting with the first. She is being hired by J. Jonah Jameson (of the Spider-Man-famous *Daily Bugle*) as an editor for his *Woman* magazine. He laments that he hasn't had enough time to devote to it and "Let me tell you, Miss Danvers, it shows. Articles on women's lib, interviews with Kate Millett, stories about careers for women—yecch . . . a woman's magazine should have articles that are useful, like new diets and fashions and recipes." Jameson tries to set her salary at $20,000, but she holds firm at $30,000 and he meets it. She ends the conversation saying, "My name is Ms. Carol Danvers. And as far as diets and recipes go, forget it!" (Gerry Conway and John Buscema 1977, #1). Jameson refers to her and a female astronaut when later exclaiming, "Women! Where'd they ever get the idea they were any good outside the kitchen anyway?" (Chris Claremont and Buscema 1977, #3).

While many letter writers responded positively to the intended feminism of the first issues, praising the female central character and the attention called to inequality, other letter writers felt that the directness of the feminist statements needed to be scaled back. "I'm employed at NASA as an electrical engineer. . . . I'm also a married and liberated woman—*and* the half owner of a comic book store. [*Ms. Marvel*] should be an action-oriented comic and not a soapbox for women's lib" (Cynthia Walker (Mrs., not Ms.), #3). Editor Conway responded:

> It's never been our purpose to preach, convert, or pontificate—only to entertain. And if along the way, we happen to talk about some of the major issues of the day . . . well, that's a little something extra that helps make us Marvel. . . . Now more than ever, you are the final editors. [The title Ms. is] more than just a symbol of quasi-political leanings—it's a long-needed simplification of abbreviations . . . it means the same thing as both Miss and Mrs.—only without any marital references. In other words, should we ever decide to have our woman wonder marry, we won't have to worry about changing the title of her book. And to our ever-lovin' production staff, that means a lot.

He not only addresses the letter itself, but also defines Marvel as a company that cares about "the world outside your window" and about its fans' opinions such that they can feel they are a part of the creative process. He acknowledges the politics of the word "Ms." and stands by it, capturing and also defusing negative reaction to the word by pitching its use as a dovetailing of political and production concerns.

Along with the costume and the use of "Ms.," the heart of the first few stories is the dichotomy that is set up in the first issue between Carol Danvers and Ms. Marvel. As noted, the explosion of the "psyche-magnitron" imbued Carol with the mind of a Kree warrior who would come to call herself Ms. Marvel. But this being was cast as separate from Carol, although within Carol's body, to the extent that "Carol" was not even aware of "Ms. Marvel." "Carol" would have a terrible headache and pass out, "Ms. Marvel" would take over, and when the superhero had completed her mission, "Carol" would reemerge with no knowledge of what "Ms. Marvel" had done. Editor/ writer Gerry Conway wrote in his column launching the title: "You might see a parallel between her quest for identity, and the modern woman's quest for raised consciousness, for self-liberation, for identity." The initial creative team saw the dual identity as an opportunity to tell a story about "the modern woman" and a more universal journey of coming into one's own.

However, the "split personality" (clinically, dissociative identity disorder) can be read as Carol Danvers' mind being much weaker than her life journey would indicate. It can imply that because she is female, she could not handle the notion of being a superhero, and so she has no memory of what she has done as Ms. Marvel. And as Carol is female, she is cast in the mold of early Jean Grey of the X-Men and Susan Storm of the Fantastic Four in that she passes out when using her powers because she is not strong enough to deal with them. This is underscored by Jameson when he sees her faint and exclaims, "Just like a woman!" (Claremont, #6). Carol, not Ms. Marvel, thinks, "I don't know who I am" (Conway, #1), "Am I losing my mind?" (Conway, #2), "I can't go on like this" (Claremont, #3), and "Why am I so afraid of her?" (Claremont, #4). Further, the verbiage that describes the differences between the two early on cast Carol in stereotypically female adjectives and Ms. Marvel in stereotypically male ones, implying that while Carol may have succeeded in a variety of ways in her civilian life (in the Air Force, at NASA, at *Woman* magazine), heroism is a male trait that she has difficulty grasping. Gibson labels Carol "the feminine" and Ms. Marvel "the feminist" and reads the split to be "representing fears about feminist activism" and a "critique of feminism in the comic" (2015: 143, 144). The early issues may point to seeing the "feminine" and the "feminist" as irreconcilable, or, as noted, of seeing "female" and "male" traits as irreconcilable and women as inherently unheroic. They may also be seen as showcasing the "feminine" Carol as clearly "feminist" in her career status and her self-advocacy, and showcasing the need to integrate the "feminine," the "masculine," and the "feminist."

Readers disagreed as to how much attention was, or needed to be, placed on the "feminine," reflecting splits within the feminist movement then and now. One wrote, "While you know Ms. Marvel is a woman, when you read the story you don't consciously preface everything she does with the idea that this is a woman doing it. She is treated as a person . . . without . . . the stereotype pigeonholing of the person as man or woman first" (Rob Allstetter, #7). But another countered with, "Please bring out the woman in her more. . . . A lady can be equal and feminine. Try watching Charlie's Angels if you don't understand what I'm trying to explain" (Ms. (and bubbling over with pride over it) Adrienne Foster, #7). In the first letter, Ms. Marvel may be more palatable to comic readers of the time as a "person," but that doesn't draw attention to the importance of a nonstereotypical portrayal of a female superhero. The latter likes the attention drawn to her as a woman, but drawing attention to her traditionally feminine attractiveness can also draw on stereotypes.

Carol's dissociative identity disorder, coupled with the initial speechifying and the shrunken distaff costume, together do display stereotypes of women. "I'm willing to believe Gerry Conway really tried to create a feminist super-heroine, but his handling of Ms. Marvel demonstrates he has no idea what feminism is" (Jana Hollingsworth, #5). Conway anticipated such criticism in his initial column, asking,

> Why is a man writing this book about a woman? Why didn't a woman create Ms. Marvel? . . . At the moment there are no thoroughly trained and qualified women writers working in the super-hero comics field. . . . Reason two is more personal. A man is writing this book because a man wants to write this book: me . . . . Reason three is—why not a man? If the women's liberation movement means anything, it's a battle for equality of the sexes. And it's my contention that a man, properly motivated and aware of the pitfalls, can write a woman character as well as a woman.

While the last statement is certainly true, the rest of this section of the column is imbued with good intentions and blind privilege. Women weren't employed in high-level writing positions because of long-standing discrimination, while a white man such as Conway can write the book simply because he "wants to," a privilege many talented women could not have employed in 1977. While, as he says, the feminist movement sought equality for all, he glosses over the fact that men had been writing women's stories—sometimes quite poorly and with rampant stereotypes—for hundreds of years such that another man writing another woman's story was not happening in a vacuum. A later letter writer tells the still-completely-male creative team to "find yourselves a feminist proofreader, and listen to her" (Suzanne Elliott, #9).

A new writer and new editor would see that the character that "originated as a cardboard feminist" grew more nuanced as time went on (Julie St. Germaine, #18). The new writer was *X-Men* scribe Chris Claremont and the new editor was future *Star Wars* writer and editor Archie Goodwin. Not unlike William Moulton Marston writing Wonder Woman in the 1940s, Claremont has the "masculine" Ms. Marvel learn from the "feminine" Carol. The latter had friends and memories of "love and beauty" while the former had only memories of "violence and hatred" (#7). It begins to feel "good" to Ms. Marvel to help others (#9), and when she next hears a cry for help, she thinks, "I can't stand by and not get involved Carol—I learned that from you" (#11). Even so, letters increasingly asked that the "split personality" situation be resolved (in #5, 10, 11, 12), and praised Claremont when he had Carol integrate what had been "two people, two souls, sharing one body" together (Claremont and Jim Mooney 1977, #5) by issue #13. New editor Goodwin wrote in response to a letter in #8, "We've been trying to eliminate as much of the blatant, preachy feminism as we can; and instead, striving to let Ms. Marvel's—and Carol Danvers'—words and actions and feelings speak for themselves." Marvel Assistant Editor (and future writer of Marvel's *Star Wars* comics) Jo Duffy penned her own letter to her colleagues about Carol, "My initial reaction to the book was pretty much what the general public's was ('Oh lord, no! Another ready-made feminist. This character was born to fail.'). And the first few issues did everything to confirm those suspicions," but, she addressed Claremont directly, "Since you've taken over, however, you've undone most of the conceptual harm and opened up dozens of intriguing possibilities, doing so credibly and in a remarkably brief time" (#11). Indeed, over the arc of the series, the singular persona becomes ever stronger. As Conway said it would, the series represents a journey of finding out who one is and the strength one has within, against a backdrop of increased consciousness-raising about equality. It can be said to demonstrate that a hero needs all of these traits—some that are traditionally thought of as masculine and some that are traditionally thought of as feminine—to succeed.

The costume was changed as well. By issue #9 in the fall of 1977, Ms. Marvel's midriff and back were covered (cover by Dave Cockrum, Joe Sinnott, and Earl Watanabe; panels by Keith Pollard). According to the editor, this was partly an aesthetic decision, but mostly a production one because it was difficult to color: "Not as sexy, perhaps (sorry, young fellas in the audience) but a lot easier to handle." The question, as with the editor's explanation of the use of "Ms.," is whether these were purposefully politically progressive decisions but described as partly production decisions to try to head off political opposition, or whether they were production decisions that were pitched as being partly political to generate goodwill among fans who would agree with their politics, or whether they were some combination of both of these.

Claremont clearly stated his goals for the character in response to a reader's letter that detailed stereotypical treatment of female superheroes in the past: "The point is not that women in comics were stereotyped in the past—they were—but that the stereotype is being broken down. Which is what *Ms. Marvel* is all about: taking a woman, giving her super-powers—and then treating that super-person with the same intelligence and respect that I would Spider-Man or the FF [Fantastic Four]" (#4). He would have Carol embrace her Ms. Marvel-ness, would widen her circle of villains and of friends both civilian and superhero. She goes on dates with a few men but commits to none. She appears in *Avengers* beginning in 1978 (#171). Not long after, she finally meets Captain Marvel, addressing him while also addressing reader comments about their ties and summing up the Ms. Marvel character:

> All my life, I've fought to be my own woman. The last thing I wanted was to become a female copy of anyone—especially you. But for better, or worse, that's what happened. I'm not griping, y'understand. I . . . like being a superhero . . . . Our powers may be similar, but our heads aren't. I'm not Kree—I'm human and proud of it. . . . Oh, hell, give us a kiss for old time's sake. (Claremont and Carmine Infantino 1978, #19)

Her origin as a romantic interest for Captain Marvel and then as a female copy of him is acknowledged, along with her own strengths as a character: her wanting to be a hero, and her humanity. Claremont fills in her backstory as well, stressing her agency. Her father pays for her brother to go to college, but not for Carol because he assumes her future lies, and should lie, solely in marriage. Increasing references are made to her need to control her stubbornness and her temper. She graduates high school in the top of her class, and upon her eighteenth birthday joins the Air Force and has her education paid for. She works with intelligence, then becomes NASA security chief. Claremont expands on the one panel in 1969's *Captain Marvel* #18 that shows Carol lying on the ground just before the "psyche-magnitron" explosion. He adds in the idea that Carol at that moment was "wishing she had the power to stand with Mar-Vell as an equal," and that is why the machine gave her the power and mind of Kree warrior.

All of this establishes her as smart, determined, and equal to any man who might take a similar path. It also reflects her privileges in terms of race and sexuality. Carol's successful path makes it seem as if such sexism is the product of individuals rather being systemic, even as the comic constantly reminds the reader of sexism by having villains and everyday people call her "woman" or "female" as well as underestimate or dismiss her as Carol and as Ms. Marvel. This detailing of Carol's backstory and expansion of her social circle, along with her having integrated her two personas while still questioning herself and striving to be a hero, greatly strengthened the storytelling and engendered strongly positive letters on each of these points.

Given that the writer was now the same as that of *X-Men*, it is unsurprising that these nuances echo the strengths of that title at the time. The parallels would increase as artist Dave Cockrum joined the book, which Claremont had requested when he began writing the title. Cockrum revamped Ms. Marvel's costume in a manner that echoed two other costumes that he had created for *X-Men*. Like Storm, Ms. Marvel would wear a black bathing suit with a high neck, and black thigh-high boots. She would tie her red scarf around her waist like Jean Grey's Phoenix. Claremont recalled, "We're trying to appeal to a female audience, trying to make her a hip, happening, 70s woman striking out on her own. . . . We say to the [pre-Cockrum] artist, 'and we need her to look sexy.' Well, his interpretation of sexy was derived from the '40s" (Howe 2012: 221). Cockrum said, "Remember she started with a female version of Captain Marvel's costume only with an open belly, and we all bitched about it because none of us could figure out a rationale for it. So they closed the belly opening." Still, he says, they wanted to pitch a new costume to Stan Lee. Cockrum recounts that he went through "fifty designs" and then "finally I did the one with the lightning bolt and sash, and I took it to Stan who said, 'That's what you should have done from the start! That's what I like: Shiny leather and tits and ass'" (Cronin 2014). She is not actually less covered in this new design, as she wears long boots and long gloves, and the new lightning bolt across her breasts doesn't draw any more attention to them than the centered Hala star they replaced. Indeed, she has more material covering her body than she did in the initial midriff-baring costume. Her breasts and buttocks, at this point in the 1970s, are not more exposed than they had been with the long-sleeved costume. But Lee's reaction about "t&a," and Claremont's direction that she had to be drawn "sexy" show that they wanted her physical appearance to appeal to an Anglo-European upper-middle-class standard of attractiveness. This costume would endure until 2012. Unfortunately, there is not much contemporary reader reaction to the costume change in letter columns, because the book was canceled shortly thereafter with issue #23 (April 1979). One would assume this was due to sales, but no sales figures were published in these issues as they were in the contemporaneous *X-Men* issues. As increasing sales allowed Claremont freer rein on *X-Men*, so that latitude extended to *Ms. Marvel* as well, albeit with different results.

The initial run of *Ms. Marvel* was embedded in late 1970s debates over feminism, and concurrent with a wave of "jiggle tv" featuring attractive, white, female protagonists with careers and opposite-sex romances. More so than its print counterpart at DC Comics at the time, *Wonder Woman*, its main character was less sexualized, more nuanced, and more purposefully progressive. Ms. Marvel's portrayals would become more mixed in the 1980s–2000s as creative teams changed, as corporate decision-making accounted for the direct market's more homogenous fan base of older males, and as these industry changes occurred within a more nationwide backlash to Second Wave feminism that spawned both more progressive and more conservative movements in its wake.

## Avenger, Binary, Warbird, survivor: Carol Danvers in the 1980s–1990s

As with other female characters at the time such as Wonder Woman and Barbara Gordon, for Carol Danvers the 1980s–90s era begins with text and ends with art that can be read as steeped in backlash to feminism and to strong female characters, while still containing nuanced elements of heroism. After *Ms. Marvel's* last issue in the spring of 1979, the character of Carol Danvers/Ms. Marvel would continue to appear in *Avengers* for about twenty issues. She would then appear in *Uncanny X-Men*, written by Chris Claremont and drawn by Dave Cockrum—the writer of most of the 1977–79 *Ms. Marvel* series and the artist who created her lightning-bolt bathing-suit costume. In *Avengers* in the late 1990s, she was written by Kurt Busiek and drawn by various artists. Throughout multiple trials in these stories, her inner strength, her high emotion, her hot temper, and increasing amounts of her body are on display, as her stories both showcase her character as well as put her in service to other characters' development.

The early 1980s *Avengers* issues, like those of the 1977–79 *Ms. Marvel*, illustrate the power of editorship and prominent authorship. *Avengers* #200 can best be summed up by the title of what has become the most famous response to its content, a piece written at the time by Carol Strickland called "The Rape of Ms. Marvel." Marvel editor-in-chief Jim Shooter, noted in Chapter 4 as having demanded that the character of X-Woman Jean Grey/Phoenix be killed, mandated the already-finished *Avengers* #200 be rewritten and redrawn, and directed a new plot of Carol having a baby. The revised issue was co-plotted by Shooter, *Avengers* writer and future *Star Wars* comics writer David Michelinie, Bob Layton, and future *Wonder Woman* writer/artist George Pérez.

When the Avengers discover that she is the equivalent of four months pregnant in a matter of hours, they don't ask why, but rather are thrilled for her. Beast offers to be the child's "teddy bear" and Wasp says, "I think it's *great*! Gosh, a real baby!" (#199). After the birth, Carol responds to Wasp's perky "You're so lucky!" by saying "Lucky? . . . I've been used! That isn't my baby! I don't even know who the father is!" (#200). She, at first, rejects the pregnancy and baby, having no memory of having become pregnant. But later, she tells Wasp she feels "like a fool" for snapping at her, and goes to meet her baby, who has grown so quickly that he is now an adult, named Marcus. "She steels herself, bracing for a resurgence of the loathing and humiliation she had felt before, waiting for the swell of fear and anger she knows will follow—but doesn't! . . . She feels instead an odd sense of calm, along with and unexplainable and undeniable attraction." "Hello, Mother," Marcus says, and recounts their time together. He himself kidnapped her to Limbo, wooed her with poetry and clothes to no avail, and then "after relative weeks of such efforts—and admittedly, with a subtle boost from Immortus' machines," which he describes to her as able to "bend your will to mine," he had sex with her and impregnated her with a version of himself. Panels show Carol's seemingly pleasure-filled face next to his monologue. He then wipes her memory and sends her back to the Avengers, pregnant. Carol doesn't ask Marcus about the kidnapping, the "subtle boost from Immortus' machines," the impregnation, or the erasure of her memory. She looks at him lovingly and says, "I feel closer to you than I've felt to anyone in a long, long time. And I think that just might be a relationship worth giving a chance." Carol leaves with Marcus. The male Avengers Hawkeye, Iron Man, and Thor watch her go, two of them saying they hope it's for the best and she's happy. Carol is written out of *Avengers* after she suffers confusion and anger over her pregnancy and her friends' lack of concern for her, gives birth, sees her kidnapper/brainwasher/rapist/mindwiper/son's face and feels "undeniable attraction" for him, and goes off with him.

The number of misogynistic tropes in this one issue is quite startling. It indicates that women's minds can be altered and that they enjoy rape, that all pregnancies are cause for joy no matter the circumstances, that women are emotional during pregnancy but, of course, will love their children as soon as they see them, that women can come to love a rapist, that romantic love and parental love are the most important things in the world to women. Strickland writes in her "Rape of Ms. Marvel" piece,

> In that issue, an all-male Marvel staff, presided by Jim Shooter and watched by the Comics Code, slaughtered Marvel's symbol of modern women, Ms. Marvel. They presented her as a victim of rape who enjoyed the process, and even wound up swooning over her rapist and joining him of her "free" will. Such a storyline might have fit into the 1950s . . . but to present such a storyline today shows a collection of medieval minds at work. Or at vicious play.

Years later, this is often talked about as the obvious reading of this now-infamous story.[4] Jim Shooter wrote on his own blog in 2011 that he finds it "heinous" and "a travesty" and doesn't remember co-plotting it but does take responsibility for signing off on it (Shooter 2011b). At the time, though, Strickland's essay engendered strikingly negative letters.

Strickland was not the only one horrified by the story. Chris Claremont was, too, finding it "callous" and cruel" (Sanderson 1982).

> There was what I felt was an egregious mistake made in *Avengers* and I wanted to set it right . . . to say what was done in the story was wrong . . . so you take the mistake, and you turn it into an asset, and you make a story out of it, and you can then take the evolution of the character from that point. (Columbia University Libraries 2012)

So in *Avengers Annual* #10 the following year, drawn by Michael Golden, Claremont rehabilitated Carol's character. Following the then-villainous Rogue's absorption of her powers and memories, Carol is rescued by Spider-Woman and taken to the X-Men. The Avengers visit her there, and she confronts them,

> Don't any of you realize . . . what Marcus did to me?!? . . . He set out to win my love and finally, as he told you, "with a subtle boost from Immortus' machines," he succeeded. . . . When I needed you most, you betrayed me. . . . Your concerns were for the baby, not for how it came to be—nor of the cost to me of that conception. You took everything Marcus said at face value. . . . You screwed up, Avengers. That's human. What is also human is the ability to learn from those mistakes. . . . If you do that, even a little, then perhaps what I went through will have a positive meaning.

They leave, and Carol stays with the X-Men. Here, Claremont exercises a privilege that fans would love to have: using the character's own voice to push back against a story he (and others) felt did an injustice to a character he cared about, and pulling that character into his orbit to continue writing her.

Written by Chris Claremont and drawn by Dave Cockrum, Carol Danvers in *Uncanny X-Men* showed her characteristic strength and courage when she went with the team on missions. She also faced the frustration over the loss of her Ms. Marvel powers and her memory due to their being absorbed by the then-villainous Rogue. But she was not superpowerless for long. The alien Brood subject her to painful "evolutionary modification" through which "she remains sane and defiant." Wolverine finds her and reassures her, but thinks "Carol isn't alright. She knows it. She looks normal, but . . . her scent's no longer human. That scares us both. But we're professionals with a job to do. So we cope as best we can" (Claremont and Cockrum 1982, #163). Carol dominates the cover of the next issue (by Dave Cockrum and Bob Wiacek) with flaming hair, shoulders, and thighs, a white Storm-shaped bathing-suit costume and boots and gloves, and a glowing red-hot face and body. "A blinding light flares within her soul, a thing apart from her that instantly becomes a part of her to form a union that will last til death. The light is power, and Carol uses it without hesitation." Unlike her superpowered beginnings in Ms. Marvel, she is unafraid and unconflicted. She has within her the power of a star, and so calls herself Binary. She single-handedly wipes out much of the Brood that had experimented on her and implanted themselves in the X-Men, and releases their victims. Now a mutant, she is invited to join the X-Men officially.

Carol's character, in some ways, is sacrificed for that of the increasingly popular Rogue. Rogue shows up at the X-mansion, begging for help in dealing with the absorption of Carol's memories and powers. Giving into her much-noted temper, Carol punches Rogue into outer space. X-Men leader Professor Xavier sees Rogue as remorseful and says he will help her. Carol calls him cruel and the rest of the X-Men are initially on her side, saying they will leave the X-Men over Xavier's decision to help Rogue. But they give in to Xavier when he argues that everyone has potential for good. As with the Avengers, what seemed to be a strong circle of peers for Carol falls away from her. She says, "I'm sorry. I'm just not that forgiving. . . . That makes my decision easy. I'm not an X-Man, and all a sudden, I'm glad!" (Claremont and Walt Simonson 1983, #171). She takes off and joins the Starjammers, space pirates led by Cyclops/Scott Summers' father. Letter writers at this point preferred the character of Binary to that of Rogue, with one saying, "Are you WACKO? There is no way that you can possibly make Rogue into an X-Man. The X-Men hate her. Binary hates her, half of the free world hates her. I hate her! Don't do it to us suffering X-Men fans" (Chuck Sottosanti, *Uncanny X-Men* #179). The conflict within Rogue, and her hero's journey, begins with *Avengers Annual* #10 in 1981, but would become a plot point from *Uncanny X-Men* #158 in 1982 to *Uncanny X-Men* #269 in 1990, all by Claremont. Along the way, "Carol" (i.e., her personality as absorbed by Rogue) would sometimes manifest herself more strongly in "Rogue." The principle is the same as it was in Ms. Marvel, that an alien psyche is alongside but not assimilated into the main character's psyche. The difference is that it is part of Rogue's story that she has to live with her own villainous actions against Ms. Marvel. The situation is resolved when the two psyches are separated into two bodies and fight one another. Jim Lee's art of their conflict was emblematic of the early 1990s Image/Bad Girl style. Both women are scantily clad and posed in unnatural positions, with Carol's black bathing suit cut high up the thighs and her large breasts straining against its fabric. While only one of them can live, Rogue will not take "Carol's" life a second time, so Magneto makes the choice for her by saving her and (off-panel) killing "Carol." This manifestation of Carol's psyche serves to shore up Rogue's heroism, as does the version of their story in 1992's *X-Men* animated series (see Chapter 4). The "real" Carol, meanwhile, also appears as Binary a few times in *Uncanny X-Men* in the early 1990s before Claremont left, and a few more times in *Avengers*.

Just as Carol's struggle with memory loss and power loss furthered Rogue's heroic arc, her abuse of alcohol furthered the development of Iron Man Tony Stark. She is hiding the trope-laden problem (for female characters) that her "Binary" powers are decreasing from having overtaxed herself saving the universe. The alcoholic Tony is concerned when she makes an excuse to him for why she is behind the bar and expresses reservations about her joining the team, but the others adamantly defend her (Kurt Busiek and George Pérez 1998, *Avengers* Vol. 3 #4). She runs through a number of new codenames, settling on Warbird after the fighter plane, linking the name to her past as an Air Force pilot. She has a sizable drink while an ice-cream-eating Scarlet Witch tells her it's too much. Carol tells her to back off and reminds her that

**Figure 6.1** Carol as Ms. Marvel, wearing her lightning-bolt bathing-suit-esque costume, in the *X-Men: The Animated Series* episode that dramatized Rogue's absorption of her powers ("A Rogue's Tale," S02E09, 1994).

ice cream goes straight to one's hips. Captain America questions her and she snaps, "Save me from men who don't think women should be able to think independently" (Busiek and Pérez 1998, #6). In other books, she is seen under the influence, lying and endangering the others. Issue #7, in which she quits the team, is titled "The Court Martial of Carol Danvers." Scarlet Witch thinks about how they failed her with Marcus, and "now it feels like we're failing her again." Warbird joins the Avengers in battle, to show them her worth, but she falls. Shaky letters read, "Guess I just didn't have what it takes . . . I need a drink!" Only three letters were printed about this issue, with one writer praising the depth of the story, and two others bemoaning it (Busiek and Pérez 1998, #11). The thread about alcoholism ran through multiple issues of *Iron Man* as well. The writer of both titles, Kurt Busiek says, "We wanted to have Tony become an AA sponsor to another alcoholic. . . . We were able to explore both Tony's struggle and Carol's" (Dalton 2011: 111). The popular character of Iron Man was an alcoholic well before this, and it certainly does not make Carol less compelling for her to live with alcoholism. But this is yet another example of when a female character's storyline is in service of male character's growth. As a package, the cattiness to Scarlet Witch, the one-dimensional "feminist" telling Captain America to mind his own business, and the drinking, which is apparently due to her being unable to handle her admittedly multiple losses, unfortunately call to mind stereotypes of women as emotional and out of control. And because there are fewer female than male characters, each female carries more representational weight than each male such that she virtually stands in (impossibly) for all women.

This is not to say that Busiek did not write a nuanced and heroic Carol and that George Pérez did not draw her as such. They did. In *Avengers*, beginning in 1998, Carol appears wearing the black bathing suit with a lightning bolt. Some artists would draw her in a sexualized way in this time period. But as drawn by George Pérez, who bucked the trends of the late 1980s–early 1990s by drawing Wonder Woman with her curves fully covered and facing front heroically, Carol looks entirely different from the 1990 *Uncanny X-Men* version described above. She still wants to be a full-time Avenger, and is committed to recovery and to taking responsibility for her actions. She appears in court to confess to endangering a plane while drunk, and announces that "with Iron Man's help and support, I've joined Alcoholics Anonymous and recently gotten my 30-day sobriety chip" (Busiek and Stuart Immonen 2000, #26). She returns to the Avengers, along with a few other new recruits, such that the team is "Four women, three men? You know, it's about time." She fills the first splash page, flying at the reader with fiery fists, saying, "All right Avengers, let's do this!" (Busiek and Pérez 2000, #28).

Busiek showcases Carol's strength and heroism by bookending issue #7 from 1998 with a seemingly identical court martial scene for Carol. But this one is different. Carol requested it for herself because she had killed a villain in battle. They decide not to punish her because there was no alternative to her actions. She says to the Scarlet Witch after, "I thought I'd be kicked out again . . . but I had to face it . . . . I feel like I've turned a corner—like after all this time I might actually *have* what it takes." Scarlet Witch replies, "You always did, Carol, and we all knew it. You just had to realize it yourself" (Busiek and Kieron Dwyer 2002, #55).

## The 2000s and 2010s: The best of the best

Carol launched into the mid-2000s and 2010s with the same personality she had always had: the resilient soldier, the self-reflective striver, the all-too-human hero. She would have two solo series during this time, as well as appearing in *Avengers*, in crossover events, and in animated series. Similar to other female superheroes, her character displays more nuance in her solo titles than in the ensemble titles or in television animation.

When Scarlet Witch completely warps reality such that both the Avengers and the X-Men are given their heart's desire (albeit not their memories of what came before), Carol is Captain—not Ms.—Marvel, the world's most beloved superhero. As much as she wants to maintain this status, she fights alongside the other heroes to change their world back to its reality. The memories and feelings of this time give her an AA-esque "moment of clarity." In the first of fifty issues (*Ms. Marvel* Vol. 2, 2006–10) written by Brian Reed, she vows, "I can do more. I know I can . . . I can be the best." This is not much different from her attitude upon integrating her Ms. Marvel and Carol Danvers personalities back in the 1970s. She enjoyed being a hero and wanted to do good. She also always "wanted to fly" and loves "the rush . . . it's what I live for" (Reed and Roberto De La Torre, #1). She becomes the leader of the Mighty Avengers and also leads a small and more independent strike team, keeps the villainous Skrulls from taking over Manhattan pretty much single-handedly, rescues mind-controlled superheroes, and protects Rogue even though she still has conflicted feelings about the woman who stole her powers and memories.

She does all of this while still wearing her black bathing-suit costume, generally higher cut on the sides and smaller across her behind, depending on the artist. From the first issue, she is alternately facing front, fiercely flying and slyly smiling, as well as being posed in more submissive ways that draw attention to her curves. Given the time period of dependence on the direct market and local comic shops, one might assume the target audience was their frequent customer base, male and heterosexual. As one letter writer said, "If you were to make any changes [to the costume] I wouldn't mind if you made the back show off her butt a little more, the way [Frank] Cho drew it in *New Avengers*. And if you made it a thong, I wouldn't complain about it either" (Greg Martino, #7). Only the first half of the fifty issues of this *Ms. Marvel* series had letters, and only 7 percent of them were from women. This could be because that is the breakdown of who was reading the comic or the breakdown of letters received, or it could be because the editors chose to portray the readership that way or to specifically cater to that audience by fostering that perception. Cho did indeed draw Ms. Marvel in his style on the first several covers of the Brian Reed run, and in the first several issues of 2007's *Mighty Avengers* as well.

In both literal and figurative ways, Ms. Marvel's most powerful adversary in this mid-2000s series—again, by a usually all-male and all-white creative team—is often herself. She does not have female allies around her except in isolated issues, and stands mostly alone with an occasional love interest as in her first title in the 1970s. She was on the side of Iron Man and having superheroes abandon secret identities and register with the government, in the Marvel crossover event series *Civil War*. This is not terribly surprising given the character's deep friendship with Iron Man and her having worked in the Department of Homeland Security for a time. Letters from fans about this particular storyline show that most of them were not pleased about which side she took in this conflict. The character shows doubts about it, arguing with herself. She also doubts herself when Rogue appears, which as writer Brian Reed noted was requested in a number of letters and also on message boards. They work together, and Rogue apologizes, "There ain't nothin' in my life I'm more sorry about than what went on between you and me," and Carol says that she's forgiven her, but internally she is not so sure (Reed and Mike Wieringo 2007, #10). She kills twice, and sadly refers to herself as a "killer" (Reed and Aaron Lopresti 2008, #24). At the end of the series, though, she wants to kill Mystique but backs away, noting that her inability to seek vengeance feels "unfair," and that she is making the more heroic choice (Reed, Sana Takeda, and Ben Oliver 2010, #50).

The other times she fights "herself" in this series, across multiple issues, are more literal and recall her earliest incarnation and "split personality." She fights an alternate-universe version of her alcoholic Warbird self who is out to kill Rogue, "You're everything I've ever fought not to be" (Reed and Wieringo 2007, #9). She fights a similar looking woman who has taken her place as Ms. Marvel and wears her old Captain Marvel-esque red-and-black costume and who declares in meta-commentary, "I've lost track of the number of photos being taken of my ass. This costume is murder" (Reed and [future *Buffy Season 10* artist] Rebekah Isaacs 2009, #38). She is seemingly dead after using too much power and is split into four beings. She then has to integrate them all back together in a recall of the first series' dissociative identity disorder arc, "My name is Catherine Donovan. My name is Carol Danvers. My name is Ms. Marvel . . . " (Reed and Takeda 2009, #42). She succeeds, and the series ends in 2010 as it began: "A while back, I said I wanted to be the best of the best. . . . Being the best of the best is not really a goal. But being the best you can be . . . that's doable. That's possible for anybody, if they put their mind to it." It is this promise of the first series, stated repeatedly in this one, which fans will cite in the mid-2010s as at the heart of their love for the character.

This nuance, the striving, the facing down adversity again and again to emerge stronger, and the occasional humor are totally lacking in the contemporaneous animated versions of the character, in *Super Hero Squad* (2009–11) and *The Avengers: Earth's Mightiest Heroes* (2010–12). The former, pitched to a younger audience, generally shows more comedic and "kiddie" versions of each character. It featured Carol Danvers as Ms. Marvel in her black bathing suit with a yellow lightning bolt adorned by a red sash, but with black tights rather than bare legs under her thigh-high boots. She stands in contrast to the more numerous male Avengers in her strident humorlessness. Thor calls her, accurately, "Ms. Crankypants." Her most prominent episodes are ones in which she is the victim of a love spell and so falls temporarily for the villain MODOK, and two others involving Captain Marvel, to whom she refers as her boyfriend (Matt Wayne 2009, "Mental Organism Designed Only For Kisses!" [S01E14]). The male Avengers are shocked that Captain Marvel is real, as they had assumed that she was lying about having a boyfriend. He is missing and she pushes the Avengers to help her find him. She is jealous when he puts his arm on another

**Figure 6.2** Ms. Marvel wears the lightning-bolt costume in *Super Hero Squad*, but with her legs completely covered. Usually the lone female and usually shrill and humorless, she is here jealous of her boyfriend Captain Marvel's attention to another woman ("Another Order of Evil Part 2," S02E02, 2010).

woman (Matt Wayne 2010, "Another Order of Evil Part 2" [S02E01]). In another, she calls Captain Marvel "sweetie" and he calls her "Masky-poo." She says that he has more cosmic energy than she does, more power than she does, and more cosmic awareness than she does. The two do work together to defeat the villain, but Captain Marvel must sacrifice himself for the victory (Charlotte Fullerton 2011, "Soul Stone Picnic" [S02E24]). In short, her character is an annoyance whose most prominent episodes cast her as "the girlfriend" and as a distaff version of a male hero. Ms. Marvel is usually the only female in *Super Hero Squad*. On the promotional poster, she is the Smurfette—a lone female with sixteen males. As such, her rather negative and clichéd representation winds up standing in for all women.

The other animated series, *Earth's Mightiest Heroes*, is pitched at an older audience and characterizes Carol in a way more akin to the comics in terms of strength and independence, but lacks well-roundedness. One episode features Carol's origin story as Ms. Marvel, and the "psyche-magnitron" explosion. She is introduced as Major Danvers, wears a military uniform with a red scarf, and is friends with the Avenger Wasp who by contrast wears a little strapless dress. Again, Carol is humorless, but in a no-nonsense way rather than a shrill way. Wasp is her foil, looking and sounding like a stereotypical teenager. Carol is active in the story, protecting Captain Marvel. The explosion that gives her powers is portrayed similarly to its original print version of 1969, in that she is unconscious and Captain Marvel picks her up and runs out. It is implied that he cares greatly for her (Joelle Sellner 2010, "459" [S01E15]). She appears in a later episode again in military garb, piloting a shuttle. She then displays her Ms. Marvel powers in a cross between her second outfit (the long-sleeve bodysuit with the Hala star), and her third (the thigh-high black boots). She is fearless and

**Figure 6.3** Ms. Marvel in *Earth's Mightiest Heroes*, wearing her second comics outfit—a bare-legged version of Captain Marvel's costume (see Figure 6.2). The first Captain Marvel wears his native uniform ("Welcome to the Kree Empire," S02E04, 2012).

confident to the point of heedlessness as in the comics, and manages to resist, blast, and punch out a seemingly invulnerable foe. At this point, she is asked to join the Avengers and does (Paul Giacoppo 2012, "Welcome to the Kree Empire" [S02E04]). Comics author Brian Reed wrote three of the *Earth's Mightiest Heroes* episodes, but not those featuring Ms. Marvel as much as the above. In *Earth's Mightiest Heroes*, Ms. Marvel and Wasp are two females alongside eight males. She is a stronger character, but still one-dimensional in her uptight military seriousness that reads as a stereotype of a "strong female character."

As with the X-Women in their animated series, cartoon Carol is more one-note than she is in print. She would appear in animated form in 2015 and 2016 as well, but as Captain Marvel, following her taking on that mantle in comics beginning in mid-2012. It is this incarnation of the character that has garnered so much attention both among comics fans and in mainstream media.

## Captain Marvel, 2012–present: Flying with her own wings

The 2012 comic relaunch of *Ms. Marvel* as *Captain Marvel* sought to capitalize on the assets of the Claremont and Reed runs of the 1970s and 2000s while purposefully steering away from the more stereotypical parts of her characterization. It marked the first time the character would have a female writer, and soon after launching, a female editor as well. The new title was directed from the top-down by editor Steve Wacker, who had edited much of the 2006–10 series as well. It was he who wanted to give Carol Danvers the title of Captain Marvel, and who wanted her to be costumed in something his daughter would like and could wear. The character would be written with a more Third Wave rather than Second Wave feminist sensibility by Kelly Sue DeConnick, a self-labeled intersectional feminist and hot-tempered Air Force brat, not unlike Carol Danvers. She assumed that given the structure of the direct market and the conventional wisdom about its fan base's noninterest in female characters, the series would run only a few issues (Phillips 2012). She sought to move the character away from her "law-and-order" characterization and toward her having pilot "swagger" along with human flaws (Women of Marvel 2014). This imperfection coupled with the willingness to go out and do her best "kicking ass" anyway is not dissimilar, she says, to the characterization of Buffy the Vampire Slayer (Siuntres 2010). Further, she sought to upend stereotypes of female military characters as being "by-the-book" "no-fun-nags," as Carol was portrayed in the animated *Super Hero Squad* and *Earth's Mightiest Heroes*. She wanted a hero for whom readers could cheer, while also seeing that she is an impatient "adrenaline junkie" prone to patting herself on the back for her "righteous indignation." None of these characteristics—the swagger, the humor, the heroism, the temper, the indignation—DeConnick felt, need be tied to masculinity but rather, could be embodied by anyone (Women of Marvel 2015). Readers would respond in unprecedented ways.

In *Captain Marvel*'s first issue in 2012, Marvel editor Steve Wacker, like Marvel editor Gerry Conway in *Ms. Marvel*'s first issue in 1977, writes a letter in the back.

He addressed two main points: the change from "Ms." to "Captain" and the change from the lightning-bolt bathing suit to a new, full-body uniform with the Hala star:

> [Changing the name] was not a change we took lightly and in fact have debated it internally at Marvel for several years. . . . With all due respect to the Ms. Marvel name, [it] is of a different era. . . . To me it made sense given her military background and the importance for Carol to feel a part of something bigger. . . . We want the comic and the character to be inspired by that same consuming need to fly higher and faster than those who came before.
>
> Here's a tip if you're ever looking to get comic fans angry on Twitter, Facebook, and various message boards . . . change Carol Danvers' costume! . . . For years, Carol wore a beautiful costume designed by the legendary Dave Cockrum. . . . The costume was definitely titillating, but again, of its time and none too practical. . . . The overt sexiness of the outfit would often—rightfully or wrongfully—cause the character to be dismissed outright by people unfamiliar with the depth and history of Carol's backstory. And to be even more blunt, it's not a costume most fathers would want their daughters dressing up in for Halloween.

The combination of these two changes, a diversifying fan base, and the outspokenness of the editors and writer about portrayals of women in comics made the new *Captain Marvel* both an immediate and sustained flashpoint for struggles over gender. The attention began before the first issue was printed. Wacker continues in #1, "What I didn't take into account was the fan reaction . . . . I'm pretty sure this is the first time a Marvel comic has gotten fan-made art BEFORE an issue has even gone on sale." Numerous issues of *Captain Marvel* displayed fan art on the letters pages, and more of it was posted on fan tumblrs. Such art, along with comments about the title and the character, pictures of cosplayers dressed like Captain Marvel, and Captain-Marvel-related crafts, would come to be tagged "#CarolCorps"—the self-named, loosely organized, active and vocal fans of the character—and be reblogged and retweeted by Kelly Sue DeConnick to her tens of thousands of tumblr and twitter followers. Fans and naysayers were primed by the costume reveal and news of the name change before issue #1 hit the stands and the digital market, and their comments spilled into the blogosphere and the comic's letter columns immediately.

Issue #1 from 2012 opens not dissimilarly to issue #1 from 1977, with a villain drawing attention to her female-ness, "Lucky me! If it ain't Captain America's secretary, Mrs. Marvel!" and referring to her as a "broad." Instead of a no-nonsense rebuttal, however, this Carol makes fun of the villain's name of Absorbing Man, which "sounds like a brand of toilet paper." Another sharp contrast to 1977 is that in 2012 the only skin exposed is her face, rather than most of her body. Captain America encourages her to take the mantle of "Captain Marvel." When logic doesn't work, he asks if she can't handle it, knowing she always rises to such bait. She reflects on the death of her idol, record-breaking pilot Helen Cobb, and Cobb's words to her in a letter would come to represent the character of Carol as well as the Carol Corps, "Higher, further, faster, more. Always more . . . . The Lord put us here to punch holes in the sky. And when a soul is born with that kind of purpose, it'll damn sure find a way. . . . We'll get there . . . and we will be the stars we were always meant to be." (Kelly Sue DeConnick and Dexter Soy 2012, *Captain Marvel* Vol. 7 #1). The first storyline, with time travel, puts her back during the Second World War with a female squadron, the Banshees. She hesitates briefly to engage, but then plunges in as usual. She travels in time again, to when Helen Cobb was a young hotheaded pilot with a secret. She has a shard of the "psyche-magnitron," the machine that blew up and gave Carol her powers, and the two of them wind up at that fateful scene.

As writer Kelly Sue DeConnick framed her first few issues, "A lot of the first volume is revisiting Carol's history and reworking it with an eye toward more agency" (White 2014b). In the original *Captain Marvel* (1969), Carol lay unconscious under debris and Captain Marvel (the alien Mar-Vell) picked her up and carried her out. In Chris Claremont's *Ms. Marvel* (1978), Carol was conscious and "wishing she had the power to stand with Mar-Vell as an equal." In DeConnick's *Captain Marvel* (2012), present-Captain Marvel/Carol rushes in to help past-Captain Marvel/Mar-Vell, "I don't go in because I'm choosing to change anything. I go because he's hurt and I can help. I go because I'm an Avenger and that's what we do" (DeConnick and Emma Rios 2012, #6). She chooses not to stop the blast that gives her her powers. As past-Captain Marvel carries out past-Carol, present-Captain Marvel/Carol carries out Helen in a parallel way. DeConnick's original plan, nixed due to the paradoxes of time travel, was to have "Mar-Vell scoop up Helen and have [older] Carol scoop up young Carol so the transfer of powers would be from her to her; she would become the source of her own power" (White 2014b). Even without this specific change, her version of the origin has Carol actively choosing to become Captain Marvel.

As the first series continued, this agency, this heroism, and a new circle of friends and allies would be on full display. A strong supporting cast would be introduced, most of them female: best friend Spider-Woman Jessica Drew, younger and efficient assistant Wendy Kawasaki, older and crustier coworker from the 1970s series Tracy Burke, adoring eight-year-old Kit and her mother Marina, and the all-female Banshee Squadron (written by DeConnick and Christopher Sebela, drawn by Soy, Rios, Filipe Andrade, Scott Hepburn, Gerardo Sandoval, and Pat Olliffe). This breadth of female characters, working together, meant that no longer would Carol have to carry the representational weight for all women. Indeed, both their looks and their characterizations were diverse. Further, Carol is motivated by her care for them. Although she is told she should no longer fly due to a growing lesion in her brain, she continues to do so to protect her friends, and so as to not let down little Kit. She realizes that the source of the lesion is a shard from the old psyche-magnitron explosion, and that the part of it that is still embedded in her head is sought after by her old nemesis, Yon-Rogg. With the pain in her head growing, Captain America tells her it's ok if she stays out of the final battle. But as is her nature, she says, "No . . . I WILL MAKE IT IF I HAVE TO CRAWL" (DeConnick, Hepburn, and Sandoval 2013, #14). Knowing what will happen to her if she does, she ends the battle by taking off into space to remove his access to the shard in her head. "I'm making a choice. I'm severing the connection to this power source and saving eight million lives. . . . I can think of worse ways to—." She screams, her eyes tearing and her body falling lifelessly. Kit's mother thinks through what to tell her daughter about the sacrifice Carol has made: "First, we tell her she's right. That she chose her hero well . . . and then we tell her what that means . . . . We tell her that heroes aren't defined by their powers or their costumes . . . but by the content of their hearts. . . . She's Captain Marvel. She's our hero" (DeConnick, Hepburn, and Sandoval 2013, #14).

Without memories, Carol survives, the parallel to the past intended by DeConnick as another intentional tweak to increase the character's agency. Akin to the 1980s storyline in which Rogue stole Carol's memories, Carol again feels nothing for those around her. But there are important differences here. First, she begins to rebuild the memories with the help of her friends, rather than having them restored by a powerful male telepath (X-Man Professor Xavier). Eight-year-old Kit makes her a comic book: "I'm going to teach you. There is nobody in the whole universe that knows more about Captain Marvel than me. . . . 'This is the story of Captain Marvel. Her many foes and challenges and how our intrepid hero became the hero we call earth's mightiest avenger . . . and how she inspired . . .'" (DeConnick and Andrade 2013, #17). DeConnick explains this move as having the Carol "relearn her personal history through the eyes of this 8-year-old girl who sees her in the best possible light—that is what [Carol] is trying to be now" (Ching 2014). Second, the plot device wipes away the years of baggage the character was saddled with: her depowering and memory loss and near-death experience due to Rogue, her rape by Marcus and her pregnancy, her betrayal by the Avengers, her alcoholism and court martial. Third, in this version of losing her memories, she was not a victim who had her memories ripped away by a villain but a hero who made the choice herself to allow it to happen as a consequence of saving millions (Ching 2014). Her core personality shines through. When best friend Spider-Woman jokingly tells her to apologize for something she has done, Carol half-complies, saying, "I'm sorry . . . sorry I'm a badass" (#16).

The combination of such relationships with the hero's non-sexualization, heroism, strength, perseverance, caring, hotheadedness, risk-taking, agency, humor, and pathos struck a chord with those who had felt alienated from mainstream superhero comics. As one comics site puts it, "Carol Danvers isn't suddenly popular after languishing in relative obscurity because she's now Captain Marvel. She's popular because Kelly Sue DeConnick has tapped into a market demographic that's been not only ignored but actively abused by publishers and fans alike" (Maggs 2015a). This described many female readers as well as others who had tired of or been offended by "broke back," secondary, and one-note female superheroes.

The first two letters published in issue #2 were perhaps a strategic choice by the editors, as both were relatively negative and reflected much of the online backlash to the new title. As Pustz notes, "Letters can reveal editors' ideas about a comic's intended audience and about how it will be read . . . [as well as] to mobilize fans" (1999: 167). Editor Steve Wacker prefaces them by saying,

> Our book has only been on sale for a few hours and we've always sold out of issue #1 and are heading back to a second printing. . . . The reaction to the book has been pretty darn loud with some people loving what we're doing, some hating it, and some not sure what to make of us yet.

Letter writer Alan Brown wrote, "I have always loved Carol Danvers [but] every time I see that new costume I want to vomit." Eric Apfel went on at more length:

> I hate it. . . . Ms. Marvel was strong-willed, powerful, and sexy. . . . You've given her a hideous new costume. . . . This new idea you guys have is only attracting attention of one small group of readers—those who know nothing about Ms. Marvel and are curious about this new female character. They aren't going to sustain this comic for more than a few months . . . . Sales are going to be bad for this title.

A third similar reaction, later noted by costumer redesigner Jamie McKelvie on his twitter, was posted to the "Captain Marvel?" section of the *MarvelMasterworksFansite* online forum by a person who had logged over 19,000 posts: "With the haircut and costume change it looks like Captain Butch. Might as well give her some more muscles, shorter legs, broad shoulders, some arm pit hair and some ugly tattoos. . . . Long sexy blonde hair with domino mask to butch hair cut with no mask. The naked thighs were just the wonderful icing on the sexcake" (FiveYearsLater 2012). Several other posters to this forum, like the letter writer Eric, predicted the title would not sell well. Such comments reflect the conventional wisdom of the 1990s–2000s: female characters must fall within a narrow definition of "sexy" and be in revealing clothing or the title will not appeal to the core direct market audience of older, heterosexual, white males. Fans perceived to be outside of this demographic group were neither "real" fans nor numerous enough to sustain such a title.

Numerous subsequent letter writers (about a third of whom were women) directly referenced these two negative letters and proclaimed their love for the title and its place in superhero comics.

> Women in comics were given the short end of the stick. None of them ever led the teams they were a part of and they always seemed to be more concerned with who they had a crush on than saving the world. . . . I love seeing Carol as a leader. . . . Shouldn't people be more concerned with the content of the story and not whether or not the costume shows enough skin? (Claire, #5)

"Here we have a United States Air Force colonel, a fighter pilot, a super hero who represents many feminist qualities, yet she fights crime with her ass hanging out. So you have no idea how thrilled I was when I saw the ad with Carol in a full body costume . . . it represents her oh so well" (Lucas Click, #5). "Finally a female comic book hero who has not been fetishized for a male readership that is largely imagined. . . . Now that it has been pretty much exposed that the 'only teenaged boys read comics' trope is a myth, it opens up the possibilities of catering to audiences like myself and my daughter and my teenaged students" (Imogen Cassidy, #6).

> The new costume is an awesome combination of sexy and commanding of respect. To be honest, the fact that the hero of this series is wearing something other than a glorified bathing suit is part of what turned me on to these comics in the first place. . . . I can see encouraging my future daughters to play pretend as her. (Kit Cox, #4)[5]

Many letter writers and tumblr posters noted that they bought the comic digitally, and had picked up or come back to comics because of it. This fan base for Carol Danvers as Captain Marvel is emblematic of the changing face of comics fandom and comics titles. Still, there is a tension inherent in reaching beyond the long-targeted group to those outside. To minimize their risk, the big companies have thus far tended to diversify their lines a little bit at the margins with new creative teams, new characters, or desexualized female characters. Having done only that much, blogs, comment spaces and forums, and social media, as noted, are full of accusations of "pandering" to "social justice warriors" who have always wanted to see nonwhite, non-male, nonheterosexual heroes and now are empowered to demand them. The irony, not lost on those advocating for more diversity, is that that the core direct market audience has been pandered to for years as comics companies catered to their presumed preferences for big action and big breasts, and only token numbers of characters of color or who were female or queer.

In the 1990s in particular, but also in the 1980s and 2000s, the print sales numbers from Diamond Comic Distributors to local comic shops were crucial to determining the health of a particular title. These figures represent the numbers of individual issues ordered by the shops in anticipation of what their particular local customers might buy. They are not reflective of what is sold through to customers. *Captain Marvel's* single-issue print sales were not blockbusting, with its #1 at about 42,000 and the next issues in the 20,000s. But the title sold well digitally and in trade paperback format in bookstores. In the 2010s, says *X-Men, Mighty Avengers,* and *Spider-Man* (Miles Morales) writer Brian Michael Bendis, "Diamond is such an inconsequential part" of total sales (Siuntres 2014). In the 2010s, bookstore sales (including online bookstores) of trade paperbacks are an increasingly important component. Digital sales are as well. Digital sales figures have not been released in any format, but one can surmise that the digital audience is more diverse than the local comic shop audience. All three of these types of sales are only a small part of the overall interest in a character—which also includes video games, merchandise, movies, and TV shows—and all of that interest can be monetized.

Not only did *Captain Marvel* and its fans get coverage in the usual places in comics journalism and engender increasing numbers of panels at conventions about diversity, but the comic and the debates around it were covered in non-comics and mainstream sites such as the *NPR,* the *New York Times, The Washington Post, The Guardian, Time, Slate,* and even *Military News.*[6] There was no mistaking the intent or effect of the comic as each of these outlets framed it the same way as its writer and editors: a new, more inclusive title that had galvanized a diverse, tech-savvy, and active fan base.

By issue #10 in February 2013, editor Sana Amanat was addressing readers as the "Carol Corps." In issue #11, she wrote, "From our Captain Marvel cosplayers to some nice reviews from fans and critics, the Carol Corps is being heard loud and clear." As Pustz notes, letter columns can be used to create community and loyalty and make fans feel as if they are helping to shape a comic (1999: 167). In the case of this comic, the issue in which Kit teaches Carol how to be Captain Marvel (#17) is a meta-showcase for the Carol Corps. They are represented on the cover as a crowd of Captain Marvel cosplayers who stand under the hero as she flies overhead with Kit. This includes renditions of writer Kelly Sue DeConnick, cover artist Joe Quinones, interior artists Filipe Andrade and Dexter Soy, colorist Jordie Bellaire, and editors Sana Amanat and Steve Wacker as well. New villain Grace Valentine seeks to harm Captain Marvel while she is being honored by a huge crowd in Times Square. Valentine (not unlike those who dislike the new uniform and title) is furious that Carol is beloved by so many: "She's an alien. An alcoholic. An undisciplined brain-damaged disaster." But in the crowd, one young dark-skinned boy pushes back, saying à la Spartacus, "I am Captain Marvel!" A chorus of "I am Captain Marvel" by countless regular people in the crowd both confuses the targeting of Valentine's machinery and represents the Carol Corps' identification with Carol. Physically hurt but defiant, Carol rises, "I'm Captain Marvel [and] I'm going to kick some ass!" The crowd, and the reader, cheer for their hero.

## Two Captain Marvels: Carol Danvers and Monica Rambeau

Kelly Sue DeConnick wanted to bring the character of Monica Rambeau into the new *Captain Marvel* title, noting, "I brought up Monica Rambeau and a group of fans in the back shrieked. It was my first really visceral understanding . . . of what representation means. At that moment I decided, first chance that I have for Monica to come in, Monica comes in" (White 2014a). Indeed, in the early 2010s, there was some dissension among fans over which character—Carol or Monica—was more deserving of the "Captain Marvel" title.

The first African American female Avenger, Monica was the second hero after the original Mar-Vell to have the moniker of Captain Marvel. Mar-Vell died of cancer in Marvel's first graphic novel, *The Death of Captain Marvel*, in 1982. From an all-white, all-male creative team, Monica launched later the same year in the *Amazing Spider-Man Annual* #16, almost the same month that Carol began as "Binary" in *Uncanny X-Men*. At this time in television, notes Gray, the face of black upward mobility was replacing that of black urban poverty (Gray 1995: 446). Monica was a New Orleans Harbor Patrol Lieutenant, her look based loosely on that of actor Pam Grier, with a long lean body and natural hair. Passed over for promotion, she accuses her boss of not wanting "to see a woman in charge of a patrol boat!" and then is described by her coworkers as being "on the warpath again" for her anger about it. Her coworkers calling out her anger marks perhaps her feminism or perhaps her blackness or their intersection, as the stereotype of "angry black woman" is not uncommon in pop culture (Tyree 2013: 49). Not unlike other black characters at the time, she is somewhat within a frame of blaxploitation due to her Grier-esque look, and she is tied to a white hero. She is not, like others, unduly exoticized or saddled with having "Black" be part of her codename (Svitavsky 2013), nor does she fit the mold of other black female media stereotypes such as mammy, jezebel, gold digger, or welfare queen (Tyree 2013). Monica, described by Spider-Man as "stunning," goes undercover in a revealing bikini to investigate a potential weapon. She destroys it and absorbs its energy, gaining the ability to transform herself into "any form of electromagnetic energy." She wears a white (described in the text as silver) long-sleeve bodysuit with a black Hala-ish star over black pants, with heeled white boots. The media label her Captain Marvel, but Monica is informed that she is not the first and says, "There was another Captain Marvel? I'm sorry. I didn't know." Monica, Spider-Man, and the Thing all express concern about her abilities, and the rest of the story concerns the Avengers trying to keep Monica from exploding. This issue characterizes her as tough and heroic, but also as a sexualized angry black woman who can't control her power.

Monica becomes the Avengers' first female African American member (Roger Stern and John Buscema 1983, #227). Often called "C.M." by her teammates, she begins as a trainee but works her way up to leading the team. Letters about "C.M." during this time, when the series was selling over 200,000 per month (#291), were all written by men and generally fall into three categories. The largest number proclaim that she is a "perfect" or "excellent" or "ideal" choice for leader. A few say that she's too powerful and needs some sort of vulnerability. And two ask for her to be paired with African American FBI agent Derek Freeman (#286–89, #291–94). The middle group got their wish. She overtaxes herself in her electrical form and simultaneously touches water (Stern and Buscema 1987, #279; Walt Simonson and Buscema 1988, #291–93). This overuse and loss of power, as noted not uncommon for female characters, would happen with Carol Danvers in her Binary form as well. Monica is brought to a hospital. Her parents arrive, and in short order, the Avengers are waving at a plane bound for New Orleans, containing the weak and physically withered Monica and her parents.

Written out of the Avengers, Monica starred in the one-off 1989 *Captain Marvel* #1 by African American Milestone Comics cofounder (and future *Justice League* writer/producer) Dwayne McDuffie and Mark Bright. She lives with her parents, works again at the Harbor Patrol, and outwits villains even though she is powerless. In McDuffie's second issue with Dwight Coye five years later, Monica speaks directly to prejudice by quoting black lesbian feminist poet Audre Lorde, "I speak without concern for the accusations that I am too much or too little woman, that I am too black or too white or too much myself." But these two issues were isolated and her appearances sporadic for several years. The character cedes the title of Captain Marvel to Mar-Vell's son and begins to call herself Photon in 1996. When he later calls himself Photon, she renames herself Pulsar. She opposes Iron Man and Ms. Marvel's pro-superhero-registration stance in *Civil War*, working on Captain America's side with Black Panther, Luke Cage, Falcon, Storm (i.e., the most prominent superheroes of color) and others. Again with Black Panther and Luke Cage, and alongside Brother Voodoo and Blade, she is part of an all-black team in then BET-President of Entertainment Reginald Hudlin and Scot Eaton's *Black Panther* that fights vampires in her hometown of New Orleans after Hurricane Katrina. In Warren Ellis and Stuart Immonen's arch 2006–07's *Nextwave: Agents of H.A.T.E.* she leads the team in a white jumpsuit and trench coat and spends quite a bit of time reminding the other characters that she used to lead the Avengers. She takes on the name "Spectrum" when she joins the 2013 *Mighty Avengers* as field leader, wearing a version of her black-and-white Hala star outfit and for the first time not sporting natural hair. A civilian comments on her straight hair, "Ms. Rambeau, I just wanted to say my daughter absolutely idolizes you . . . and thanks to you, she finally agreed to let me straighten her hair . . . and it only burned a little bit, didn't it honey?" (Al Ewing and Valerio Schiti 2014, #6) Monica is upset, but keeps her new look because she took it on as an escape from some events in *Nextwave* that she would prefer not to remember. Except for the issues by Dwayne McDuffie and Reginald Hudlin, Monica, not unlike Carol Danvers, was conceived and written by white men with varying degrees of stereotypicality and nuance.

The character appears in two issues of Kelly Sue DeConnick's *Captain Marvel*. Similar to Joss Whedon or Gail Simone, DeConnick uses humor to both address and defuse the contention about the title "Captain Marvel." Names are addressed immediately as Monica keeps calling Carol "Captain Marvel." Carol finally replies, "Give me a break! You don't go by Captain Marvel! You haven't used it in years—it wasn't yours to begin with." Monica responds, "All I'm saying is, you should have called. It's like . . . you want to date my ex? . . . you call" (DeConnick, Sebela, and Soy 2012, #7). Carol apologizes. And they work together well, Monica regaining confidence and using her powers in a way she hadn't, "I am back, baby! Monica is back!" (DeConnick, Sebela, and Soy 2012, #8). Sporting her *Nextwave* white jumpsuit and trench coat and dreadlocks, her skin tone is not much darker than Carol's and their body type is the same. Well received, these two issues did face some previously simmering criticism from Monica Rambeau fans who felt that the character of Carol had usurped the title from Monica—the first female Captain Marvel—in a way that smacked of racism and lacked understanding from creators and from the fans in the Carol Corps. Monica had not always been treated well in her stories, and there were and are a dearth of black female superheroes. Kelly Sue DeConnick addressed such fans on her tumblr, saying that the book was "always a Carol Danvers book," then became a Captain Marvel book. Further, she said, Monica Rambeau was set for the *Mighty Avengers* title (http:// kellysue.tumblr.com/post/109223187053/this-is-how-i-see-the-carol-corps; see also Rosberg 2015, ArdentTomatoStudio 2014). As pointed out by the Wasp in her first issue, Monica was unrelated to the original Captain Marvel. The *Captain Marvel* issues with Monica are about teamwork, as Monica turns herself into light and Carol, who can absorb energy, absorbs her. Their merged body defeats that day's threat. Together, they are much more powerful, making the point that women can be both competitive and friendly, an underrepresented relationship in popular culture. Together, Monica and Carol are two of the five core members of the *Ultimates* (2015–)comic team.

Along with pairing her with Monica in *Ultimates*, Marvel capitalized on and broadened the profile of Carol Danvers in several other ways as well: launching the new *Ms. Marvel* comic; relaunching the *Captain Marvel* comic twice more with #1 issues to draw in new readers; celebrating Carol Danvers' 100th solo issue with David Lopez' cover mimicking that of *Ms. Marvel* #1, except with Carol in her full-coverage 2012 uniform rather than her midriff- and leg-baring 1977 one; crossing her story over with that of the blockbusting *Guardians of the Galaxy*; having Carol appear in the high-profile *Avengers Assemble* comic, also written by Kelly Sue DeConnick; centering her character in the *Civil War II* event comic series; publishing a young adult *Captain Marvel* novel by Newbury award-winning author Shannon Hale and her husband Dean; giving her a role (albeit as the only female superhero among several male ones, who never speaks to the only other female character) in Marvel's animated special,

**Figure 6.4** Carol as Captain Marvel, wearing her redesigned uniform in 2015's *Frost Fight*.

"Frost Fight," and in its animated series *Avengers: Ultron Revolution*; and announcing a *Captain Marvel* feature film written by Nicole Perlman and Meg LeFauve. "It's not an exaggeration to suggest that the Carol Corps is at least partly responsible for the *Captain Marvel* movie announcement" (McMillan 2014). Editor Jeanine Schafer echoed this to fans, "We've been able to have this kind of diversity because you guys are asking for it and you're following up on it" (Tomaszewski 2014). The demographic shift in readership and the support of Captain Marvel had a ripple effect. Several more female Marvel characters began to appear with redesigned costumes and/or with less sexualization. Thor's role was taken up by Jane Foster. An all-female X-Men team and an all-female Avengers team were launched, as would new solo titles for a dozen Marvel female characters. The most successful would be the new *Ms. Marvel*.

## The new Ms. Marvel:
## Whoever saves one person has saved all of mankind

The great test of Marvel's new strategy of diversification would occur in 2014. Enter Kamala Khan as the new Ms. Marvel: an entirely new character, a young female, and a Pakistani-American Muslim written by G. Willow Wilson and drawn by Adrian Alphona (with a few issues by Jake Wyatt, Takeshi Miyazawa, and Elmo Bondoc). Having a character of color take on the title of a previously existing white character was not a new idea. Green Lantern John Stewart, Atom Ryan Choi, Iron Man James Rhodes, Captain America Sam Wilson, Spider-Man Miles Morales, and Captain Marvel Monica Rambeau had all done it before Kamala, in moves meant to increase diversity and update an old character, while easing acceptance of change among longtime fans through familiarity and by showing the original to be superior to the "copy" (Svitavsky 2013: 18).

In her specific demographic profile, though, this new Ms. Marvel embodied a combination of multiple aspects of comic characters that supposedly would never sell. Yet it has been selling well beyond expectations. Its first issue went into an extremely unusual seventh printing and several issues thereafter went into multiple prints as well. Within the first few issues, it was Marvel's top digital seller (#6) and remained so a year later (MacDonald 2014). It became Marvel's top international seller. Over a year after *Ms. Marvel*'s launch, when digital retailer Comixology had a "buy one, get one free" sale, four of the top ten issues purchased were Ms. Marvel #9–12.[7] It has very strong trade paperback sales. Marvel publisher Dan Buckley confirms, "*Ms. Marvel* is a legitimate top-selling title for us in all channels" (ICV2 staff 2015). Indeed, "All the female-led books sell better in digital format than in print" (Lynnskey 2015). Ms. Marvel is in the 2016 cartoon *Avengers: Ultron Revolution*, shepherded by the same Steve Wacker who edited *Ms. Marvel* in the 2000s and conceived of *Captain Marvel* in the 2010s, who had moved from print editor to animation VP (SDCC Women of Marvel Panel 2015 (July 12)). And *Ms. Marvel* marks the first-time Graphic Audio has made a direct adaptation of a Marvel comic story for an audio–book.

*Captain Marvel* and *Ms. Marvel* editor Sana Amanat recounts, "We were inspired by the Carol Corps members. Kamala was empowered by Carol and was something that was very organic to what the story was supposed to be" (Sunu 2014). The character of Kamala Khan, in other words, is a member of the Carol Corps within her comic. Hence, "Even before the first issue was published there was already a Kamala Korps waiting to buy it" (Oler 2014). As with *Captain Marvel*, the response was overwhelming before the first issue came out. In the back of that first issue, writes Amanat, they "couldn't predict how immediate, how immense, and how overwhelmingly positive the reaction would be. It seemed we had tapped into some global subconscious desire that had gone ignored for far too long. . . . Thank you . . . for making this series such an international media sensation" (*Ms. Marvel* Vol. 3 #1). All of the fan letters in this issue, written before it came out, specifically praise the concept and the representation of diversity in it.

*Ms. Marvel* writer G. Willow Wilson has repeatedly cited the combination of other prominent female writers (such as *Batgirl* and *Birds of Prey* writer Gail Simone, *Astonishing X-Men* writer Marjorie Liu, and *Captain Marvel* writer Kelly Sue DeConnick) and fans pushing conversations about diversity, Marvel editors Sana Amanat and Steve Wacker, as well as the fan "zeitgeist" as enabling the launch of Ms. Marvel,

> All of this change has been fan-driven more than anything else. I can remember when I started out back in the mid-2000s; a lot of these conversations were not being had. There were very sympathetic editors . . . who were passionate about getting more female heroes on the page dressed in things you could actually get into a fight in. There just wasn't a ton of fan support for that kind of stuff. Now that the fans are engaged, that's what I think is driving the change. (Gilly 2015, see also Nerdist Comics Panel 2014, Lynnskey 2015, Weiland 2014)

As with *Captain Marvel*, the assumption was that the title would not sell well. But, says Wilson,

> We've sort of disproven a lot of industry math: New characters don't sell; female characters don't sell; minority characters don't sell. When you can sort of break that down and show that these kinds of characters can be marketable, that there can be audiences for these kinds of stories, then that's a good thing. That holds the door open for hopefully more stories that speak to a broad range of people. (Weiland 2014)

Amanat did a Ted Talk about it, telling a wide audience that

> the big idea behind *Ms. Marvel* [was] very much about minority representation, the bigger idea was about finding your authentic self . . . it's a universal story. . . . It seems like you all found that to be true too. . . . You wrote in from all over the world, you're of all ages, races, and genders. (#6)

Kamala is Pakistani-American, Muslim, female, and straddling the worlds of her high school and her family, which for so many teenagers do not mix. Numerous letter writers reflect the fandom described by Amanat. Many of them, young and stating their ages in their letters, were thrilled to see someone who looked like them and came from a similar background, and thanked the creators. Just as many found a more universal story. One says of her identification with Kamala, "I am half Gujarati and half Filipino. Half-Hindu and half-Catholic. Half super-heroine, half-nerd. All American . . . I am different and special in my own way, yet like everyone else I desperately want to fit in and make a difference. And I will" (Leela A.V., 13 years old, Charlottesville, VA, #2). Another wrote, "I'm a white dude. But I'm also a gay man. I've faced discrimination before. I've felt like an outsider for who I am . . . .I feel like Kamala was in part made for me" (Steven Ennis, 24, #6). "As an awkward Hispanic teenager, I'm completely overjoyed when any good character arrives to punch stereotypes in the face. . . . She feels me" (Jasmin, #15).

In the first issue, Kamala is a teen who adores the Avengers and particularly Captain Marvel, writes fan fiction, and has made her own Ms. Marvel cosplay jacket. She is exposed to a mist that activates her powers. As it is happening, she sees "what she needs to see," which is a vision of Captain Marvel flanked by Iron Man and Captain America. When Captain Marvel asks her what she wants to be, she replies, "I want to be you. Except I would wear the classic politically incorrect uniform and kick butt in giant wedge heels." She thinks, "There's this ayah from the Quran . . . whoever saves one person, it is as if he has saved all of mankind," and uses her new shapeshifting powers and strength to save a classmate who looks down on Kamala and her heritage. Kamala transforms from her short, brown, brunette self into the tall, white, blonde Captain Marvel and soon finds out that "being someone else isn't liberating. It's exhausting. I always thought that if I had amazing hair, if I could pull off great boots, if I could fly, that would make me feel strong, that would make me happy. But the hair gets in my face, the boots pinch, and this leotard is giving me an epic wedgie." The comment on the impracticality of the costume also serves as an observation about the impossibility of being someone else and needing to be oneself. She does change her appearance into that of Captain Marvel in her full-coverage uniform after this, but soon makes her own costume that suits her young age and her forming identity.

Like Captain Marvel's costume, the new Ms. Marvel's was designed by artist Jamie McKelvie, to "mix in a bit of her own style, a bit of Captain Marvel (her hero), and a little of the classic Cockrum Ms. Marvel costume" (http://mckelvie.tumblr.com/post/66212034034/hey-so-you-know-theres-a-new-ms-marvel-series). Kamala's costume, grounded in a traditional South Asian silhouette, is based on her Ms. Marvel cosplay outfit and her modest bathing costume: blue shift with a yellow lightning bolt, with red long sleeves, red leggings, and a flowing red scarf. Her girlishness calls to mind the TV stars of the 1990s–2000s such as Buffy the Vampire Slayer, with her Third Wave feminist quipping and style. But more like Kitty Pryde of the X-Men, Kamala aspires to look as fashionable and cool as someone like Buffy or Barbara Gordon while forging her own individualized look for her heroism, thus showcasing a different form for her "girl power." Artist Adrian Alphona captures her strength, her awkwardness, her joy in doing good, her worries about friends and family. But he in no way sexualizes or exoticizes Kamala, whereas other female superheroes of color tend to be drawn in such ways (Brown 2013: 137). Her personality is similar to Peter Parker and to Willow from *Buffy* in being a tech-savvy high school nerd, similar to Kitty Pryde and Buffy in being a petite girl with remarkable physical strength who wants to do good, and similar to all four in being a young point-of-view character who marvels at the world around her and jokes about it, but yearns to find her place in it as well.

Kamala's family and their Sheikh subtly subvert American stereotypes of Islam and of Muslims as associated with terrorism while embodying the immigrant experience. Her parents have taught her "to think about the greater good, to defend people who can't defend themselves" (Wilson and Alphona 2014, #3). They are kind and worried about their move to the United States. Her brother turns to religion for solace, her Pakistani Muslim first love betrays her, her white blonde friend Zoe is more of a frenemy, her Turkish friend Nakia feels like Kamala is hiding something, and her Italian Catholic best friend Bruno is in love with her and supportive. At first, unlike Captain Marvel, Buffy, early Wonder Woman, Barbara Gordon in *Birds of Prey*, and the 1980s and 2010s X-Women, but more common to female characters such as these same ones in their 1960s and 1990s incarnations, Kamala's supporting cast was more male than female, placing the same heavy representational burden on Kamala that other female characters have had to carry for decades. Later, Zoe and Nakia are closer to her, and along with the newer characters Mike, Tyesha, and Ms. Norris, these female characters and their families represent more of a spectrum of gender, sexuality, ethnicity, religion, and ability.

## Conclusion: The changing face of comics . . . at the margins

In the end, "The success of Ms. Marvel and Captain Marvel has little to do with identity politics and everything to do with great storytelling" (Lynskey 2015). Kamala keeps learning about her powers and their limits as she meets and works with other superpowered beings including her hero Captain Marvel as well as the Avengers (whom she joins in *All-New All-Different Avengers*), she inspires her fellow teens, and she faces her own fears and insecurities and keeps moving forward. Both *Captain Marvel* and *Ms. Marvel* have been nominated for comics' Eisner Awards. Their characters are not "sexy lamps" who are mere window dressing to the plot, but rather, they are "strong" female characters" in that they have internal lives, friends and family, conflicts, moments of doubt, quirks, strength, humor, and heroism.

Marvel editor-in-chief Axel Alonso has said, "Fans of all colors and creeds are embracing Kamala Khan because her story is universal. She is a direct descendent of Peter Parker" and Peter Parker is the most popular superhero in the world by far in terms of sales of merchandise (Block 2014).[8] He continued, "Fans' appetite for diversity and change is re-shaping the market. . . . We've gone into a seventh printing of [*Ms. Marvel*] #1, and the digital sales are off the charts. We've got plenty more to come" (Alonso 2014). Captain Marvel's creative team continued to reach out to its fandom with a miniseries titled *Captain Marvel and the Carol Corps*. Both *Ms. Marvel* and *Captain Marvel* were relaunched in 2015 with new #1s, along with the rest of the Marvel superhero line. They may not be high sellers in print, the traditional benchmark of comics' success, but they are digital high sellers and convention favorites with dedicated and active fan bases. The *Captain Marvel* movie is on the way, partly due to the structure of Marvel's licensing deals (i.e., unlike X-Men and Spider-Man, profits from a *Captain Marvel* movie would all come back to Marvel studios), and partly due to the assumed fan base. The company can showcase a superhero and her amazing feats, capitalize on its perceived progressivism, and marketize the feminism inherent in Carol Danvers' story.

"These are books that dare to imagine that comic book readers represent a full spectrum of human beings" (Oler 2014). But other excellent books have failed in the past. Why these two 2010s titles, both launched with hopes that they would reach at least six issues, have succeeded also has to do with the numerous changes that have broadened and diversified comics fandom, both enabling and reinforcing Captain Marvel and Ms. Marvel's popularity.

Despite the fears of some very vocal fans from the more homogenously male and white fan base of the 1990s–2010s, all of the much-touted and fought-over changes in the Big Two comics world are still at the margins. Of the seventy titles launched or relaunched in the "All-New All-Different Marvel" initiative, fifteen have female leads, up from zero only four years previous. *A-Force* has an entirely female cast while Marvel's other team books with female members have one or two women and a larger number of men. About a quarter of them have characters of color. Unlike *Ms. Marvel* and *Captain Marvel*, over 90 percent of them are being written and/or drawn by white men. DC Comics' 2015 "DC You" initiative of twenty-five continuing titles and twenty-four new ones purported to cater to all types of fans. Only six of the forty-nine, four of which were new, had female leads. Their 2016 "Rebirth" initiative of thirty-two titles (more accurately, forty-nine issues per month because some of them double-shipped) had six female leads. Women were writers or artists on only four of the six female-led titles, and on zero male-led titles. These issues—changing fandom and increasing diversity, the backlash to that diversity and the marketing of diversity with caution and at the margins—are taken up in the conclusion.

# Notes

1  This phrase repeats at least three times in Captain Marvel and Ms. Marvel stories. It is in editor Steve Wacker's letter in the back of *Captain Marvel* #1. It is stated by Spider-Woman Jessica Drew to Captain Marvel in *Avengers Enemy Within* #1. And it is thought by Ms. Marvel Kamala Khan in *Ms. Marvel* #2.
2  Marvel.com credits Carla Conway as the author of *Ms. Marvel* #1.
3  Not to be confused with Fawcett Comics' Golden Age male superhero who transforms from a boy into a powerhouse by speaking the word "Shazam." The company that would become DC Comics sued Fawcett for basically creating a knockoff of Superman, and they won. Fawcett paid them and closed down. Marvel claimed the trademark with the creation of the new male Captain Marvel discussed in this chapter. DC then secured rights to the original Captain Marvel/Shazam from Fawcett but had to call the character Shazam.
4  See, e.g., Brian Cronin 2013 (March 3) on *Comic Book Resources*: http://goodcomics. comicbookresources.com/2013/03/03/meta-messages-chris-claremont-sticks-up-for-ms-marvel/; FNord's 2011 review on *SuperMegaMonkey*: http://www.supermegamonkey.net/chronocomic/entries/avengers_200.shtml; Meredith Woerner 2011 (December 8) on *io9*: http://io9.com/5866330/a-video-breakdown-of-the-sad-history-of-ms-marvel-sex-slave; Michael Westgarth 2013 (April 25) on *GeekInsider*: http://www.geekinsider.com/on-the-rape-of-ms-marvel/; *Jay & Miles X-Plain the X-Men* #17 "The Island of Dr. Corbeau": http://www.xplainthexmen.com/2014/08/17-the-island-of-dr-corbeau/.
5  Kit Cox would emerge as an organizing force in the Carol Corps and the character of Kit in the comic is assumed to be named for her. She later worked at DeConnick and her husband's production company.
6  See, e.g., Ching 2013, Wheeler 2014, Field 2014, Maggs 2015, Pantozzi 2015 from comics news sites. See Tomaszewski 2014, Sunu 2014, Campbell 2014 and various panel discussions from conventions. See Edidin 2014, Oler 2014, Baker-Whitelaw 2014a, Lynskey 2015, Betancourt 2014, McMillan 2014, Parrish 2014 for more mainstream coverage.
7  Of the other six, two were the female *Thor*, one was *Silk*. The other three were two *Star Wars* issues and one *Darth Vader* issue.
8  Indeed, Spider-Man merchandise pulls in more than the next three most popular characters/teams *combined*: Batman, then Superman, and then the Avengers.

# Conclusion: Gender, Power, and Representation

The Captain Marvel, Ms. Marvel, X-Women, Princess Leia, Batgirl, and Wonder Woman of the 2010s have commonalities with all of their previous incarnations. They are mostly white, able-bodied, and heterosexual. They are conventionally attractive, strong, and capable. They do the same things that male superheroes do. Still, and unlike male superheroes, attention is called to their gender both within the texts themselves as well as outside of them. They are more nuanced in print, where the production costs are lower so the company's risk in changing their old formulas is smaller than on the small or big screen. There are differences as well. For the most part, the stereotypical and one-note "strong woman" limited by her "femininity" from the 1950s to the 1970s has fallen away, and the pose-oriented sexualization from the 1990s to the 2000s has decreased. The younger characters—Buffy, Batgirl, Ms. Marvel, Princess Leia, and (in the mid-2010s) Jean Grey of the X-Men—are powerful and no less subversive of gendered inequalities than their older counterparts, Captain Marvel, Storm, and Wonder Woman. They are not as alone as they used to be, with many of them surrounded by new and more diverse supporting characters, so each no longer has to stand-in for "all" women as they did so often in previous decades. More of them are being written or drawn by women. More of them are written and drawn less as "sexy lamps" serving no purpose other than eye candy, and more as plot-driving characters with agency and nuanced personalities. Their power is located not just in their physicality, but also in their love, empathy, sisterhood, families, perseverance, and forgiveness. These are the elements that create loyal readers: good stories in which female superhero characters are portrayed with complexity and with care. Fans have become increasingly active and organized in pushing for more diversity among creators, against objectification of female characters, and for more diverse representation in terms of both the demographics and characterizations of those characters.

There are more female superheroes starring in mainstream comics and more female writers and artists working on comics in the mid-2010s than in the last seventy years. Yet, these titles are a small percentage of superhero comics, about 11–12 percent. This is an improvement over their percentage in decades past, which was usually in the single digits. On the one hand, representation of female superheroes has doubled, which is significant growth. On the other hand, they are still only a fraction of the overall output in the genre. Similarly, the percentage of female writers and artists still hovers at about 10–11 percent of writers and 6–8 percent of artists at Marvel and DC, the "Big Two" of superhero comics. At Boom! and Dynamite, the percentage of writers is slightly higher, more in the mid-teens. Their percentage of female artists is about 20 percent and 8 percent, respectively. Image Comics' writers and artists are about 10 percent female, and Valiant's hover at or near 0 (Hanley 2015). The percentage of women writing or producing or directing TV shows and films is similarly low. Across media, almost all of these women are white. Racial and ethnic diversity is rising for mainstream superhero comics, but so far, almost entirely among male creators. Things have changed, but overall, slowly and at the margins.

## "This isn't affirmative action. This is capitalism."

A big part of the change has to do with the changing fan base for superhero characters and its relationship to comics production and distribution. Decisions about characters and their representation are not solely top-down from a company nor solely bottom-up from fans. Rather, there is a complex interplay in the arenas of production, distribution, representation, and audience reception and action. "Economic factors affect not only which media products get created, but also the content of those products, who is represented in them and how, and which audiences get their interests catered to" (Duncan and Smith 2012: 146). In the 1940s when comics were sold on newsstands, companies knew they had to appeal to many different types of people to remain afloat. The direct market model of the 1980s–2000s by contrast, in which local comic shops were the customers for the comics publishers, played a role in concentrating the fan base to the point that it was, as DC copublisher Jim Lee puts it, "perceived as monolithic" (Ching 2015). In both eras, the types of comics produced catered to the assumed fan bases: one wide, one narrow. The direct market may have saved the comics industry, but it also fostered stories with stereotypes and objectification of female characters, as well as a culture in many shops of exclusivity and gate-keeping.[1] But "the synergy between comic book stores and comic books, which had developed relatively seamlessly from the end of the 1970s to the mid-1990s, now belongs to the past" (Gabilliet 2010: 210).

Distribution methods have changed. With digital downloads of comics, there's always a "comic book store in your pocket."[2] Fans can buy trade paperbacks of comic issues in a bookstore, or borrow them from a library, without having to go into a comic shop. Hundreds of female comic book retailers organized as the Valkyries and their sister organization of librarians and bookstore retailers known as the Valhallans are recommending titles more friendly to new readers and diverse readers. Bolstering these changes in distribution methods as well as being encouraged by them, more creators and more fans, some of whom are older fans who want to share the medium with their children, have pushed for the inclusion of more character diversity in terms of gender, race, ethnicity, sexuality, and ability. White male support for diversity within and outside of comics' companies nudges those companies as well. Many of these people have connected with other fans as well as with creators at far more frequent and safer conventions, which are approaching gender parity, and have joined other fans in speaking out about diversity at an increasing number of panels at those conventions. Fans have also used social media or podcasts or comics journalism websites' comment spaces or other electronic forums to communicate with creators and with each other, "a new more symbiotic relationship between creator and fan" (Lackaff and Sales 2013: 73). Comics companies are taking note.

DC's Lee observes, "You see a lot more women that are into comics, at comic book shops and conventions. Our own studies have shown there's a lot more people looking for a lot more flavors and diversity in our line than we're currently doing" (Ching 2015; O'Leary 2015). Marvel publisher Dan Buckley has made similar comments: "Just from going to cons, feedback from social media, the old method of letters, emails . . . there's a diversifying of the readership base" (ICV2 staff 2015).

At the end of the day for these companies, it's about money. And sales are up. Print sales for comic books and graphic novels overall (not just for superhero titles), adjusted for inflation, are higher than they've been in twenty years. Only a little more than half of the total sales are through comic book stores, with the rest through online and brick-and-mortar bookstores, newsstands, and digital (Miller 2015). When digital platform Comixology held a "buy one get one free" sale in the spring of 2015, seven of the top ten selling titles were female-led and the other three were *Star Wars* titles (Pantozzi 2015). Outside of single-issue comics sales are other potential fans. Nine of the ten *New York Times* best-selling graphic novels in the summer of 2015—none from Marvel or DC—were by female creators featuring female characters. The tenth, by two men known for their well-written and well-drawn female characters, Kieron Gillen and Jamie McKelvie, features women as well (http://www.nytimes.com/best-sellers-books/2015-07-26/paperback-graphic-books/list.html). Films, TV shows, video games, and merchandise are consumed by both males and females, with increasing protests at the gendering of these media and products toward males. Conventions have an economic impact of several billion dollars while comic sales themselves hover at about one billion (Siuntres 2015). Marvel editor-in-chief Axel Alonso acknowledges the company has a "larger game plan [including] animation divisions, video games, movies [and] digital sales." Therefore, he says, "the traditional method of determining whether or not a book is gonna be around next month," print orders by local comic shops through the direct market, "is obsolete" (Lynnskey 2015).

The new (or newly active and vocal) fans are proving that they can support—with their dollars, not just their letters, emails, tumblrs, instagrams, and tweets—a different kind of character from that which the medium had been putting out for the previous twenty to thirty years. *Captain Marvel* writer Kelly Sue DeConnick comments on the industry's years of narrow marketing to a narrow fan base: "From a business standpoint, it's just stupid. Women control the purse strings in families very often. Young women have their own income and love to shop and read. Why would you leave money on the table?" (Phillips 2012). Marvel editor Sana Amanat has said the same: "You can't ignore half the market, right? That's pure finance and economics speaking" (Maggs 2015b). Marvel's Alonso, who by all accounts has sought to increase the diversity of creative teams as well as characters, has said, "This isn't affirmative action. This is capitalism" (FanBros 2015).

It's both affirmative action and capitalism. The former is a systemic means to speed diversity after centuries of systemic discrimination. It requires being conscious of historic vectors of discrimination such as gender, race, ethnicity, religion, sexuality, and disability in hiring creators, and a similar consciousness in creating and fleshing out characters. While writers, artists, and editors might be interested in change for a variety of reasons, the profit motive is the incentive for the parent companies to engage in diversification of creative teams and of characters. *Archie* publisher Jon Goldwater said of introducing gay character Kevin Keller, "It was a cultural decision and business decision. They go hand in hand" (Schmidt 2015). A superhero-character-owning company will diversify their staffs or their characters not solely because it benefits other people, because it is the right thing to do, nor because it's an idea whose time has come. They will do it because it's in their interest too.[3]

This particular arena allows the furthering of more equal representation through its purchase by individuals' dollars, and those dollars can serve to uphold the unequal economic, political, and social systems in which the superhero genre is embedded. The numbers of people on each side are irrelevant: if those pushing for inequality have more dollars than those pushing for equality, the former will be catered to by superhero-producing companies. Democracy and capitalism can be, and often in world history have been, at cross-purposes. Individual dollars for individual comics or movies cannot guarantee systemic change; collective political action that empowers formerly marginalized groups can. Comics and other fiction-producing media are among many institutions in our world, and broad-based change toward more equity requires attending to other institutions and other methods for change as well as this one.

In this arena, the companies are being told, directly and repeatedly, that they will get more dollars from certain organized and vocal fans if they create, highlight, or strengthen characters that are more demographically representative, preferably through hiring a wider variety of creators. The fans are being told that they are being heard, and that changes are coming. As Henry Jenkins writes, "The media industries have to change to accommodate the demands of consumers even as they seek to train consumers to behave in ways that are beneficial to their interests. Media companies act differently today because they have been shaped by the increased visibility of participatory culture" (2007: 362–63). There is money to be made, the companies have discovered, from diversifying—at least at the margins.

## Struggling over gender

There has been negative reaction to the diversification, even though it is still only in its baby steps. Image Comics cofounder Erik Larsen encapsulated it with a 2015 tweet,

> I'm tired of the big two placating a vocal minority at the expense of the rest of the paying audience by making more practical women outfits . . . vocal critics on the web who get in a tizzy every time a woman character looks attractive. . . . There is a portion of the audience that would dearly love frumpy, plain looking female characters whose love interests are all impossibly handsome men. Kind of a wish fulfillment thing, I suppose.

In an interview used to expand upon his comments, he referred to readers as "mouthy amateurs [whose] suggestions should largely be treated like the witless ramblings of an insane person" (Bechtloff 2015a).

This casts those (read: women) who want "practical women outfits" as others, as outsiders: unduly loud, unduly overwrought, a small number, unattractive, and pathetic. There is no reference to the fact that vocal segments of the 1990s–2000s direct market audience apparently wanted their female characters to be "impossibly" attractive and so comics creators delivered what that particular audience wanted at that particular time. Again, the repetition of a specific female body type in specific poses in comics made it appear timeless and natural, but it was and is neither. Numerous comics creators and fans pushed back at Larsen to the point that he removed his tweets, although not before they were captured on other sites. Others against change have claimed that comics companies are now suffused with "killjoy political correctness" and "progressive hand-wringing and misandry" (quoted in Lynskey 2015 and Binder 2015), by "moralizing busybodies" and "joyless harpies" who are "killing comics" and also "making them suck" (Bechtloff 2015b). Still others have issued rape threats and death threats to those whom they label "social justice warriors" for having pointed out that male characters are idealized for their athleticism and female characters for sexual availability, replicating power asymmetries from everyday life into fandom.[4] *Captain Marvel* writer Kelly Sue DeConnick notes that the "social justice warrior" term shouldn't have a negative connotation in comic fandom because superheroes "ARE social justice warriors!" and those missing that "need to read it again" (Maggs 2015). One of the targets of such threats, former DC editor Janelle Asselin, writes, "Times are changing. Fans and pros who are angry about it are not victims. They've dominated the comics industry for decades. Now they too must learn to live with a world where not every single book is made for them" (2015).

Discomfort about "the place of women" has been embedded in the superhero genre for decades. Letter columns of *Superman* or *Batman* or *X-Men* don't have passionate arguments about how the male characters perform "manliness," or "masculinity," or how they should be more or less sexualized. The letters tend to be about plot points. But with the female characters, so many letters and blog/board posts and podcast comments—especially for Wonder Woman, Batgirl/Oracle, Leia and Padmé, Storm, Buffy, and Ms. Marvel/Captain Marvel—are about how they perform their gender, and how it looks and sounds on the page and on the screen, and whether or not that meshed with the fans' ideas of how women are supposed to look, supposed to talk, and supposed to behave. Readers and viewers have shown themselves to be inspired, delighted, surprised, offended, and threatened by the gender performance of these characters in ways that they have not been with male characters. Fans don't seem to approach Batman or Spider-Man as making a political statement about whiteness or maleness because we have been taught to think of "white and male and powerful" as some kind of natural, neutral norm, and anyone who's not that but who still seeks to exert power as having a political agenda, as pushy, as uppity, as aggressive. Those who are against more diversity among comics creators and comics characters decry diversification and inclusion as "political," without recognizing that discrimination and exclusion are just as political.

No one asks comic creators, "How do you write such strong male characters?" because male characters are always already assumed to be strong, and readers and viewers have seen countless examples of them. There are no seeming contradictions in those characters. There is apparently nothing "tricky" about writing them. But people do ask, all the time of writers and artists, "How do you create such strong female characters?" Somehow the "strong female character" is a mystery, an anomaly, a contradiction requiring explanation because she has been so little seen, across all media, for countless years.

When *X-Men* writer Chris Claremont is asked how he writes strong female characters, he usually says, "I just started writing women and girls like the ones I knew" (Kaplan, Pekar, and Waldman 2008: 120). *Wonder Woman* writer Greg Rucka was asked so many times, he finally wrote an article called "Why I Write Strong Female Characters" in 2012. "I write characters. Some of those characters are women," and, "I write them the way I write all of my characters. With consideration, with respect, with honesty" (Rucka 2012). He says authenticity is important, but so is respect for the story and the audience, and so is research. When *Captain Marvel*'s Kelly Sue DeConnick is asked for advice on how to write a strong female character, she has taken to saying, "First, pretend we're people" (NYCC 2014, "Carol Corps and Beyond: The Future of Female Fandom" panel). Second, "if you can take out your female character and replace her with a sexy lamp and your plot still functions, you're doing it wrong" (Dockterman 2014). *Buffy*'s Joss Whedon echoes all of these sentiments: "I like strong women. I was raised by one . . . . I've always been comfortable with women as people, and I was surprised when I realized how few people—writers and filmmakers—actually think of them as people" (Ervin-Gore 2001).

Rucka says that when people ask him how or why he writes strong female characters, he thinks that "what they're really asking is, why aren't more men doing it? Why is it that so many male writers, when trying to write strong female characters, fail? Why do they default to a shorthand, lazy equation, where strong equals bitch?" (Rucka 2012). Why, asks, DeConnick, is it so easy to some male writers to write a male alien from another planet and so difficult to write a woman from planet Earth, when "we're not so very different" (NYCC 2014, "Carol Corps and Beyond: The Future of Female Fandom" panel). There have been so few examples of female characters to use as models, and so little diversity across that small number. So many of them, in a variety of media, have been written stereotypically, as secondary characters positioned as different from, or lesser than, the heroic male main character. This is why, when Joss Whedon is asked, "Why do you write strong female characters?" he answers, "Because you're still asking me that question" (Whedon 2006).

## Moving forward: Countering stereotypes and making mirrors

Depictions of many characters described in this book have been written poorly at various times—weak, emotional, (hetero)romance-driven caricatures of "feminine," or strident, humorless, one-note cardboard cutouts of "feminist." But "feminine" need not be conflated with weak, and "feminist" with strong as if they are total opposites. "Strong female character" doesn't have to mean "emotionless," or "badass," or "flawless," although these seem to have been initial steps in subverting long-standing stereotypes.

Rather, "strong" can encompass any characters who are nuanced rather than stereotyped, authentic rather than caricatured. They have to be more numerous so that a range of characterizations can be written without fear that the one woman or the two women have to stand in and carry the representative weight for half the world. If there is only one woman on a team and she isn't "strong," one runs the risk of having stereotyped the woman as the "weak" one on that team. But with a number of female characters, one can be strong, one can be weak, one can be flawed and striving, one can be vulnerable and decisive, one can be unrepentantly villainous, or all or none of the above. They have to be well written, with depth and quality. And although there are many excellent white male creators who write all types of characters well and should continue to do so, it is essential to also have people from groups that have been historically discriminated against tell their own stories and tell others' stories too. Not only for more equity in the workplace, for more authenticity, for a wider variety of characters and stories, and for more points of identification for readers, but also to challenge that white men have been telling their own and everyone else's stories for a very long time.

In the past, even when female comic characters were made central and made powerful, their power was counterbalanced with exaggerated sexualization, priming the reader to associate that female-ness with being a sex object. Male superheroes were not, and are not, ever in such clothing or poses. The near nudity, the "broke back" posing, and the lack of nuance pushed readers to continue to trivialize such characters as objects, as playthings, as side characters to look at and act on rather than identify with or empathize with. Women and people of color, extremely underrepresented or represented only stereotypically in media, still consumed it—either reading against the grain and spinning characters who looked like them as best they could, or identifying with characters who looked unlike them. This is both a shame and a means to an important skill. It is a shame because there is no denying the importance, especially to children, of seeing characters who look like them and with whom they can strongly identify. It is important because it builds empathy for those who look quite different but to whose humanity the reader still can relate. Those from dominant groups need to see heroes who do not look like them. And those from more marginalized groups need to see heroes who do look like them.

As Pulitzer Prize-winning author Junot Díaz has said in speaking with young people:

> You guys know about vampires? You know, vampires have no reflections in a mirror? There's this idea that monsters don't have reflections in a mirror. And what I've always thought isn't that monsters don't have reflections in a mirror. It's that if you want to make a human being into a monster, deny them, at the cultural level, any reflection of themselves. And growing up, I felt like a monster in some ways. I didn't see myself reflected at all. I was like, "Yo, is something wrong with me? That the whole society seems to think that people like me don't exist?" And part of what inspired me was this deep desire that before I died, I would make a couple of mirrors. That I would make some mirrors so that kids like me might see themselves reflected back and might not feel so monstrous for it. (Donohue 2009)

This making of mirrors in fiction, by and for formerly disempowered groups, is occurring in the world of superheroes, still in small numbers but with growing frequency beginning in the 2010s. Increasingly active fans, enabled by broader political gains coupled with different comics distribution methods and social media technologies, are pushing for change. They are invested in superheroes. They are inspired by them. They are communicating that "symbolic annihilation" (Tuchman 1978) and "cinematic racism" (hooks 1992) are no longer acceptable, that women, and queer people, and people of color cannot be omitted, trivialized, condemned, or stereotyped in fiction anymore. But, as comics writer Kelly Sue DeConnick has said, while there have been gains, "Nobody sit down. We're not done yet" (Baldwin 2015).

# Notes

1   On the distribution system as affecting the output of comics companies, see, for instance, Duncan and Smith 2012: 146, Lopes 2009: xiii.
2   Quote from Kelly Sue DeConnick 2014 (October 10): "Carol Corps and Beyond: The Future of Fandom" NYCC Panel. See also Howe 2014, ICV2 staff 2015, Johnson 2007, Lynskey 2015, Salkowitz 2012, Wilson 2014.
3   This is "interest convergence" theory, named by critical race theorist Derrick Bell in talking about why whites finally allowed blacks some measure of equality beginning in the 1950s (Bell 1980).
4   See note 3 in the Introduction.

# Bibliography

Adichie, Chimamanda Ngozi, 2014. "The Danger of a Single Story." *Everyday Feminism* (October 25): http://everydayfeminism.com/2014/10/the-danger-of-a-single-story/.

AfterEllen.com staff. 2009a (April 6). "Interview with Gail Simone Part 1." http://www.aft erellen.com/movies/48255-interview-with-wonderwomans-gail-simone-part-1.

AfterEllen.com staff. 2009b (April 8). "Interview with Gail Simone Part 2." http://www. afterellen.com/people/48372-interview-with-wonder-womans-gail-simone-part-2

Alaniz, José. 2014. *Death, Disability, and the Superhero: The Silver Age and Beyond.* Jackson, MS: University Press of Mississippi.

Allstetter, Rob. 1997 (August). "The Dark Knight Returns." *Wizard* 72: 50–54.

Alonso, Axel. 2014 (October 24). "AXEL-IN-CHARGE: Teasing Marvel Events, Bringing 'She-Hulk' to a Close." *Comic Book Resources*: http://www.comicbookresources. com/?page=article&id=56590.

Amy B. 2013 (July 24). "What's Wrong with Barbara Gordon as Batgirl." *Comics Bulletin*: http://comicsbulletin.com/whats-wrong-barbara-gordon-batgirl/.

Andersen, Michael. 2013. "X-Men and X-Factor United." *Uncanny X-Men.Net*: http:// www.uncannyxmen.net/secrets-behind-the-x-men/x-men-and-x-factor-united.

Anderson, Kevin, and Rebecca Moesta. 1998. *Crisis at Crystal Reef.* Boulevard.

Ardent Tomato Studio. 2014 (November 2): http://ardenttomatostudio.tumblr.com/ post/101616118111/ive-been-sad-and-angry-lately-so-i-drew-these.

Asselin, Janelle. 2014 (July 8). "Some Quick Convention Attendance Math:" http:// gimpnelly.tumblr.com/post/91230004080/some-quick-convention-attendance-math.

Asselin, Janelle. 2015 (March 17). "The 'Vocal Minority' and Artistic Integrity in Comics." *Comics Alliance*: http://comicsalliance.com/the-vocal-minority-and-artistic-integrity-in-comics/?trackback=tsmclip.

Associated Press. 2014 (16 December). "Black Captain America Leading Comic Book Diversity." *The New York Times*: http://www.nytimes.com/aponline/2014/12/16/us/ politics/ap-us-diverse-superheroes.html.

Aubrey, Jennifer Stevens, and Kristen Harrison. 2004. "The Gender-role Content of Children's Favorite Television Programs and Its Links to Their Gender-related Perceptions." *Media Psychology* 6 (2): 111–46.

Ausiello, Michael. 2008 (March 21): "Laughter, Tears, and (Yikes!) Tension at Buffy Reunion." *TV Guide*: http://www.tvguide.com/news/laughter-tears-yikes-8507/).

Backman, Russell. 2014. "In Franchise: Narrative Coherence, Alternates, and the Multiverse in X-Men." In *Superhero Synergies: Comic Book Characters Go Digital*, edited by James Gilmore and Matthias Stork, 201–20. Lanham, MD: Rowman & Littlefield.

Bajac-Carter, Maja, Norma Jones, and Bob Batchelor, eds. 2014. *Heroines of Comic Books and Literature: Portrayals in Popular Culture.* Lanham: Rowman & Littlefield.

Baker, Kaysee, and Arthur A. Raney. 2007. "Equally Super? Gender-Role Stereotyping of Superheroes in Children's Animated Programs." *Mass Communication & Society* 10 (1): 25–41.

Baker-Whitelaw, Gavia. 2014a (November 9). "Captain Marvel Wants YOU for the Carol Corps." *The Daily Dot*: http://kernelmag.dailydot.com/issue-sections/features-issue-sections/10785/captain-marvel-carol-corps/#sthash.xsmFFG2k.dpuf.

Baker-Whitelaw, Gavia. 2014b (December 30). "An Illustrated Guide to Superhero Movies that Pass the Bechdel Test." *The Daily Dot*: http://www.dailydot.com/geek/superhero-movie-bechdel-infographic/.

Baldwin, Dianna. 2015 (July 1). "An Interview with Kelly Sue DeConnick." *Destroy the Cyborg*: http://www.destroythecyb.org/an-interview-with-kelly-sue-deconnick-20638.htm.

Barnes, Brooks. 2015 (April 17). "For Lucasfilm, the Way of Its Force Lies in Its 'Star Wars' Fans." *The New York Times*: http://www.nytimes.com/2015/04/18/business/media/for-lucasfilm-the-way-of-its-force-lies-in-its-star-wars-fans.html.

Barr, Tricia. 2011 (July 18). "Does Slave Leia Weaken or Empower Women?" *Fangirl Blog*: http://fangirlblog.com/2011/07/slave-leia-empower-women/.

Barr, Tricia. 2012 (February 21). "The Power to Save Padmé." *Fangirl Blog*: http://fangirlblog.com/2012/02/the-power-to-save-padme/.

Barr, Tricia. 2014 (June 28). "Did Geena Davis Convince J.J. Abrams to Gender-Swap and Episode VII Character?" *Fangirl Blog*: http://fangirlblog.com/2014/06/did-geena-davis-convince-j-j-abrams-to-gender-swap-an-episode-vii-character/.

Baumgartner, Jennifer, and Amy Richards. 2000. *Manifesta: Young Women, Feminism, and the Future*. New York: Farrar, Straus, and Giroux.

Bechtloff, Chris. 2015a (March 21). "Erik Larsen Speaks On Online Outrage, Women In Comics And "Sexist" Costume Designs." *Reaxxion*: http://www.reaxxion.com/6512/erik-larsen-speaks-on-online-outrage-women-in-comics-and-sexist-costume-designs.

Bechtloff, Chris. 2015b (April 10). "How Frank Cho Told Feminists to Shut Up and Go Away: One Man Resists the SJW Hordes." *Reaxxion*: http://www.reaxxion.com/7442/how-frank-cho-told-feminists-to-shut-up-and-go-away.

Beerbohm, Robert (beerbohmrl@gmail.com). 2015 (January 27). "Early 1970s Comic Book Market." COMIXSCHOLARS-L@lists.ufl.edu.

Bell, Derrick. 1980. "Brown v. Board of Education and the Interest-Convergence Dilemma." *Harvard Law Review* 93: 518–33.

Bellafante, Ginia. 2001 (June 24). "Bewitching Teen Heroines." *Time*: http://www.time.com/time/magazine/article/0,9171,137626,00.html.

Berlatsky, Noah. 2015. *Wonder Woman; Bondage and Feminism in the Marston/Peter Comics, 1941-48*. New Brunswick: Rutgers University Press.

Binder, Matt. 2015 (March 24). "The New Gamergate: Angry White Men Are Trying To Shut Down Diverse Comics: Female Thor and Muslim Ms. Marvel Are Saving the Comic Book Industry, and the Misogynist Trolls Are Pissed." *Salon*: http://www.salon.com/2015/03/24/the_new_gamergate_angry_white_men_are_trying_to_shut_down_diverse_comics/.

Block, Alex Ben. 2014 (November 13). "Which Superhero Earns $1.3 Billion a Year?" *The Hollywood Reporter*: http://www.hollywoodreporter.com/news/superhero-earns-13-billion-a-748281.

Bolland, Brian. 2013 (December 1). http://brianbolland.blogspot.com/2013/12/heres-page-i-drew-for-killing-joke.html.

Bowman, Stella. 2011 (June 10). "Episode 22, 'Chuck Dixon and Scott Beatty'." *Batgirl to Oracle Podcast*: http://thebatmanuniverse.net/episode-22-chuck-dixon-and-scott-beatty-interview/.

Box Office Mojo. 2015. "Franchises: X-Men." http://www.boxofficemojo.com/franchises/ chart/?id=xmen.htm.

Brereton, Dan and Christopher Golden (w), and Joe Bennett (a). 2007. "Buffy: The Origin." [adapted from Joss Whedon's original screenplay in 1999] In *Buffy the Vampire Slayer Omnibus*, edited by Scott Allie, 35–102. Milwaukie, OR: Dark Horse Books.

Brooker, Will. 2000. *Batman Unmasked: Analyzing a Cultural Icon*. London: Continuum.

Brooker, Will. 2001. "Readings of Racism: Interpretation, Stereotyping and *The Phantom Menace*." *Continuum: Journal of Media & Cultural Studies* 15 (1): 15–32.

Brooker, Will. 2002. *Using the Force: Creativity, Community, and Star Wars Fans*. London: Continuum.

Brooker, Will, and Deborah Jermyn, eds. 2002. *The Audience Studies Reader*. New York: Routledge.

Brown, David Garrett. 2015 (December 13). "*Star Wars* Lost $4.2 Million Because Of Our Reporting That Identified It As SJW Propaganda." *Return of Kings*: http:// www.returnofkings.com/76356/star-wars-lost-4-2-million-because-of-our- reporting-that-identified-it-as-sjw-propaganda?utm_source=facebook&utm_ medium=facebook&utm_campaign=sumome_share.

Brown, Jeffrey. 2000. *Black Superheroes, Milestone Comics, and Their Fans*. Jackson, MS: University Press of Mississippi.

Brown, Jeffrey. 2004. "Gender, Sexuality, and Toughness: The Bad Girls of Action Film and Comic Books." In *Action Chicks: New Images of Tough Women in Popular Culture*, edited by Sherrie Inness, 47–74. Gordonsville, VA: Palgrave Macmillan.

Brown, Jeffrey. 2011. *Dangerous Curves: Action Heroines, Gender, Fetishism, and Popular Culture*. Jackson, MS: University Press of Mississippi.

Brown, Jeffrey. 2013. "Panthers and Vixens: Black Superheroines, Sexuality, and Stereotypes in Contemporary Comic Books." In *Black Comics: Politics of Race and Representation*, edited by Sheena Howard and Ronald Jackson II, 133–50. London: Bloomsbury, 2013.

Burlingame, Russ. 2015 (July 27). "Exclusive: Marvel's Star Wars To Sell More than 200,000 Copies in Collected Edition," *Comicbook.com*: http://comicbook.com/2015/07/27/ marvels-star-wars-to-sell-more-than-200-000-copies-in-collected-/.

Butler, Judith. 1990. *Gender Trouble: Feminism and the Subversion of Identity*. New York: Routledge.

Butler, Karen. 2003 (June 11). "James Marsters on Life after *Buffy*." United Press International: http://www.upi.com/Odd_News/2003/06/11/James-Marsters-on-Life- After-Buffy/32631055349874/.

Byrne, John. 2005. Post in response to reader question "Who were Nightcrawler's parents supposed to be?" *Byrne Robotics* (blog). Last modified January 20, 2005: http://www. byrnerobotics.com/FAQ/listing.asp?ID=2&T1=Questions+about+Comic+Book+Proj ects#136.

Caldwell, Carol. 1983 (July 21/August 4). "Space Cadet: A Few Words with Carrie Fisher." Interview in *Rolling Stone*, issue no. 400/401, p. 10.

Camron, Marc. 2007. "The Importance of Being the Zeppo: Xander, Gender Identity, and Hybridity in *Buffy the Vampire Slayer*." *Slayage: The Journal of the Whedon Studies Association* 6: http://slayageonline.com/PDF/Camron.pdf.

Carter, Kelly. 2015 (December 13). "Why Lupita Nyong'o Didn't Want To Be Seen in *Star Wars*." *Buzzfeed*: http://www.buzzfeed.com/kelleylcarter/lupita-nyongo-didnt-want- you-to-see-her-face-in-star-wars?utm_term=.jpKbnPP1xV#.bre8NDDEV0.

Case, Sue Ellen. 1988. *Feminism and Theatre*. New York: Routledge.

Casey, Dan. 2015 (April 15). "How *Star Wars* Saved Marvel Comics From Bankruptcy": http://nerdist.com/how-star-wars-saved-marvel-comics-from-bankruptcy/.

Cavelos, Jeanne. 2006. "Stop Her, She's Got a Gun: How the Rebel Princess and the Virgin Queen Became Marginalized and Powerless in George Lucas' Fairy Tale." In *Star Wars on Trial: Science Fiction and Fantasy Writers Debate the Most Popular Science Fiction Films of All Time*, edited by David Brin and Matthew Woodring Stover, 305–27. Dallas, TX: Ben Bella Books.

Charlton, James. 2010. "The Dimensions of Disability Oppression." In *The Disability Studies Reader*, 3rd ed., edited by Lennard J. Davis, 147–59. New York and London: Routledge. Reprint from *Nothing About Us Without Us: Disability Oppression and Empowerment*. Berkeley: University of California Press, 1998.

Ching, Albert. 2013 (February 8). "Captain Marvel Keeps Her Feet on the Ground in New Arc." *Newsarama*: http://www.newsarama.com/10911-captain-marvel-keeps-her-feet-on-the-ground-in-new-arc.html.

Ching, Albert. 2014 (February 13). "DeConnick Deploys Captain Marvel on an Outer Space Journey of Self-Discovery". *Comic Book Resources*: http://www.comicbookresources.com/?page=article&id=50883.

Ching, Albert. 2015. (March 10). "Lee & DiDio Call June Launches 'First of Many Steps' in Building the 'New' DC Comics." *Comic Book Resources*: http://www.comicbookresources.com/article/lee-didio-call-june-launches-first-of-many-steps-in-building-the-new-dc-comics.

Clare, Eli. 2009. *Exile and Pride: Disability, Queerness, and Liberation*, 2nd ed. Cambridge, MA: South End Press.

Claremont, Chris (w), Paul Smith, Dave Cockrum, John Byrne, and Brent Anderson (p). 2011. *Essential X-Men Volume 4*, 2nd ed., collecting *Uncanny X-Men*, 162–79. New York: Marvel.

Clarke, M.J. 2011. "The Production of the Marvel Graphic Novel series: The Business and Cutlure of the Early Direct Market." *Journal of Graphic Novels and Comics* 5 (2): 192–210.

Cocca, Carolyn. 2003. "First Word, 'Jail,' Second Word, 'Bait': Adolescent Sexuality, Feminist Theories, and *Buffy the Vampire Slayer*." *Slayage: The Journal of the Whedon Studies Association* 3: http://slayageonline.com/PDF/cocca.pdf.

Cocca, Carolyn. 2014a. "The Broke Back Test: A Quantitative and Qualitative Analysis of Portrayals of Women in Mainstream Superhero Comics, 1993-2013." *Journal of Graphic Novels and Comics* 5 (4): 411–28.

Cocca, Carolyn. 2014b. "'It's About Power and It's About Women': Gender and the Political Economy of Superheroes in *Wonder Woman* and *Buffy the Vampire Slayer*." In *Heroines of Film and Television: Portrayals in Popular Culture*, edited by Maja Bajac-Carter, Bob Batchelor, and Norma Jones, 215–35. Lanham, MD: Rowman & Littlefield.

Cocca, Carolyn. 2014c (January). "Negotiating the Third Wave of Feminism in *Wonder Woman*." *PS: Political Science and Politics* 47 (1): 98–103.

Cocca, Carolyn. 2014d. "Re-Booting Barbara Gordon: Oracle, Batgirl, and Feminist Disability Theories." *ImageText* 7 (4): http://www.english.ufl.edu/imagetext/archives/v7_4/cocca/.

Cocca, Carolyn. 2016. "Containing the X-Women: De-powering and De-queering Female Characters." In *The X-Men Films: A Cultural Analysis*, edited by Claudia Bucciferro, 79–91. Lanham, MD: Rowman & Littlefield.

Cohen, Cathy J. 1997. "Punks, Bulldaggers, and Welfare Queens: The Radical Potential of Queer Politics?" *GLQ* 3: 437–65.

Coleman-Brown, Lerita. 2010. "Stigma: An Enigma Demystified." In *The Disability Studies Reader*, 3rd ed., edited by Lennard J. Davis, 179–92. New York and London: Routledge.

Columbia University Libraries. 2012 (March 24). "Keynote [Chris Claremont and Louise Simonson]: Comic NY—A Symposium." Columbia University Libraries: https://www.youtube.com/watch?v=WEpZrZNtgxE.

Comeford, AmiJo, Ian Klein, and Elizabeth Rambo. 2012. "Academics Assemble: A Report on New Scholarship at SC5." *Slayage: The Journal of the Whedon Studies Association* 34: http://slayageonline.com/essays/slayage34/Comeford_Klein_Rambo.pdf.

Comic Book Queers. 2012 (April 8). "Have You Seen What They Did to Wonder Woman?" *Comic Book Queers Podcast*: http://www.comicbookqueers.com/?p=3327.

Comic Shenanigans. 2015 (April 13). "A Conversation with Chris Claremont." *Comic Shenanigans Podcast*: http://comicshenanigans.podbean.com/e/episode-260-a-conversation-with-chris-claremont/.

Cooperative Children's Book Center, School of Education, University of Wisconsin-Madison. 2014 "Children's Books by and about People of Color Published in the United States." http://ccbc.education.wisc.edu/books/pcstats.asp.

Costello, Matthew. 2009. *Secret Identity Crisis: Comic Books and the Unmasking of Cold War America*. London: Continuum.

Cotton, Mike. 2004 (January). "Last Call: Preparing for Retirement, Alan Moore Reflects on His Accomplishment." *Wizard* 147: 57–68.

Crenshaw, Kimberle, Neil Gotanda, Gary Peller, and Kendall Thomas, eds. 1996. *Critical Race Theory: The Key Writings That Formed the Movement*. New York: New Press.

Cronin, Brian. 2011 (October 28). "Comic Book Legends Revealed #338." *Comic Book Resources*: http://goodcomics.comicbookresources.com/2011/10/28/comic-book-legends-revealed-338/.

Cronin, Brian. 2014 (March 14). "Comic Book Legends Revealed #462." *Comic Book Resources*: http://goodcomics.comicbookresources.com/2014/03/14/comic-book-legends-revealed-462/2/.

Cunningham, Elaine. 2002. *The New Jedi Order: Dark Journey*. New York: Del Rey.

Dalton, Russell. 2011. *Marvelous Myths: Marvel Superheroes and Everyday Faith*. St. Louis, MO: Chalice Press.

Daniels, Les. 2000. *Wonder Woman: The Complete History*. New York: DC Comics.

Darowski, Joseph. 2014a. "When Business Improved Art: The 1975 Relaunch of Marvel's Mutant Heroes." In *The Ages of the X-Men: Essays on the Children of the Atom in Changing Times*, edited by Joseph Darowski, 37–45. Jefferson, NC: McFarland and Company, Inc.

Darowski, Joseph. 2014b. *X-Men and the Mutant Metaphor: Race and Gender in the Comic Books*. Lanham, MD: Rowman & Littlefield. 2014.

Davidson, Michael. 2010. "Universal Design: The Work of Disability in an Age of Globalization." In *The Disability Studies Reader*, 3rd ed., edited by Lennard J. Davis, 132–46. New York and London: Routledge.

Davis, Lennard J. ed. 2010a. *The Disability Studies Reader*, 3rd ed. New York and London: Routledge.

Davis, Lennard. 2010b. "Constructing Normalcy." In *The Disability Studies Reader*, 3rd ed., edited by Lennard J. Davis, 3–19. New York and London: Routledge. Reprint from *Enforcing Normalcy: Disability, Deafness, and the Body*. New York: Verso, 1995.

Davis, Lennard. 2010c. "The End of Identity Politics: On Disability as an Unstable Category." In *The Disability Studies Reader*, 3rd ed., edited by Lennard J. Davis, 288–315. New York and London: Routledge. Reprint from *Bending Over Backwards: Disability, Dismodernism and Other Difficult Positions*. New York: New York University Press, 2002.

DC Women Kicking Ass. 2011. "A chat with former Batgirl writer Barbara Randall Kesel." *DC Women Kicking Ass*: http://dcwomenkickingass.tumblr.com/post/5871466489/brkinterview.

DCE Editorial [Jim Lee and Dan DiDio].2011 (July 29). "We Hear You:" http://www.dccomics.com/blog/2011/07/29/we-hear-you.

Deis, Christopher. 2007. "May the Force (Not) Be With You: 'Race Critical' Readings and the *Star Wars* Universe." In *Culture, Identities, and Technology in the Star Wars Films: Essays on the Two Trilogies*, edited by Carl Silvio and Tony Vinci, 77–108. Jefferson, NC: McFarland and Company, Inc.

Delgado, Richard. 2000. "Storytelling for Oppositionists and Others: A Plea for Narrative." In *Critical Race Theory: The Cutting Edge*, 2nd ed., edited by Richard Delgado and Jean Stefancic, 60–70. Philadelphia: Temple University Press.

Delgado, Richard, and Jean Stefancic, eds. 2013. *Critical Race Theory: The Cutting Edge*, 3rd ed. Philadelphia: Temple University Press.

DeLullo, Tara. 2003 (March). "That Was Excellent: A Conversation With Buffy Writer Jane Espenson." *TVZone Online Magazine*: http://www.atnzone.com/tvzone/features/buffywriter.shtml.

Denaill. 2004. "Forty Questions with Boyd Kirkland." *X-Men Beyond Evolution*: http://x-men.toonzone.net/qaboyd.php.

Denison, Rayna. 2007. "It's a Bird! It's a Plane! No, it's DVD!: Superman, Smallville, and the Production (of) Melodrama." In *Film and Comic Books*, edited by Ian Gordon, Mark Jancovich, Matthew Mcallister, 160–79. Jackson, MS: University Press of Mississippi.

Denning, Troy. 2005. *Dark Nest I: The Joiner King*. New York: Del Rey.

Denning, Troy. 2008. *Legacy of the Force: Invincible*. New York: Del Rey.

Denning, Troy. 2012. *Fate of the Jedi: Apocalypse*. New York: Del Rey.

Denver Comic Con. 2013 (June 7). "Spotlight on Denny O'Neil" Panel.

DiPaolo, Marc. 2011. *War, Politics, and Superheroes: Ethics and Propaganda in Comics and Film*. Jefferson, NC and London: McFarland and Company, Inc.

Dockterman, Eliana. 2014 (November 4). "Meet Captain Marvel: Fighter Pilot, Feminist and Marvel's Big Gamble." *Time*: http://time.com/3554606/captain-marvel-movie-kelly-sue-deconnick/.

Dockterman, Eliana. 2015 (February 6). "Why Marvel Decided to Create an All-Female Superhero Team." *Time*: http://time.com/3699450/marvel-aforce-secret-wars-superhero-female/.

Dominguez, Diana. 2007. "'Feminism and the Force' Empowerment and Disillusionment in a Galaxy Far, Far Away." In *Culture, Identities, and Technology in the Star Wars Films: Essays on the Two Trilogies*, edited by Carl Silvio and Tony Vinci, 109–33. Jefferson, NC: McFarland and Company, Inc.

Donaldson, Thomas. 2013. "Ineffectual Lass among the Legions of Superheroes: The Marginalization and Domestication of Female Superheroes 1955-70." In *Ages of Heroes, Eras of Men: Superheroes and the American Experience*, edited by Julian Chambliss, William Svitavsky and Thomas Donaldson, 139–52. Newcastle: Cambridge Scholars Publishing.

Donohue, Brian. 2009 (October 21). "Pulitzer Prize-winning Author Junot Diaz Tells Students His Story." *NJ.com*: http://www.nj.com/ledgerlive/index.ssf/2009/10/junot_diazs_new_jersey.html.

Duggan, Lisa. 2000. *Sapphic Slashers: Sex, Violence, and American Modernity*. Durham, NC: Duke University Press.

Duggan, Lisa. 2003. *The Twilight of Equality? Neoliberalism, Cultural Politics, and the Attack on Democracy*. Boston: Beacon Press.

Duncan, Randy, and Matthew Smith. 2009. *The Power of Comics: History, Form and Culture*. New York: The Continuum International Publishing Group Ltd.

Durand, Kevin. 2000. *Buffy Meets the Academy: Essays on the Episodes and Scripts as Text*. Jefferson, NC: McFarland and Company, Inc.

Durham, Meenakshi, and Douglas Kellner, eds. 2012. *Media and Cultural Studies: Keyworks*, 2nd ed. Hoboken: Wiley-Blackwell.

Dyce, Andrew. 2016 (January 21). "X-Men Apocalypse's Four Horsemen Explain Their Roles." *Screen Rant*: http://screenrant.com/x-men-apocalypse-four-horsemen-explained/.

Early, Frances. 2001. "Staking Her Claim: Buffy the Vampire Slayer as Transgressive Woman Warrior." *The Journal of Popular Culture* 35: 11–27.

Early, Frances, and Kathleen Kennedy. 2003. "Introduction." In *Athena's Daughters: Television's New Warrior Women*, edited by Frances Early and Kathleen Kennedy, 1–12. Syracuse: Syracuse University Press.

Edgar, Joanne. 1972. "Wonder Woman: Revisited." *Ms.* (July): 50–55.

Edidin, Jay Rachel. 2014 (April 19). "The Minor League Superhero Who Changed the Face of Fandom." *Wired*: http://www.wired.com/2014/04/captain-marvel-carol-corps/.

Edidin, Jay Rachel, and Miles Stokes. 2015. "Tag Archive for Yukio." *Jay & Miles X-Plain the X-Men*: http://www.xplainthexmen.com/tag/yukio/.

Edwards, Gavin. 2004 (June 7). "Whedon, Ink." *New York*: http://nymag.com/nymetro/arts/9218/.

Eisner, Joel. 2011 (November 17). "The Batscholar on Season Three." *To The Batpoles Blogspot*: http://tothebatpoles.blogspot.com/2011/11/batscholar-on-season-three.html.

Elliott, Timothy, and Robert Dennis Watkins. 2014. "Sexy Art, Speculative Commerce: The *X-Men* #1 Launch Extravaganza." In *The Ages of the X-Men: Essays on the Children of the Atom in Changing Times*, edited by Joseph Darowski, 105–15. Jefferson, NC: McFarland and Company, Inc.

Ellis, Kathleen. 2003. "New World, Old Habits: Patriarchal Ideology in Star Wars: A New Hope." *Australian Screen Education* 30: 135–38.

Emad, Mitra. 2006. "Reading Wonder Woman's Body: Mythologies of Gender and Nation." *The Journal of Popular Culture* 39 (6): 954–84.

Emerald City Comicon. 2014 (May 8). "ECCC 2014 Survey Gender Identification." http://emeraldcitycomicon.tumblr.com/post/85161983740/as-you-may-remember-we-asked-emerald-city-comicon.

Ervin-Gore, Shawna. 2001. "Interview with Joss Whedon." *Dark Horse News*: http://web.archive.org/web/20080211141837/http://www.darkhorse.com/news/interviews.php?id=737.

EUCantina.net. 2013. "Interview with Sue Rostoni:" http://www.eucantina.net/interviews/sue-rostoni2.

Faircloth, Kelly. 2014 (June 5). "The Disney Store will get with the Program and add Leia items." http://jezebel.com/the-disney-store-will-get-with-the-program-and-add-prin-1586640232.

Faircloth, Kelly. 2014 (May 27). "No Princess Leia dolls? Disney thinks Star Wars is just for boys." http://jezebel.com/no-princess-leia-dolls-disney-thinks-star-wars-is-just-1582028327.

FanBros. 2015 (January 8). "The Axel Alonso (Marvel Comics Editor in Chief) Episode." *Fan Bros Podcast*: http://fanbros.com/axel-alonso-episode/.

Faraci, Devin. 2014 (July 22). "Why I Believe Gwendoline Christie's Star Wars Episode VII Role Was Gender Swapped." *BirthMoviesDeath.com*: http://birthmoviesdeath.com/2014/07/22/why-i-believe-gwendoline-christies-star-wars-episode-vii-character-was-gend.

Fawaz, Ramzi. 2011. "'Where No X-Man Has Gone Before! Mutant Superheroes and the Cultural Politics of Popular Fantasy in Postwar America." *American Literature* 83 (2): 355–88.

Fiske, John. 2002 [1989]. "We're Here, We're Queer." In *The Audience Studies Reader*, edited by Will Brooker and Deborah Jermyn, 112–16. New York: Routledge.

FiveYearsLater. 2012 (May 20). Post to "Captain Marvel?" section of *MarvelMasterworksFansite*: http://marvelmasterworksfansite.yuku.com/reply/547139/Re-Captain-Marvel#.Va-R-flViko.

Fleisher, Michael. 1976. *The Original Encyclopedia of Comic Book Heroes, Volume Two, Featuring Wonder Woman*. New York: DC Comics.

Foucault, Michel. 1976 [1990]. *The History of Sexuality: Volume 1, an Introduction*. Translated by Robert Hubley. New York: Vintage.

Fritz, Steve. 2009. (February 5). "NYCC 09—Mike Jelenic: Bringing Wonder Woman to DVD Life." *Newsarama*: http://www.newsarama.com/2127-nycc-09-mike-jelenic-bringing-wonder-woman-to-dvd-life.html.

Frohard-Dourlent, Helene. 2010. "'Lex-Faux Representations: How Buffy Season 8Navigates the Politics of Female Heteroflexbility." In *Sexual Rhetoric in the Works of Joss Whedon*, edited by Erin Waggoner, 31–47. Jefferson, NC: McFarland and Company, Inc.

Fuchs, Cynthia. 2007. "'Did Anyone Ever Explain to You What Secret Identity Means?' Race and Displacement in Buffy and Dark Angel." In *Undead TV: Essays on Buffy the Vampire Slayer*, edited by Elana Levine and Lisa Parks, 96–115. Durham: Duke University Press.

Fury, David. 2000. "The 'I' in Team." *Buffy the Vampire Slayer*, Season 4, Episode 13. DVD. 20th Century Fox.

Gabilliet, Jean-Paul. 2010. *Of Comics and Men: A Cultural History of Comic Books*. Translated by Bart Beaty and Nick Nguyen. Jackson, MS: University Press of Mississippi.

Galvan, Margaret. 2014. "From Kitty to Cat: Kitty Pryde and the Phases of Feminism." In *The Ages of the X-Men: Essays on the Children of the Atom in Changing Times*, edited by Joseph Darowski, 46–62. Jefferson, NC: McFarland and Company, Inc.

Garland-Thomson, Rosemarie. 1997. *Extraordinary Bodies: Figuring Physical Disability in American Culture and Literature*. New York: Columbia University Press.

Garland-Thomson, Rosemarie. 2002. "Integrating Disability, Transforming Feminist Theory." *NWSA Journal* 14 (3): 1–23.

Garland-Thomson, Rosemarie. 2005a. "Disability and Representation." *PMLA* 120 (2): 522–27.

Garland-Thomson, Rosemarie. 2005b. "Feminist Disability Studies." *Signs* 30 (2): 1557–87.

Gavaler, Chris. 2015. *On the Origin of Superheroes: From the Big Bang to Action Comics #1*. Iowa City, IA: University of Iowa Press.

Ghee, Kenneth. 2013. "Will the Real Black Superheroes Please Stand Up?!: A Critical Analysis of the Mythological and Cultural Significance of Black Superheroes." In *Black Comics: Politics of Race and Representation*, edited by Sheena Howard and Ronald Jackson II, 223–38. London: Bloomsbury.

Gibson, Mel. 2015. "Who Does She Think She Is? Female Comic-Book Characters, Second-Wave Feminism, and Feminist Film Theory." In *Superheroes and Identities*, edited by Mel Gibson, David Huxley and Joan Ormrod, 135–46. London: Routledge.

Gill, Rosalind. 2009. "From Sexual Objectification to Sexual Subjectification: The Resexualisation of Women's Bodies in the Media." *Monthly Review* 61 (1): http://mrzine.monthlyreview.org/2009/gill230509.html.

Gilly, Casey. 2015 (June 23). "Gillen, Wilson, Lark and Huehner on Creative Process, Sexy Art and Challenging Stereotypes—Part 2." *Comic Book Resources*: http://www.comicbookresources.com/article/gillen-wilson-lark-huehner-on-creative-process-sexy-art-and-challenging-stereotypes-part-2.

Goodwin, Archie (w), Al Williamson (a). 1996. *Classic Star Wars Volume 1: In Deadly Pursuit* [collected newspaper strips 1981–84]. Milwaukie, OR: Dark Horse.

Gordon, Ian. 2012. "Writing to Superman: Towards an Understanding of the Social Networks of Comic Book Fans." *Participations: Journal of Audience and Reception Studies* 9 (2): 120–32.

Gordon, Ian, Mark Jancovich, and Matthew McAllister, eds. 2007. *Film and Comic Books*. Jackson: University Press of Mississippi.

Gosling, Victoria. 2007. "Girls Allowed? The Marginalization of Female Sport Fans." In *Fandom: Identities and Communities in a Mediated World*, edited by Jonathan Gray, Cornel Sandvoss, and C. Lee Harrington, 250–60. New York: New York University Press.

Gottlieb, Allie. 2002 (September 26). "Buffy's Angels." *Metroactive*: http://www.metroactive.com/papers/metro/09.26.02/buffy1-0239.html.

Gray, Herman. 2012. "The Politics of Representation in Network Television." In *Media and Cultural Studies: Keyworks*, 2nd ed., edited by Meenakshi Durham and Douglas Kellner, 70-92. Hoboken: Wiley-Blackwell. Reprint from *Watching Race: Television and the Struggle for Blackness*. Minneapolis: University of Minnesota Press, 1995.

Gray, Jonathan, Cornel Sandvoss, and C. Lee Harrington. 2007a. "Introduction." In *Fandom: Identities and Communities in a Mediated World*, edited by Jonathan Gray, Cornel Sandvoss, and C. Lee Harrington, 1–12. New York: New York University Press.

Gray, Jonathan, Cornel Sandvoss, and C. Lee Harrington, eds. 2007b. *Fandom: Identities and Communities in a Mediated World*. New York: New York University Press.

Greenberger, Robert. 2010. *Wonder Woman: Amazon, Hero, Icon*. New York: Universe Publishing.

Grossman, Lev. 2005 (September 25). "Interview with Joss Whedon and Neil Gaiman." *Time*: http://www.time.com/time/arts/article/0,8599, 1109313,00.html.

Habermas, Jurgen. 1962. *The Structural Transformation of the Public Sphere an Inquiry into a Category of Bourgeois Society*. Translated by Thomas Burger. Boston: Massachusetts Institute of Technology.

Hains, Rebecca. 2012. *Girl Power: Girlhood on Screen and in Everyday Life*. New York: Peter Lang.

Hajdu, David. 2008. *The Ten-Cent Plague: The Great Comic Book Scare and How It Changed America*. New York: Macmillan.

Halberstam, Judith. 1998. *Female Masculinity*. Durham, NC: Duke University Press.

Hall, Donald and Annamarie Jagose, with Andrea Bebell and Susan Potter, eds. 2012. *The Routledge Queer Studies Reader*. New York: Routledge.

Hall, Kim Q. 2011. *Feminist Disability Studies*. Bloomington and Indianapolis: Indiana University Press.

Hall, Stuart, ed. 2003a [1997]. *Representation: Cultural Representations and Signifying Practices*. London: Sage.

Hall, Stuart. 2003b [1997]. "Introduction." In *Representation: Cultural Representations and Signifying Practices*, edited by Stuart Hall, 1–11. London: Sage.

Hanley, Tim. N.d. "Straitened Circumstances:" https://thanley.wordpress.com/.

Hanley, Tim. 2015. *Wonder Woman Unbound: The Curious History of the World's Most Famous Heroine*. Chicago: Chicago Review Press.

Heflick, Nathan, and Jamie Goldenberg. 2009. "Objectifying Sarah Palin: Evidence That Objectification Causes Women To Be Perceived As Less Competent and Less Fully Human." *Journal of Experimental Social Psychology* 45 (3): 598–601.

Heldman, Caroline, and Michael Cahill. 2007. "The Beast of Beauty Culture: An Analysis of the Political Effects of Self-Objectification." Paper presented at the Western Political Science Association conference, Las Vegas, March 8–10. Retrieved from http://hilo.hawaii.edu/~tbelt/pols433-reading-thebeastofbeautyculture.pdf.

Helford, Elyce Rae. 2000. "Introduction." In *Fantasy Girls: Gender in the New Universe of Science Fiction and Fantasy Television*, edited by Elyce Rae Helford, 1–9. Lanham: Rowman & Littlefield.

Helford, Elyce Rae. 2002. "My Emotions Give Me Power: The Containment of Girls Anger in Buffy." In *Fighting the Forces: What's at Stake in Buffy the Vampire Slayer*, edited by Rhonda Wilcox and David Lavery, 18–34. Lanham, MD: Rowman & Littlefield.

Heywood, Leslie, and Jennifer Drake, eds. 1997. *Third Wave Agenda: Being Feminist, Doing Feminism*. Minneapolis: University of Minnesota.

Hickey, Walt. 2014 (October 13). "Comic Books Are Still Made by Men, for Men, about Men." *FiveThirtyEight*: http://fivethirtyeight.com/features/women-in-comic-books/.

Hidalgo, Pablo. 2012. *Star Wars: The Essential Reader's Companion*. New York: Ballantine Books.

Hollon, Marina. 2012. "Superheroine History 1959-1984; Wonder Woman and Supergirl." https://csusm-dspace.calstate.edu/handle/10211.8/261.

hooks, bell. 1981. *Ain't I a Woman: Black Women and Feminism*. Boston: South End Press.

hooks, bell. 1992. *Black Looks: Race and Representation*. Boston: South End Press.

Howard, Sheena, and Ronald Jackson II, eds. 2013. *Black Comics: Politics of Race and Representation*. London: Bloomsbury.

Howe, Sean. 2012. *Marvel Comics: The Untold Story*. New York: Harper Collins.

Hudson, Laura. 2012 (March 19). "Kelly Sue DeConnick on the Evolution of Carol Danvers to Captain Marvel [Interview]." *Comics Alliance*: http://comicsalliance.com/kelly-sue-deconnick-captain-marvel/?trackback=tsmclip.

Hull, Gloria, Patricia Bell-Scott, and Barbara Smith, eds. 1982. *All the Women Are White, All the Blacks are Men, But Some of Us Are Brave: Black Women's Studies*. Old Westbury, NY: Feminist Press.

Hunt, Darnell, and Ana-Cristina Ramon. 2015. *2015 Hollywood Diversity Report: Flipping the Script*: http://www.bunchecenter.ucla.edu/wp-content/uploads/2015/02/2015-Hollywood-Diversity-Report-2-25-15.pdf.

Hunt, Darnell, Ana-Christina Ramon, and Zachary Price. 2014. *2014 Hollywood Diversity Report: Making Sense of the Disconnect*. Ralph Bunche Center for African American Studies at UCLA: http://www.bunchecenter.ucla.edu/wp-content/uploads/2014/02/2014-Hollywood-Diversity-Report-2-12-14.pdf.

ICV2 staff. 2015 (January 19). "Interview with Marvel Publisher Dan Buckley, Part 2: The Changing Audience and Transmedia and Comics." *ICV2*: http://icv2.com/articles/news/view/30662/interview-marvel-publisher-dan-buckley-part-2.

Inness, Sherrie A. 1998. *Tough Girls: Women Warriors and Wonder Women in Popular Culture*. Philadelphia: University of Pennsylvania Press.

Inness, Sherrie A. 2004. "'Introduction' Boxing Gloves and Bustiers: New Images of Tough Women." In *Action Chicks: New Images of Tough Women in Popular Culture*, edited by Sherrie Inness, 1–20. Gordonsville, VA: Palgrave Macmillan.

Jankiewicz Pat. N.d. "Interview with Yvonne: Recalling Batgirl." *Yvonnecraig.com*: https://yvonnecraig.com/up_close_interview.html.

Jenkins, Henry. 2007. "Afterword." In *Fandom: Identities and Communities in a Mediated World*, edited by Jonathan Gray, Cornel Sandvoss, and C. Lee Harrington, 357–64. New York: New York University Press.

Jennings, Dana. 2014 (November 28). "The Force Was With Them: How Star Wars Saved Marvel Comics from Financial Ruin." http://www.nytimes.com/2014/11/30/books/how-star-wars-saved-marvel-from-financial-ruin.html?_r=1.

Jimenez, Phil. 2013 (4/24), comment on "The Problem With Wonder Woman is Complete Pants," at *Comics Beat*: http://comicsbeat.com/the-trouble-with-wonder-woman-is-complete-pants/#comment-461908.

Johnson, Derek. 2007a. "Fan-tagonism: Factions, Institutions, and Constitutive Hegemonies of Fandom." In *Fandom: Identities and Communities in a Mediated World*, edited by Jonathan Gray, Cornel Sandvoss, and C. Lee Harrington, 285–300. New York: New York University Press.

Johnson, Derek. 2007b. "Will the Real Wolverine Please Stand Up? Marvel's Mutation form Monthlies to Movies." In *Film and Comic Books*, edited by Ian Gordon, Mark Jancovich, and Matthew McAllister, 64–85. Jackson: University Press of Mississippi.

Jones, Amelia, ed. 2010. *The Feminism and Visual Culture Reader*. New York: Routledge.

Jones, Norma, Maja Bajac-Carter, and Bob Batchelor, eds. 2014. *Heroines of Film and Television: Portrayals in Popular Culture*. Lanham, MD: Rowan & Littlefield.

Jowett, Lorna. 2005. *Sex and the Slayer: A Gender Studies Primer for the Buffy Fan*. Middletown, CT: Wesleyan University Press.

Kaplan, Arie, Harvey Pekar, and J. T. Waldman. 2008. *From Krakow to Krypton: Jews and Comic Books*. Philadelphia, PA: Jewish Publication Society.

Kaveney, Roz. 2001. *Reading the Vampire Slayer: An Unofficial Critical Companion to Buffy and Angel*. New York: Tauris Park.

Kaveney, Roz. 2008. *Superheroes: Capes and Crusaders in Comics and Films*. London: I. B. Taurus.

Keith, Lois. 1996. "Encounters with Strangers: The Public's Responses to Disabled Women and How This Affects Our Sense of Self." In *Encounters with Strangers: Feminism and Disability*, edited by Jenny Morris, 69–88. London: The Women's Press.

Kellner, Douglas, and Meenakshi Gigi Durham. 2012. "Adventures in Media and Cultural Studies: Introducing the Keyworks." In *Media and Cultural Studies: Keyworks*, 2nd ed., edited by Meenakshi Gigi Durham and Douglas Kellner, 1–26. Hoboken: Wiley-Blackwell.

Kelly, Elizabeth. 2005. "Review Essay: A New Generation for Feminism? Reflections on the Third Wave." *New Political Science* 27 (2): 233–43.

Kennedy, Fred. 2013 (February 1). "Brian Azzarello." *Fredcast Podcast*: https://itunes.apple.com/us/podcast/fredcast/id496916593?mt=2.

Kinser, Amber. 2004. "Negotiating Spaces For/Through Third Wave Feminism." *National Women's Studies Association Journal* 16 (3): 124–53.

Knight, Gladys L. 2010. *Female Action Heroes: A Guide to Women in Comics, Video Games, Film, and Television*. Santa Barbara, CA: ABC-CLIO/Greenwood.

Kociemba, David. 2006. "'Over-identify much?' Passion, 'Passion', and the Author-Audience Feedback Loop in *Buffy the Vampire Slayer*." *Slayage: The Journal of the Whedon Studies Association* 5: http://slayageonline.com/PDF/kociemba.pdf.

Krensky, Stephen. 2008. *Comic Book Century: The History of American Comic Books*. Minneapolis: Twenty-First Century Books.

Lackaff, Derek, and Michael Sales. 2013. "Black Comics and Social Media Economics: New Media, New Production Models." In *Black Comics: Politics of Race and Representation*, edited by Sheena Howard, and Ronald Jackson II, 65–78. London: Bloomsbury.

LaVorgna, Bria. 2013 (July 13). "Diversity in Star Wars." *Tosche Station*: http://tosche-station.net/diversity-in-star-wars/.

LaVorgna, Bria. 2015 (October 1). "Baltimore Comic Con 2015: Interview with Mark Waid." *Tosche Station*: http://tosche-station.net/baltimore-comic-con-2015-interview-with-mark-waid/.

Leaper, Campbell, Lisa Breed, Laurie Hoffman, and Carly Ann Perlman. 2002. "Variations in the Gender-Stereotyped Content of Children's Television Cartoons Across Genres." *Journal of Applied Social Psychology* 32 (8): 1653–62.

Lepore, Jill. 2015. *The Secret History of Wonder Woman*. New York, NY: Vintage.

Lewis, A. David. 2012. "The Militarism of American Superheroes after 9/11." In *Comic Books and American History: An Anthology*, edited by Matthew Pustz, 223–36. London: Continuum.

Lewis, Andy. 2015 (April 21). "Trailer Report: 'Star Wars: The Force Awakens' Crushes 'Ant-Man'." *The Hollywood Reporter*: http://www.hollywoodreporter.com/heat-vision/trailer-report-star-wars-force-790540.

Liedl, Janice. 2012. "Teen Queen: Padme Amidala and the Power of Royal Women." In *Star Wars and History*, edited by Nancy Reagin and Janice Liedl [written in collaboration with George Lucas and Lucasfilm], 151–76. New York: John Wiley & Sons, Inc.

Lien-Cooper, Barb. 2002. "The Ultimate Writer: Mark Millar." *Sequential Tart*: http://www.sequentialtart.com/archive/mar02/millar2.shtml.

Linton, Simi. 2010. "Reassigning Meaning." In *The Disability Studies Reader*, 3rd ed., edited by Lennard J. Davis, 223–36. New York and London: Routledge. Reprint from *Claiming Disability: Knowledge and Identity*. New York: New York University Press, 1998.

Lippincott, Charles. 2015 (March 31). "Marvel Star Wars Comics Part 2." *From the Desk of Charles Lippincott*: http://therealcharleslippincott.blogspot.com/2015/03/marvel-star-wars-comics-part-2-a.html.

Longmore, Paul K. 2003. *Why I Burned My Book and Other Essays on Disability*. Philadelphia: Temple University Press.

Lopes, Paul. 2009. *Demanding Respect: The Evolution of the American Comic Book*, 223–36. Philadelphia: Temple University Press.

Lorde, Audre. 1984. *Sister Outsider*. Freedom, CA: Crossing.

Lynch, Kevin. 2015 (April 27). "Furious 7 Speeds Past Avatar To Take the Fastest $1Billion Box Office Gross World Record." http://www.guinnessworldrecords.com/news/2015/4/furious-7-speeds-past-avatar-to-take-fastest-1billion-box-office-gross-world-rec-377519.

Lynskey, Dorian. 2015 (March 25). "Kapow! Attack of the Feminist Superheroes." http://www.theguardian.com/books/2015/mar/25/feminist-superheroes-she-hulk-ms-marvel-thor.

MacDonald, Heidi. 2014 (November 4). "Ms. Marvel is Marvel's "#1 Digital Seller." *The Beat*: http://www.comicsbeat.com/ms-marvel-is-marvels-1-digital-seller/.

Madrid, Mike. 2009. *The Supergirls: Fashion, Feminism, Fantasy, and the History of Comic Book Heroines*. Minneapolis, MN: Exterminating Angel Press.

Maggs, Sam. 2015a (April 3). "ECCC's "Being Non-Compliant" Panel Brought The Bad-Ass Women Of The Comics Internet Together, And It Was Beautiful." *The Mary Sue*: http://www.themarysue.com/being-non-compliant-panel-eccc/.

Maggs, Sam. 2015b (April 8). "The Mary Sue Exclusive Interview: Marvel's Sana Amanat and Author James Patterson on Why YA Lit Fans Will Love the Complex Female Characters of Max Ride: First Flight." *The Mary Sue*: http://www.themarysue.com/interview-max-ride-first-flight/.

Magoulick, Mary. 2006. "Frustrating Female Heroism: Mixed Messages in *Xena, Nikita,* and *Buffy.*" *The Journal of Popular Culture* 39: 729–55.

Marston, William Moulton (w), Harry Peter (a). 1941. *All Star Comics* #8 (December to January). New York: DC Comics.

Marston, William Moulton (w), Harry Peter (a). 1942. *Wonder Woman* Vol. 1 #1 (Summer). New York: DC Comics.

Martins, Nicole, and Kristen Harrison. 2012. "Racial and Gender Differences in the Relationship Between Children's Television Use and Self-Esteem: A Longitudinal Panel Study." *Communication Research* 39 (3): 338–57.

Marx, Christy. 2006. "Why I Didn't Grow Up To Be Marvel Girl." In *The Unauthorized X-Men*, edited by Len Wein and Leah Wilson, 171–82. Dallas, TX: Ben Bella Books.

McAllister, Matthew P., Edward H. Sewell, and Ian Gordon. 2001. "Introducing Comics and Ideology." In *Comics and Ideology*, edited by Matthew P. McAllister, Edward H. Sewell, and Ian Gordon, 1–13. New York: Peter Lang.

McAllister, Matthew P., Ian Gordon, and Mark Jancovich. 2006. "Blockbuster Meets Superhero Comic, or Art House Meets Graphic Novel?" *Journal of Popular Film and Television* 34 (3): 108–14.

McCabe, Janice, Emily Fairchild, Liz Grauerholz, Bernice A. Pescosolido, and Daniel Tope. 2011. "Gender in Twentieth-Century Children's Books: Patterns of Disparity in Titles and Central Characters." *Gender & Society* 25 (2): 197–226.

McMillan, Graeme. 2014 (October 28). "Who Is Captain Marvel? A Brief History of Marvel Studios' First Leading Lady." *Hollywood Reporter*: http://www.hollywoodreporter.com/heat-vision/who-is-captain-marvel-a-744562.

McRuer, Robert. 2006. *Crip Theory: Cultural Signs of Queerness and Disability*. New York: New York University Press.

Meltzer, Brad, and Ed Benes. 2007. *Justice League of America: The Tornado's Path* [collecting #1-7 and including additional interview material]. New York: DC Comics.

Metropolitan Museum of Art. 2008 (June 22). "Costume Designers Panel." *Superheroes: Fashion and Fantasy Conference*: https://www.youtube.com/watch?v=UfYkCJTmZb4&feature=youtu.be&t=3m14s.

Miczo, Nathan. 2014. "Punching Holes in the Sky: Carol Danvers and the Potential of Superheroinism." In *Heroines of Comic Books and Literature*, edited by Maja Bajac-Carter, Norma Jones, and Bob Batchelor, 171–83. Lanham, MD: Rowman & Littlefield.

Mikosz, Philip, and Dana Och. 2002. "Previously on Buffy the Vampire Slayer . . ." *Slayage: The Journal of the Whedon Studies Association* 2: http://slayageonline.com/PDF/mikosz_och.pdf.

Milestone, Katie, and Anneke Meyer. 2012. *Gender and Popular Culture*. Cambridge: Polity Press.

Miller, John Jackson. 1997. "A Look Back at Marvel's Star Wars Comics by John Jackson Miller." *Comic Buyer's Guide* #1216: http://www.cbgxtra.com/columnists/john-jackson-miller-longbox-manifesto/cbg-1216-97-a-look-back-at-marvels-star-wars-comics#sthash.eYvI8Ibw.dpuf.

Miller, John Jackson. 2014 (December 10). "Marvel Star Wars #1 Top 1 Million, Matching Title's 1977 Feat; Some Historical Context." *Comichron*: http://blog.comichron.com/2014/12/marvel-star-wars-1-sales-to-top-1.html.

Miller, John Jackson. 2015 (June 20). "Comics and Graphic Novel Sales Hit New Twenty-Year High in 2014." *Comichron*: http://blog.comichron.com/2015/06/comics-and-graphic-novel-sales-hit-new.html.

Miller, Karen. 2010. *Clone Wars Gambit: Stealth*. New York: Del Rey.

Miller, Laura. 2003 (May 20). "The Man Behind the Slayer." *Salon*: http://www.salon.com/2003/05/20/whedon/.

Mintz, Susannah. 2007. *Unruly Bodies: Life Writing by Women with Disabilities*. Chapel Hill, NC: University of North Carolina Press.

MIT [Massachusetts Institute for Technology]. 2009 (April 21). "Opening Doors, Building Worlds: The Origins of the X-Men." MIT Comparative Media Studies and Writing Podcast: http://cmsw.mit.edu/chris-claremont-the-origins-of-the-x-men/.

Mitchell, David, and Sharon Snyder. 2010. "Narrative Prosthesis." In *The Disability Studies Reader*, 3rd ed., edited by Lennard J. Davis, 274–87. New York and London: Routledge. Reprint from *Narrative Prosthesis: Disability and the Dependencies of Discourse*. Ann Arbor, MI: University of Michigan Press.

Moradi, Bonnie, and Yu-Ping Huang. 2008. "Objectification Theory and Psychology of Women: A Decade of Advances and Future Directions." *Psychology of Women Quarterly* 32 (4): 377–98.

Moraga, Cherríe, and Gloria Anzaldúa, eds., 1981. *This Bridge Called My Back: Writings by Radical Women of Color*. Watertown, MA: Persephone Press.

Morrison, Grant. 2011. *Supergods: What Masked Vigilantes, Miraculous Mutants, and a Sun God from Smallville Can Teach Us About Being Human*. New York: Spiegel and Grau.

Morrison, Peter. 2012 (May 9). "Gender and the Star Wars Expanded Universe." *RebelsReport.com*: http://lightsaberrattling.com/gender-and-the-star-wars-expanded-universe-editorial-and-analysis/.

Moss, Gabrielle. 2001. "From the Valley to the Hellmouth: Buffy's Transition from Film to Television." *Slayage: The Journal of the Whedon Studies Association* 1: http://slayageonline.com/PDF/moss.pdf.

Mullaney, Dean, ed. 2014. *Wonder Woman: The Complete Dailies 1944-45* [by William Moulton Marston and Harry G. Peter]. Library of American Comics, DC Entertainment, and IDW Publishing.

Murray, Ross. 2011. "The Feminine Mystique: Feminism, Sexuality, Motherhood." *Journal of Graphic Novels and Comics* 2 (1): 55–66.

Nerdist Comics Panel. 2014 (October 11). "Nerdist Comics Panel [NYCC]: G. Willow Wilson and Greg Pak:" http://nerdist.com/nerdist-comics-panel-67-g-willow-wilson-and-greg-pak/.

Nestle, Joan, Clare Howell, and Riki Wilchins, eds. 2002. *GenderQueer: Voices from Beyond the Sexual Binary*. Los Angeles and New York: Alyson Books.

*Newsarama* staff. 2006. "Interview with Mike Deodato." Archived at http://www.comicbloc.com/forums/archive/index.php?t-29878.html.

Nicholson, Max. 2013 (October 24). "Wonder Woman Movie Not Called 'Wonder Woman?'" IGN: http://www.ign.com/articles/2013/10/25/wonder-woman-movie-not-called-wonder-woman.

Nolen-Weathington, Eric. 2004. *Modern Masters Volume 3: Bruce Timm*. Raleigh, NC: TwoMorrows Publishing.

Nowakowska, Maggie. 1989. "The Incomparable Jundland Wastes." *Alliance*. Archived at http://fanlore.org/w/images/b/ba/JundlandWastes-rollup_2009-1.pdf.

Nussbaum, Emily. 2002 (September 22). "Must-see Metaphysics." *The New York Times Magazine*: http://www.nytimes.com/2002/09/22/magazine/22WHEDON.html?8hpib.

Nussbaum, Martha. 1999. *Sex and Social Justice*. New York: Oxford University Press.

O'Leary, Shannon. 2015 (June 5). "Comics Retailer Survey: Good Sales Get Better in 2015. Goodbye 2014, Hello 2015 Paradigm Shift." *Publisher's Weekly*: http://publishersweekly.com/pw/by-topic/industry-news/comics/article/67045-comics-retailer-survey-good-sales-get-better-in-2015.html#path/pw/by-topic/industry-news/comics/article/67045-comics-retailer-survey-good-sales-get-better-in-2015.html.

Oler, Tammy. 2014 (April 7). "Marvelous: Ms. Marvel and Captain Marvel Are Changing the Way Readers (and Publishers) Think About Who Can Be a Superhero." *Slate*: http://www.slate.com/articles/arts/books/2014/04/kamala_khan_as_ms_marvel_and_carol_danvers_as_captain_marvel_female_nonwhite.html.

Ono, Kent. 2000. "To Be a Vampire on *BTVS*: Race and ('Other') Socially Marginalizing Positions on Horror TV." In *Fantasy Girls: Gender in the New Universe of Science Fiction and Fantasy Television*, edited by Elyce Rae Halford, 163–79. London: Rowman & Littlefiel.

Ostrander, John. 2008. "Comic Reality Bytes by John Ostrander." Comicmix, (June 19): http://www.comicmix.com/news/2008/06/19/comic-reality-bytes-by-john-ostrander/.

Pantozzi, Jill. 2011. "Gail, Jill and Babs: A Conversation about Batgirl and Oracle." *Newsarama* (June 9): http://www.newsarama.com/7777-gail-jill-and-babs-a-conversation-about-batgirl-oracle.html.

Pantozzi, Jill. 2014 (March 11). "The Mary Sue's In-depth Talk with Dark Horse Comics' Editor in Chief on Women in Comics." *The Mary Sue*: http://www.themarysue.com/dark-horse-scott-alli-interview/.

Pantozzi, Jill. 2015 (April 8). "The Mary Sue Exclusive: Comixology's Recent Marvel Sale Boasted 7 Out of 10 Female-Led Titles in the Top 10." *The Mary Sue*: http://www.themarysue.com/exclusive-comixology-marvel-women-top-10/.

Parrish, Master Sgt. Brannen. 2013 (July 4). "Air Force Brat Breathes Life, Experiences into Comic Book Heroine." *Military News*: http://military-online.blogspot.com/2013/07/air-force-brat-breathes-life.html.

Patton, Tracey Owens. 2006. "Hey Girl, Am I More Than My Hair? African American Women and Their Struggles with Beauty, Body Image, and Hair." *Feminist Formations* [formerly *NWSA Journal*] 18 (2): 24–51. Reprinted in Alma Garcia, ed. *Contested Images: Women of Color in Popular Culture*, 111–36. Lanham, MD: Altamira Press. 2012.

Payne-Mulliken, Susan, and Valerie Renegar. 2009. "Buffy Never Goes it Alone: The Rhetorical Construction of Sisterhood in the Final Season." In *Buffy Meets the Academy: Essays on the Episodes and Scripts as Text*, edited by Kevin Durand, 57–77. Jefferson, NC: McFarland and Company, Inc.

Pender, Patricia. 2002. "'I'm Buffy, and You're History': The Postmodern Politics of Buffy." In *Fighting the Forces: What's at Stake in Buffy the Vampire Slayer*, edited by Rhonda Wilcox and David Lavery, 35–44. Lanham, MD: Rowman & Littlefield.

Pennell, Hillary, and Elizabeth Behm-Morawitz. 2015. "The Empowering (Super) Heroine? The Effects of Sexualized Female Characters in Superhero Films on Women." *Sex Roles* 72 (5/6): 211–20.

Peters, Brian Mitchell. 2003. "Qu(e)erying Comic Book Culture and Representations of Sexuality in *Wonder Woman*." *Comparative Literature and Culture* 5 (3): http://docs.lib.purdue.edu/clcweb/vol5/iss3/6.

Phelan, Peggy. 1993. *Unmarked: The Politics of Performance*. New York: Routledge.

Phillips, Jevon. 2012 (August 16). "Captain Marvel: DeConnick on Carol Danvers and the Comics Industry." *Los Angeles Times*: http://herocomplex.latimes.com/comics/captain-marvel-deconnick-on-carol-danvers-and-the-comics-industry/#/0.

Playden, Zoe-Jane. 2001. "'What You Are, What's to Come': Feminisms, Citizenship and the Divine." In *Reading the Vampire Slayer: An Unofficial Critical Companion to Buffy and Angel*, edited by Roz Kaveney, 120–47. New York: Tauris Park.

Pollitt, Katha. 1991 (April 7). "Hers; The Smurfette Principle." *The New York Times*: http://www.nytimes.com/1991/04/07/magazine/hers-the-smurfette-principle.html.

Portwood, Jerry. 2012 (September 10). "Exclusive: Buffyverse Gets Its First Male Slayer." *Out*: http://www.out.com/entertainment/popnography/2012/09/10/buffy-comics-billy-first-gay-male-slayer?page=0,0.

Purvis, Jennifer. 2004. "Grrrls and Women Together in the Third Wave: Embracing the Challenges of Intergenerational Feminism(s)." *National Women's Studies Association Journal* 16 (3): 93–123.

Pustz, Matthew. 1999. *Comic Book Culture: Fanboys and True Believers*. Jackson: University of Mississippi Press.

Reed, Jennifer. 2009. "Reading Gender Politics on *The L Word*: The Moira/Max Transitions." *Journal of Popular Film and Television* 37 (4): 169–78.

ReedPop. 2014. "NYCC Sales Kit:" http://www.reedpop.com/RNA/RNA_ReedPop/documents/2013/2013Recap_NYCC_SalesKit_web.pdf?v=635197868146432773.

Richard, Olive. 1942 (August 14). "Our Women Are Our Future," *Family Circle*: http://www.castlekeys.com/Pages/wonder.html.

Robbins, Trina. 1996. *The Great Women Superheroes*. Northampton: Kitchen Sink Press.

Robbins, Trina. 2002. "Gender Differences in Comics." *Image [&] Narrative* 4 (September): http://www.imageandnarrative.be/inarchive/gender/trinarobbins.htm.

Robbins, Trina. 2008. "Wonder Woman: Queer Appeal." *International Journal of Comic Art* 10 (2): 89–94.

Robbins, Trina. 2013. *Pretty in Ink: North American Women Cartoonists: 1896-2013*. Stamford, CT: Fantagraphics.

Robbins, Trina. 2014. "Wonder Woman: Lesbian or Dyke? Paradise Island as a Woman's Community." In *Heroines of Comic Books and Literature: Portrayals in Popular Culture*, edited by Maja Bajac-Carter, Norma Jones, and Bob Batchelor, 145–52. Lanham, MD: Rowman & Littlefield.

Robinson, Lillian. 2004. *Wonder Women: Feminisms and Superheroes*. New York: Routledge.

Robinson, Tasha. 2007 (August 8). "Interview: Joss Whedon." *AV Club*: http://www.avclub.com/articles/joss-whedon,14136/.

Rohaly, Jeff, and Matthew Wohaske. 2004. "Nielsen Ratings for Buffy the Vampire Slayer, Angel, and Firefly:" http://web.archive.org/web/20080216043137/http://home.insightbb.com/~wahoskem/buffy.html.

Roper, Caitlin. 2015 (January 23). "George Lucas on How His New Film is Like Star Wars for Girls." *Wired*: http://www.wired.com/2015/01/george-lucas-strange-magic/.

Rosberg, Caitlin. 2015 (April 27). "Marvel learned the wrong lessons from the Carol Corps." *AV Club*: http://www.avclub.com/article/marvel-learned-wrong-lessons-carol-corps-218003.

Ross, Sharon. 2004. "'Tough Enough': Female Friendship and Heroism in Xena and Buffy." In *Action Chicks: New Images of Tough Women in Popular Culture*, edited by Sherrie Inness, 231–55. Gordonsville, VA: Palgrave Macmillan.

Rucka, Greg. 2012 (May 22). "Why I Write Strong Female Characters." *IO9*: http://io9.com/5912366/why-i-write-strong-female-characters.

Russell, Emily. 2011. *Reading Embodied Citizenship: Disability, Narrative, and the Body Politic*. Piscataway, NJ: Rutgers University Press.

Ryan, Mike. 2015 (January 5). Reprinting letter column of Marvel's Star Wars #24, June 1979: http://uproxx.com/movies/2015/01/heres-a-star-wars-fan-complaining-about-not-enough-luke-leia-romance-in-a-1979-letter-to-the-editor/.

Salkowitz, Rob. 2012. *Comic-Con and the Business of Pop Culture: What the World's Wildest Trade Show Can Tell Us about the Future of Entertainment*. New York: McGraw Hill.

Salvatore, R. A. 1999. *The New Jedi Order: Vector Prime*. New York: Del Rey.

Sanderson, Peter. 1982. *The X-Men Companion II*. Stamford, CT: Fantagraphics.

Scharf, Lindzi. 2015 (August 8). "*Batman v Superman* Costume Designer Reveals One of the Superhero Suits Will Have Hidden Kryptonian Script—Exclusive." *People's Choice*: http://blog.peopleschoice.com/2015/08/18/batman-v-superman-costumes-michael-wilkinson-interview/.

Schmidt, Gregory. 2015 (July 5). "Pow! Gay Comic Book Characters Zap Stereotypes." *The New York Times*: http://www.nytimes.com/2015/07/06/business/pow-gay-comic-book-characters-zap-stereotypes.html?smid=nytcore-iphone-share&smprod=nytcore-iphone.

Schur, Lisa. 2004. "Is There Still a Double Handicap? Economic, Social, and Political Disparities Experienced by Women with Disabilities." In *Gendering Disability*, edited by Bonnie G. Smith and Beth Hutchison, 253–68. New Brunswick, NJ: Rutgers University Press.

Scott, A. O. 2015 (July 10). "At Comic-Con, It Feels Like the Year of the Woman" *The New York Times*: http://www.nytimes.com/2015/07/11/movies/at-comic-con-it-feels-like-the-year-of-the-woman.html?smid=nytcore-iphone-share&smprod=nytcore-iphone.

Scott, Jason. 2013. "Star Wars as a Character-Oriented Franchise." In *Fan Phenomena: Star Wars*, edited by Mika Elovaara, 10–19. Bristol, UK: Intellect Ltd.

Shah, Diane. 1978 (March 20). "Superwomen Fight Back!" *Newsweek*, 91 (12): 75.

Shooter Jim. 2011a (July 5). "Roy Thomas Saved Marvel:" http://www.jimshooter.com/ 2011/07/roy-thomas-saved-marvel.html.

Shooter, Jim. 2011b (December 11). "Avengers #200:" http://www.jimshooter.com/ 2011/12/avengers-200.html.

Showalter, Elaine. 1971. "Women and the Literary Curriculum." *College English* 32 (8): 855–62.

Showden, Carisa. 2009. "What's Political about the New Feminisms?" *Frontiers* 30 (2): 166–98.

Siebers, Tobin. 2010. "Disability and the Theory of Complex Embodiment." In *The Disability Studies Reader*, 3rd ed., edited by Lennard J. Davis, 316–35. New York and London: Routledge. Reprint from *Disability Theory*. Ann Arbor: University of Michigan Press, 2009.

Signorielli, Nancy. 2012. "Television's Contribution To Stereotyping: Past, Present, Future." In *Handbook of Children and the Media*, 2nd ed., edited by Dorothy Singer and Jerome Singer, 321–40. Thousand Oaks, CA: Sage Publications.

Simone, Gail. 1999. "Women in Refrigerators:" http://lby3.com/wir/.

Simone, Gail. 2008. "Five Questions with Phil Jimenez:" http://fivequestionswith. wordpress.com/phil-j/.

Simone, Gail. 2010 (5/28). Comment on "Amazon Courtship Initiation" at *Comic Book Resources* Forums: http://forums.comicbookresources.com/showthread.php?323912-Amazon-Courtship-Initiation.

Simone, Gail. 2014a (June 5). Untitled post at "Ape in a Cape" tumblr: http://gailsimone. tumblr.com/post/87900145385.

Simone, Gail. 2014b (August 24). Untitled post at "Ape in a Cape" tumblr: http:// gailsimone.tumblr.com/post/95662306760/hey-i-dont-know-if-you-get-this-question-often-or.

Simone, Gail. 2015 (July 20). Untitled post at "Ape in a Cape" tumblr: http://gailsimone. tumblr.com/post/124560954485/why-do-you-think-a-romantic-relationship-between.

Singh, Arune. 2002. "Wonder Man: Phil Jimenez talks Wonder Woman." *Comic Book Resources* (January 23): http://www.comicbookresources.com/?page=article&id=796.

Siuntres, John. 2007 (January 1). "Dwayne McDuffie, Justified." *Word Balloon Podcast*: http://wordballoon.libsyn.com/dwayne_mc_duffie_justified.

Siuntres, John. 2010 (June 1). "'Girl in the Clubhouse' Kelly Sue DeConnick." *Word Balloon Podcast*: http://wordballoon.libsyn.com/girl_in_the_clubhouse_kelly_sue_ deconnick.

Siuntres, John. 2012 (January 25). "2012 Comic Book Industry Watch with Stephen Wacker and Marty Pasko." *Word Balloon Podcast*: http://wordballoon.blogspot. com/2012/01/2012-comic-book-industry-watch-with.html.

Siuntres, John. 2013 (September 15). "Scott Allie, Mike Norton, Gabe Hardiman, Jenny Frison, Steve Seeley, Mike Gallagher." *Word Balloon Podcast*: http://wordballoon.libsyn. com/word-balloon-podcast-scott-allie-mike-norton-gabe-hardman-jenny-frison-steve-seeley-mike-gallagher.

Siuntres, John. 2014 (August 26). "Ninth Anniversary Show Hosted by Brian Michael Bendis." *Word Balloon Podcast*: http://wordballoon.libsyn.com/word-balloon-9th-anniversary-show-hosted-by-brian-m-bendis.

Siuntres, John. 2015 (July 16). "San Diego Comic Con Panels With Greg Pak Calvin Reid Heidi MacDonald and Rob Salkowitz." *Word Balloon Podcast*: http://wordballoon.

libsyn.com/san-diego-comic-con-panels-with-greg-pak-calvin-reid-heidi-macdonald-and-rob-salkowitz.

Skir, Robert. 2005. "X-ing the Rubicon." In *The Unauthorized X-Men: SF and Comic Writers on Mutants, Prejudice, and Adamantium*, edited by Len Wein and Leah Wilson, 19–28. Dallas, TX: Benbella Books.

Smith, Anna Marie. 1994. *New Right Discourses on Race and Sexuality: Britain, 1968-1990*. New York: Cambridge University Press.

Smith, Bonnie G. 2004. "Introduction." In *Gendering Disability*, edited by Bonnie G. Smith and Beth Hutchison, 1–6. New Brunswick, NJ: Rutgers University Press.

Smith, Matthew, and Randy Duncan. 2012. *Critical Approaches to Comics. Theories and Methods*. New York: Routledge.

Smith, Stacy, and Crystal Allene Cook. 2008. *Gender Stereotypes: An Analysis of Popular Films and TV*. Geena Davis Institute on Gender and Media. http://seejane.org/wp-content/uploads/GDIGM_Gender_Stereotypes.pdf.

Smith, Stacy, Marc Choueiti, and Katherine Pieper, with Yu-Ting Liu and Christine Song. 2014. *Gender Bias Without Borders: An Investigation of Female Characters in Popular Films Across 11 Countries*. Geena Davis Institute on Gender and Media. http://seejane.org/wp-content/uploads/gender-bias-without-borders-full-report.pdf.

Smith, Stacy, Marc Choueiti, and Katherine Pieper. 2014. *Gender Stereotypes: An Analysis of Popular Films and TV*. Annenberg School for Communication and Journalism at USC: http://seejane.org/wp-content/uploads/gender-bias-without-borders-full-report.pdf.

Smith, Stacy, Marc Choueiti, and Katherine Pieper. 2015. *Inequality in 700 Popular Films: Examining Portrayals of Gender, Race, & LGBT Status from 2007 to 2014*. Annenberg School for Communication and Journalism at USC: http://annenberg.usc.edu/pages/~/media/MDSCI/Inequality%20in%20700%20Popular%20Films%2081415.ashx.

Snyder, R. Claire. 2008. "What is Third Wave Feminism? A New Directions Essay." *Signs* 34 (1): 175–96.

Snyder, Sharon L., and David T. Mitchell 2005. *Cultural Locations of Disability*. Chicago: University of Chicago Press.

South, James B., ed. 2003. *Buffy the Vampire Slayer and Philosophy: Fear and Trembling in Sunnydale*. Chicago: Open Court Press.

Spangler, William. 2006. "Fighting Princesses and Other Distressing Damsels." In *Star Wars on Trial: Science Fiction and Fantasy Writers Debate the Most Popular Science Fiction Films of All Time*, edited by David Brin and Matthew Woodring Stover, 329–38. Dallas, TX: Ben Bella Books.

Spicer, Arwen. 2002. "'Love's Bitch but Man Enough to Admit It': Spike's Hybridized Gender." *Slayage: The Journal of the Whedon Studies Association* 2: http://slayageonline.com/PDF/spicer.pdf.

Springer, Kimberly. 2002. "Third Wave Black Feminism?" *Signs* 27 (4): 1059–82.

Stackpole, Michael. 2000. *The New Jedi Order: Dark Tide: Onslaught*. New York: Del Rey.

Stanley, Kelli. 2005. "'Suffering Sappho!': Wonder Woman and the (Re)invention of the Feminine Ideal." *Helios* 32 (2): 143–71.

Star Wars. 2014 (December 5). "Thank You, #StarWars Fans for 100 Million Global Views" *Twitter*: https://twitter.com/starwars/status/541043256369217536.

Stover, Matthew. 2005. *Revenge of the Sith*. New York: Random House.

Strickland, Carol. 1980. "The Rape of Ms. Marvel:" http://carolastrickland.com/comics/msmarvel/[first published in comic magazine *LOC* #1].

Stromberg, Fredrik. 2003. *Black Images in the Comics: A Visual History*. Stamford, CT: Fantagraphics.

Stroup, Tim (tstroup@coldcut.com). 2015 (January 27). "Early 1970s Comic Book Market." Post on Comix-scholars list serve COMIXSCHOLARS-L@lists.ufl.edu.

Stuller, Jennifer. 2010. *Ink-Stained Amazons and Cinematic Warriors: Superwomen in Modern Mythology*. London: I. B.Tauris.

Sunu, Steve. 2014 (April 19). "WC14: Creators Discuss All-New Marvel NOW!" *Comic Book Resources*: http://www.comicbookresources.com/?page=article&id=52278.

Superhero Hype. 2003. "Halle Berry on X-Men 3 and Catwoman" [Reprinting article in *Courier-Post of* November 16, 2003]. Last modified December 21, 2003: http://www.superherohype.com/features/84095-halle-berry-on-x-men-3-catwoman.

Svitavsky, William. 2013. "Race, Superheroes, and Identity: 'Did you Know he was Black?'" In *Ages of Heroes, Eras of Men: Superheroes and the American Experience*, edited by Julian Chambliss, William Svitavsky, and Thomas Donaldson, 153–62. Newcastle: Cambridge Scholars Publishing.

Symonds, Gwyn. 2004. "'Solving Problems with Sharp Objects': Female Empowerment, Sex, and Violence in *Buffy the Vampire Slayer*." *The Journal of the Whedon Studies Association* 3: http://slayageonline.com/PDF/symonds.pdf.

Talking Comics. 2013a (April 13). "Greg Rucka Interview." *Talking Comics Podcast*: http://talkingcomicbooks.com/2013/04/05/special-issue-greg-rucka-interview/.

Talking Comics. 2013b (August 29). "Wonder Woman Panel," *Talking Comics Podcast*: http://talkingcomicbooks.com/2013/08/29/women-comics-podcast-wonder-woman-panel/.

Taylor, Aaron. 2007. "'He's Gotta Be Strong, and He's Gotta Be Fast, and He's Gotta Be Larger Than Life': Investigating the Engendered Superhero Body." *The Journal of Popular Culture* 40 (2): 344–60.

Taylor, Chris. 2014. *How Star Wars Conquered the Universe: The Past, Present, and Future of a Multibillion Dollar Franchise*. New York: Basic Books.

Three Chicks Review Comics. 2012 (September 9). "Episode 43." *Three Chicks Review Comics Podcast*: http://goodcomics.comicbookresources.com/2012/09/10/3-chicks-review-comics-episode-043/.

Tilley, Carol. 2012. "Seducing the Innocent: Fredric Wertham and the Falsifications That Helped Condemn Comics." *Information & Culture: A Journal of History* 47 (4): 383–413.

Tomaszewski, Alexa. 2014 (September 14). "Fan Expo: Marvel All Access Talks Female Heroes, Wolverine's Death." *Comic Book Resources*: http://www.comicbookresources.com/?page=article&id=55271.

Tosche Station. 2015a (July 15). "Dark Disciple with Christie Golden." *Tosche Station Radio Podcast*: http://tosche-station.net/tosche-station-radio-122-dark-disciple-with-christie-golden/.

Tosche Station. 2015b (August 7). "Guide to New-Canon Comics." *Tosche Station Radio Podcast*: http://tosche-station.net/tosche-station-radio-124-guide-to-new-canon-comics/.

Travis, Erika. 2013. "From Bikinis to Blasters: The Role of Gender in the Star Wars Community." In *Fan Phenomena: Star Wars*, edited by Mika Elovaara, 48–59. Bristol, UK: Intellect Ltd.

Tremain, Shelley Lynn, ed. 2005. *Foucault and the Government of Disability*. Ann Arbor: University of Michigan Press.

Tuchman, Gaye. 1978. "Introduction: Symbolic Annihilation of Women in the Mass Media." In *Hearth and Home: Images of Women in Mass Media*, edited by Gaye Tuchman, Arlene Kaplan Daniels, and James Benet, 3–38. Oxford: Oxford University Press.

Tung, Charlene. 2004. "Gender, Race, and Sexuality in La Femme Nikita." In *Action Chicks: New Images of Tough Women in Popular Culture*, edited by Sherrie Inness, 95–121. Gordonsville, VA: Palgrave Macmillan.

Tyree, Tia C. M. 2013. "Contemporary Representations of Black Females in Newspaper Comic Strips." In *Black Comics: Politics of Race and Representation*, edited by Sheena Howard and Ronald Jackson, 45–64. London: Bloomsbury.

Valcour, Francinne. 2013. "Retiring Romance: The Superheroine's Transformation in the 1960s." In *The Ages of Wonder Woman: Essays on the Amazon Princess in Changing Times*, edited by Joseph Darowski, 66–78. Jefferson, NC and London: McFarland and Company, Inc.

Veronese, Keith. 2011 (September 15). "How Star Wars Saved Marvel and the Comic Book Industry." http://io9.com/5840578/how-star-wars-saved-the-comic-book-industry.

Vulture. 2015 (December 1). "Women Don't Talk Much in *Star Wars*." https://www.youtube.com/watch?v=ODgwL7DJ9dY.

Walker, Rebecca. 1992. "Becoming the Third Wave." *Ms.* (January): http://www.msmagazine.com/spring2002/BecomingThirdWaveRebeccaWalker.pdf.

Walker, Rebecca, ed. 1995. *To Be Real: Telling the Truth and Changing the Face of Feminism*. New York: Doubleday.

Weber, Erik. 2014 (December 2). "New Star Wars Teaser is the Fastest Growing Trailer Ever." *Zefr: A View into Culture on youtube and Beyond*: http://blog.zefr.com/star-wars-trailer-fastest-growing-ever/.

Weiland, Jonah. 2014 (May 21). "Cliff Chiang on Wonder Woman's Design and His Almost Law Career." *Comic Book Resources*: http://www.comicbookresources.com/?page=article&id=52952.

Weiland, Jonah. 2014 (October 16). "G. Willow Wilson Taps into the Zeitgeist with Ms. Marvel." *Comic Book Resources:* http://www.comicbookresources.com/?page=article&id=56339.

Wein, Len. 2006. "Introduction." In *The Unauthorized X-Men: Science Fiction and Comic Writers on Mutants, Prejudice, and Adamantium*, edited by Len Wein and Leah Wilson, 1–8. Dallas, TX: Benbella Books.

Wendell, Susan. 2010. "Toward a Feminist Theory of Disability." In *The Disability Studies Reader*, 3rd ed., edited by Lennard J. Davis, 336–52. New York and London: Routledge. Reprint from *Hypatia* 4 (2): 104–22, 1989.

Wendig, Chuck. 2015 (September 7). "Star Wars: Aftermath—Reviews, News, and Such." *Terribleminds*: http://terribleminds.com/ramble/2015/09/07/star-wars-aftermath-reviews-news-and-such/comment-page-1/#comments.

Wertham, Frederic. 2008 [1954]. "Excerpt from *Seduction of the Innocent*." In *A Comics Studies Reader*, edited by Jeet Heer and Kent Worcester, 53–57. Jackson, MS: University Press of Mississippi.

West, Carolyn. 2008. "Mammy, Jezebel, Sapphire, and Their Homegirls: Developing an 'Oppositional Gaze' Toward the Images of Black Women." In *Lectures on the Psychology of Women*, 4th ed., edited by Joan Chrisler, Carla Golden, and Patricia Rozee, 286–99. New York: McGraw Hill.

Whedon, Joss. 1998 (December 3). Comment at *The Bronze*, now archived at http://www.cise.ufl.edu/cgi-bin/cgiwrap/hsiao/buffy/get-archive?date=19981203.

Whedon, Joss. 2000 (May 4). Comment at *The Bronze*, now archived at http://www.cise. ufl.edu/cgi-bin/cgiwrap/hsiao/buffy/get-archive?date=20000504.

Whedon, Joss. 2006. "Equality Now: Acceptance Speech." *YouTube*: https://www.youtube. com/watch?v=cYaczoJMRhs.

Wheeler, Andrew. 2014a (June 30). "Freak Like Me: Understanding the Queerness of the X-Men [Mutant and Proud Part III]." *Comics Alliance*: http://comicsalliance.com/ mutant-proud-xmen-lgbt-rights-identity-queerness-transformation/.

Wheeler, Andrew. 2014b (November 10). "Oh Captain, My Captain: How Carol Danvers Became Marvel's Biggest Female Hero." *Comics Alliance*: http://comicsalliance.com/ captain-marvel-carol-danvers-marvel-biggest-female-hero/.

Whipple, Blair. n.d. "Interview: Shannon Farnon, Super Friends' Original Wonder Woman." *Polar Blair's Den*: http://www.polarblairsden.com/cartoonsfarnon.html.

Whitbrook, James. 2015a (February 18). "Hasbro Flounders When Asked About the Lack of Female *Star Wars* Toys:" http://toybox.io9.com/hasbro-flounders-when-asked-about-the-lack-of-female-st-1686572897.

Whitbrook, James. 2015b (February 27). "Rejoice, The New Star Wars Figures Come With A Non-Slave Leia:" http://toybox.io9.com/rejoice-the-new-star-wars-figures-come-with-a-non-slav-1688428658/+riamisra.

White, Brett. 2014a. (March 10). "Take Flight With Captain Marvel part 1:" http://marvel. com/news/comics/22114/take_flight_with_captain_marvel_pt_1.

White, Brett. 2014b. (March 11). "Take Flight With Captain Marvel part 2:" http://marvel. com/news/comics/22121/take_flight_with_captain_marvel_pt_2.

Wilcox, Rhonda. 2002. "'Who Died and Made Her the Boss?' Patterns of Mortality in *Buffy the Vampire Slayer*." In *Fighting the Forces: What's at Stake in Buffy the Vampire Slayer*, edited by Rhonda Wilcox and David Lavery, 3–17. Lanham, MD: Rowman & Littlefield.

Wilcox, Rhonda, and David Lavery, eds. 2002. *Fighting the Forces: What's at Stake in Buffy the Vampire Slayer*. Lanham, MD: Rowman & Littlefield.

Williams, Patricia. 1999 (June 17). "Racial Ventriloquism." *The Nation*: http://www. thenation.com/article/racial-ventriloquism#.

Williams, Walter John. 2002. *The New Jedi Order: Destiny's Way*. New York: Del Rey.

Wilson, Veronica. 2007. "Seduced by the Dark Side of the Force: Gender, Sexuality, and Moral Agency in George Lucas's Star Wars Universe." In *Culture, Identities, and Technology in the Star Wars Films: Essays on the Two Trilogies*, edited by Carl Silvio and Tony Vinci, 134–52. Jefferson, NC: McFarland and Company, Inc.

Wilts, Alissa. 2009. "'Evil, Skanky, and Kinds Gay': Lesbian Images and Issues." In *Buffy Goes Dark: Essays on the Final Two Season of Buffy the Vampire Slayer on Television*, edited by Lynne Edwards, Elizabeth Rambro, and James South, 41–56. Jefferson, NC: McFarland and Company, Inc.

Women of Marvel. 2014 (June 23). "Kelly Sue DeConnick." *Women of Marvel Podcast*: http://marvel.com/news/comics/22734/kelly_sue_deconnick_joins_the_women_of_marvel_podcast.

Women of Marvel. 2015 (June 26). "Thank You to Kelly Sue DeConnick." *Women of Marvel Podcast*: http://marvel.com/news/comics/24783/the_women_of_marvel_say_thank_you_to_kelly_sue_deconnick.

Wookieepedia. 2008 (16 April). "Interview with Kevin J. Anderson:" http://starwars.wikia. com/wiki/Wookieepedia:Interview/Kevin_J._Anderson. 4/16/08.

Wright, Bradford. 2001. *Comic Book Nation: The Transformation of Youth Culture in America*. Baltimore, MD: The Johns Hopkins University Press.

Yu, Mallory. 2014 (October 10). "Where's Thor When You Need Her? Women in Comics Fight an Uphill Battle." *National Public Radio*: http://www.npr.org/2014/10/10/353497842/wheres-thor-when-you-need-her-women-in-comics-fight-an-uphill-battle.

Zingsheim, Jason. 2011. "X-Men Evolution: Mutational Identity and Shifting Subjectivities." *Howard Journal of Communications* 22: 223–39.

# Index